Windows Server® 2008 R2 Hyper-V™

Windows Server® 2008 R2 Hyper-V™

Insiders Guide to Microsoft's Hypervisor

John Kelbley

Mike Sterling

Wiley Publishing, Inc.

Acquisitions Editor: Agatha Kim
Development Editor: Stef Jones
Technical Editor: Manjnath Ajjampur
Production Editor: Elizabeth Ginns Britten
Copy Editor: Kim Wimpsett
Editorial Manager: Pete Gaughan
Production Manager: Tim Tate
Vice President and Executive Group Publisher: Richard Swadley
Vice President and Publisher: Neil Edde
Book Designer: Maureen Forys, Happenstance Type-O-Rama; Judy Fung
Compositor: Craig Woods, Happenstance Type-O-Rama
Proofreader: Word One, New York
Indexer: Ted Laux
Project Coordinator, Cover: Lynsey Stanford
Cover Designer: Ryan Sneed

ISBN: 978-0-470-62700-6
ISBN 978-0-470-88033-3 (ebk)
ISBN 978-0-470-88035-7 (ebk)
ISBN 978-0-470-88034-0 (ebk)

For general information on our other products and services or to obtain technical support, please contact our Customer Care Department within the U.S. at (877) 762-2974, outside the U.S. at (317) 572-3993 or fax (317) 572-4002.

Wiley also publishes its books in a variety of electronic formats. Some content that appears in print may not be available in electronic books.

Library of Congress Cataloging-in-Publication Data is available from the publisher.

10 9 8 7 6 5 4 3 2 1

Dear Reader,

Thank you for choosing *Windows Server 2008 R2 Hyper-V: Insiders Guide to Microsoft's Hypervisor.* This book is part of a family of premium-quality Sybex books, all of which are written by outstanding authors who combine practical experience with a gift for teaching.

Sybex was founded in 1976. More than 30 years later, we're still committed to producing consistently exceptional books. With each of our titles, we're working hard to set a new standard for the industry. From the paper we print on, to the authors we work with, our goal is to bring you the best books available.

I hope you see all that reflected in these pages. I'd be very interested to hear your comments and get your feedback on how we're doing. Feel free to let me know what you think about this or any other Sybex book by sending me an email at nedde@wiley.com. If you think you've found a technical error in this book, please visit http://sybex.custhelp.com. Customer feedback is critical to our efforts at Sybex.

Best regards,

Neil Edde
Vice President and Publisher
Sybex, an Imprint of Wiley

Acknowledgments

Writing a book about a new technology is a complex task, and like most such labors, it has been a team effort. As the front cover notes, this book has (at least) two authors, with contributions from many others. Sincere thanks go out to everyone involved and their families (who suffered much like mine!). Dividing the book into separate sections allowed us to, we hope, produce a better book more quickly than either of us could have on our own. Writing a book sounds like a great idea before you start (and it is), but it takes far longer to complete and requires a great deal more effort than I ever would have imagined. My wife, Sylvia, and my sons, Andrew and Alexander, have been more than patient with me the last few years while I put off other commitments and borrowed computer capacity from the infrastructure at home.

Many co-workers and friends helped out (including many members of the Virtualization Nation), but I am most grateful for the feedback from the technical titans who were willing to read, critique, or contribute to my chapters (Manjnath Ajjampur, Jason Buffington, Arno Mihm, Alexander Lash, James O'Neill, Ben Herman, Alex Kibkalo, Matt Lavallee, and a guy named Bob). The dialogues with James and Ben in particular on the scripting chapters were great for the book (and for me), with my regret being that we didn't write an entire book about Hyper-V scripting. There just isn't enough space in two chapters for all the suggestions from James, Ben, and Alex.

Thanks to the patient, professional editors for the first and second editions (Agatha Kim, Stef Jones, and Liz Britten), as well as others at Wiley who turned our ideas, sentences, and cocktail-napkin class diagrams into things more intelligible. The editorial process is still largely a mystery to me—a testament to the quality of their work!

—*John Kelbley*

When I sat down with John for dinner in Houston, I had no idea what I was getting myself into. "Hey Mike, want to help me write a book?" After a couple glasses of wine, he had convinced me that writing a book was a great idea. Now that the book is complete, I can heartily agree.

Having worked with virtualization since the beginnings of Virtual PC for the Macintosh, I've seen huge advancements made with the usage of virtualization. No longer is it just a fun tool for your friends on your Mac—we've moved on to server virtualization and even more wide-scale adoption of what was previously a niche technology. This book is a way for me to try to get some of the information that has sat in my head for the last 13 years onto paper.

No acknowledgments section would be complete without a list of people I need to thank. First and foremost, I need to thank my wife, Nancy, and my son, Maxwell—the reasons why I had enough time to write my portions of the book. Thank you for supporting me through the late nights that were necessary to get this done. My co-author, John, was immensely helpful in making sure we covered everything. Our technical reviewers, Manjnath and James, did a great job of keeping us honest. My team members, off whom I bounced countless ideas and who verified many of my thoughts, deserve many of my thanks. Last, I need to thank the editorial staff—Agatha, Stef, and Liz—who have done an exceptional job of taking our words and crafting them into something that people want to read.

—*Mike Sterling*

About the Authors

John Kelbley is a senior technical product manager with Microsoft's Platform Tech Strategy team based in the Northeastern United States. He joined Microsoft in 2002 after working at a number of large enterprises as a management consultant, IT manager, and infrastructure architect. John has more than 20 years of computing industry experience with a focus on infrastructure architecture. This is the first book he has authored since leaving grade school.

Mike Sterling is a program manager in the Windows Server team at Microsoft, focused exclusively on virtualization. Prior to this role, Mike spent 10 years in software testing, working on products such as Virtual PC, Virtual Server, and Hyper-V. When he's not working, he can be found playing World of Warcraft or taking photographs.

Contents at a Glance

Contents

Introduction

Welcome to the best book we've ever written about Microsoft's hypervisor technology, Hyper-V! Hyper-V is a foundational virtualization technology released in 2008 by Microsoft, and this book is intended to be a resource for systems administrators looking to use it in a cost-effective and efficient manner. We have worked hard to update the book to cover the changes and enhancements in Hyper-V incorporated in Windows Server 2008 R2.

The book covers the essentials of using Hyper-V, giving you the information necessary to get up and running quickly. The book includes technical depth (some not found anywhere else), but it isn't intended as a comprehensive guide to all aspects of Hyper-V.

What Is Virtualization?

At its simplest, *virtualization* is the abstraction of computing from computers. Separating software from hardware isn't a new concept. Administrators have done it for many years on all sorts of platforms. Nearly any system or system component can be somehow pulled away or separated from the hardware or software on which it depends. In Windows-centric environments, complete operating system instances can be virtualized using Hyper-V, Virtual Server, and Virtual PC. Windows systems can also be virtualized with products from other companies, including VMware. This full-system virtualization is only one type of computing abstraction.

Virtualization can happen at nearly any computing boundary within a system. The broad definition and interpretation of virtualization has led to a virtualization frenzy in all forms. It seems as if every software and hardware company has a virtualization offering of some kind. For good or for bad, the word *virtualization* has been tagged onto products and solutions across the computing industry. It sounds like virtualization is the *next great thing* in computing. It's already here, so it actually *was* the next great thing! In all its current forms, virtualization is providing value to enterprises and individuals and has been doing so for some time.

Microsoft's Approach to Virtualization

Some software companies address virtualization from a single direction. VMware, for example, focuses on virtualizing and managing operating system instances. Microsoft has been more thoughtful and less myopic in its approach. Microsoft's articulated virtualization direction is in five key areas:

Server Hyper-V and Virtual Server 2005 for server services

Desktop Virtual PC for client-centric, local operating system instances

Presentation Terminal Services (now called Remote Desktop Services in Windows Server 2008 R2) providing remote desktop and application access

Application SoftGrid/AppV for application encapsulation

Profile Roaming profiles for personal-experience encapsulation

All these approaches are tied together by Windows as a platform and managed by the System Center family of products to enable administration of virtual and physical resources.

You can benefit from this multipronged approach to virtualization, which is unified by a common platform and management suite.

It's All Windows

The great thing about virtualization technology from Microsoft is that it's integrated with Windows. Windows is a platform well known to administrators and users alike. You don't need special training to use Microsoft's virtualization offerings because they're already familiar. You don't need to be a virtualization specialist to use Hyper-V, Terminal Services RDS, or AppV (as you might with VMware). You can have virtualization as a competency, just as you might with other focus areas of Windows administration.

System Center Manages All Worlds Well

You manage and monitor each of these virtualization offerings with the same System Center tools that you may already have in your environment for physical system management. Some virtualization management tools provide insight only into the virtualization layer and can't dive further into running operating systems or applications (they're essentially half-blind). Using a unified, familiar tool set that can correlate data between physical, virtual, and application software can magnify the benefits of virtualization.

Mixing and Matching with Virtualization

You can use these separate directions of virtualization together with the others to provide more value. You can combine the different focuses of virtualization—server, desktop, presentation, application, and profile—to meet the needs and requirements of changing enterprises. Why not rapidly provision Hyper-V–based virtual machines for thin-client access to meet dynamic demands? How about combining AppV with Terminal Services RDS to alleviate application coexistence issues and reduce server count?

Where Hyper-V Fits

Hyper-V is Microsoft's efficient hypervisor that enables operating system virtualization in a server environment. Hyper-V is a core technology pillar of Microsoft's virtualization strategy and the focus of this book. It's an installable feature of Windows Server 2008/Windows Server 2008 R2 and is available as a no-cost download as Hyper-V Server 2008 R2. Even with other virtualization solutions already installed, Hyper-V can be part of any contemporary Windows Server infrastructure, based on availability and price.

Why We Wrote This Book

Just before the release of Hyper-V, we realized there were few books on the horizon addressing this important and industry-altering technology. We agreed that a book should be written to bring together the combined available information and knowledge we had in developing, using, and managing Hyper-V. We had all read books written by professional authors about technology and thought the insight of those closer to the product (not professional authors) could serve the needs of administrators well.

When Windows Server 2008 R2 was nearing release, we realized that there had been substantial enhancements to Hyper-V. We addressed these updates by revising our first book and developed this second edition.

Who Should Read This Book

Everyone and anyone interested in understanding Hyper-V and how to use it should read this book. We developed the content specifically for Windows administrators. IT professionals with some experience using Windows Server 2003 or Windows Server 2008 will get the most out of the book. Some chapters are more technical than others, but notes, tips, and pointers to necessary resources are included to make every (aspiring server administrator) reader productive.

Readers are expected to be familiar with Windows and have some experience with and understanding of Windows Server 2008 or Windows Server 2008 R2. You don't need extensive server administration experience to benefit from the book, only a desire to learn more about Hyper-V and how to use it.

How the Book Is Organized

The book is organized and written with a "crawl, walk, run" philosophy. We'll introduce you to server virtualization and Hyper-V administration and then lead you along to expose you to enterprise management concepts and tools for virtualization. We've purposely organized the book into three distinct sections to address separate levels of interest and to provide you with three different perspectives on Hyper-V.

The first section (Chapters 1 through 5), or the "crawling" section, is geared toward making you productive with Hyper-V as quickly as possible. These chapters are focused on introducing Hyper-V, setting it up, and running virtual hosts in an efficient and secure manner using little more than the Hyper-V console.

Chapter 1: Introducing Hyper-V

Chapter 2: Installing Hyper-V and Server Core

Chapter 3: Configuring Hyper-V

Chapter 4: Virtualization Best Practices

Chapter 5: Hyper-V Security

The second, "walking" section (Chapters 6 through 10), builds on knowledge from the earlier chapters. The middle of the book dives into more advanced manual administration tasks and concepts. Here we wade into complicated and necessary topics including virtual machine migration, backup and recovery, failover clustering, and automation through scripting. We show you how to handle advanced administration tasks manually or through custom automation.

Chapter 6: Virtual Machine Migration

Chapter 7: Backing Up and Recovering VMs

Chapter 8: High Availability

Chapter 9: Understanding WMI, Scripting, and Hyper-V

Chapter 10: Automating Tasks

The final section of the book (Chapters 11 through 13) is the "running" or "soaring with eagles" part of the book. These chapters introduce you to the most effective way to manage an enterprise virtualization environment with several members of the Microsoft System Center family of products. One chapter is devoted to each of three products that are commonly used for server virtualization management (Operations Manager, Virtual Machine Manager, and Data Protection Manager):

Chapter 11: Using System Center Virtual Machine Manager 2008

Chapter 12: Protecting Virtualized Environments with System Center Data Protection Manager

Chapter 13: Using System Center Operations Manager 2007

Final Thoughts

The best way to learn about Hyper-V is to be hands-on with it. If you can, take some time to load Windows Server 2008 R2 with Hyper-V on a capable system. This book provides lots of great tips and tricks for using Hyper-V, and trying them firsthand is a great way to develop your understanding and expertise.

Inexpensive systems available today include hardware-assisted virtualization support (as well as x64 support) and make serviceable Hyper-V test systems. You don't even need new systems for Hyper-V—just a host with Intel VT or AMD-V support. Many of the examples in the book were developed and tested on laptops and desktop systems more than three years old. An older desktop or laptop may not be in any way suitable for production use with Hyper-V, but it can be perfect for you to build a better understanding of this important and useful virtualization technology.

Chapter 1

Introducing Hyper-V

With the release of Windows Server 2008, Microsoft has included a built-in virtualization solution, Hyper-V. Hyper-V is a role of Windows Server 2008 that lets administrators create multiple virtual machines. A *virtual machine* is a separate, isolated environment that runs its own operating system and applications.

Virtual machine technology isn't new—it's been available from Microsoft in both Virtual PC and Virtual Server since late 2003 and from other vendors since the 1970s. By including it in the operating system, Microsoft has made an extremely feature-rich product available at no extra cost.

Hyper-V takes the concept of virtualization to the mainstream IT environment by including it in the operating system. Previous Microsoft virtualization solutions ran on top of the operating system—a significant difference from the way Hyper-V is designed. Inclusion in the operating system also provides a seamless management experience when paired with the System Center family of products.

In this chapter, we'll review the following elements of Hyper-V:

◆ Scenarios for Hyper-V

◆ Architecture of Hyper-V

◆ Features of Hyper-V

◆ Hardware and software requirements for Hyper-V

Scenarios for Hyper-V

Hyper-V was developed with several key scenarios in mind. When Microsoft started developing Hyper-V, the development team spent a great deal of time meeting with customers who were using virtualization—small businesses, consultants who implement virtualization on behalf of their customers, and large companies with multimillion-dollar IT budgets. The following key scenarios were developed as a result of those meetings; they represent customer needs, demands, and wants.

Server Consolidation

Systems are becoming increasingly powerful. A couple of years ago, quad-processor servers started to enter the mainstream market at enterprise-friendly prices. Now, with major processor manufacturers providing multicore functionality, servers have more and more processing power. Multicore technology combines multiple processor cores onto a single die, enabling a single physical processor to run multiple threads of execution on separate cores. Virtualization and multicore technology work great together. If you're combining multiple workloads onto a single server, it makes sense to have as much processing power as possible. Multicore processors help provide the optimal platform for virtualization.

Businesses are increasingly likely to need multiple systems for a particular workload. Some workloads are incredibly complex, requiring multiple systems but not necessarily using all the power of the hardware. By taking advantage of virtualization, system administrators can provide a virtualized solution that better utilizes the host hardware, thus allowing administrators to get more out of their expenditure.

Workloads aren't the only driving item behind virtualization. The power and cooling requirements of modern servers are also key driving factors. A fully loaded rack of servers can put out a significant amount of heat. (If you've ever stood behind one, you're sure to agree—it's a great place to warm up if you've been working in a cold server room.) All that heat has to come from somewhere. The rack requires significant power.

But for companies in high-rise buildings in the middle of major cities, getting additional power is incredibly difficult, if not impossible. In many cases, the buildings weren't designed to have that much power coming in, and the companies can't add more power without extensive retrofitting. By deploying virtualization, more workloads can be run on the same number of servers.

Testing and Development

For people working in a test or development role, virtualization is a key to being more productive. The ability to have a number of different virtual machines (VMs), each with its own operating system that's ready to go at the click of a mouse, is a huge time-saver. Simply start up whichever VM has the operating system that you need. You no longer need to continually reinstall the OS for every test session; instead, you can revert to a known good state to start the test cycle over. Also, by using the snapshot functionality, users can quickly move between known states in the VM.

With Hyper-V's rich Windows Management Interface (WMI) interfaces, testing can start automatically. By scripting both Hyper-V and the operating system to be tested, testers can run a script that starts the VM, installs the latest build, and performs the necessary tests against it.

A Hyper-V virtual machine is also portable. A tester can work in the VM; if an issue is found, the tester can save the state of the VM (including the memory contents and processor state) and transfer it to the developer, who can restore the state at their convenience. Because the state of the VM is saved, the developer sees exactly what the tester saw.

Business Continuity and Disaster Recovery

Business continuity is the ability to keep mission-critical infrastructure up and running. Hyper-V provides two important features that enable business continuity: live backup and quick or live migration.

Live backup uses Microsoft Volume Shadow Services functionality to make a backup of the entire system without incurring any downtime, as well as provide a backup of the VM at a known good point in time. The system backup includes the state of all the running VMs. When a backup request comes from the host, Hyper-V is notified, and all the VMs running on that host are placed into a state where they can be backed up without affecting current activity; they can then be restored at a later time.

Quick migration and *live migration* offer the ability to move a VM from one host to another in a cluster using Microsoft Failover Cluster functionality at no extra cost. During a quick migration, you save the state of the VM, move storage connectivity from the source host to the target host, and then restore the state of the VM. During a live migration, the state of the VM is transferred over the network from the source host to the target host, which ensures the VM remains active and responsive through the process. Windows Server 2008 added support for the virtual machine resource type to the Failover Cluster Manager tool, enabling you to make a VM highly available using functionality included with the operating system. For more information about both of these features of Hyper-V, refer to Chapter 6, "Migrating Virtual Machines," and refer to Chapter 7, "Backing Up and Recovering VMs."

Disaster recovery is becoming a requirement for increasing numbers of businesses. You must consider more than just big disasters, though—small disasters or even simple configuration issues can lead to a mission-critical service being unavailable. Hyper-V includes support for geographically dispersed clusters (a new feature of Windows Server 2008).

Dynamic IT

Microsoft's idea of a dynamic IT infrastructure involves self-managing dynamic systems— systems that adjust automatically to the workload they're running. By using Hyper-V in conjunction with the systems management functionality present in the System Center family of products, enterprises can take advantage of the benefits of virtualization to meet the demands of a rapidly changing environment.

Now that we've covered Hyper-V's key targeted scenarios, we'll cover the architecture of Hyper-V and explain how Microsoft has implemented support for those scenarios.

Architecture of Hyper-V

Before we cover the architecture of Windows Server 2008 with the Hyper-V role, it's useful to understand how Windows Server 2008 works without this role.

As shown on the next page in Figure 1.1, Windows Server 2008 operates in both kernel mode and user mode. *Kernel mode* (also known as Ring 0) is where the Windows kernel lives, as well as all the device drivers for the hardware installed in the system. *User mode* (Ring 3) is where applications are run. This ring separation is a key feature of the x86 architecture—it means that a rogue application shouldn't be able to take down the operating system.

A *role* in Windows Server 2008 is a task for the server, whereas a *feature* can (and often does) supplement a role. A great example of this role/feature distinction is a web server. Internet Information Services (IIS) functionality is a role of Windows Server 2008, and features that go hand in hand with IIS include Network Load Balancing and Windows PowerShell. Each of those features can be installed on an as-needed basis.

A default installation of Windows Server 2008 doesn't include any active roles or features. Windows Server 2008 was designed to be as secure as possible. As part of the development process, Microsoft worked with and received feedback from many users about how they deploy servers. A frequent customer request was an easy way to deploy a server to perform a particular task—for example, a file server or print server. That's where the concept of a role or feature came into play.

Now that you understand the meaning of roles and features in Windows Server 2008, we'll talk about the Hyper-V role. We'll cover installation of the role in Chapter 2, "Installing Hyper-V and Server Core."

Figure 1.2 on page 5 shows that once the role is installed, some pretty significant changes happen to the installed copy of Windows Server 2008.

FIGURE 1.1
Simplified archi-
tecture for a clean
install of Windows
Server 2008

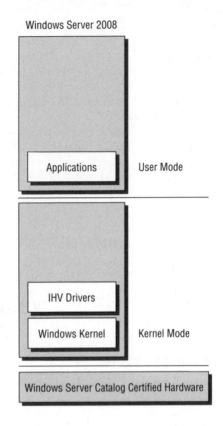

Looks quite a bit different, doesn't it? Let's break down each of the changes.

Parent Partition

The installation of Windows is now running on top of the Windows hypervisor, which we'll describe later in this chapter. One of the side effects of running on top of the hypervisor is that the installation is technically a VM. We'll refer to this as the *parent partition*.

The parent partition has two special features:

◆ It contains all the hardware device drivers, as well as supporting files, for the other VMs. (We'll look at the functions of each of those drivers in "Kernel Mode Drivers" later in this chapter.)

◆ It has exclusive direct access to all the hardware in the system. In conjunction with the virtualization service providers, the parent partition executes I/O requests on behalf of the VM—sending disk traffic out over a Fibre Channel controller, for example.

The following best practices provide a secure and stable parent partition, which is critical to the VMs running on the host. We'll cover other best practices in Chapter 4, "Virtualization Best Practices."

◆ Don't run any other applications or services in the parent partition. This may seem like basic knowledge for system administrators, but it's especially crucial when you're running multiple VMs. In addition to possibly decreasing stability, running multiple roles, features, or applications in the parent partition limits the amount of resources that can otherwise be allocated to VMs.

◆ Use the Windows Server 2008 Core installation option as the parent partition. We'll discuss Windows Server Core in Chapter 2.

FIGURE 1.2

Simplified architecture for Windows Server 2008 with the Hyper-V role added

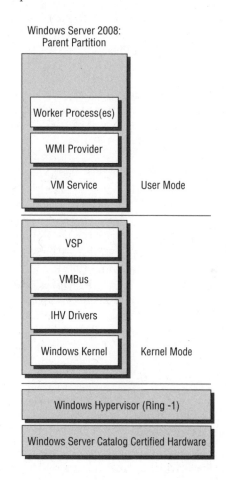

Windows Server 2008:
Parent Partition

Worker Process(es)

WMI Provider

VM Service — User Mode

VSP

VMBus

IHV Drivers

Windows Kernel — Kernel Mode

Windows Hypervisor (Ring -1)

Windows Server Catalog Certified Hardware

WINDOWS HYPERVISOR

The Windows *hypervisor* is the basis for Hyper-V. At its heart, the hypervisor has only a few simple tasks: creating and tearing down partitions and ensuring strong separation between the partitions. (A partition is also known as the basis for a VM.) It doesn't sound like much, but the hypervisor is one of the most critical portions of Hyper-V. That's why the development of the hypervisor followed the Microsoft Security Design Lifecycle process so closely—if the hypervisor is compromised, the entire system can be taken over, because the hypervisor runs in the most privileged mode offered by the x86 architecture.

One of Microsoft's design goals was to make the Microsoft hypervisor as small as possible. Doing so offered two advantages:

◆ The Trusted Computing Base (TCB) is smaller. The TCB is the sum of all the parts of the system that are critical to security. Ensuring that the hypervisor is small reduces its potential attack vectors.

◆ The hypervisor imparts less overhead on the system. Because all VMs (as well as the parent partition) are running on top of the hypervisor, performance becomes a concern. The goal is to minimize the hypervisor's overhead.

KERNEL-MODE DRIVERS

A Windows kernel-mode driver is one of two types of drivers in Windows. Kernel-mode drivers execute in Ring 0. Because this type of driver is executing in kernel mode, it's crucial that these drivers be as secure as possible. An insecure driver, or a crash in the driver, can compromise the entire system.

Hyper-V adds two kernel-mode drivers:

VMBus   VMBus is a high-speed, in-memory bus that was developed specifically for Hyper-V. Each instance of VMBus is a point-to-point connection and is not shared between virtual machines—each virtual machine has its own instance. VMBus acts as the bus for all I/O traffic that takes place between the VMs and the parent partition. VMBus works closely with the virtualization service provider and virtualization service client.

Virtualization Service Provider (VSP)   The Virtualization Service Provider (VSP) enables VMs to securely share the underlying physical hardware. The VSP initiates I/O on behalf of all VMs running on the system. It works in conjunction with the hardware vendor drivers in the parent partition—which means that no special "virtualization" drivers are necessary. If a driver is certified for Windows Server 2008 or R2, it should work as expected with Hyper-V. Each class of device has a VSP present—for example, a default installation of Hyper-V has a networking VSP as well as a storage VSP. The VSPs communicate with the matching Virtualization Service Client (VSC) that runs in the VM over VMBus. We'll cover the VSC when we cover the different types of drivers for virtual machines in the section "Synthetic Device Drivers."

USER-MODE APPLICATIONS

User-mode applications, as might be expected, are applications that run in user mode. They execute in Ring 3, which is where all unprivileged instructions are run. Many of the applications that run in Windows are user-mode applications—for example, the copy of Notepad that you use to look at a text file is executing in user mode.

Hyper-V has a number of user-mode applications:

Virtual Machine Management Service (VMMS)   The VMMS acts as the single point of interaction for all incoming management requests. It interacts with a number of processes, two of which we'll refer to here.

WMI providers   Hyper-V has a rich set of WMI interfaces. They provide a way to manage the state and health of the VMs as well as get settings information and some performance information. All the WMI interfaces are fully documented on `http://msdn.microsoft.com`. Search for *Hyper-V WMI reference*.

Worker processes   When a VM is started, a worker process is created. The worker process represents the actions that are taking place in the virtual processor, as well as all emulated devices and the virtual motherboard. Each VM that is running on a host has a worker process.

Now that we've shown you what's happening in the parent partition, let's look at the VMs. After you create a VM and power it on, you can install a wide variety of x86/x64-based operating systems. Even though these are VMs, they can run the same operating systems as a physical computer. But operating systems that are supported by Microsoft include new synthetic drivers, which work in conjunction with the matching VSP running in the parent partition.

Let's examine how a virtualized operating system handles I/O.

Virtual Machine

A VM can have two different types of devices: emulated and synthetic. Although synthetic devices are better than emulated devices because of their superior performance, they aren't available for all operating systems. Emulated devices are present in Hyper-V mainly for backward compatibility with nonsupported operating systems. VMs running certain distributions of Linux have synthetic device support as well. Let's examine both types of device.

EMULATED DEVICES

Emulated devices in a Hyper-V VM exist primarily for backward compatibility with older operating systems. In an ideal world, all applications would run on the latest version of the operating system they were designed for, but that's far from reality. Many companies have systems in production that run on older copies of operating systems because one of their applications doesn't run on anything newer. An older operating system may not be supported under Hyper-V, which means it can't take advantage of the high-performance I/O. That's not a total loss, however. If you consolidate those older systems onto a newer Hyper-V host, the advantages of moving to a more up-to-date hardware platform can provide a performance boost.

Emulated devices have another key role. During the installation of the VM, operating systems don't have support for the synthetic devices that may be installed in the VM. For that reason, you must use emulated devices—otherwise, the operating system installation can't function. For Hyper-V, it's easy to move from emulated to synthetic devices.

The emulated devices presented to a VM are chosen for their high degree of compatibility across a wide range of operating systems and in-box driver support. As you can see in Figure 1.3, the video card is seen as a Standard VGA Graphics Adapter, and the network card is an Intel 21140-based Ethernet adapter.

FIGURE 1.3
Device Manager for a Windows Server 2008 virtual machine, showing emulated devices

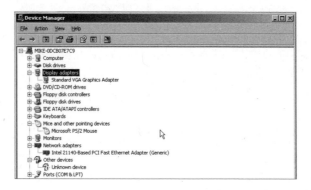

Emulated devices under Hyper-V don't perform as well as the new synthetic devices. Thanks to part of the work that was done to harden the entire virtualization stack, emulated devices execute in the worker process—specifically, in user mode in the parent partition.

How does I/O happen with emulated devices?

Figure 1.4 goes into considerable detail about how emulated storage requests are handled. Emulated networking is handled in a similar fashion.

We want to point out a few specific items:

◆ Context switches are used. A *context switch* occurs when a particular process instruction stops executing in kernel mode and begins executing in user mode. When paired with virtualization, a context switch is an "expensive" operation. There's no money involved, but the CPU cost for such an operation is very high. That time could be spent doing other tasks.

◆ The path that the data packet traverses is long, especially compared to the synthetic case (which we'll review next).

◆ The path illustrated in Figure 1.4 is repeated hundreds of times for a 10 KB write to disk. Imagine if you're doing a large SQL transaction that involved writing hundreds of megabytes to disk or running a popular website being served up from IIS running in the VM. You can see that it won't scale well.

FIGURE 1.4
I/O for emulated storage devices

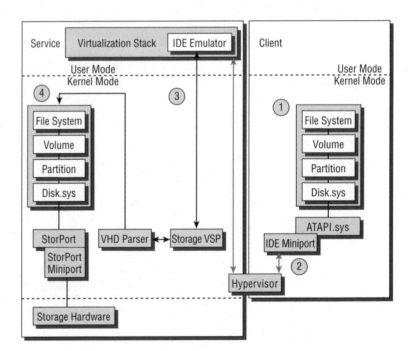

SYNTHETIC DEVICE DRIVERS

Synthetic devices provide much higher performance than their emulated counterparts. By taking advantage of VMBus, synthetic devices can execute I/O transactions at a much faster rate than emulated devices.

Synthetic devices, such as the Microsoft Virtual Machine Bus Network Adapter shown in Figure 1.5, don't have real-world counterparts. They are purely virtual devices that function only with Hyper-V—loading the drivers on a physical system can't be done. These new synthetic devices rely on VMBus.

FIGURE 1.5

Device Manager for a Windows Server 2008 virtual machine, showing synthetic devices

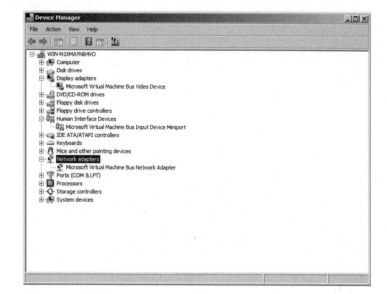

Synthetic device drivers are available only for operating systems that are supported by Microsoft. (For reference, a list of supported operating systems for Hyper-V is available in Knowledge Base article 954958 at `http://support.microsoft.com/kb/954958`). If you're running an operating system in the VM that isn't supported by Microsoft, you'll need to use the emulated devices in the VM.

Much like the emulated storage request chart shown earlier in Figure 1.4, Figure 1.6 (on the next page) presents a lot of data.

Here are a few key differences:

♦ In the beginning, the data path is similar to the emulated data path. However, the synthetic storage device in Hyper-V is a SCSI-based device (or IDE if the Integration Services are installed), so the last driver it hits before getting put on VMBus is the StorPort driver.

♦ When a packet makes it to the miniport driver, it's put on VMBus for transport to the Storage VSP in the parent partition. Because VMBus is a kernel-mode driver, no context switches are necessary.

◆ After the data packet crosses over to the parent partition, the correct destination is determined by the VSP, which routes the packet to the correct device. In Figure 1.6, the destination is a virtual hard disk (VHD) file.

FIGURE 1.6
I/O for synthetic storage devices using VMBus

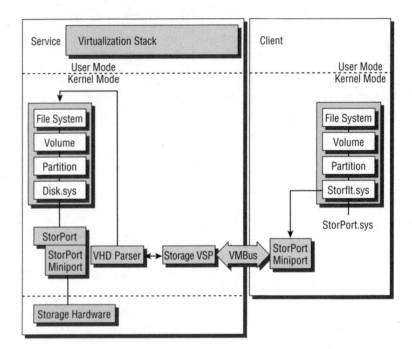

It's easy to install synthetic device drivers in the VM. After you've installed the operating system, select Action ➤ Insert Integration Services Setup Disk. An installer launches and automatically installs the drivers for you. When you reboot, the VM can take advantage of the new architecture. If the host is running Windows Server 2008 R2 and the VM is running Windows Server 2008 SP2 or Windows Server 2008 R2, the integration services are already installed.

NOTE A special synthetic driver technology deals with the boot process: Optimized Boot Performance, also known as *fastpath boot*. Because the synthetic drivers rely on VMBus, you can't boot off hard drives that are connected to the SCSI controller. All isn't lost—during the boot process, after the VMBus driver is loaded, all the IDE boot traffic is automatically routed through the same infrastructure that is used for SCSI traffic. This means the boot process and all disk traffic (reads and writes) perform at the same accelerated speed.

LINUX DEVICE DRIVERS

No, that's not a typo—certain distributions of Linux are supported under Hyper-V. Not only is the operating system supported, but a full set of device drivers also enable synthetic device support under Linux (see Figure 1.7 on the next page). We'll go into more detail in Chapter 4.

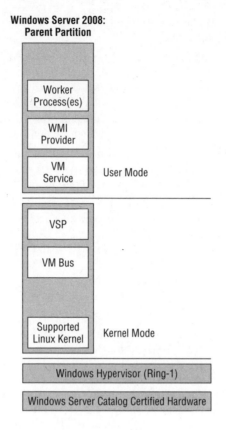

FIGURE 1.7
Synthetic
device support
under Linux

**Windows Server 2008:
Parent Partition**

Worker Process(es)

WMI Provider

VM Service

User Mode

VSP

VM Bus

Supported Linux Kernel

Kernel Mode

Windows Hypervisor (Ring-1)

Windows Server Catalog Certified Hardware

Features of Hyper-V

Now that we've gone over both the scenarios and architecture of Hyper-V, let's dive into some of the features of Microsoft's virtualization platform. First you'll learn about the general features of Hyper-V, and then you'll learn about the new features in Windows Server 2008 R2.

General Features

The following are the general features of Hyper-V:

32-bit (x86) and 64-bit (x64) VMs   Hyper-V provides support for both 32-bit and 64-bit VMs. This lets users provision both architectures on the same platform, easing the transition to 64-bit and providing legacy 32-bit operating systems.

Large memory support (64 GB) within VMs   With support for up to 64 GB of RAM per virtual machine, Hyper-V scales out to run the vast majority of enterprise-class workloads. Hyper-V can also use up to a total of 1 TB of RAM on the host for Windows Server 2008 or can use up to 2 TB on Windows Server 2008 R2.

SMP virtual machines   Symmetric Multi Processor (SMP) support allows VMs to recognize and utilize up to four virtual processors in certain supported operating systems. As a result, server applications running in a Hyper-V VM can take full advantage of all the host system's processing power.

Integrated cluster support for quick migration, live migration, and high availability
Windows Server 2008 Hyper-V and high availability (HA) go hand in hand. As we'll discuss in Chapter 8, "Achieving High Availability," it is easy to create a failover cluster of VM hosts that your VMs can live on. After you set up the failover cluster, you can quickly and easily move a VM from one host to the other from the Failover Cluster Manager or from other management tools (such as System Center Virtual Machine Manager).

Volume Shadow Services integration for data protection   Hyper-V includes a Volume Shadow Services (VSS) provider. As we discussed earlier in the list of scenarios, VSS lets backup applications prepare the system for a backup without requiring the applications (or VMs) to be shut down.

Pass-through high-performance disk access for VMs   When a physical volume is connected directly to the VM, disk I/O–intensive workloads can perform at their peak. If the Windows Server 2008 system can see the volume in the Disk Management control panel, the volume can be passed through to the VM.

Although you'll see faster performance with pass-through disk access, certain features (such as snapshots, differencing disks, and host-side backup) that you get from using a VHD file aren't available with pass-through disks.

VM snapshots   Snapshots let administrators capture a point in time for the VM (including state, data, and configuration). You can then roll back to that snapshot at a later point in time or split from that snapshot to go down a different path. The snapshot is a key feature for the test and development scenario, because it lets users easily maintain separate points in time. For example, a user may install an operating system inside a VM and take a snapshot. The user can perform a number of tasks and then take a second snapshot. Then, the user can return to either of those snapshots later, saving configuration time and effort.

New hardware-sharing architecture (VSP/VSC/VMBus)   By using the new VMBus communication protocol for all virtual devices, Hyper-V can provide higher levels of performance than were previously seen with Microsoft virtualization products.

Robust networking: VLANs and NLB   Virtual Local Area Network (VLAN) tagging—also referred to as the IEEE standard 802.1Q—provides a secure method for multiple networks to use the same physical media. Hyper-V supports VLAN tagging (802.1Q) on the virtual network interfaces and specifies a VLAN tag for the network interface.

Network Load Balancing (NLB) support in Hyper-V allows VMs to participate in an NLB cluster. An NLB cluster is different from a failover cluster, such as those used for VM quick migration. NLB clusters are configured with front-end nodes that handle all incoming traffic and route it to multiple servers on the back end.

DMTF standard for WMI management interface   The Distributed Management Task Force (DMTF) is a standards body that provides a uniform set of standards for the management of IT environments. Microsoft has worked closely with the DMTF to ensure that all the management interfaces for Hyper-V adhere to the standards, allowing management tools from multiple vendors to manage the system.

Support for full or Server Core installations   Hyper-V can run on a full installation of Windows Server 2008 as well as the Server Core option of installation.

New Features in Windows Server 2008 R2

With the release of Windows Server 2008 R2, some significant new functionality has been added to the Hyper-V role:

Live migration   Offers the ability to move a virtual machine from one cluster node to another without any user-perceptible downtime

Support for 64 logical processors   Allows you to take full advantage of the newest multi-core processors

Processor compatibility mode   Allows administrators to use nonmatching systems in a Failover Cluster configuration

Enhanced processor functionality support   Provides support for Second Level Address Translation functionality in newer processors, reducing the work that the hypervisor has to do

Hot-add/remove of storage   Allows dynamic storage growth inside the virtual machine

TCP Offload/VM queue support   Enables the virtual network adapter to offload tasks to the host's network adapter, enhancing network performance

We'll cover all of these items in later chapters. Now that we've covered the list of Hyper-V features, we'll talk about the system requirements.

ADVANTAGES OVER VIRTUAL SERVER

Windows Server 2008 Hyper-V has a number of advantages over Virtual Server 2005 R2 SP1:

◆ Support for SMP and 64-bit VMs. Virtual Server was limited to 32-bit uniprocessor virtual machines.

◆ Support for more than 3.6 GB of RAM per VM.

◆ Support for mapping a logical unit number (LUN) directly to a VM.

◆ Increased performance from VSP/VSC architecture.

◆ Hyper-V management via a Microsoft Management Console (MMC)–based interface instead of the web-based console.

However, it's impossible for users who have only 32-bit hardware in their environment to move to Hyper-V (because it's a feature of the 64-bit version of Windows Server 2008).

Hardware and Software Requirements for Hyper-V

Because Hyper-V is included as a role of Windows Server 2008 x64 edition, it inherits the same hardware requirements. However, a few areas require special attention for Hyper-V.

Hardware Requirements and Best Practices

Some of the requirements for Hyper-V are hard requirements, such as the type of processor, whereas others are best practices to ensure that Hyper-V performs optimally.

PROCESSOR

Hyper-V requires a 64-bit capable processor with two separate extensions: hardware-assisted virtualization and data-execution prevention.

Hardware-assisted virtualization is given a different name by each vendor—Intel calls it Virtualization Technology (VT), and AMD calls it AMD Virtualization (AMD-V). Almost all processors now ship with those features present, but check with your processor manufacturer to make sure.

Although the functionality is required in the processor, it's also required to be enabled in the BIOS. Each system manufacturer has a different way of exposing the functionality, as well as a different name for it. However, most, if not all, manufacturers provide a way to enable or disable it in the BIOS. You can enable it in the BIOS, but some systems don't enable the feature unless there's a hard-power cycle—shutting off the system completely, for example. *We recommend that the system be completely powered off.*

Data-execution prevention (DEP) goes by different names depending on the processor manufacturer—Intel calls it eXecute Disable (XD), and AMD refers to it as No eXecute (NX). DEP helps protect your system against malware and improperly written programs by monitoring memory reads and writes to ensure that memory pages marked as *Data* aren't executed. Because you'll be running multiple VMs on a single system, ensuring stability of the hosting system is crucial.

STORAGE

As we talked about earlier, Hyper-V's architecture lets you use standard Windows device drivers in conjunction with the VSP/VSC architecture. As such, any of the storage devices listed in the Windows Server Catalog will work with Hyper-V. These include SCSI, SAS, Fibre Channel, and iSCSI—if there's a driver for it, Hyper-V can use it. Of course, you'll want to take some considerations into account when planning the ideal Hyper-V host. We'll talk about those more in Chapter 4, "Virtualization Best Practices."

Here are some of the areas where extra attention is necessary:

Multiple spindles and I/O paths Most disk-intensive workloads, such as database servers, need multiple spindles to achieve high performance. Hyper-V's storage architecture enables those workloads to be virtualized without the traditional performance penalty. When multiple disk-intensive workloads share the same disk infrastructure, they can quickly slow to a crawl.

Having multiple disks (as well as multiple I/O paths) is highly recommended for disk-intensive workloads. Even two workloads sharing a host bus adapter with a single Fibre Channel can saturate the controller, leading to decreased performance. Having multiple controllers also can provide redundancy for critical workloads.

Disk configurations for optimal performance Hyper-V has a number of ways to store the VM's data, each with its own pros and cons:

◆ Pass-through disks

  ◆ *Pros*: Pass-through disks generally provide the highest performance. The VM writes directly to the disk volume without any intermediate layer, so you can see near-native levels of performance.

  ◆ *Cons*: Maintaining the storage volumes for each VM can be extremely challenging, especially for large enterprise deployments. Additionally, snapshots can't be used with pass-through disks.

- Fixed virtual hard disks

  - *Pros*: These are the best choice for production environments using VHD files. Because you allocate all the disk space when you create the VHD file, you don't see the expansion penalty that occurs with the dynamically expanding VHD. With Windows Server 2008 R2, performance is nearly on par with a pass-through disk.

  - *Cons*: Because all the space for the VHD is allocated at creation, the VHD file can be large.

- Dynamic virtual hard disks

  - *Pros*: A dynamically expanding VHD expands on demand, saving space on the system until it's needed. Disks can remain small. Dynamic virtual hard disk files are great for use in development and test environments but are not recommended for production.

  - *Cons*: There is a small performance penalty when a disk is expanded. If large amounts of data are being written, the disk will need to be expanded multiple times.

Snapshots   Snapshots are extremely useful in the test and development environment. However, what can be helpful in one environment can be harmful in another. You shouldn't use snapshots in a production environment, because rolling back to a previous state without taking the proper precautions can mean data loss!

NETWORKING

Much like storage, networking with Hyper-V inherits the rich driver support of Windows Server 2008. Many of the caveats for storage apply to networking as well—ensure that multiple network interface cards (NICs) are present so a single interface doesn't become the bottleneck.
  The following list identifies areas where you should pay special attention with networking:

- Hyper-V supports Ethernet network adapters, including 10, 100, 1000, and even 10Gb-E network adapters. Hyper-V can't use ATM or Token Ring adapters, and it can't use wireless (802.11) adapters to provide network access to the VMs.

- During the Hyper-V role installation (which we'll cover in Chapter 2), you can create a virtual network for each network adapter in your system.

- We recommend that you set aside a single NIC to manage the host. That NIC shouldn't be used for any VMs (no virtual switch should be associated with it). Alternatively, you can use out-of-band management tools to manage the host. Such tools typically use an onboard management port to provide an interface to the system.

Software Requirements

Hyper-V is a feature of Windows Server 2008 x64 edition and Windows Server 2008 R2 only. There's no support for Hyper-V in the x86 (aka 32-bit) edition or the Itanium versions of Windows Server 2008. The x64 edition is required for a couple of reasons:

Kernel address space   The 64-bit version of Windows Server 2008 provides a much larger kernel address space as compared to the 32-bit edition. This directly translates into the support of larger processes, which is crucial for virtualization.

Large amount of host memory   Windows Server 2008 Hyper-V supports up to 1 TB of RAM on the host. x86 versions of Windows Server 2008 support only up to 64 GB of RAM on the host, which would severely limit the number of VMs you could run. With Windows Server 2008 R2 Hyper-V, this limitation has been removed, and Hyper-V supports up to 2 TB of RAM.

We're frequently asked to explain the differences with Hyper-V between editions of Windows Server 2008. There's no difference—the features of Hyper-V are the same, regardless of whether you're running the Standard, Enterprise, or Datacenter product. However, differences in the editions of Windows Server 2008 affect key virtualization scenarios:

Processor sockets   Windows Server 2008 Standard is limited to four sockets, whereas Enterprise supports eight sockets.

Memory   Windows Server 2008 Standard supports up to 4 GB of RAM on 32-bit editions and up to 32 GB of RAM on 64-bit editions. Windows Server 2008 Enterprise supports up to 2 TB of RAM.

Failover clustering   Windows Server 2008 Standard doesn't include the failover-clustering functionality required for quick migration.

Virtual image use rights   Windows Server 2008 includes the rights to run additional instances of the installed operating system. The number and type of those virtual images are tied to the edition, as illustrated in Table 1.1. The edition of the operating system can be the installed operating system or a lower-level edition. For example, a Windows Server 2008 R2 Enterprise license grants four virtual image use rights that can be Enterprise or Standard. Windows Server 2008 R2 Datacenter provides unlimited virtual image use rights, and the virtual images can be Datacenter, Enterprise, or Standard. For more information on Windows Server downgrade rights, refer to www.microsoft.com/windowsserver2008/en/us/downgrade-rights.aspx.

TABLE 1.1:   Virtual Image Usage Rights

EDITION	VIRTUAL IMAGE USAGE RIGHTS	EDITIONS SUPPORTED AS VIRTUAL IMAGES
Standard	1	Standard
Enterprise	4	Enterprise, Standard
Datacenter	Unlimited	Datacenter, Enterprise, Standard

Summary

In this chapter, we've provided a great deal of information about Hyper-V. From its scenarios to its architecture to its features, we've laid the groundwork. In the upcoming chapters, we'll go into depth about many of the items we touched on here. Keep reading to find out why you should deploy Hyper-V in your environment.

Chapter 2

Installing Hyper-V and Server Core

In Chapter 1, "Introducing Hyper-V," we spent a great deal of time talking about the "why" for Hyper-V. Now let's look at how to actually start using Hyper-V. Because Hyper-V is a built-in role of the operating system, installation is quite simple. However, you need to take certain steps to ensure that you're using the latest version of Hyper-V.

In this chapter, we'll cover three different usage scenarios. First, we'll look at a clean installation—installing Windows Server 2008 and Hyper-V on a clean system. Then, we'll look at upgrading from the beta version of Hyper-V included with Windows Server 2008 to the final version of Hyper-V. For those of you running Windows Server 2008 SP2 or Windows Server 2008 R2, though, you don't need to update.

Finally, we'll end with a discussion of using Windows Server Core as a host operating system and address some of the common pitfalls that system administrators run into when getting used to this new installation option of Windows Server 2008. We'll also cover some of the significant benefits that using Windows Server Core brings to administrators.

We'll cover the following topics in this chapter:

- Performing a clean installation of Hyper-V

- Updating from the beta version to the final version of Hyper-V

- Installing Windows Server Core

- Installing Windows Server 2008 as a Core installation

Performing a Clean Installation of Hyper-V

Use these instructions if you do not have Hyper-V already installed and do not have any virtual machines. If you do have virtual machines and you want to preserve them, go to the "Updating from the Beta Version to the Final Version of Hyper-V" section later in this chapter.

You can install Hyper-V in two ways. Both installation methods result in the same binaries being installed—which one you prefer depends on how you as an administrator perform system updates. Although some of the intermediate steps are different, both installation paths begin and end the same way.

Before we get started, let's address perhaps the most burning question—why didn't the final version of Windows Server 2008 have the final version of Hyper-V? When Windows Server 2008 shipped, it included the beta version of Hyper-V. In a perfect world, the Windows Server 2008 media would have included the final version of Hyper-V. However, software development is rarely a perfect world, so it was decided that the Hyper-V Release to Manufacturing (RTM) update would be released after Windows Server 2008 shipped.

These instructions will cover how to install the RTM update for Microsoft Hyper-V.

Meeting the Installation Requirements

Before starting the installation of Windows Server 2008 or Windows Server 2008 R2, confirm that the system meets the requirements of the version that's being installed. Each version of Windows Server 2008 has a different set of hardware requirements as well as supported features.

For example, the Standard edition of Windows Server 2008 doesn't include the failover clustering functionality (required for Quick Migration and Live Migration, covered in Chapter 8, "Achieving High Availability"). The other editions, Enterprise and Datacenter, include that functionality (which enables Quick Migration and Live Migration) as well as additional virtualization usage rights. Table 2.1 covers the processor sockets, memory, virtual image rights, and other features across all three editions of Windows.

TABLE 2.1:   Comparison of Windows Server 2008 x64 Editions

FEATURE	WINDOWS SERVER 2008 STANDARD	WINDOWS SERVER 2008 ENTERPRISE	WINDOWS SERVER 2008 DATACENTER
Processor sockets supported	4	8	64
Memory	32 GB	2 TB	2 TB
Virtual image rights	1	4	Unlimited
Failover Clustering	Not included	Included	Included

TIP   Microsoft has a tool that helps system administrators evaluate their current IT infrastructure and provides an easy-to-read report specifying what Microsoft technologies are best for the given environment. You can download the Microsoft Assessment and Planning Toolkit Solution Accelerator from http://go.microsoft.com/fwlink/?LinkId=111000.

To install Windows Server 2008 or Windows Server 2008 R2, follow these simple steps:

1. Start up your system with the Windows Server 2008 or R2 DVD in the drive, or boot the system to a Pre-boot eXecution Environment (PXE) deployment server over the network.

2. If you're prompted to enter a product key, enter the key that came with the copy of Windows Server 2008 or R2.

3. After you type in the product key, you're presented with a list of available installation choices. Select the version for which the system is licensed.

4. The installer automatically proceeds and reboots a few times. After the installation is complete, the login screen appears.

> **WINDOWS SERVER VS. WINDOWS SERVER CORE**
>
> Another installation option for Windows Server 2008, called Windows Server Core, has some significant differences that may make you think twice about using a full installation of Windows Server 2008.
>
> Windows Server Core is a new minimal installation option that contains a subset of the roles and features of a full installation of Windows Server 2008. A Core installation offers lower overhead and a reduced attack surface, making it an ideal partition for virtualization. For more information, see the "Installing Windows Server Core" section later in this chapter.

Installing the Hyper-V Role

Installing the Hyper-V role is the same on both Windows Server 2008 and Windows Server 2008 R2. However, if Windows Server 2008 is used, then it's necessary to update the Hyper-V functionality to the final RTM version. Now that you have installed the base OS, you have two different ways to update the installed version of Hyper-V to the final release.

If you have, or plan to install, Windows Server 2008 SP2, you don't need to do this update. Go to the "Adding the Hyper-V Role" section later in this chapter.

UPDATING VIA WINDOWS UPDATE (FOR PRE-SP2 VERSIONS OF WINDOWS SERVER 2008)

Windows Update is one of the ways that Microsoft distributes updates. You can configure it a number of ways; for example, you can apply updates automatically or only after the approval of an administrator. Updates that are posted to Windows Update are assigned a priority, ranging from Optional to Recommended.

To update from the installed beta version of Hyper-V to the RTM version via Windows Update, follow these steps:

1. Open Windows Update. Browse to Start ➤ All Programs ➤ Windows Update.

2. By default, Automatic Updating is turned off. You can enable it by clicking the Turn On Now button. Clicking the button will caused updates to be installed automatically every day at 3 a.m.

If you want the updates to be installed at different times or if you want to approve updates before they are installed, click the Change Settings link. You're presented with a number of options for how Windows Update will update the system. These options provide more control over what updates are applied, at the cost of manual approval of updates.

NOTE   Group Policy settings can set the default action and block users from making changes.

Regardless of the choice, you need to make one before you can proceed.

3. To do a manual check for updates, click the Check For Updates button. Doing so contacts either the Microsoft Update server or the local Windows Software Update Services (WSUS) server for a listing of the updates that apply to the system.

4. In the list of applicable updates, Update For Windows Server 2008 x64 Edition (KB950050) should be listed. Ensure that the check box is selected. This option updates the offline package store on the system so that when the Hyper-V role is added, the RTM version will be used.

5. Select any other updates to be applied, and click the Install button.

UPDATING VIA DOWNLOAD CENTER (FOR PRE-SP2 VERSIONS OF WINDOWS SERVER 2008)

If your system doesn't have access to the Internet (and therefore can't use the Windows Update functionality), you can, using another system with Internet access, download the Hyper-V RTM update from the following website:

```
http://support.microsoft.com/kb/950050
```

Copy the downloaded file to the new Hyper-V host, and run it. Doing so updates the offline package store on the system so when the role is added, the final version will be used.

NOTE Don't download the update from any website other than Microsoft's.

TIP If you're installing on a number of systems, it's possible to slipstream the Hyper-V RTM update into the installation media. For more information, refer to the "Hyper-V Installation Tricks – Part 3: Integrated Installation and The Beauty of the Win6 Servicing Stack" article on the blog Virtual Varia at the following URL:

```
http://blogs.msdn.com/mikekol/archive/2008/03/27/hyper-v-installation-tricks-part-3-
integrated-installation-and-the-beauty-of-the-win6-servicing-stack.aspx
```

The author reviews how to integrate the final version of Hyper-V into the installation media.

Adding the Hyper-V Role

To add the Hyper-V role, you use Server Manager (see Figure 2.1), which is a central console for most administration tasks against a host computer.

Follow these steps:

1. From the Start menu, open Server Manager, and expand the Roles option on the left side of the window.

2. Server Manager uses a wizard to walk you through adding a role to a system. Click the Add Roles link on the right to start the wizard.

3. After an introductory page, the Add Roles Wizard lists all the roles that are available to add to the server. Select the Hyper-V role, and then click Next.

After the introductory page for Hyper-V appears, which describes what Hyper-V does, you see the screen shown in Figure 2.2.

FIGURE 2.1

Server Manager on a clean install of Windows Server 2008

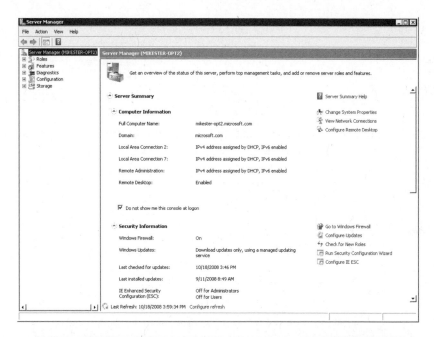

FIGURE 2.2

Create Virtual Networks screen in Server Manager

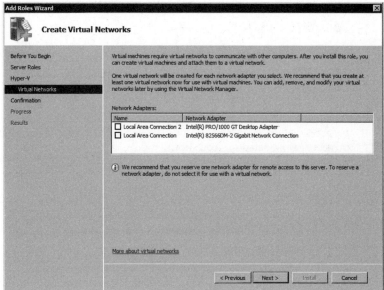

As we'll discuss in Chapter 3, "Configuring Hyper-V," a virtual machine has three types of virtual networks that can be used for network traffic. The setup process for Hyper-V provides an easy-to-use method for creating external virtual networks; this process allows virtual machines to send traffic over physical network adapters that are installed on the host.

NOTE   What if Hyper-V isn't listed? There are a few possible causes for this:

◆ Are you using the x64 version of Windows Server 2008? Hyper-V isn't included in the x86 versions of Windows Server 2008. Windows Server 2008 R2 is available in the x64 edition only.

◆ Did you use an installation disc that has Windows Server 2008 without Hyper-V? This product no longer exists with Windows Server 2008 R2.

◆ When you add the role, does the Hyper-V Manager say *beta*? If so, the update didn't apply successfully.

4. To create a virtual network, select the check box next to the name of the Ethernet card installed on the host.

NOTE   It's highly recommended that you set aside one network interface card (NIC) for remote administration of the host and that you not create a virtual network on it. We'll cover this topic in more detail in Chapter 4, "Utilizing Virtualization Best Practices."

5. Select the virtual networks to be created, and click Next.

After confirming the installation choices, the system performs the installation and then reboots. (In some cases, the system will reboot twice.) The Hyper-V role has now been installed.

6. Browse to Administrative Tools in the Start menu, and launch the Hyper-V Manager to start using Hyper-V.

Updating from the Beta Version to the Final Version of Hyper-V

As we discussed earlier, the final version of Windows Server 2008 included the beta version of Hyper-V. Before you update to the final version of Hyper-V, you must perform several steps to protect against data loss. You should follow these instructions if you want to upgrade to the final version without losing your existing virtual machines.

Performing the Pre-update Configuration

Unfortunately, there is no central site for configuration data. Therefore, you must follow the following four steps for basic configuration before you apply the update:

1. *Record the static IP configuration*: If the virtual machine is set up to use a static IP address, write it down. As part of the upgrade process, the virtual machine will need to be re-created using the old virtual hard disk (VHD). Because the new virtual machine will have a new Media Access Control (MAC) address for the Ethernet controller, the old static IP address won't be recognized.

2. *Shut down all virtual machines*: Saved states from earlier versions of Hyper-V can't be used when moving forward to a newer version.

3. *Commit all snapshots*: Snapshots aren't compatible between the beta version and the RTM of Hyper-V. Additionally, because virtual machines will need to be re-created, actively using a snapshot when the RTM update is applied can possibly lead to data loss.

4. *Record virtual network names*: Any virtual networks that were created under the beta of Hyper-V will need to be re-created. If you want to maintain the same names after the update is applied, record the name of each virtual network so it can be re-created after updating.

Now, follow the steps outlined earlier in this chapter to apply the Hyper-V RTM update to your host via Windows Update or the Microsoft Download Center.

Performing the Post-update Configuration

After you've applied the Hyper-V RTM update, follow these steps to configure your system:

1. *Re-create virtual networks*: Create any custom virtual networks that were present in the earlier version of Hyper-V. We'll cover how to do this in Chapter 3.

2. *Re-create virtual machines*: If virtual machines were running on the host before you updated to the RTM version of Hyper-V, they will need to be re-created. Follow the steps in Chapter 3 to create a virtual machine from an existing VHD file.

3. *Update integration components*: The Hyper-V RTM update includes new integration components that need to be updated in the virtual machine. You can find information about how to apply the updated integration components in Chapter 4.

Upgrading Hyper-V from Windows Server 2008 to Windows Server 2008 R2

If you have an existing installation of Windows Server 2008 Hyper-V and want to upgrade to R2, that's a fully supported upgrade. There are three ways to do it.

◆ *Do an in-place upgrade to Windows Server 2008 R2*: This is by far the easiest way to upgrade. By performing an in-place upgrade, your virtual machines will be preserved in the Hyper-V Manager and your settings will be maintained. You must check the following three items before performing the upgrade:

  ◆ You must be running the RTM version of Hyper-V. You can check to see whether KB950050 is installed. If KB950050 is not installed, then the upgrade is blocked.

  ◆ All the virtual machines must be shut down, because the saved states are not compatible.

  ◆ Any snapshots that were taken when the virtual machine was powered on need to be committed to the parent disk.

◆ *Export your virtual machines from a Windows Server 2008 host to a Windows Server 2008 R2 host*: If you have another host that is already running Windows Server 2008 R2, then a virtual machine can be exported to that new host. However, before exporting, make sure that the virtual machine is shut down and that any snapshots are merged.

◆ *Back up and restore the VM*: Back up the virtual machine running on Windows Server 2008 using the Hyper-V VSS writer, and restore the VM from the backup on a Windows Server 2008 R2 host.

After the host operating system has been upgraded successfully, make sure Integration Services is updated in the virtual machine. For more information on Integration Services, refer to Chapter 4.

NOTE If you have an existing failover cluster that's providing high availability of Hyper-V virtual machines for Quick Migration, then refer to the following link for information specifically aimed at migrating a cluster from Windows Server 2008 to Windows Server 2008 R2: http://support.microsoft.com/kb/957256.

Installing Windows Server Core

Windows Server Core is an installation option of Windows Server 2008.

A full installation of Windows Server 2008 includes the full user interface. This is the only installation option that has been present for Windows Server until now.

Windows Server Core removes the Windows Explorer shell from the operating system and instead presents only a command line (see Figure 2.3). Windows Server Core is included in all the Windows Server 2008 editions—Standard, Enterprise, Datacenter, and Web.

FIGURE 2.3
Windows Server
2008 Enterprise
in the Core
installation

Exploring the Windows Server Core Architecture

The architecture of Windows Server Core is extremely similar to a full installation of Windows Server 2008. Windows Server Core uses the same device drivers, has the same kernel installed on disk, and behaves the same way as a full installation of Windows Server. The main difference is that the graphical subsystem of Windows, as well as other products and services, are absent from a Server Core installation. This means that any application that relies on any of those pieces of functionality won't run. Some applications, such as SQL Server 2008, also won't work on a Windows Server 2008 Server Core installation. Additionally, items such as Internet Explorer and Windows Mail have been removed. With Windows Server 2008 R2, the .NET Framework has been added to Windows Server Core. By including the .NET Framework, Windows PowerShell and a subset of the ASP.NET framework are now available in a Core installation.

ADVANTAGES

Windows Server Core offers a number of benefits, regardless of its intended use:

Reduced maintenance By default, a Windows Server Core system has very few binaries installed. No longer will your Windows Servers need updates for Internet Explorer, Outlook, or other little-used components. Systems running Windows Server Core can see up to 40 percent fewer patches compared to systems running Windows Server 2003.

Reduced attack surface Because fewer applications and services are running on the server, there are fewer avenues to exploit. Exploits aimed at components that don't exist on the server don't get a chance to work.

Reduced management Because fewer components are installed on the system, there's less administrative overhead.

Less disk space required Fewer binaries being installed on disk mean that less disk space is required. Windows Server Core requires only around 2 GB of disk space, as opposed to around 10 GB for a full installation of Windows Server 2008.

Reduced memory Because fewer components are installed by default and there's no GUI overhead, Windows Server Core typically uses 500 MB to 1 GB less memory than a full installation. This memory savings can be used for more or larger virtual machines.

DISADVANTAGES

Although the benefits of the Server Core installation option sound great, administrators need to be aware of the following concerns:

Remote management requirement Because Windows Server Core provides no local GUI-based administration tools, you perform the bulk of administration for the system from another system with a full installation of Windows Server 2008 or enterprise management tools. Many of the Windows administration tools that are accessed through the Microsoft Management Console (MMC) can be configured to administer other computers in either a workgroup or a domain setting.

Command-line interface only The only interface presented at a console or remote logon on a Windows Server Core system is the command line. For some administrators, that's preferred— and those administrators probably use batch files (`.bat`) and command scripts (`.cmd`) to perform mundane administration tasks. Not all administrators prefer that approach, however.

No PowerShell (Windows Server 2008 only) Because Windows Server 2008 Core doesn't include the .NET Framework, the PowerShell feature isn't available. You can still use PowerShell from another system to perform administrative tasks against the Windows Server Core system via Windows Management Interface (WMI).

Inability to upgrade from Server Core to full A Windows Server Core installation can't be "upgraded" to a full installation of Windows Server. To move to a full installation of Windows Server 2008, you must reinstall the system.

Configuration challenges Changing some vendor-specific settings for certain drivers, such as network or storage drivers, requires modifying the Windows registry. Some vendors have provided command-line functionality, but not all have—check with the hardware vendor for the latest drivers.

Managing Windows Server Core

You can manage Windows Server Core in a number of ways:

Local command prompt   Many of the command-line utilities present in a full installation of Windows Server 2008 also exist in a Server Core installation. This allows administrators to perform the same tasks using a common tool set.

Remote Desktop Services   Windows Server Core supports Remote Desktop Services Administration mode. Administrators can connect to the Server Core system from another Windows system for administrative purposes. The user experience is identical—the user logging in from the remote system will only get a command prompt in their Remote Desktop session.

NOTE   Remote Desktop Services Administration is disabled by default, just as it is on a full installation of Windows Server 2008. We provide instructions on how to enable Remote Desktop Services Administration later in Chapter 4.

WS-Management   Web Services for Management (WS-Management) is a relatively newly defined standard in the IT world. It provides a common method for systems to access and exchange management information across the entire IT infrastructure. Many management tools, including System Center Virtual Machine Manager, use WS-Management to communicate between the client and the server.

Windows Remote Shell   By adding this feature, administrators can execute commands on a Server Core system from another system via the command line. Windows Remote Shell uses WS-Management to pass the commands from one system to another.

To add Windows Remote Shell, follow these steps:

1. From the Windows Server Core system, run the following command:

    ```
    WinRM quickconfig
    ```

2. Now, from a separate Windows Server 2008 or Windows Vista or Windows 7 system, you can execute commands against the Windows Server Core system like this:

    ```
    Winrs -r:<server_core_system> dir
    ```

This generates a directory listing of the remote Windows Server Core system.

Windows Script Host   Windows Server Core includes the `cscript.exe` application, allowing you to run scripts for administrative purposes. You can write scripts in a variety of different languages—Jscript, VBScript, and so on (providing the scripting engine for that language is installed).

Microsoft Management Console (MMC) and Server Manager   By adding the Windows Remote Server Administration Toolkit on a Windows Vista or Windows 7 system, a Windows Server Core system can be administered remotely by using the Server Manager MMC snap-in. A Windows Server Core installation can also be administered from a full installation of Windows Server.

Installing Windows Server 2008 as a Core Installation

We've spent a great deal of time talking about the advantages and disadvantages of Windows Server Core. Now we'll show how to deploy Hyper-V on a Windows Server 2008 Core installation.

Installation Considerations and Requirements

As we detailed in the previous section, there are pros and cons to running Windows Server Core. Before you implement Windows Server Core, system planners should ensure that their tools and scripts work as expected in the Windows Server Core environment and that administrators are comfortable in the command-line environment. Additionally, you should confirm system management and antivirus tool functionality. Management agents can't have any dependencies on the Windows shell or GUI, and they can't use managed code.

The installation requirements for Windows Server Core are nearly the same as for a full installation of Windows Server 2008, which we talked about earlier in this chapter (see Table 2.2). The main difference is in the amount of disk space required. Because Windows Server Core has fewer binaries on disk, it requires less disk space.

TABLE 2.2: Installation Requirements for Full Installation vs. Core Installation

	WINDOWS SERVER: FULL	**WINDOWS SERVER: CORE**
Processor	1.4 GHz or faster processor minimum, 2 GHz or faster recommended.	1.4 GHz or faster processor minimum, 2 GHz or faster recommended.
Memory	512 MB minimum. Maximum supported memory depends on edition.	512 MB minimum. Maximum supported memory depends on edition.
Disk	20 GB space minimum, 40 GB or more recommended.	10 GB space minimum, 40 GB or more recommended.
Other	DVD-ROM drive, keyboard, mouse.	DVD-ROM drive, keyboard, mouse.

Performing a Core Installation

Installing Windows Server Core is the same as performing a full installation:

1. Start the system with the Windows Server 2008 DVD in the drive, or boot the system to a PXE deployment server over the network.

2. If you're prompted to enter a product key, enter the key that came with the copy of Windows Server 2008.

3. After you type in the product key, you're presented with a list of available installation choices (see Figure 2.4). Select the version for which the system is licensed in the Server Core installation—this will install Windows Server 2008 in the Server Core configuration.

FIGURE 2.4
Installation
options for Win-
dows Server 2008

4. Select the volume for installation, and the installer automatically proceeds and reboots a few times. After the installation is complete, the login screen appears. In the full server install only, you must set the password for the administrator as the initial step.

Doing the Initial Configuration

Because Windows Server Core has no graphical elements, you need to use the command line to configure the system. We'll cover some of the most common configuration steps in this section. You can find additional information about configuration at the Windows Server site: www.microsoft.com/windowsserver2008. If you use Windows Server 2008 R2, see the section "Windows Server 2008 R2: Introducing sconfig" later in this chapter.

Activate a Windows Server Core system To activate a Windows Server Core system, run the following command:

```
cscript.exe %windir%\system32\slmgr.vbs -ato
```

This command attempts to activate the installed copy of Windows over the Internet or against a local Key Management Services (KMS) server.

Configure a static IP address for a management NIC We'll talk about a management NIC in more detail in Chapter 4. With Windows Server Core, you have no graphical tools for the configuration of the NIC's properties—you must configure it from the command line. Specifically, the netsh command-line tool provides the functionality to set the IP addresses on the NIC, among other things. To set the management NIC to use a static IP address, run the following commands:

```
Netsh interface ipv4
show interfaces
```

```
set address name="ID" source=static address=StaticIP mask=SubnetMask
gateway=DefaultGateway
add dnsserver name="ID" address=DNSIP index=1
netsh interface set interface name name="OLD_NAME" newname="Management NIC"
```

Set the machine name   To set the name of the Windows Server Core system, run the following command:

```
Netdom.exe renamecomputer %computername% /newname:<new_computer_name>
```

Join a domain (if desired)   Use `netdom.exe` to join the system to a domain. Run the following command:

```
Netdom.exe join %computername% /domain:<domain_name> /userd:<user_name> /
password:<password>
```

Add users to the administrator's group   Logging in as the local administrator, especially in a domain environment, is usually a very bad idea. By adding individual administrators to the administrator's group, you can audit actions in case of issues.

To add a user account to the administrator's group, run the following command:
```
net localgroup administrators /add <user_account>
```

OTHER HELPFUL SCRIPTS FOR THE COMMAND LINE

Here are a few extra tips that aren't related to virtualization but are still good techniques to know.

To enable Remote Administration, run the following command:

```
Cscript.exe \windows\system32\scregedit.wsf /ar 0
```

To enable Remote Administration to accept connections from systems before Windows Vista or Windows Server 2008, run the following command:

```
Cscript.exe \windows\system32\scregedit.wsf /cs 0
```

To enable Automatic Updating, run the following commands:

```
Cscript.exe \windows\system32\scregedit.wsf /au 4
net stop wuauserv
net start wuauserv
```

To disable the Windows Firewall, run the following command:

```
netsh firewall set opmode disable
```

You can find additional functionality in the `\windows\system32\scregedit.wsf` script.

Installing Hyper-V Under Windows Server 2008 Server Core

Installing Hyper-V under Windows Server Core requires the same series of steps as installing Hyper-V on a full installation of Windows Server 2008. We covered those steps earlier in this chapter in "Adding the Hyper-V Role." However, because of the command-line interface, there are a few differences.

PREREQUISITE STEPS IF YOU'RE RUNNING WINDOWS SERVER 2008

Follow these steps if you're installing Hyper-V on Windows Server 2008.

1. Apply the Hyper-V RTM update. The released media for Windows Server 2008 includes the beta version of Hyper-V and must be updated. You can update the role by copying the MSU package that was downloaded from the Microsoft support site—KB950050.msu—to the Windows Server Core system and then running it from the command prompt (see Figure 2.5).

FIGURE 2.5

Applying the Hyper-V RTM update on Windows Server 2008 Core

2. Browse to where the file is located, and run it. For the Hyper-V final update, the filename is Windows6.0-KB950050-x64.MSU.

3. After the update succeeds, you must restart the system.

NOTE   If you ran Automatic Updating via Windows Update, then the Hyper-V RTM update may have been applied already, depending on your Windows Update settings.

INSTALLING THE ROLE

These steps apply to both Windows 2008 and Windows 2008 R2. To install the role, follow these steps:

1. After the system starts up, log in. When the command prompt appears, run one of the following commands:

    ◆ If you're running Windows Server 2008 Hyper-V:

```
Start /w ocsetup Microsoft-Hyper-V
```

◆ If you're running Windows Server 2008 R2 Hyper-V:

```
Dism /online /enable-feature /featurename:Microsoft-Hyper-V
```

NOTE The capitalization of this command is critical—the command will fail if it isn't capitalized exactly as shown in step 1.

The system installs all the necessary files for Hyper-V. After it completes, a dialog box appears, as shown in Figure 2.6.

FIGURE 2.6
Reboot dialog box after successful addition of the Hyper-V role

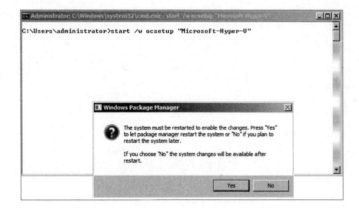

2. Click Yes to reboot the system.

NOTE As part of the installation of the Hyper-V role, all firewall ports required by Hyper-V are opened.

3. After the reboot, the system is ready to run virtual machines. From another system, use the Hyper-V Manager to connect as the local administrator account on the Server Core host.

NOTE Ensure that the system where the Hyper-V MMC is being used has also been updated to the RTM version of Hyper-V. Administration of an RTM Hyper-V host from an earlier version of the Hyper-V Manager MMC isn't supported.

4. Before you create a virtual machine, you must create virtual networks. From the Hyper-V Manager MMC, select the Hyper-V host on the left, and then select Virtual Network Manager in the Actions section at right. From there, create the necessary external, internal, and private virtual networks for the virtualized workloads on the host (see Figure 2.7).

NOTE Ensure that an external virtual network isn't created on the NIC being used as the management NIC.

FIGURE 2.7
Virtual Network
Manager showing
no virtual net-
works created

For more information about the different types of virtual networks, refer to Chapter 3.
Congratulations! You can now use the system to run virtualization workloads on top of a
Windows Server Core system.

New in Windows Server 2008 R2: Introducing sconfig

With the release of Windows Server 2008 R2, a new configuration tool has been added to
Core installations. Called sconfig, it provides an easy way to perform basic configuration
of a newly installed system (see Figure 2.8).

FIGURE 2.8
Main window of
sconfig, provid-
ing a multitude of
options to configure
Windows Server
2008 R2 core

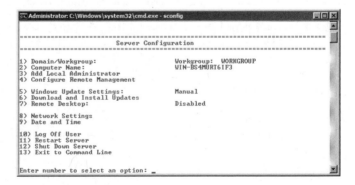

To use `sconfig`, after installing Windows Server 2008 R2, simply run `sconfig` from the command line. The `Server Configuration` window will appear, allowing you to do the following:

- `Domain/Workgroup`: Change the membership of the newly installed server to a specific domain or workgroup.

- `Computer Name`: Change the name of the host.

- `Add Local Administrator`: Give a user account on the host administrative rights, or add a domain account as an administrator.

- `Configure Remote Management`: Allow the host to be managed remotely via the Server Manager MMC snap-in (on a full installation of Windows Server 2008 R2), or grant a remote instance of PowerShell the ability to administer the local host.

- `Windows Update Settings`: Enable or disable the ability for Windows to automatically update itself via Windows Update.

- `Download and Install Updates`: Launch the Windows Update client, which can be used to update the host.

- `Remote Desktop`: Enable or disable the Remote Desktop functionality, and also set the security level for Remote Desktop Protocol (RDP) access.

- `Network Settings`: Configure the IP address and other related settings for the network adapters present in the host.

- `Date and Time`: Set the date and time for the host.

Summary

In this chapter, we detailed how administrators can lay the groundwork for implementing virtualization in your environment. By having Hyper-V as a role of Windows Server 2008, Microsoft has provided an easy deployment scenario, allowing users to add the virtualization layer to Windows.

For production servers where the host is running only the Hyper-V role, Windows Server Core is easily the best choice. By removing from the system a number of the applications that are rarely used and pairing the system with the targeted role and feature functionality of Windows Server 2008, you've got the base platform for a great virtualization host. It may take a little while to adjust to the command-line equivalents of graphical tools you're used to using, but the benefits of Windows Server Core make it the optimal platform for your production virtualization needs.

Chapter 3

Configuring Hyper-V

In the first two chapters, we introduced why system administrators and developers would want to use virtualization, and specifically Hyper-V.

In this chapter, we'll cover the Hyper-V Manager, the main administration console for Hyper-V. The Hyper-V Manager is a powerful management interface that provides easy-to-use wizards for tasks such as new virtual machine creation, shows an all-up view of all virtual machines on a host, and has multiple host management built in.

After we review the Hyper-V Manager, we'll dig into how to create a new virtual machine using the New Virtual Machine Wizard. We'll edit the settings of the newly created virtual machine and then finish by covering some more advanced topics.

Ready? Let's get started! In this chapter, we'll cover the following topics:

- Getting started: the Hyper-V MMC
- Creating a new virtual machine
- Virtual machine settings
- New Virtual Hard Disk Wizard
- Virtual Network Manager
- Hyper-V settings

Getting Started: The Hyper-V MMC

To start working with Hyper-V, click the Start menu, select Administrative Tools, and then select Hyper-V Manager (see Figure 3.1). If the Hyper-V Manager isn't present, or for information about adding the Hyper-V Manager to a system not running the Hyper-V role, keep reading.

Although the initial window for the Hyper-V Manager is sparse, it'll fill up quickly when you begin creating virtual machines (VMs). Let's look at each area of the Microsoft Management Console (MMC).

On the left is a list of all the Hyper-V hosts managed by this instance of the Hyper-V Manager. By default, only one host is listed: the local host on which the MMC is running. To add hosts to the MMC, right-click Hyper-V Manager, and select Connect To Server. After typing the host name in the Another Computer text box, you can perform all Hyper-V administrative tasks against that system.

FIGURE 3.1
Window for
Hyper-V Manager

The center of the Hyper-V Manager window is broken up into three sections:

Virtual Machines   The top section lists all the VMs that are registered on the selected host. If you haven't created any VMs, this list is empty. This section also lists the status of all the VMs, including the state (running, off, saved, and so on), central processing unit (CPU) utilization, the amount of time the VM has been running, and operations that are currently taking place against the VM.

Snapshots   The middle section lists all the snapshots for the selected VM. The snapshot functionality is one of the new features in Hyper-V. A *snapshot* is a point-in-time representation of a VM. As an administrator, you can move back and forth between snapshots and easily perform tasks such as resetting a test environment.

NOTE   You should not use snapshots as a backup tool in a production environment. For more information about snapshots, see Chapter 7, "Backing Up and Recovering VMs."

Details   The bottom section provides a small thumbnail of the virtual machine console session, as well as the VM's created date and notes. We'll cover where to enter notes later in this chapter.

On the right is a list of actions that you can take against the selected host. These include creating a VM (which we'll cover next) as well as changing the host settings and starting/ stopping the Hyper-V service. If you create a VM and select it here, more options appear below; these are actions you can take against the selected VM and are dependent on the state of the VM.

ADDING THE HYPER-V MANAGER

It's possible to add the Hyper-V Manager to a Windows Server 2008, Windows Vista SP1, or Windows 7 system that isn't running the Hyper-V role. This enables you to remotely configure and control a Hyper-V host.

WINDOWS SERVER 2008/R2

To add the Hyper-V Manager on a Windows Server 2008 system, launch Server Manager from the Start menu. Select Features, and then select Add Features. Under Remote Server Administration Tools, browse to Role Administration Tools, select Hyper-V Tools, and then click Install. After installation, you can launch the Hyper-V Manager by selecting Administrative Tools ➤ Hyper-V Manager.

WINDOWS VISTA SP1

To add the Hyper-V Manager on a Windows Vista SP1 system, download the Update for Windows Vista (KB952627) from the Microsoft Download Center. After installation, you can launch the Hyper-V Manager by selecting Administrative Tools ➤ Hyper-V Manager. (Make sure you select the correct package to download—packages for both x86 and x64 architectures are available.)

WINDOWS 7

To add the Hyper-V Manager on a Windows 7 system, download the Remote Server Administration Tools for Windows 7 (KB958830) from the Microsoft Download Center. After installation, browse to Control Panel ➤ Programs ➤ Programs And Features, and click Turn Windows Features On Or Off. Scroll down to Remote Server Administration Tools, and select Hyper-V Tools under Role Administration Tools.

Creating a New Virtual Machine

To create a new VM, you use the New Virtual Machine Wizard. Follow these steps:

1. To launch this wizard, select New ➤ Virtual Machine. It will walk you through the initial configuration of the VM.

2. The Before You Begin page of the wizard is a simple introduction that provides an overview of the wizard (see Figure 3.2). It also provides a check box that you can select to prevent the page from appearing again, which can be a time-saver if you're creating multiple VMs. Click Next to continue.

3. On the Specify Name And Location page, you can set the VM's name as well as the location of its supporting files (see Figure 3.3).

NOTE The name of the VM as set here is separate from the name that will be assigned to the virtual operating system that is installed. One common gotcha is assigning the same name to two different VMs. Because the displayed name is a friendly form for a long, globally unique identifier behind the scenes, Hyper-V Manager doesn't check to see whether the name already exists.

FIGURE 3.2
First page of
the New Virtual
Machine Wizard

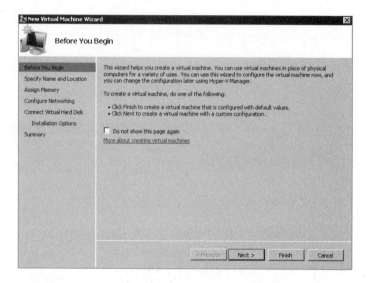

FIGURE 3.3
Specify Name And
Location page in
the wizard

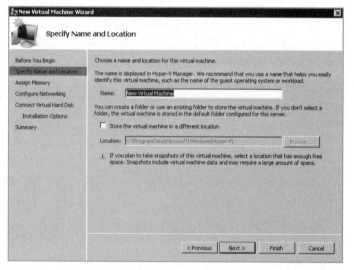

The VM's location is where the configuration file and all the associated files will be created. These files include the `.bin` and `.vsv` files. When a VM is powered on, both `.bin` and `.vsv` files are created. The `.bin` file is used when the VM is powered on, and it's the same size as the memory assigned to the VM. This file ensures that, in case of a system shutdown, the VM can be saved. When the state of the VM is saved, the `.bin` file is deleted, and the contents of memory are written to the `.vsv` file so it can be restored at a later time.

One common reason to change the default location of the VM is so you can create a *highly available* VM. If you're going to do so, then you need to create the VM on a shared volume. We'll cover that more in Chapter 8, "Achieving High Availability."

4. On the Assign Memory page, the memory assigned to the VM is set. By default, it's set at 512MB of RAM (see Figure 3.4). The maximum amount of RAM that can be assigned is one of two values: the amount of memory installed in the host or 64GB (whichever is smaller). Hyper-V will prevent you from assigning too much memory to the VM (an amount that could prevent the host from normal operation). For more information on host memory reserves, refer to Chapter 4, "Virtualization Best Practices."

FIGURE 3.4
Assign
Memory page

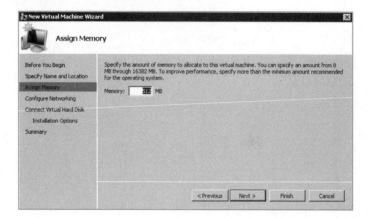

5. By default, the wizard will add a single virtual network adapter to the VM, as you can see on the Configure Networking page shown in Figure 3.5. The network adapter can be connected to any virtual network that has already been created. For instructions on creating a virtual network, see "Virtual Network Manager" later in this chapter. If you're going to install the operating system (OS) via Pre-boot eXecution Environment (PXE), then make sure you select a valid virtual network on this page. If you leave the Connection option set to Not Connected, PXE can't be used for OS installation (as you'll see in step 6).

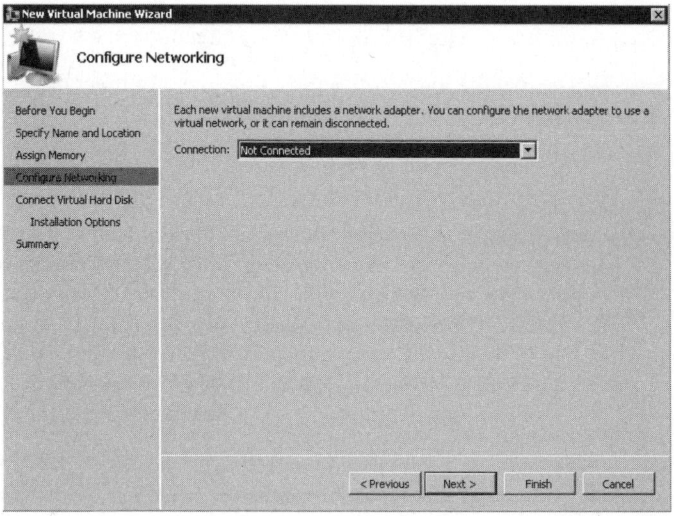

FIGURE 3.5
Configure Net-
working page

6. The Connect Virtual Hard Disk page controls where the OS for the VM will go. There are three options, two of which deal with virtual hard disk (VHD) files (see Figure 3.6).

FIGURE 3.6
Options available
on the Connect
Virtual Hard
Disk page

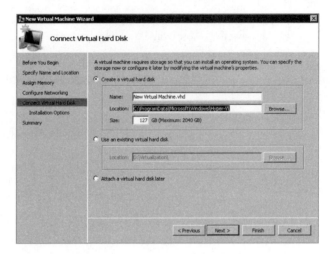

◆ *Create A Virtual Hard Disk*: This option creates a new VHD file for OS installation. The newly created VHD is completely blank. You can set the location as well as the size here.

When you create a new VM via the wizard, the VHD type is a dynamically expanding disk. For other types, such as a fixed-size disk or a physical disk, you must configure the VM's settings after the wizard completes. (For more information, see "New Virtual Hard Disk Wizard" later in this chapter.)

◆ *Use An Existing Virtual Hard Disk*: This option allows you to use a VHD that you've already created. We'll cover how to create a library of VHD files in Chapter 4.

◆ *Attach A Virtual Hard Disk Later*: Select this option if you plan to add a VHD file later. If you select this option, you can modify the VHD in the settings for the VM.

7. The Installation Options page provides a number of ways that you can install the OS within the VM (see Figure 3.7).

◆ *Install An Operating System Later*: If you choose this option, the virtual machine will be created, but no operating system will be installed.

◆ *Install An Operating System From A Boot CD/DVD-ROM*: You can install operating systems either by using the physical CD/DVD-ROM drive on the host computer or by using an ISO file. An ISO file is an exact file copy of the contents of a physical piece of CD/DVD-ROM media. Many software companies now ship electronic copies of OSs in the ISO file format. Installs that take place from an ISO file are generally faster than from the physical CD/DVD-ROM drive, because the installation is reading from a fast disk as opposed to a slower optical drive. Additionally, you can set up a central network share for multiple systems to access a library of ISO files.

NOTE The Installation Options page appears only if you created a new VHD in step 5. If you select a VHD file that already exists, the wizard assumes that the existing VHD has an OS installed.

FIGURE 3.7
Installation
Options page

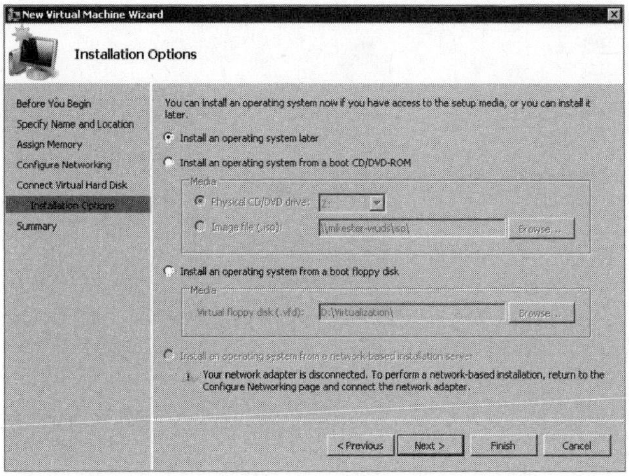

NOTE Only one VM at a time can install an OS from the physical CD/DVD-ROM drive.

NOTE If you have a network share with operating system ISO files, you can share them with all the Hyper-V hosts in your environment. Simply add the machine account to the share permissions—for example, HYPERV1$. If you are using Hyper-V in a domain, then the use of constrained delegation is necessary.

◆ *Install An Operating System From A Boot Floppy Disk*: Some operating systems require the use of a boot floppy disk to start the installation. If you select this option, you must use a virtual floppy disk (VFD) file. A VFD file is similar to an ISO file—it's a file-based representation of the physical medium.

NOTE Hyper-V can't directly access the physical floppy disk drive on the host computer.

◆ *Install An Operating System From A Network-Based Installation Server*: Hyper-V includes the capability to boot the VM over the network using the PXE protocol. You can install a variety of operating systems over the network by using the PXE protocol, including Windows Server 2008. To perform a network-based installation, you must use a legacy network adapter.

If you selected a virtual network earlier in the setup process and you then select the Install An Operating System From A Network-Based Installation Server option, the network adapter added to the VM will be a legacy network adapter, and the boot order will be modified to boot over the network first.

8. The Completing The New Virtual Machine Wizard page appears next. Finally, the VM creation is complete. The last screen summarizes the newly created VM (see Figure 3.8). Click Finish to close the wizard.

FIGURE 3.8
Completing
The New
Virtual Machine
Wizard page

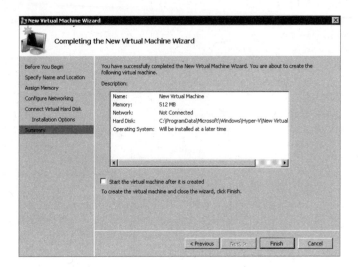

Virtual Machine Settings

Now that you've created a new VM using the wizard, let's look at the VM's settings. To do so, select the newly created VM in the Hyper-V Manager, and click Settings.

The Settings dialog box is broken into two sections: Hardware and Management. The hardware options control the hardware that's available to the VM, and the management options control the VM's administrative tasks. We'll cover all the options available.

Hardware

Just like a physical system, a VM consists of a variety of (virtual) hardware devices. In the settings for a VM, you can modify that hardware, including adding processors, network adapters, and hard disks.

ADD HARDWARE

You can modify the configuration of the VM by adding hardware, such as a small computer system interface (SCSI) controller or additional network interface, to the VM (see Figure 3.9). The VM must be powered off to add hardware to the VM, with the exception of virtual hard disks connected to a SCSI controller. After you add the virtual hardware to the VM and power on the VM, the OS will recognize the new hardware.

BIOS

Hyper-V doesn't allow direct access to the Basic Input/Output System (BIOS), so the only BIOS settings you can modify are exposed here (see Figure 3.10).

◆ *Num Lock*: Selecting this check box triggers Num Lock in the VM to be active on boot.

◆ *Startup Order*: This option controls the order in which devices will be queried for boot. The topmost option will be tried first, and if it fails, then the next option will be tried. By default, the boot order is CD, IDE, Legacy Network Adapter, and then Floppy.

FIGURE 3.9
Adding hardware
for a new VM

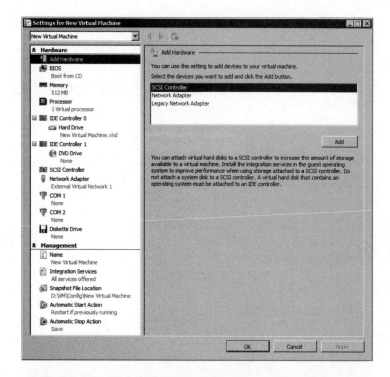

FIGURE 3.10
Looking at the
BIOS for a new VM

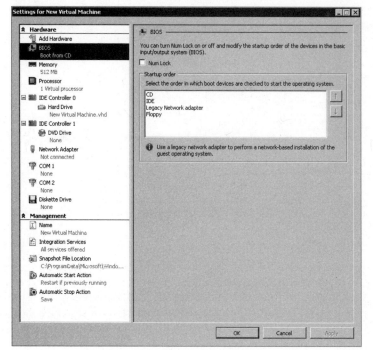

MEMORY

You can adjust the amount of memory allocated to the VM (see Figure 3.11). This can range from 8MB to the maximum amount of RAM in the system. There are some caveats.

FIGURE 3.11

Allocating memory

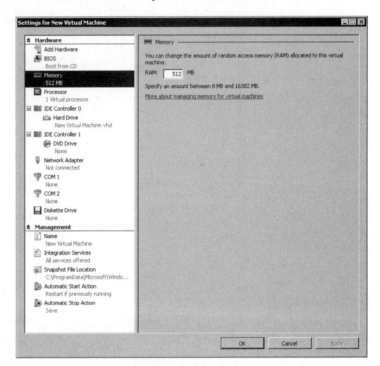

♦ Once the VM is powered on, the memory is allocated to the VM and can't be reclaimed until the VM is saved or turned off.

♦ Memory allocated to a VM can't be shared. If multiple VMs are running the same OS, Hyper-V doesn't provide the capability to share common pages of memory between the VMs.

♦ Hyper-V doesn't provide support for allocating more memory than is available on the host. The amount of memory available for VMs is about 1GB less than the maximum amount of RAM in the host.

We'll discuss some of the best practices for memory in Chapter 4.

PROCESSOR

You have a number of processor settings, as you can see in Figure 3.12.

As we discussed in Chapter 1, "Introducing Hyper-V," Hyper-V supports up to four virtual processors in the VM. Those virtual processors are scheduled as threads on the physical processors. A VM can't have more virtual processors allocated than are present in the host. This means that in order to create a four-core VM, the host system must have at least four cores.

FIGURE 3.12

Modifying the number of processors for a new VM

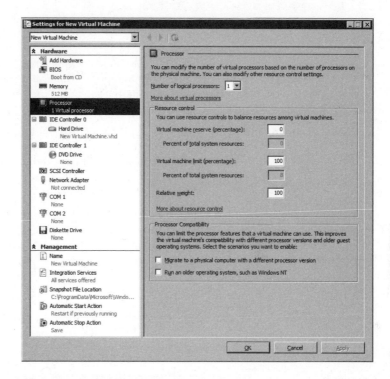

LOGICAL PROCESSORS AND VIRTUAL PROCESSORS

It's important to know the differences between a *logical processor* and a *virtual processor*. Logical processors are the foundation of today's multicore processors. A system with a single core and without hyperthreading has a single logical processor. Adding more cores increases the logical processor count. For example, a system with two physical processors, each processor having two cores, has a total logical processor count of four. A virtual processor is seen on the host as a single thread of execution, which can then be scheduled on any of the logical processors in the system.

The upper limit on the number of virtual processors that you can allocate on a host is 8 times the number of logical processors, up to a maximum of 512 virtual processors. A single dual-socket, dual-core server (exposing 4 processors to the host) can support a total of 32 virtual processors.

NOTE You should keep a very close eye on performance to ensure that the system can handle all the running VMs as well as the host.

Additionally, the Processor tab is where you set the resource-control options for the VM. This screen includes the following options:

◆ *Virtual Machine Reserve*: This reserves a set amount of processor power for the VM. You can think of this reserve as a guaranteed amount of processor resources.

- ◆ *Virtual Machine Limit*: This is a hard cap on the amount of processor power that the VM can take from the host.

- ◆ *Relative Weight*: The relative weight is another method of assigning a value of importance between multiple VMs. You can set this option to any value from 1 to 10,000. If two VMs have the same VM reserves and limits, the VM with a higher relative weight will receive more processing power.

- ◆ *Migrate To A Physical Computer With A Different Processor Version (Windows Server 2008 R2 feature)*: If you enable this option, the processor that is available inside the virtual machine is stripped of many of its advanced features. This is useful for performing live migrations between cluster nodes with different processor revisions. For more information on this feature, refer to Chapter 8.

- ◆ *Limit Processor Functionality (Windows Server 2008 feature)/Run An Older Operating System, Such As Windows NT (Windows Server 2008 R2 feature)*: The last check box in the processor settings controls the processor functionality. By selecting this option, you'll let older OSs, such as Windows NT or earlier, work with Hyper-V.

IDE CONTROLLER

Hyper-V includes a dual-channel IDE controller much like many standard hardware PCs. By default, a single VHD is connected to the primary IDE controller in the primary connection, with a CD/DVD drive connected to the primary connection of the secondary controller (see Figure 3.13).

FIGURE 3.13
IDE controller options

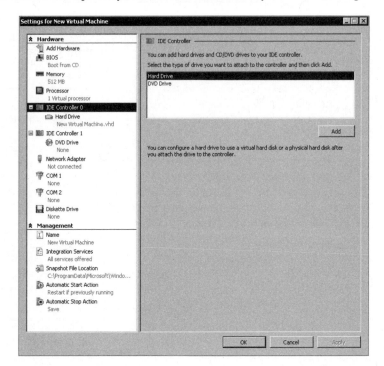

The VM can boot only from a VHD connected to the IDE controller. Although this does seem strange and counterintuitive for performance reasons, this arrangement is necessary because of the architecture of Hyper-V. The synthetic devices in Hyper-V aren't seen in the OS without the integration services being installed.

NOTE   After you install the integration services in the VM, you'll notice near-identical performance from disks connected to the IDE controller and disks connected to the SCSI controller.

By clicking the IDE controller, you can add a new hard disk or DVD drive to the specific IDE controller. (DVD drives can be connected only to the IDE controllers, not to SCSI controllers.) If you select a hard disk, you have a number of options to choose from.

At the top, you can select the specific location where the VHD file will be connected the top (see Figure 3.14). If no SCSI controllers have been added to the VM, then you can add the new VHD to one of the preexisting IDE controllers only. However, if you added a SCSI controller to the VM's configuration, then the SCSI controller and all available locations will be listed as well.

FIGURE 3.14
Specifying the path for a VHD with the IDE controller

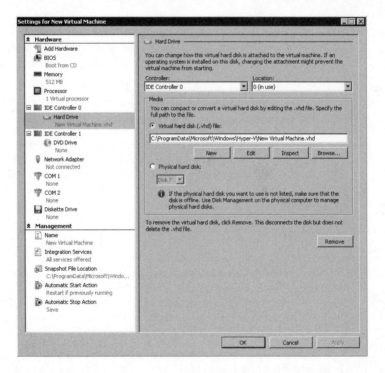

After you've assigned the new VHD to a specific location and clicked the New button, you can set up the specifics of the disk. A number of hard drive settings are available, including creating a new VHD, using an existing disk, or editing or inspecting an existing disk.

The New, Edit, and Inspect buttons all map back to the New Virtual Hard Disk Wizard. This wizard provides a one-stop interface for all tasks having to do with VHD files. (For more information, see "New Virtual Hard Disk Wizard" later in this chapter.)

The bottom option, Physical Hard Disk, lets you directly connect a physical logical unit number (LUN) to a VM. This feature, commonly referred to as pass-through disks, allows the VM to directly use storage volumes that are connected to controllers on the host—including Fibre Channel, Internet SCSI (iSCSI), or direct-attached SCSI storage. Support for physical hard disks lets you treat your VMs the same way as physical machines, and you get an increase in performance compared to the default dynamically expanding VHD.

To connect a physical hard disk to a VM, you must mark the physical disk Offline on the host. You can do this by opening the Disk Management MMC snap-in, selecting the disk, and then right-clicking it and selecting Offline.

NOTE   Take care that you don't bring the same volume online while the VM has it mounted, or you may lose data.

SCSI CONTROLLER

If you need more storage for the virtual machine than the dual-channel IDE controller can provide, you can add a SCSI controller to the virtual machine. Each SCSI controller can have up to 64 devices connected to it, and there is a maximum of 4 controllers per virtual machine.

In Windows Server 2008 R2 Hyper-V, a SCSI controller is added by default to each newly created virtual machine.

NOTE   To use any devices connected to the SCSI controller, the Integration Services must be installed within the virtual machine. For more information on installing the integration services, refer to Chapter 4.

Devices connected to the virtual SCSI controller take advantage of the Virtualization Service Provider/Virtualization Service Client architecture that we reviewed in Chapter 1.

NETWORK ADAPTER

Two separate types of network adapters can be added to a virtual machine: a synthetic network adapter (referred to in the user interface as a *network adapter*) and an emulated network adapter (referred to as a *legacy network adapter* in the UI).

It's recommended that synthetic network adapters be used over legacy network adapters for those operating systems that have integration services available, because the performance of the synthetic devices is significantly better than the legacy (emulated) devices.

NOTE   There can be a total of 12 network adapters in a virtual machine: 8 synthetic and 4 legacy.

You have several items to choose in the Network Adapter settings window, and you can change the same settings regardless of the type of network adapter—normal or legacy (see Figure 3.15).

◆ *Network*: Each network adapter defined in the Settings dialog can be connected to a single virtual network.

◆ *MAC Address*: The Media Access Control (MAC) address of a network adapter is what makes each network adapter unique. The role of the MAC address in the network stack is beyond the scope of this book.

FIGURE 3.15
Network
Adapter tab

Hyper-V gives you the ability to assign a static MAC address to each network adapter in the VM or to use a dynamically generated MAC address. Some applications use the MAC address of a system for a number of purposes. To set a static MAC address, click the Static radio button, and enter the value.

Dynamic MAC addresses under Hyper-V always start with 00:15:5D, with the last three octets randomly chosen based on the MAC address of the host's physical adapter.

◆ *Enable Spoofing Of MAC Addresses (Windows Server 2008 R2 feature)*: This new option in Windows Server 2008 R2 enables the following features:

   ◆ The virtual machine can send and receive traffic using any MAC address. This is necessary for some advanced scenarios, such as the use of Network Load Balancing (NLB) within the virtual machine.

   ◆ The virtual machine can override the MAC address that is assigned in the VM configuration.

If you enable this feature, flooded unicast packets can enter the virtual machine. This is a security risk, so it's best to not enable this feature unless it's necessary.

◆ *Enable Virtual LAN Identification*: If the VM needs to communicate over a specific virtual local area network (VLAN) using the 802.1q protocol, enter the VLAN ID here. Multiple virtual network adapters can be connected to different VLANs.

COM PORT

Access to the COM ports of the virtual machine is typically used for debugging options. The virtual machine's COM ports cannot be mapped directly to the COM port of the host. The COM ports in the VM can either be left unconnected (the default selection) or be connected to a named pipe (see Figure 3.16). *Named pipes* are a special way of communicating between two different systems.

FIGURE 3.16
Setting the
COM ports

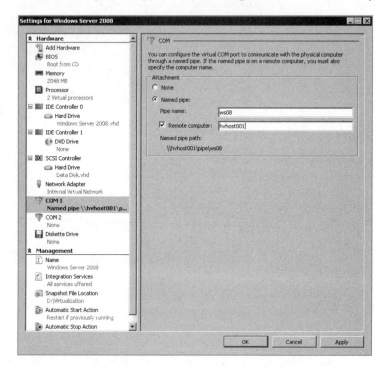

To connect a virtual COM port to a named pipe on the local system, enter the name of the pipe in the Pipe Name text box. There's no need to format it in the traditional \\.*pipe**pipe* syntax; Hyper-V takes care of that.

To connect to a remote pipe on another system, select the Remote Computer check box, and enter the name of the computer.

FLOPPY

A VM has a single virtual floppy disk drive (see Figure 3.17). The virtual floppy drive has no access to the physical floppy disk drive—rather, it uses virtual floppy disks (VFD files). You can create VFD files by using the Virtual Disk Wizard (New ➢ Floppy Disk).

NOTE To use the same VFD file in multiple VMs, make sure the file is locked in Windows Explorer. To lock a file, right-click the file, select Properties, and select the Read-Only check box.

FIGURE 3.17
Setting the virtual
floppy disk

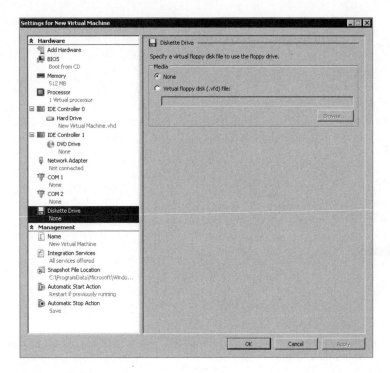

Virtual Machine Management

Now that we've covered all of the VM's hardware settings, we'll cover the management options available in the VM's configuration.

NAME

The name, as you would expect, controls the display name of the VM. Additionally, the text box lets you enter notes about the VM; these can include the OS installed, the patch level, and the applications installed. These notes are displayed in the Hyper-V MMC (see Figure 3.18).

INTEGRATION SERVICES

When integration services are installed in a VM, they provide a number of additional features to the OS (if the OS supports them). You can select which of those features are enabled on a per-VM basis, as shown in Figure 3.19. These features include the following items:

◆ Operating System Shutdown. When you select Shut Down in the Hyper-V Manager, the integration services attempt to shut down the OS cleanly. If you don't select this option, then the only way to shut down a VM is to log in and manually issue a shutdown command (or to turn off the power to the VM).

◆ *Time Synchronization*: By default, Hyper-V syncs the clock of the VM and the host when the VM is first powered on. If the integration services are installed, the time synchronization functionality will keep the two clocks in sync.

◆ *Data Exchange*: The data exchange component allows the host and the VM to exchange data via a set of registry key pairs. This data includes the host on which the VM is running on as well as the name of the VM as defined in the Hyper-V Manager. You can obtain additional data via the data exchange component, including the version of the OS in the VM and the values for the `GetVersionEx` function defined in MSDN.

◆ *Heartbeat*: The heartbeat service allows the Hyper-V host to identify whether a VM is running. If the heartbeat integration component is running in the VM and the check box is selected, then the VM sends a heartbeat back to the host every two seconds. The state of the heartbeat is displayed in the bottom panel of the Hyper-V Manager, and you can query it through Windows Management Interface (WMI) to determine whether the VM is still active and responding.

◆ *Backup (Volume Snapshot)*: Hyper-V includes a Volume Shadow Services (VSS) writer that, when signaled by a VSS-aware backup application, prepares the VM for backup and signals the VSS request into the VM. This ensures that when the VM is restored from the backup medium, it's in an application-consistent state from which it can recover.

FIGURE 3.18

Setting the display name for a VM

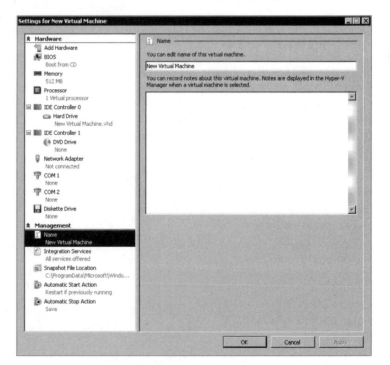

FIGURE 3.19

Choosing integration services

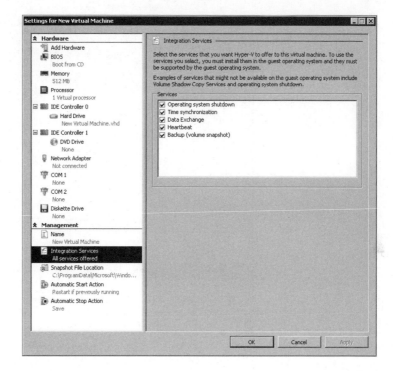

SNAPSHOT FILE LOCATION

By default, snapshot files are created in the same location where the VM is created. You can modify the location of snapshot files on a per-VM basis by changing the path (see Figure 3.20). If you're going to take a large number of snapshots, it's recommended that the location have sufficient disk space.

AUTOMATIC START ACTION

You can set the action that the VM performs when the Hyper-V host system starts (see Figure 3.21). These actions include Nothing, Automatically Start If It Was Running When The Service Stopped (default), and Always Start This Virtual Machine Automatically. If you select the default option, you can also choose a delay time; doing so helps prevent disk contention if multiple VMs are set to start at the same time.

AUTOMATIC STOP ACTION

Similar to specifying the action that the VM performs when the host starts, you can specify what action the VM takes when the Hyper-V host system is shut down (see Figure 3.22). These include Save The Virtual Machine State (default), Turn Off The Virtual Machine, or Shut Down The Guest Operating System. To shut down the OS automatically, the integration services must be installed in the guest OS.

FIGURE 3.20
Setting the snapshot file location

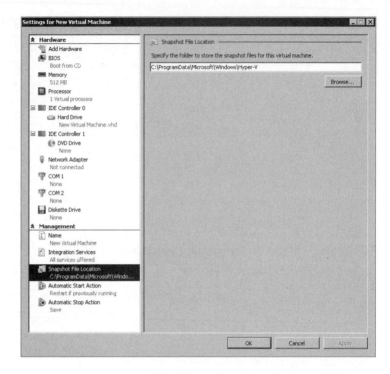

FIGURE 3.21
Settings for Automatic Start Action option

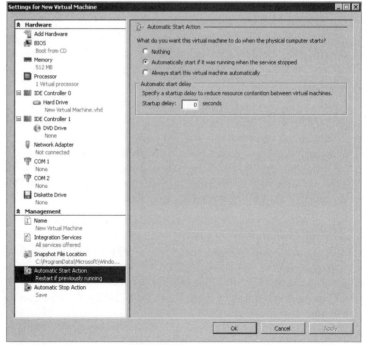

FIGURE 3.22
Settings for Automatic Stop Action option

NOTE If the host experiences a loss of power, then all the VMs will be turned off as well.

New Virtual Hard Disk Wizard

We'll cover two more important items in the Hyper-V Manager: the Virtual Network Manager and the New Virtual Hard Disk Wizard. Both of these items are important for different reasons: the New Virtual Hard Disk Wizard covers advanced disk configurations, including fixed disks and differencing disks. You'll learn more about the Virtual Network Manager in the next section.

You start the New Virtual Hard Disk Wizard by selecting New ➢ Hard Disk from the main page of the Hyper-V Manager.

NOTE When starting the New Virtual Hard Disk Wizard, ensure that the correct Hyper-V host is selected from the list in the left pane of the Hyper-V Manager.

When the New Virtual Hard Disk Wizard starts, an introductory page appears. Clicking Next provides three separate choices of VHDs to create (see Figure 3.23). You follow the same steps to set up a dynamic or a fixed VHD. However, one step is different when you set up a differencing VHD. Let's start by reviewing each type of VHD.

Exploring Types of Virtual Hard Disks

A *dynamic* VHD starts off small (approximately 1MB) but will expand to the maximum size specified as data is written to the disk. These types of disks are great for scenarios such as test and development where disk space is at a premium (see Figure 3.24). However, they're not recommended for production use. If a dynamically expanding virtual hard disk file runs out of space on the host volume, the VM will pause.

FIGURE 3.23
Choosing the type of VHD

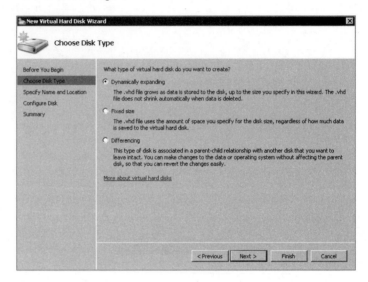

FIGURE 3.24
Dynamic VHD

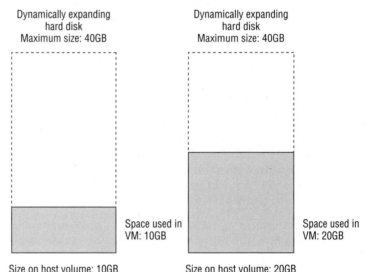

A *fixed-size* VHD has all the space allocated on the host's disk when the disk is created (see Figure 3.25). This obviously requires that the space exist on the host system. A fixed-size VHD is ideal for production deployments.

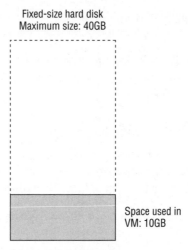

FIGURE 3.25
Fixed VHD

A *differencing* VHD is a special type. This is a disk that stores all the changes to a parent disk to a separate disk. Differencing disks are another great tool for test and development environments, where multiple VMs can be started from a single parent disk that contains a preinstalled OS. Differencing disks do present a number of unique concerns, which we'll discuss in Chapter 4.

Now that we've reviewed the three types of disks that can be created via this wizard, we'll walk you through the wizard.

Using the Wizard to Create Virtual Hard Disks

The first step to creating a new VHD is to identify the type of virtual hard disk.

NOTE   If a dynamic VHD can't expand because of lack of space on the volume where it resides, then the VM will pause, and an event will be logged in the Event Viewer notifying the administrator of the issue.

The next step depends on the type of disk you're creating:

Dynamic disk or fixed-size disk   For these two types of disk, you have two options: you can set the maximum size of the disk (the maximum size of a VHD file is a little less than 2TB), or you can select an existing physical disk. If you select an existing physical disk, then a new VHD file is created that is the same size as the existing physical disk. After the disk is created, the contents of the physical disk are copied to the new VHD file.

NOTE   If you're creating a dynamic disk, ensure that there's enough space on the volume where the disk is being placed to hold the fully expanded disk.

Differencing disk   For differencing disks, the next step after entering the name and location of the new disk is to define the parent. The *parent* VHD is the disk that the new VHD reads from while redirecting all writes to the newly created differencing disk.

After defining the type of the disk, you have the opportunity to name the virtual hard disk as well as choose the location where it will be stored. The name should give some sort of indication as to the contents of the VHD file.

The final page is a summary that details the actions selected during previous steps of the New Virtual Hard Disk Wizard. This page lets you confirm that the selected actions are correct before they're executed.

Virtual Network Manager

The Virtual Network Manager is the central administration point for ensuring that VMs have access to the correct network resources. Virtual networks differ from the virtual network adapters that are defined in the configuration—the virtual network adapters connect to the virtual networks. Multiple VMs, and multiple virtual network adapters, can connect to the same virtual network.

You access the Virtual Network Manager from the Actions pane of the Hyper-V Manager. There are three types of virtual network, and each has a specific function:

External An external network is bound to the selected physical network adapter. This type of virtual network provides access to the network to which the physical network is connected. If a VM is serving data to other physical computers, for example, an external virtual network is the type to use.

Internal An internal virtual network isn't bound to a physical network adapter. A VM that's connected to an internal virtual network can communicate with all the VMs that are connected to the virtual network, as well as the host computer. An internal virtual network provides the functionality to connect from the host to the VM(s).

Private A private virtual network, like an internal virtual network, isn't bound to a physical network adapter. Private virtual networks only allow communication between all the VMs connected to the virtual network. This is incredibly useful for virtualized environments where the need to keep data from going out "over the wire" is critical.

Creating a virtual network is simple:

1. From the Hyper-V Manager, select Virtual Network Manager on the right under Actions. A list of all the virtual networks appears on the left, with an option at the right to create a new virtual network.

2. Click the Add button to open the settings for the new virtual network (see Figure 3.26).

   ◆ *Name*: This is the display name for the virtual network. It's recommended that it reference the virtual network's intended use as well as the physical network connection (if it's an external network).

   ◆ *Notes*: This field is for notes regarding the virtual network. Again, providing a description of the virtual network is highly recommended in case you need to troubleshoot.

   ◆ *Connection Type*: Set this to the type of virtual network you're creating.

   ◆ *Allow Management Operating System To Share This Network Adapter (External Virtual Networks Only), Windows Server 2008 R2 feature*: If this check box is selected, a new virtual network adapter will be created in the parent partition. This network adapter is technically shared by both the parent partition and all the guests running on the host. It's recommended that this not be used except for cases where there is only a single network adapter in the system. We'll review this more in Chapter 4.

◆ *Enable VLAN Identification For Parent Partition*: This is a different setting from the setting in the virtual network adapter. If you're using the same network adapter both for VM traffic (as an external virtual network) and to provide network access to the host on a specific VLAN, then enter the correct VLAN ID here.

FIGURE 3.26
Virtual network properties

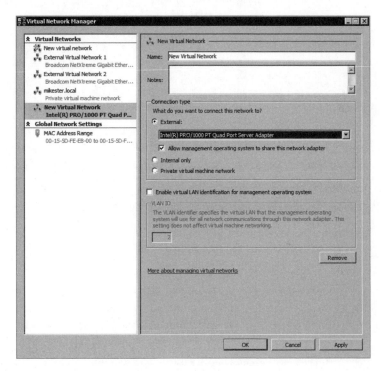

NOTE If an external virtual network is created on a host remotely using the Hyper-V Manager, there is a possibility of a loss of connection. The Virtual Network Manager will alert you to that fact before it's created.

3. After you enter all the correct data, click OK to create the virtual network and close the Virtual Network Manager.

Hyper-V Settings

In addition to the settings for the virtual machine, there are settings for the Hyper-V role on a per-server basis. In the Hyper-V Manager, click Hyper-V Settings in the Actions pane (see Figure 3.27).

FIGURE 3.27

Hyper-V Settings

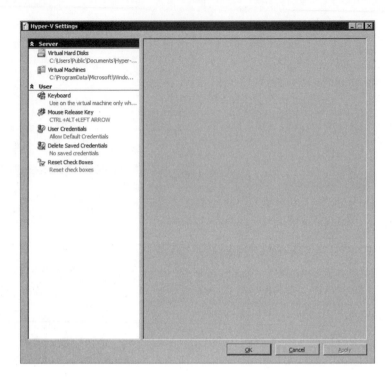

You can make settings in the following areas:

◆ *Virtual Hard Disks*: Specify the default folder to store virtual hard disk files. By default, virtual hard disk files are stored on the system volume. If you have a large number of virtual machines on a host, it's likely that you'll want to change the default location to a SAN array or some other storage location.

◆ *Virtual Machines*: Specify the default folder to store virtual machine configurations. As we mentioned earlier, when a virtual machine is created, a `.bin` file and a `.vsv` file are created in the same location. Those files can be rather large, because they are the size of the amount of memory assigned to a running virtual machine. Changing the location to a larger volume helps ensure that the system won't run out of space on the system drive.

◆ *Keyboard*: When using the Virtual Machine Connect (VMConnect) application to connect to the console of the virtual machine, there is occasionally a need to pass Windows key combinations (such as Windows+E to launch a Windows Explorer window). This setting allows you to modify how those keystrokes are handled. You can choose whether the VM or the host gets the keystrokes.

◆ *Mouse Release Key*: When running VMConnect in windowed mode with an operating system not running the integration services, clicking the mouse will "lock" the mouse to the window. To break out of the window, the key combination selected here must be entered. By default, the key combination is Ctrl+Alt+Left Arrow.

◆ *User Credentials*: By default, VMConnect will use the credentials that were used to log into the host as the credentials to connect to the console of the VM. Deselecting this check box will force the entry of credentials each time VMConnect is used to connect to a virtual machine.

NOTE If a smart card is used to log in to the host, it's unlikely that the smart card can be used to log in with VMConnect. It's recommended that this check box be deselected if a smart card is used.

◆ *Delete Saved Credentials*: This clears any saved credentials that were entered.

◆ *Reset Check Boxes*: This restores all previously hidden dialog boxes.

Summary

By now, you should have a good grasp of the Hyper-V Manager—what it does, how to create VMs, and how to modify the settings of the VMs you create. Additionally, we reviewed the New Virtual Hard Disk Wizard and Virtual Network Manager, which provide even more control and functionality for complex configurations. We'll cover more advanced configurations, including best practices, later in this book.

Chapter 4

Virtualization Best Practices

After you put Hyper-V into use in an environment, the next logical step is to look at performance and how you can use Hyper-V more efficiently. Tuning a Hyper-V host isn't much different from tuning any other high-performance server. In addition to checking the host's performance, though, it's critical to tune the virtual machines being used.

We'll cover best practices from two points of view: that of the host, including processor, memory, networking, and storage; and that of the virtual machine, including integration services, using the Sysprep tool, and patching virtual machines.

In this chapter, we'll cover the following topics:

◆ Host best practices

◆ Virtual machine best practices

Host Best Practices

Once you decide to deploy Hyper-V in a production role, a number of areas need advanced planning and thought. Because the Hyper-V host will be running multiple production workloads, it's critical that such planning take place before the system is put into use.

NOTE Microsoft offers a series of planning guides for a variety of infrastructure services in a data center. One such set of guides specific to the virtualization of the data center is entitled "Infrastructure Planning and Design Guides for Virtualization" and is available on the Microsoft TechNet web site at `http://technet.microsoft.com`.

By identifying the workloads that will be run in virtual machines (VMs) on the host, planning can help you identify potential bottlenecks in the host system. These best practices help in two key areas:

◆ Host sizing

◆ Ongoing host performance

This chapter will help with both areas.

Choosing a Processor

Hyper-V provides support for up to 24 logical processors (Windows Server 2008) or 64 logical processors (for Windows Server 2008 R2) in the parent partition. A *logical processor* is a unit of processing power. Both Intel and AMD have released processors that consist of multiple processor cores on a single processor. These processors plug into sockets on the computer's motherboard. Having multiple processor cores on a single die allows even a single-socket system to execute multiple threads on discrete processors at the same time. Although 24 or 64 logical processors sounds like a lot of processing power (and in most cases, it certainly is!), virtualization can easily use all of it.

With support for 64 logical processors, Hyper-V has support for up to 384 running virtual machines at a time, as well as a total of 512 virtual processors allocated to all running virtual machines. Getting to either 384 or 512 might sound challenging, but it can be broken down a number of ways:

- 384 single virtual processor virtual machines (maximum of 384 running virtual machines)
- 256 dual virtual processor virtual machines (maximum of 512 virtual processors: 256 × 2)
- 128 quad virtual processor virtual machines (maximum of 512 virtual processors: 128 × 4)

NOTE   The maximums listed here assume a system running Windows Server 2008 R2 Enterprise or Datacenter edition. Windows Server 2008 R2 Standard edition supports only 4 processors, which would provide (at the time of this writing) a maximum of 32 logical processors; 32 logical processors would provide up to 256 virtual processors, given the support boundary of 8:1 virtual processors to physical processors.

You must consider three key factors about processors as you work through the planning stages:

- Number of processors in the system
- Number of cores on the processors in the system
- Speed of the processors in the system

Because one of the key benefits of virtualization is the ability to achieve higher density (running multiple VMs on a single physical host), administrators naturally gravitate toward the processor as a key bottleneck. After all, if a host runs out of processing power, those virtualized workloads may not be able to keep up with the demand being placed on them.

You need to answer a couple of key questions for the host:

- How many processors are necessary for this virtualization host?
- Do the processors need to provide two, four, or even six cores per processor?

The answer to these two questions is usually "It depends." Two schools of thought apply here, which brings up two more questions: Do you want to use more dual-socket systems, which usually have a lower price point? Or do you want to achieve maximum consolidation by going with quad-socket systems?

The price advantage of dual-socket systems is significant. At the time of this writing, you can deploy three physical dual-socket systems for the price of one quad-socket system. You can then cluster those three dual-socket systems together in a high-availability configuration to ensure continuous uptime for the workloads running in the VMs. With the three-system configuration, however, you need to consider some other costs. Having three systems means further expenses for operating system licenses, management software licenses, and the administration of three servers. You also need to factor in the power costs of the three servers.

The other option, which uses only one quad-socket virtualization host, doesn't provide any sort of backup or high availability—meaning that if the single host goes down, all the virtualized workloads will go down with it. But quad-socket servers generally provide a bit more in terms of expansion and I/O scalability, which could result in additional VMs being deployed on a single host.

Some enterprises are also considering the use of blade servers. Although the up-front cost of the enclosure is higher, the ability to use 14 systems in 7 units of rack space (for example) could be a better fit for some companies. One of the downsides of blade servers is a lack of local storage. Most blades generally have only one or two local disks, which isn't enough for many virtual machines. Many blade servers rely on having higher-cost enterprise-grade storage, such as Fibre Channel or iSCSI.

As you can see, there's no simple answer when you're deciding on the best configuration for your host.

FASTER PROCESSORS AND PERFORMANCE

In some cases, the speed of the processors leads to better performance. However, this isn't always the case. For example, let's consider a VM created by using a physical-to-virtual conversion. This workload was previously running on an older Pentium 3 Xeon processor at 700 MHz and is running a custom line-of-business (LOB) application.

Now that it's in a VM, will the workload run more quickly? Depending on the type of application, it may not. That doesn't mean the extra processing power from faster processors goes to waste, because it provides extra headroom for workloads to grow and provides a resource for other VMs. But you do need to take this fact into account.

VIRTUALIZATION-SPECIFIC PROCESSOR ENHANCEMENTS

With the R2 release of Hyper-V, a new feature was added that reduces the memory required by the hypervisor for each running virtual machine and also provides a performance boost. By taking advantage of functionality built in to newer processors from both Intel and AMD, Hyper-V can enable the Second Level Address Translation (SLAT) functionality.

SLAT requires a processor that supports either Extended Page Tables (for Intel processors) or Rapid Virtualization Indexing (for AMD processors). With that functionality, the processor itself takes over the placekeeping of virtual machine memory and how it maps to the memory on the host. By letting the processor perform this operation, the hypervisor uses less memory, and the amount of processor power required is decreased.

CPU-BOUND OR I/O-BOUND WORKLOADS

Not all workloads are capped by the processing power available to the VM. Some workloads, such as a SQL server, are generally bound to a greater extent by the limits of memory and the disk subsystem than by the processor. In this case, buying a faster processor won't necessarily provide faster performance to the VMs—use the money you save to invest in memory or a faster storage subsystem.

Once the host has been deployed, administrators often use management tools to determine how the host is performing. But because of the virtual nature of the processors, monitoring a virtual system isn't as simple as looking at Task Manager.

PERFMON

Traditionally, administrators used Windows Task Manager to get a quick glance at what was happening on the system (see Figure 4.1). However, because of the architecture of Hyper-V, Task

Manager doesn't show the CPU usage of VMs. Task Manager running in the parent partition has no way of displaying that information; instead, you need to use Perfmon.

FIGURE 4.1
Windows Task Manager shows system performance.

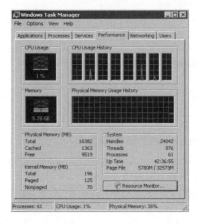

WHAT'S PERFMON?

Perfmon, short for Performance Monitor, is Microsoft's tool to examine performance data. This data can be as simple as CPU utilization or as complex as context switches between Ring 0 and Ring 3.

By looking at the Hyper-V performance counters through Perfmon, you can determine whether the system has room for more VMs or, conversely, whether the system is oversubscribed (too many VMs running on the host).

Using Perfmon to monitor the host is easy. From the Start menu, select Administrative Tools, and then select Reliability And Performance Monitor. Click Performance Monitor in the list on the left (see Figure 4.2).

FIGURE 4.2
Performance Monitor for VMs

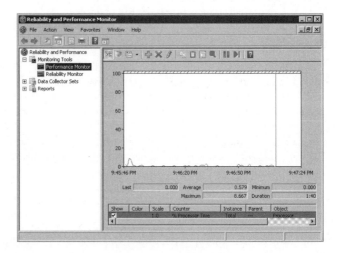

By default, only one item is tracked in Perfmon: % Processor Time. Unless you're interested in the processor utilization of the parent partition only, you'll need to add some counters.

The processor performance counters refer to the number of logical processors (LPs) in the system. A *logical processor* is a unit of processing power; for example, if you have a system with a single CPU socket and a single-core, nonhyperthreaded processor, you have one LP. Change that processor to a dual-core processor, and you have two LPs. Adding hyperthreading? Make it four logical processors.

NOTE   Before you add a virtualization-related counter, make sure a VM is running. If no VMs are running, the counters won't appear.

To add a performance counter, you click the green plus (+) sign or press Ctrl+I. A large number of Hyper-V–related performance counters are available, but we're interested in a couple in particular. Figure 4.3 shows the result of adding the counters.

FIGURE 4.3

Processor counters for a Hyper-V host

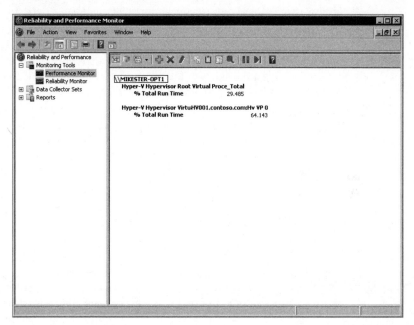

Hyper-V Hypervisor Virtual Processor, % Total Run Time   Under Instances Of Selected Object in the Perfmon window, you'll see a few options. For example, _Total provides a sum of all the VPs allocated to all running VMs. You can also add individual VPs allocated to a VM.

Hyper-V Hypervisor Root Virtual Processor, % Total Run Time   This is the percentage of time that the logical processors selected are executing instructions in non-hypervisor-based code in the root/parent partition.

Adding these two values gives you the total CPU utilization of the host executing virtualization-related code. The closer the value gets to 100 percent, the more heavily loaded the system is.

How Much Memory Is Enough?

Memory is another key area to consider when you set up virtualization. After all, you can have all the processing power in the world, but unless you have enough memory to run those VMs at the same time, processing power will remain unused.

Hyper-V doesn't support the concept of allocating more memory than is available in the host system. This prevents you from affecting the performance of the host. (If you started a VM using 4GB on a system with 2GB of RAM, the system would need to use virtual memory to provide the extra memory beyond what was available on the host.)

How much memory is necessary for the host? The usual answer applies—it depends on a number of factors, some of which are listed here:

Number of VMs running and their allocated memory   How many VMs will be running on the host, and how much memory will be allocated to each one? The amount of memory each VM needs is entirely dependent on the workload running within the VM. A SQL Server running in a VM will require much more memory than a departmental file server.

Other workloads running on the host   Although it's recommended that Hyper-V be the only role running on the host, it's possible that this won't be the case. If so, it's critical that enough memory be available to service all the other workloads running on the system. Refer to the memory requirements of the other workload(s) that will be running on the host, and add that amount to the total amount of memory required for the VM.

Host reserves   It's recommended that you set aside at least 512 MB of RAM for the host. That memory is used by Hyper-V's virtualization stack that runs in the parent partition, as well as by any services running in the parent partition. Hyper-V won't allow a VM to launch unless at least 32 MB of RAM is available. Each virtual machine has memory overhead as well—a good baseline figure is 32 MB of RAM for the first gigabyte of virtual RAM allocated, plus 8 MB for each additional gigabyte of virtual RAM.

NOTE   For more information on performance tuning for Hyper-V, refer to the Performance and Tuning Guide for Windows Server 2008, available at www.microsoft.com/whdc/system/ sysperf/Perf_tun_srv-R2.mspx.

Other VMs (for quick migration or live migration scenarios only)   If the host is part of a Windows Server 2008 cluster for quick or live migration, ensure that there are sufficient resources across all nodes of the cluster in case one node goes down. If a node hosting VMs goes offline for any reason, those VMs will attempt to restart across all other nodes in the cluster. However, if there's not enough memory on the cluster's remaining active nodes, the VMs may not be able to start. For more information, refer to Chapter 6, "Migrating Virtual Machines," which covers quick migration in depth.

NOTE   In some rare cases, a VM may not be able to start even when plenty of memory is available. This is most commonly seen when large file copies are performed in the parent partition. Microsoft has released a hotfix for this as KB953585, which can be downloaded from http://support.microsoft.com/kb/953585.

Luckily, monitoring the amount of available memory on a Hyper-V host is significantly easier than monitoring processor utilization, because memory utilization appears in Task Manager. You can also monitor the host's memory utilization using the Memory ➢ Available Mbytes counter.

Storage: How Many Drives Do I Need?

Storage can be one of the most complicated areas to plan for virtualization deployments. It's rare that you'll know exactly how large your VMs will grow, which may lead to either too much or not enough storage being allocated to a particular virtualization host. You can avoid both situations with some planning and monitoring.

When you're planning a virtualization deployment, knowing the basics of the workload and expected growth is critical to ensuring that enough storage is provisioned to the host. However, the way that storage is provisioned is as critical as the amount. Allocating 2 TB of storage to a host for VM usage may sound great; however, if it's two 1 TB drives connected to a Serial Advanced Technology Attachment (SATA) controller on the motherboard, it's highly unlikely that it will perform under load, because two disks generally can't keep up with a high-performance workload.

Storage planning involves two main areas of concern: storage controllers and the number of drives connected to those controllers. The type of storage on the back end also matters. These factors are listed here:

Storage controllers   An inadequate number of storage controllers installed in the system is a common bottleneck. A VM will do as much I/O as a physical system. If a VM is doing significant amounts of I/O, it can and will saturate the storage controller. Performance will suffer for any other VMs that are using virtual hard disks (VHDs) available from that storage controller.

That's why it's absolutely critical to have multiple paths available to the storage pool, for both performance reasons and failover in case of a loss of connection. Having multiple controllers available eliminates the single point of failure that can cripple a large-scale virtualization deployment.

Multipath I/O (MPIO)   Multipath I/O (also known as MPIO) is a technology that utilizes redundant components—adapters, cables, and switches—to provide multiple "paths" to the same storage array. This provides redundancy in case a connection is lost, because the traffic continues to flow. This functionality is provided for free with Windows Server. MPIO works with both Fibre Channel and iSCSI connections and is highly recommended for a production virtualization deployment.

Number of drives   As we mentioned earlier, provisioning storage for virtualization doesn't always mean getting the largest drive available. In many cases, just as with many high-performance workloads, it's preferable to have multiple smaller disks as opposed to fewer larger disks. A Redundant Array of Independent Disks (RAID) lets you spread the work across multiple disks in a controlled and secure manner.

Storage type   The type of storage connected to the host is of slightly less importance. As long as the storage is on the Windows Server 2008 hardware compatibility list, it will work with Hyper-V. This includes Small Computer System Interface (SCSI), serial-attached SCSI (SAS), Internet SCSI (iSCSI), Fibre Channel, and even Intelligent Drive Electronics (IDE) and Serial ATA (SATA).

You'll see performance differences based on the rotational speed of the disk as well as the amount of cache available on the disk. The performance gains of moving from a 7,200 RPM disk to a 10,000 RPM or even 15,000 RPM disk are significant and can increase even more past that level. Similarly, moving from 4 MB or 8 MB of cache to 16 MB or 32 MB will increase performance.

Volume management with quick migration When you pair storage with highly available VMs, the best practices get a bit more complicated. VMs that are made highly available as part of failover clustering have a limitation of one VM per logical unit number (LUN) if individual failover per VM is desired. This means you must carefully plan the provisioning of LUNs. This limitation doesn't apply if you're using live migration and Clustered Shared Volumes (CSV). We'll discuss this more in Chapter 6.

After your Hyper-V host is up and running, you should watch a few performance counters related to storage:

◆ Physical Disk, % Disk Read Time

◆ Physical Disk, % Disk Write Time

◆ Physical Disk, % Idle Time

These three counters provide a good high-level view of disk activity. If the read and write times are high (consistently greater than 75%), then disk performance is likely to be affected. These are the additional counters to monitor:

◆ Physical Disk, Avg. Disk Read Queue Length

◆ Physical Disk, Avg. Disk Write Queue Length

High levels for these counters (greater than 2) may indicate a disk bottleneck.

Networking

Networking requires a significant amount of planning for virtualization. You need to account for a number of different scenarios, and all of them depend on the workloads running in the VM on any given host.

Some questions you'll need to answer include the following:

◆ Does the server have an out-of-band server management controller?

◆ How many VMs will be running on the host, and what is their network utilization?

◆ Is iSCSI-based storage in use?

◆ How much network bandwidth is available on the back end?

With the R2 release of Hyper-V, Microsoft added some significant new features that help with improving network performance when used with Hyper-V. These features include:

◆ Jumbo Frame Support: The virtual network adapter now supports packets larger than 1500 frames, which increases the amount of data that can be contained in a single packet.

◆ Virtual Machine Queue (VMQ) support: This allows a network card to bypass the VMBus data path and instead use DMA (direct memory access) to copy packets directly from the physical NIC to the NIC in the VM. This requires specific hardware support.

◆ NIC Teaming: NIC Teaming is now a supported option from hardware vendors.

All of these features should be taken into account when planning your network infrastructure for Hyper-V.

For the purposes of this section, let's assume you have a host system that is hosting three VMs. The host has four network adapters and doesn't have an out-of-band management controller. We'll examine how you can best put these interfaces to use in a number of scenarios, while answering the previous questions.

NOTE Microsoft has published a white paper on networking best practices for Hyper-V called "Understanding Networking with Hyper-V." It's available at www.microsoft.com/downloads.

HOST MANAGEMENT

The first area to consider is host management. Because the system doesn't have an out-of-band management controller, which would let you access the host and act like you were sitting in front of it, you need to dedicate one interface for host management. You can do so in one of two ways:

◆ During installation, leave one of the interfaces on the host unselected (see Figure 4.4).

FIGURE 4.4
Leaving a physical network adapter unselected for host management while adding the Hyper-V role

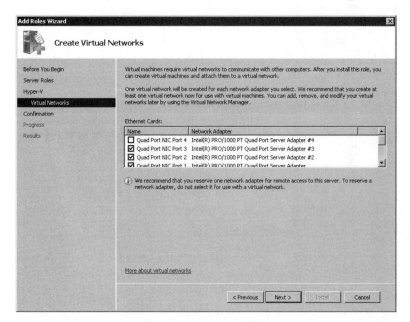

◆ If the installation has already taken place, delete the virtual network that's bound to the network adapter you want to use for managing the host.

For users of Hyper-V R2, one networking best practice that should be followed is to disable the virtual NIC in the parent partition for all external networks. This can be easily toggled— open the Virtual Network Manager, and for each external network, make sure the "Allow management operating system to share the network adapter" checkbox is not checked.

LIMITING REMOTE DESKTOP FOR ADMINISTRATION TO A SINGLE INTERFACE

If you have a server with multiple interfaces but want to limit Remote Desktop for Administration to a single interface, it's possible. This is generally helpful if there are multiple interfaces connected to the same network. Follow these steps to limit Remote Desktop for Administration to a dedicated management network adapter:

1. Open Remote Desktop Session Host Configuration under Start ➤ All Programs ➤ Administrative Tools ➤ Remote Desktop Services.

2. In the Configuration For Server window, under Connections, right-click the RDP-Tcp item, and select Properties.

3. Click the Network Adapter tab.

4. In the Network Adapter drop-down, select the network adapter that will be used for Remote Desktop for Administration.

WORKLOADS

Optimizing the network performance of the host is only half the battle. If network-intensive workloads are running within the virtual machine, improper network configuration can impact the performance.

Let's look at the workloads running in the VMs on this host. Three VMs are running, and analyzing the data indicates that two of the VMs don't generate much network traffic and that the third generates a significant network load. You decide to create two virtual networks—one for the VMs that don't generate significant network traffic and one for the VM that does.

You can do this three ways:

◆ During installation, select two ports on the Create Virtual Networks page (see Figure 4.5).

◆ If the installation has already taken place, use the Virtual Network Manager to modify the existing virtual networks.

iSCSI

The next step for proper network planning and utilization involves iSCSI. Will the VMs be using iSCSI, or will the host be using iSCSI? Whether it's a host or a guest, you should set aside a separate interface for each instance of iSCSI traffic. If the host is using iSCSI (for failover clustering, for example), then it should have a separate adapter port that is different from any adapter port being used for guest VMs using iSCSI. If you're using iSCSI in the host, it's recommended that MPIO be used as well.

NOTE iSCSI can be used in a VM—in fact, it's the only way to set up a cluster of VMs. If a VM is using iSCSI, it's recommended you create a separate virtual network to ensure sufficient bandwidth.

FIGURE 4.5

Leaving two physical network adapters unselected for iSCSI usage while adding the Hyper-V role

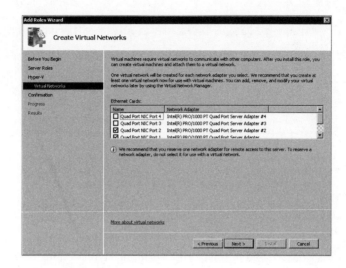

VLAN Tagging

Will any of the VMs be using virtual local area networks (VLANs)? *VLAN tagging,* also known as 802.1q, assigns a specific *tag* to packets. This tag allows separate traffic streams to go out over the same wire while maintaining isolation, because the packets can't be snooped or sniffed. This is especially useful in larger deployments of Hyper-V in enterprises with the infrastructure already in place.

As we discussed in Chapter 3, "Configuring Hyper-V," you can use VLAN tagging on each virtual adapter that's assigned to a VM. To do so, select the network adapter from the settings for the VM, and enter the correct VLAN ID.

Switch Uplink Bandwidth

Until now, we've been covering the adapters that are available on the host, as well as the virtual adapters available to the VM. There's one area that we haven't touched on: the hub or switch that the physical interfaces are plugged in to. A wide variety of switches are available, and each of them is slightly different. It's important that the switch have enough bandwidth to support multiple-gigabit interfaces and to send the data upstream. If a switch has eight 1 GB network ports and each port is sending 1 GB of traffic, a single-gigabit uplink port won't be able to handle all the traffic coming out of the switch, leading to less than optimal performance.

Virtual Network Monitoring

Monitoring virtual networks in Hyper-V is relatively painless. In Perfmon, the Hyper-V Virtual Network Adapter provides counters for each virtual network you've created. Careful monitoring of those counters can alert you to the saturation of a particular virtual network.

> **"What If My System Has Only a Single Network Adapter?"**
>
> This question comes up frequently for users in a test/development scenario. In this case, many of the items we've discussed don't apply.
>
> If only a single Ethernet port is available, all the traffic from all VMs will share the same port. It's recommended that at least two network interfaces be available on the system, which lets you reserve one network adapter for host administration.

Host Operating System Best Practices

Now that we've covered hardware best practices, we'll cover what you can do on the software side.

Run Hyper-V on Windows Server 2008 Core

As we discussed in Chapter 2, "Installing Hyper-V and Server Core," you can run Hyper-V on either a full installation of Windows Server 2008 or a Core installation. Each installation has its benefits and drawbacks, but the core Hyper-V binaries are exactly the same, regardless of your installation choice.

For a more secure and possibly more stable virtualization platform, using Windows Server 2008 Core is your best choice. Windows Server 2008 Core has a smaller attack surface and slightly less overhead for the parent partition. Those benefits help provide a more robust virtualization platform for large deployments.

Avoid Running Other Applications or Services in the Parent Partition

Two additional factors can help reduce bottlenecks in the parent partition and lead to faster performance:

◆ Don't run any applications in the parent partition.

◆ Don't run other server roles in the parent partition.

Running other applications or server roles in the parent partition can degrade performance. It's critical to keep the parent partition as unencumbered as possible. Keeping the parent partition lean and mean means more resources are available to the VMs.

NOTE   Running a lean parent partition is generally acceptable for a data center–based deployment of Hyper-V, but branch offices typically deploy only a few servers per branch. With limited processing power available, you might be tempted to run lightweight workloads on the parent partition alongside the Hyper-V role. Doing so can impact the stability of the Hyper-V role, so it's generally best to run those workloads inside VMs.

Minimize the Performance Impact of Virus Scanners

You should set your virus scanners to ignore virtualization-related files. If a virus scanner is running in the parent partition, constant scanning of virtualization-related files may slow disk performance. Many antivirus programs don't have a way to look at the contents of those files, so it's best to set up scanning exemptions in your antivirus software of choice.

The process varies depending on the antivirus software you use. You can typically block scanning either by file type or by folder. The following file types should be excluded from scanning (see Figure 4.6):

◆ Virtual hard disk (.vhd)

◆ Memory placeholder file (.bin)

◆ Saved-state files (.vsv)

◆ File-based representations of physical CD/DVD media (.iso)

FIGURE 4.6
Possible file extensions to exclude when using an antivirus scanner

Alternatively, you can exclude a directory from real-time scanning and then set the engine to ignore the configuration and VHD directories as defined in the host settings (see Figure 4.7).

FIGURE 4.7
Excluding directories

In addition to file type exclusions, it's also best to exclude the Hyper-V processes from virus scanning. This will help ensure that those processes are not slowed down. This includes the following processes:

◆ vmms.exe

◆ vmwp.exe

◆ vmmAgent.exe (if using System Center Virtual Machine Manager to manage a host)

Virtual Machine Best Practices

You've seen that you can do a significant amount of work on the host to ensure that your VMs are performing as well as possible. You can also do quite a bit of work within the VM.

In addition to sizing the VM correctly, running integration services in the VM increases performance significantly.

You can also set up a library of VHD files that have been prepared for quick deployments. If the operating systems running in the VM are Microsoft Windows, then those VHD files should be Sysprepped for hands-off deployment.

Finally, after you've created a library of Sysprepped images, how do you keep them up-to-date? Microsoft has a tool to help, called the Offline Virtual Machine Servicing Tool. We'll cover how this tool updates VHDs.

Integration Services: Guest Drivers

Integration services are a set of drivers and services that run in the VM. They're installed after you install the operating system in the VM. (We discussed integration services briefly in Chapter 1, "Introducing Hyper-V.")

Integration services are available for the following operating systems:

◆ Windows Server 2008, x86 and x64 editions

◆ Windows Server 2008 R2, x64 editions

◆ Windows Server 2003 SP2, x86 and x64 editions

◆ Windows 2000 Server/Advanced Server

◆ Windows 7 Business, Enterprise, or Ultimate, x86 and x64 editions

◆ Windows Vista SP1, x86 and x64 editions

◆ Windows XP SP2 or 3, x86 and x64 editions

◆ SUSE Linux Enterprise Server 10 SP3, x86 and x64 editions

◆ SUSE Linux Enterprise Server 11, x86 and x64 editions

◆ Red Hat Enterprise Linux 5.2, 5.3, and 5.4, x86 and x64 editions

These services contain the following drivers:

IDE   This driver provides optimized paths for IDE traffic, redirecting such traffic from the emulated device path to the synthetic (Virtual Machine Bus [VMBus]) device path.

SCSI   This driver provides support for the synthetic SCSI device in the VM. SCSI controllers in Hyper-V can have up to 64 devices per controller, with a maximum of 4 controllers per VM.

Networking   This driver provides support for the Microsoft VMBus network adapter, which provides much greater performance than the older emulated device.

Video/mouse   The video and mouse drivers work together to provide a seamless experience when you use VMConnect to access a VM.

In addition to the optimized virtualization drivers, additional services are made available to the VM once you install the integration components:

Operating System Shutdown   Operating System Shutdown lets you shut down the operating system within the VM without having to log in. It's similar to pushing the power button on a hardware system to power it down.

Time Synchronization   Time Synchronization keeps the VM's clock and the host clock in sync. When the VM is powered on, the clock in the VM is synced to the clock on the host. This driver keeps the two in sync afterward.

Data Exchange   By using the Key Value Pair (KVP) mechanism, VMs and their hosts can communicate by key pairs. This allows both systems to get information from each other—for example, the VM can query the registry and get the name of the host the VM is running on. The VM can modify only the `HKEY_LOCAL_MACHINE\Software\Microsoft\Virtual Machine\Guest` keys. This functionality is available only on Windows-based VMs.

Heartbeat   If integration services are installed in the VM, a Heartbeat service will run in the VM. That Heartbeat service sends a notification to the host if the virtual machine is still responding. You can observe the heartbeat status in the Hyper-V Manager as well as through the Windows Management Interface (WMI) interfaces.

Online Backup   The Online Backup component is a Volume Shadow Services (VSS) writer. VSS provides a method for taking a backup of the state of a disk at any given point in time; the backup is application-consistent. When you start a VSS backup, all running VMs with integration services installed are notified, and data is flushed to disk.

Newer Microsoft operating systems, including Windows Server 2008 R2 and Windows 7, have the integration services already installed. When you boot up a VM running one of those operating systems on a Windows Server 2008 R2 system, all the synthetic devices and integration services are available.

Other operating systems require that the integration services be installed manually. To install integration services in the VM, start up the Virtual Machine Connect application, and select Action ➤ Insert Integration Services Setup Disk. Doing so mounts the installation image in the VM. When that's complete, the autorun functionality in Windows starts the installer. If autorun is disabled, browse to the `support\x86` directory, and double-click `setup.exe`.

NOTE   Installing integration services in a Linux VM requires a download, because the components aren't included in the box with Hyper-V. For more information about integration services for Linux, go to www.`microsoft.com/virtualization`, and search for *Linux Integration Components for Windows Server 2008 Hyper-V.*

Sysprep: Creating a Master Base Image

Fore environments where you must rapidly deploy VMs, a library of prebuilt drive images can be a real time-saver. If those VMs are running Windows, though, it's not as simple as installing Windows once and then copying the VHD file. You need to remove the name and unique identifier of the operating system that's installed. Microsoft has made a tool available that will perform those tasks; it's called *Sysprep.*

When you Sysprep a VM, certain information is deleted and marked for re-creation on the first boot. This information includes the username, the product key, and your acceptance of the end user license agreement (EULA). This process makes it extremely easy to create a library of prebuilt VMs—and then deploy them without having to install a new copy of the operating system.

Sysprepping a VM is a very quick process. With newer versions of Windows (Windows Vista, Windows 7, Windows Server 2008, and Windows Server 2008 R2), the tool is included in the operating system. (For older operating systems, refer to the documentation to learn where Sysprep is located.) Open a command window, browse to `%WINDIR%\system32\sysprep`, and launch `sysprep.exe`.

The Sysprep tool, when run with its defaults as shown in Figure 4.8, clears the VM's security identifier (SID) and removes the registered owner. It also sets the operating system to enter what Microsoft calls *Mini-Setup*, which lets you set some parameters for the VM such as the machine name and the new administrative password.

NOTE   To create a master copy of a Windows operating system in a VHD file and prepare it for future deployments, it's best to perform a clean install of the operating system, apply any available updates and/or patches, and install the integration services. Then, run the Sysprep tool (shown here), and select Shutdown Options ➢ Shutdown. When the VM shuts down, you have a clean master copy of the operating system that can be saved for future deployment.

FIGURE 4.8
Using Sysprep to prepare a virtual machine for creating a master copy.

Offline Patching

After you follow the steps we've discussed and create a library of VMs, you need to keep them up-to-date with patches. Microsoft has released a solutions accelerator called the Offline Virtual Machine Servicing Tool 2.1. This tool works in conjunction with System Center Virtual Machine Manager (SCVMM) and either Windows Server Update Services (WSUS) 3.0 or System Center Configuration Manager 2007 (SCCM) to provide a safe and secure method for applying updates to VM images.

The workflow for the tool is simple:

1. The VM is deployed on a maintenance host—a special host type defined by SCVMM.

2. A job is triggered within the VM that starts the software-update cycle.

3. The VM is shut down and returned to the library, fully patched.

To find out more about the Offline Virtual Machine Servicing Tool or to download your free copy, browse to www.microsoft.com/solutionaccelerators.

Summary

In this chapter, we covered a number of ways that you can configure your systems for optimal performance. By ensuring that the physical system is tuned and can stand up to the VMs running on the host, you can ensure that the choice to deploy virtualization results in a positive experience for users and administrators alike.

Chapter 5

Hyper-V Security

In the first four chapters of this book, we covered a wide variety of topics, including installing Hyper-V, creating virtual machines, and following best practices. Now that we've covered the basics and set up a level playing field, let's dig into the security features of Hyper-V.

Security is a hot-button topic these days, especially when it comes to virtualization. With workload consolidation happening on a major scale after virtualization is deployed, you want to ensure that virtualized workloads are well isolated and that you grant the right access privileges to the right people.

In this chapter, we'll cover the following:

◆ The Hyper-V security model

◆ The virtualization machine access security model

◆ Working with the Authorization Manager

The Hyper-V Security Model

Because the hypervisor sits below all other components (see Chapter 1, "Introducing Hyper-V," for the architectural overview), it's naturally the first attack target of those looking to compromise a Hyper-V host.

One of the most talked-about items related to the security of hypervisors (not specific to Hyper-V) is the *blue pill*, which harks back to the film *The Matrix*. If you ingested the blue pill, you had no idea that you actually lived inside the Matrix. The blue pill concept was first written about by Joanna Rutkowska and presented at the Black Hat Security Conference in 2006; it refers to the possibility of malware being injected into a hypervisor-aware platform without the user's knowledge. Needless to say, it caused quite a stir when people learned that a hypervisor could be subverted so easily.

Hyper-V was developed with a number of security assumptions in mind:

◆ The parent partition is trusted by the hypervisor, and the virtual machines (child partitions) trust the parent partition.

◆ None of the virtual machines (VMs) running on a host are trusted. They can be used for nefarious deeds.

◆ The code running in VMs must be run unmodified, must use all features of the x86 instruction set, and can execute in any ring necessary.

◆ The hypercall interface, which child partitions can use to access functions of the hypervisor, is publicly available and fully documented. A (potentially) untrusted VM can attempt to execute any of the hypercalls.

◆ A VM can detect that it's running on a hypervisor.

We'll now review the security of the hypervisor as well as the security of the virtualization stack.

Hypervisor Security

Microsoft has done a number of things to ensure a secure hypervisor:

Security Development Lifecycle   The Microsoft Security Development Lifecycle (SDL) is one of the main ways that Microsoft assures quality software. In place since 2004, the SDL has improved product quality by implementing strict quality gates, process improvements, and other guidance throughout the entire software development process. By being put in place at the earliest possible time, before a line of code has been written, the SDL helps eliminate security issues before the product ships, before they can affect users.

For more information, you can read the white paper entitled "Microsoft Security Development Lifecycle (SDL)," available at www.microsoft.com/downloads. The latest version is 4.1a. This paper provides guidance on how Microsoft implemented the SDL.

Keep in mind that this is only a guide and that not all the steps Microsoft followed are publicly available.

Separate address spaces   Both the hypervisor and the host operating system maintain separate address spaces. An *address space* refers to a specific location in memory. By ensuring that there are separate address spaces for both components, the host operating system can't read or access the hypervisor address space, and vice versa.

No third-party code   The hypervisor included as part of Hyper-V doesn't include any third-party code. Other hypervisors include device drivers or other drivers that were submitted by third parties.

By having all code in the hypervisor go through the SDL, Microsoft can ensure the stability of the hypervisor as a whole.

Guest-to-guest communication   No communication that takes place between guests over synthetic devices goes through the hypervisor. This reduces the chance of a man-in-the-middle attack in the hypervisor, where someone injects a driver at the hypervisor level that sniffs data going between two VMs.

No shared memory between guests   Each guest has its own memory space. This means the memory allocated to those VMs is exclusive and can't be accessed from other VMs.

Inability of guests to affect hardware I/O   All I/O for synthetic devices in VMs is handled in the Virtualization Service Provider/Virtualization Service Client (VSP/VSC) model, which sits above the hypervisor layer. Also, the I/O model of the VSP/VSC architecture sends out requests on behalf of the VM—the VM itself doesn't send I/O requests.

Hypervisor access   The host and guests are unable to write to the hypervisor; rather, they communicate with the hypervisor via the well-defined Hypercall API. This ensures that the hypervisor can't be modified.

TIP Microsoft has published a useful Hyper-V security guide at the following URL: http://technet.microsoft.com/en-us/library/dd569113.aspx.

Virtualization Stack Security

The security work that Microsoft did with Hyper-V didn't stop at the hypervisor level:

◆ All of the binaries that are included as part of the Hyper-V role have gone through the SDL process. One part of this process adds Address Space Layout Randomization (ASLR), which, when enabled, loads critical DLLs in random pages of memory at each boot. This helps alleviate exploits that target DLLs that load in the same memory location every time.

◆ The worker processes that represent the virtual processor to the VM have a number of safeguards—they run in user mode with reduced privileges, and each worker process is separate from the others.

◆ Each VM has its own instance of a virtual device. No two VMs can use the same virtual network adapter; when a VM is created, a new virtual network adapter is created for that VM.

◆ By requiring the Execute Disable/No Execute bit in the host's processor, the chance of malicious buffer overflow attacks is reduced.

Other components, such as the VSP/VSC architecture, have additional security measures in place:

◆ Each VM that is powered on has a separate instance of Virtual Machine Bus (VMBus).

◆ VMBus is a point-to-point connection between the VSP in the parent and the VSC in the guest.

◆ Because the VSC doesn't have access to the physical device, direct memory access (DMA) attacks can't take place.

The Virtual Machine Access Security Model

Of course, when it comes to security, ensuring your binaries and software are secure is only half the battle. One of the core tenets of security is to ensure a user has no more access than is absolutely necessary for a particular task. As we've been saying all along, this is even more important after you bring virtualization into play. In a shared host environment, for example, an administrator for the accounting department shouldn't be able to shut off the VM for the HR department. You can achieve this separation by working with the Authorization Manager (AzMan), which is part of Windows Server 2008.

Previously with Virtual Server 2005, this security was granted via access rights on the configuration file and on the virtual hard disk (VHD) file. However, with the changes made for Hyper-V, security and access rights moved into the AzMan. Rest assured, everything you could do previously with Virtual Server, you can still do with Hyper-V.

Working with the Authorization Manager

The AzMan functionality was first included with Windows Server 2003. It's undergone some enhancements with Windows Server 2008. At its heart, it's a simple role-based security architecture that allows compatible applications, such as Hyper-V, to grant users access to functionality without granting them administrative rights to the host system.

Understanding the Terminology

You need to become familiar with some terms before you get started working with AzMan:

- *Role*: A set of permissions that's necessary to perform a job.

- *Operation*: The lowest level of actions you can take against a Hyper-V host. Examples of operations include creating a VM, modifying a virtual network, and viewing a list of the VMs on the host. You can't modify operations, but you can group them into tasks.

- *Task*: A group of operations. You can create tasks that group necessary operations for a particular task. An example task would include the ability to create and power on a VM.

- *Policy*: A definition of the interdependencies between roles, tasks, and operations.

Using the Authorization Manager for Hyper-V Security

The Authorization Manager (AzMan) is where all access policies for Hyper-V are defined. Using AzMan, you can specify which users have access to different operations on the host.

NOTE If you're using System Center Virtual Machine Manager (SCVMM) 2008, these steps don't apply. SCVMM replaces the default store with its own authorization scheme and structure. You'll need to manage access rights, as well as all other rights, via SCVMM. System Center Virtual Machine Manager 2008 R2 uses the default store.

For more information about SCVMM, refer to Chapter 11, "Using System Center Virtual Machine Manager."

In this example, the Contoso corporation has deployed a new Hyper-V host. This host will be hosting VMs for multiple departments. Each group has an administrator. The company's IT administrator wants to provide each group's administrator with the ability to turn the group's VM on or off or reset it. The first group to get a VM provisioned on this host is the HR group.

To give the group administrator this ability, you need to follow these steps as the IT administrator:

1. Open the default store.

2. Create a new role definition in the master scope.

3. Create a new child scope for the HR organization.

4. Create a role definition for the HR team in the child scope.

5. Assign access for the HR administrator account to the role definition.

6. Assign a VM to the newly created scope.

To start with, you need to open the default authorization store. This contains all the default roles, operations, and tasks. In this store, you'll make the changes necessary for the first set of tasks.

OPENING THE DEFAULT STORE

To open the default store, follow these steps:

1. Click the Start menu, and type **azman.msc** in the text box. Alternatively, open a new MMC console, select Add/Remove Snap-In, and add the Authorization Manager snap-in. Next, select Action ➢ Open Authorization Store to open the window shown in Figure 5.1.

FIGURE 5.1
Opening the authorization store

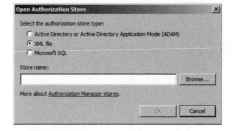

NOTE If you're modifying the access rights to a Windows Server Core system, you need to do so from a full installation of Windows Server 2008. Browse to the Windows Server Core host, and select the authorization store there.

2. Browse to the authorization store. The default authorization store is kept in the following location: C:\programdata\microsoft\windows\hyper-v\initialstore.xml.

Now that you have the store open, you can start with the changes necessary to support your scenario. Before you start, let's get familiar with the AzMan UI (see Figure 5.2).

FIGURE 5.2
The Authorization Manager UI

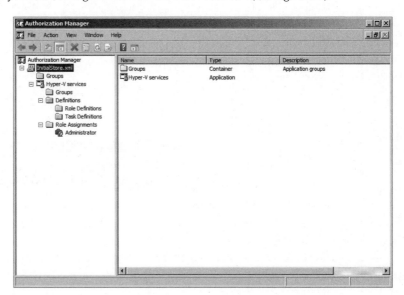

By default, a single scope is defined, named Hyper-V Services. Each child scope to the primary scope is independent of the other, but each child scope can inherit from the primary scope. Later in this exercise, you'll create a new scope.

In the Definitions folder are two items: Role Definitions and Task Definitions. By right-clicking those folders, you can create new definitions.

ASSIGNING ROLES

To get started, you need to create a new role definition. This role definition will give a user access to the VM Management Service (VMMS) and the Virtual Switch Management Service:

1. Right-click Role Definitions, and select New Role Definition.

2. For the name, type **VM Manager Access**. Click the Add button, select the Operations tab, and select the Read Service Configuration and View Virtual Switch Management Service check boxes (see Figure 5.3). Click OK to close the New Role Definition dialog box.

FIGURE 5.3
Creating a new
role definition

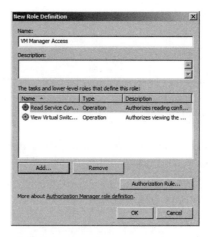

Now that you've created the role definition, you need to create a role assignment based on that role definition.

3. In the Authorization Manager window, right-click Role Assignments, and select New Role Assignment from the pop-up menu. Select the VM Manager Access check box, and click OK (see Figure 5.4).

FIGURE 5.4
Creating a new
role assignment

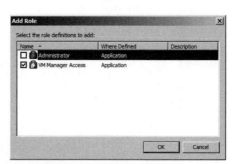

The last step adds a user account to the new role assignment you just created.

4. Right-click the VM Manager Access role assignment, and select Assign Users And Groups ➤ From Windows And Active Directory. Type the name of the account you want to add. In Figure 5.5, the HR team has an account called HRAdmin that they'll be using for this purpose.

FIGURE 5.5
Adding a user account to the role assignment

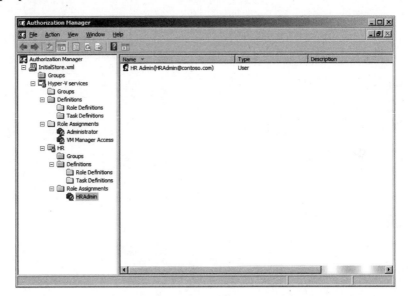

NOTE If you're interested in just adding users to Hyper-V without requiring administrative rights to the host, add the user account to the Administrator role assignment. This grants the user administrative rights on the Hyper-V host, allowing them to perform actions against all VMs that are registered on the host.

CREATING A CHILD SCOPE

The next steps involve creating a child scope that will handle all the access permissions for the HR organization. In the scope, you'll create a new role definition that's specific to that scope. This scope will let you delegate control of the HR team's VM to the HR administrator:

1. In AzMan, right-click Hyper-V Services, and select New Scope. Name the new scope **HR** (see Figure 5.6). This creates a child scope to the master Hyper-V Services scope.

2. In the HR scope, click Role Definitions, and then select New Role Definition. You'll name the new role definition **HRAdmin**.

3. Click the Add button, and then select the Operations tab. On this tab, you can add all the options you want HRAdmin to be able to perform against all VMs that will be assigned to the scope. Select the check boxes next to the following items:

   ◆ Allow Input To Virtual Machine

   ◆ Allow Output From Virtual Machine

◆ Pause And Restart Virtual Machine

◆ Start Virtual Machine

◆ Stop Virtual Machine

FIGURE 5.6
Creating a new
child scope

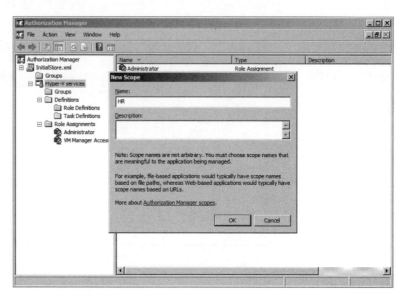

The end result should look like Figure 5.7.

FIGURE 5.7
Creating a new role
definition in the
child scope

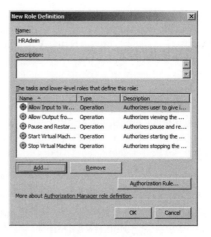

4. Like last time, you need to create a new role assignment for the role you just created.
Right-click Role Assignments in the HR scope, and select New Role Assignment. Select
the HRAdmin check box (see Figure 5.8), and click OK.

FIGURE 5.8
Creating a role assignment in the child scope

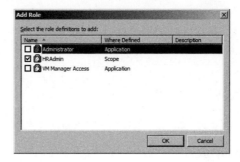

5. Right-click the new role assignment, and select Assign Users And Groups ➢ From Windows And Active Directory. Add the HRAdmin account in the dialog box, and click OK (see Figure 5.9).

FIGURE 5.9
Adding the user account to the role assignment in the child scope

SETTING THE SCOPE OF A VIRTUAL MACHINE WITH SCRIPTS

At this point, the HRAdmin user has access to the Hyper-V host. The account doesn't have the access necessary to create a VM, though. You need to create a new VM and set the scope of the VM to the HRAdmin account. Hyper-V doesn't have any graphical way to set the scope of a particular VM, so you'll use a script here.

You'll need four scripts for these next steps. These scripts, shown in Listings 5.1 through 5.4, were written by Tony Soper and posted on the Microsoft TechNet forums; refer to http://social.technet.microsoft.com/Forums/en-US/ITCG/thread/3d0888e2-7538-4578-b16c-97b73c8e0f96 for more information.

LISTING 5.1   CreateVMInScope.vbs

```
Option Explicit

Dim WMIService

Dim VMManagementService

Dim VMName

Dim VMScope

Dim VMSystemGlobalSettingData

Dim Result

Dim inParameters

VMName = InputBox("Specify the name for the new virtual machine:")

VMScope = InputBox("Specify the scope to be used for the new virtual

machine:")

'Get an instance of the WMI Service in the virtualization namespace.

Set WMIService = GetObject("winmgmts:\\.\root\virtualization")

'Get a VMManagementService object

Set VMManagementService = WMIService.ExecQuery("SELECT * FROM

Msvm_VirtualSystemManagementService").ItemIndex(0)

' Initialize the global settings for the VM

Set VMSystemGlobalSettingData =

WMIService.Get("Msvm_VirtualSystemGlobalSettingData").SpawnInstance_()
```

```vbscript
'Set the name and scope

VMSystemGlobalSettingData.ElementName = VMName

VMSystemGlobalSettingData.ScopeOfResidence = VMScope


' Create the VM

VMManagementService.DefineVirtualSystem(VMSystemGlobalSettingData.GetText_(1

)
```

LISTING 5.2   `DisplayVMScopes.vbs`

```vbscript
Option Explicit


Dim WMIService

Dim VMList

Dim VM

Dim VMSystemGlobalSettingData

Dim Message


'Setup start of message string

Message = "Virtual Machines and their scope of residence" & chr(10) _

        & "======================================="



'Get instance of 'virtualization' WMI service on the local computer

Set WMIService = GetObject("winmgmts:\\.\root\virtualization")



'Get all the MSVM_ComputerSystem object
```

```
Set VMList = WMIService.ExecQuery("SELECT * FROM Msvm_ComputerSystem")


For Each VM In VMList

   if VM.Caption = "Virtual Machine" then

      Set VMSystemGlobalSettingData =

(VM.Associators_("MSVM_ElementSettingData",

"Msvm_VirtualSystemGlobalSettingData")).ItemIndex(0)

      Message = Message & chr(10) & "VM:        " & VM.ElementName

      Message = Message & chr(10) & "Scope:   " &

VMSystemGlobalSettingData.ScopeOfResidence

      Message = Message & chr(10)

   end if

Next


wscript.echo Message
```

LISTING 5.3   ClearVMScope.vbs

```
Option Explicit


Dim WMIService

Dim VMList

Dim VM

Dim VMSystemGlobalSettingData

Dim VMManagementService
```

```
Dim Result


'Get instance of 'virtualization' WMI service on the local computer

Set WMIService = GetObject("winmgmts:\\.\root\virtualization")


'Get a VMManagementService object

Set VMManagementService = WMIService.ExecQuery("SELECT * FROM

Msvm_VirtualSystemManagementService").ItemIndex(0)


'Get all the MSVM_ComputerSystem object

Set VMList = WMIService.ExecQuery("SELECT * FROM Msvm_ComputerSystem")


For Each VM In VMList

    if VM.Caption = "Virtual Machine" then

        Set VMSystemGlobalSettingData =

(VM.Associators_("MSVM_ElementSettingData",

"Msvm_VirtualSystemGlobalSettingData")).ItemIndex(0)

        VMSystemGlobalSettingData.ScopeOfResidence = ""

        Result = VMManagementService.ModifyVirtualSystem(VM.Path_.Path,

VMSystemGlobalSettingData.GetText_(1))

    end if

Next
```

LISTING 5.4   ChangeVMScope.vbs

```
Dim WMIService

Dim VM

Dim VMManagementService

Dim VMSystemGlobalSettingData

Dim VMName

Dim VMScope

Dim Result


'Setup variables for the VM we are looking for, and the scope to assign it to

VMName = InputBox("Specify the virtual machine to change scope on:")

VMScope = InputBox("Specify the new scope to be used:")


'Get an instance of the WMI Service in the virtualization namespace.

Set WMIService = GetObject("winmgmts:\\.\root\virtualization")


'Get a VMManagementService object

Set VMManagementService = WMIService.ExecQuery("SELECT * FROM

Msvm_VirtualSystemManagementService").ItemIndex(0)


'Get the VM object that we want to modify

Set VM = (WMIService.ExecQuery("SELECT * FROM Msvm_ComputerSystem WHERE

ElementName='" & VMName & "'")).ItemIndex(0)
```

```
'Get the VirtualSystemGlobalSettingsData of the VM we want to modify

Set VMSystemGlobalSettingData = (VM.Associators_("MSVM_ElementSettingData",

"Msvm_VirtualSystemGlobalSettingData")).ItemIndex(0)


'Change the ScopeOfResidence property

VMSystemGlobalSettingData.ScopeOfResidence = VMScope


'Update the VM with ModifyVirtualSystem

Result = VMManagementService.ModifyVirtualSystem(VM.Path_.Path,

VMSystemGlobalSettingData.GetText_(1))
```

After you create the scripts, you can execute them from the command line. Each script has a specific function:

♦ CreateVMInScope creates a new VM with the specified name in the specified scope. For example, you can use this script to create a new VM named HR VM in the HR scope.

♦ DisplayVMScopes enumerates all the VMs on the host and displays their names as well as their scopes. If the scope field is empty, then it's accessible by all users who have access to the Hyper-V system.

♦ ClearVMScope removes the scope assignment from a particular VM.

♦ ChangeVMScope changes the scope assignment for a particular VM.

For the purposes of this section, let's assume that you already have a VM provisioned for the HR team named HRVM001. As an administrator on the Hyper-V host, from the command prompt, run ChangeVMScope.vbs. A dialog box appears, asking for the name of the VM on which the scope will be changed. Type in the name of the VM (**HRVM001**), and then click OK. Next, enter the scope you set up earlier (HR), and click OK.

To confirm that the scope was set correctly, run DisplayVMScopes.vbs. The scope of the VM should be set to HR (see Figure 5.10).

FIGURE 5.10
Confirming the scope for a virtual machine

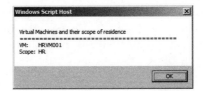

From a Hyper-V Manager console, when logged in as HRAdmin, connect to the Hyper-V host. Only one VM should be listed: HRVM001. You should be able to power on the VM as well as perform all the operations that were specified when you set up the permissions for the HR scope. You also shouldn't be able to create a new VM; if you try, an error is returned that says "Cannot create a VM in the default authorization scope."

Using Alternative Tools

The process that we've just covered is manual and involved. If you're looking for a shortcut, the Hyper-V Remote Management Configuration Utility greatly simplifies these steps. The tool (available for download from `http://code.msdn.microsoft.com/HVRemote`) was written by one of the program managers on the Hyper-V team and provides a command-line interface to all the commands you used earlier.

Using the tool is extremely easy. To grant a user access to a Hyper-V host, run the following command:

```
hvremote /add:domain\user
```

Note, however, that this grants access only to the host. If you want to restrict access by user account to a VM, then you still need to set up scopes and assign VMs to those scopes. Additional options are available that you can access by executing the following command:

```
cscript hvremote.wsf /?
```

NOTE If you're in a domain environment, it's highly recommended that you use `hvremote` for granting access to a host.

Storing the AzMan Store in Active Directory

You can place the AzMan store in one of two locations—either in a XML file on the local system being managed or in Active Directory. Moving the AzMan store into Active Directory provides a central repository for all systems as well as provides replication in the Active Directory schema.

However, if you create the AzMan store on a local system and then choose to move it into Active Directory, that poses its own unique set of challenges. There's an unsupported application from the AzMan developers that can provide that functionality. It's part of the Windows software development kit (SDK). For more information, refer to the Directory Services team blog at `http://blogs.technet.com/askds` and search for *How to Migrate the AzMan Store*.

Summary

In this chapter, we covered the work Microsoft has done to ensure a secure virtualization stack. All the components that are included as part of Hyper-V have undergone a strict security overview and in-depth analysis. We also provided examples for granting access to a Hyper-V host without allowing administrative access to the rest of the system.

Chapter 6

Virtual Machine Migration

Existing physical systems inevitably become targets for virtualization, thanks to the savings and value it provides. Loading and configuring applications on top of a freshly installed, contemporary operating system yields the best performance and stability but may not always be feasible.

The goal of this chapter is to introduce the steps and processes required to migrate an existing system into a Hyper-V virtual machine. The chapter includes a walkthrough of the manual process to move a physical system into a virtual machine.

The best approach for converting any existing supported Windows system into a virtual machine is to use System Center Virtual Machine Manager (SCVMM). SCVMM is covered in Chapter 11, "System Center Virtual Machine Manager."

After you virtualize systems on top of Hyper-V, you may need to migrate virtual machines between physical hosts. In this chapter, we'll also discuss migrating virtual machines from one Hyper-V host to another using the provided export and import functionality.

We'll cover the following topics in this chapter:

- Migration challenges and drivers
- Migration considerations
- Preparing a system for migration
- Capturing, transposing, and deploying system configurations
- Capturing and deploying disk images
- Updating images
- Walking through a physical-to virtual migration
- Exporting and importing in Hyper-V

Migration Challenges and Drivers

The challenges presented by a virtual migration are similar to those you would encounter moving a system from one physical host to another. Relocating (via backup/restore or disk imaging) a Windows Server 2003–based Exchange Server from an HP DL365 to a Dell 1955 might be a risky proposition. The two systems can have significant variations in hardware including CPU manufacturer, CPU architecture, CPU core count, network interface cards, disk controllers, video controllers, management services/tools, and other components. Some of the variations are insignificant. Other changes can (we hope) be detected by the operating system and addressed. Some differences in network and storage configuration often require expert attention from either specialized migration software or a knowledgeable administrator.

You may face similar configuration challenges when you move a server from a physical or virtual environment to create a new virtual instance. No physical system in the world has an exact match for the network adapter, Small Computer System Interface (SCSI) controller, Intelligent Drive Electronics (IDE) controller, and video controller presented to a Hyper-V virtual machine (VM). You need to add optimized drivers to a migrated system just as they might be required in a physical migration. Network-configuration information (static IP address, name-resolution servers, gateways, and so on) may need to be set, just as if you were installing a new network interface card (NIC) in a physical system.

NOTE Some hardware components simply can't be virtualized. Specialized boards to perform data collection, provide voice integration, or function as interfaces to industrial equipment don't have equivalents in the virtual world. Hyper-V lacks USB support for VMs, so USB-based devices don't function (which is important for some license-key dongle devices). Although older networking adapters including Token Ring and Attached Resource Computer Network (ARCNET) cards can't be virtualized, the Ethernet adapters found in Hyper-V may be able to provide suitable replacement network service.

With all these challenges, why migrate an existing system to a VM rather than build a clean, fresh install? A new operating system could be installed, patched, and configured to provide an up-to-date platform for applications and services. It sounds like a great approach, but often building a new system isn't feasible. Reasons for pursuing a server migration rather than a replacement vary. Sometimes the expertise for configuring a system or application is no longer available. Installation source for a program may not be accessible (install disks have been lost, or the vendor is out of business). A system's configuration may be deemed too fragile to risk a reinstallation. A catastrophic hardware failure may have left only an old backup image of a system.

Whatever the reasons might be, the pain and suffering you incur to build a system can be greater than the risk and effort to forklift the system into a VM. Drivers to migrate such systems (legacy hardware maintenance costs, backup costs, recovery risk, power cost, performance limitations, and so forth) can easily justify the effort to migrate. After the system is virtualized, risks and challenges posed by a future migration are largely eliminated, because virtualized systems are portable (via export and import) and more easily recovered.

The high-level steps necessary to successfully migrate from one system to another are largely the same, regardless of the tools you use:

1. Assess the existing configuration.

2. Capture the configuration.

3. Capture the disk image(s).

4. Transpose the disk image(s).

5. Disable the legacy system.

6. Transpose the configuration.

Conversion from an existing physical host to a VM is frequently the goal of a migration, but it isn't the only type of virtualization-related system migration. In some situations, you may want to move from one virtualization platform to another or migrate a VM to physical hardware.

Physical to Virtual (P2V) Migration

You use a physical to virtual (P2V) conversion to decouple a system from its hardware and create a new virtual system instance. Targets for a P2V migration often include older systems. Hardware maintenance costs and spare-part availability can conspire with vintage operating systems and application software to increase operations risk. Deep in the heart of a computer room, you may find ancient servers with unclear but critical business functions. Failure may not be an option for these systems, but fail they will—some day.

Converting the system in order to decouple it from its stone-age hardware can breathe new life into it and bring necessary longevity. Virtualizing such a system not only can extend its life by enabling it to run on contemporary hardware but also can enable entirely new backup and recovery scenarios. Often, legacy applications lacked integrated backup and recovery awareness. Successfully completing a P2V migration of such a system allows for the backup of the encapsulated VM, as detailed in Chapter 7, "Backup and Recovery."

NOTE Migrating an older, unsupported system to a VM and hosting it on Windows Server 2008 in Hyper-V doesn't extend support from Microsoft or other vendors. If the platform or application is out of support, virtualization probably won't change its support status. But a P2V migration can still *drastically reduce the risk of failure* to your organization. Regardless of vendor support status, eliminating high-risk hardware can be a good thing, and you should consider it.

Not all candidates for P2V migration are long in the tooth, high-risk servers. Contemporary mainstream systems may also be candidates for conversion to a VM. P2V processing can move you closer to the reality of a virtualized environment in conjunction with building and configuring new VMs. An automated P2V tool like that included in System Center Virtual Machine Manager (SCVMM) can save you substantial time and effort.

Virtual to Virtual (V2V) Migration

You may have an existing VM environment that doesn't leverage Hyper-V. Perhaps you use Virtual Server 2005, a VMware product, or another virtualization layer. Performance, software costs, or corporate standards can drive the need to move to Hyper-V, necessitating a virtual to virtual (V2V) migration.

V2V conversions are often less complicated than P2V migrations. Virtual machines don't leverage the vast array of hardware available in the physical world. The potential hardware presented to a VM is limited, so the assessment of the source VM isn't as extensive.

Common file formats used between virtualization platforms can also simplify V2V migrations. Virtual Server 2005 and Hyper-V share a common file format for virtual disks (.vhd). Moving a virtual hard disk (VHD) file from Virtual PC / Virtual Server to Hyper-V or Hyper-V R2 eliminates the need to capture and convert an existing disk-image file. In this case, additional configuration is required both outside the VM (to configure similar virtual hardware resources) and within it (removing additions, installing or updating integration components, and re-creating network configuration). It's important to note that you can't migrate a *saved* VM from one virtualization platform to another. The details of how running systems work vary by virtualization platform (how memory is mapped and managed, for example) and can't be easily converted from an in-flight operating system instance. You must typically shut down a VM for a successful V2V migration.

TIP Matthijs ten Seldam created a Virtual Server to Hyper-V configuration migration tool, which is available via his blog at `http://blogs.technet.com/matthts/archive/2008/09/12/vmc-to-hyper-v-import-tool-available.aspx`. It does a nice job of converting the configuration information, but it doesn't remove additions or install Integration Components (ICs). SCVMM does a more complete job of V2V migrations in this case.

You can easily automate V2V migrations to Hyper-V from other virtualization platforms such as Virtual Server and VMware ESX. SCVMM includes support for Virtual Server or VMware ESX to Hyper-V conversion.

You can move existing Hyper-V–based VMs from one host to another in a number of ways, and it really isn't considered a V2V migration. You can migrate VMs from one Hyper-V host to another using failover clustering, using export/import, or leveraging SCVMM. We'll discuss and demonstrate failover clustering in Chapter 8, "High Availability," and we cover SCVMM in Chapter 11. Export and import are discussed at the end of this chapter.

Virtual to Physical (V2P)

Occasionally, you may want to migrate a VM to dedicated physical hardware. Most often, you need to address performance requirements that can't be met from a virtual system. Although a virtual to physical (V2P) conversion is possible, it's more challenging to accomplish or automate than a P2V or V2V migration.

P2V and V2V conversions have the benefit of a known target system. The end state and target hardware come from the same pool of hardware for every migration, simplifying driver integration. The possible variations for V2P target hardware configurations are enormous and difficult to anticipate.

You must take a great deal of care to complete a successful V2P migration. Microsoft doesn't provide any supported means of performing a V2P conversion, but third parties including Acronis and Vizioncore provide tools for V2P as well as P2V and V2V. You can also use common backup and recovery tools as well as the manual processes shown later in the chapter.

Migration Considerations

As is the case when you're creating a new VM, it's important to know the performance characteristics required for a migrated system before you undertake a conversion. Assessing the system to be migrated is an important step in the overall process. Consider the following questions before you begin migration:

◆ How much RAM is required for the VM?

◆ What are the disk requirements and anticipated growth?

◆ How many network connections are required? Do the Media Access Control (MAC) addresses need to be preserved?

◆ Does the system require significant CPU capacity?

◆ How many processors can the system use or does it require?

◆ Is any software installed that may be looking for hardware that won't be in the VM?

You have to understand the constraints of the virtualization platform as well as the migration method and tools. It may be obvious to you that a physical system requiring (for example) a video-capture card to function properly won't virtualize well. It may be less clear that a network-based image-capture and -deployment tool could fail to run within Hyper-V because it lacks a suitable Hyper-V–compatible network driver. Understanding all the components of the migration process up front will save you time and effort later.

Capturing the Configuration

Creating an inventory of the physical source hardware is a common practice before undertaking a migration. Automated tools (like Microsoft's SCVMM and the older Virtual Server Migration Toolkit [VSMT]) do a thorough analysis of the source system before proceeding.

Creating a Manual Inventory

You can manually create an inventory of your physical virtualization candidates. This doesn't mean you have to shut down the system, open it up, and inspect the physical parts (although that's a good idea). Most of the important system information can be collected while the system is running, using available commands and tools. Common information to collect about the source system includes the following:

◆ Processor configuration including CPU type; quantity, speed, and number of cores; bus speed; and cache size

◆ NIC information, including MAC address, protocols, and IP address settings

◆ Amount of RAM

◆ Disk controller type(s)—SCSI, IDE, Serial ATA, and Serial-Attached SCSI (SAS) including Redundant Array of Independent Disks (RAID) support—and driver information

◆ Physical and logical disk sizes and file-system information

◆ Operating-system version and patch levels

◆ Installed applications

◆ Installed management tools

You might not need all of this information for a successful P2V migration, but it's best to collect it anyway, in case you need it later. By doing so, you'll ensure that sufficient capacity exists on the Hyper-V host (including processor, RAM, disk, and networking). Modern versions of Windows can handle many of the system-reconfiguration tasks, but some system settings, like static TCP/IP configuration settings, are tied to a physical network card and will be lost if not recorded for reconfiguration purposes.

You can gather information locally or remotely from a system using Windows Management Instrumentation (WMI) and by perusing the source system's Registry. WMIC, the WMI command-line tool included in Windows XP, Windows Server 2003, and newer versions of Windows, is a convenient way to capture much of the information. The following example commands capture some configuration information for a remote system named dquad to local text files:

```
wmic /node:dquad os > c:\dquad_os.txt
wmic /node:dquad qfe > c:\dquad_patches.txt
wmic /node:dquad baseboard > c:\dquad_baseboard.txt
wmic /node:dquad cpu > c:\dquad_cpu.txt
wmic /node:dquad nic > c:\dquad_nic.txt
```

Using the MAP Toolkit

An automated tool that is free to download may provide a more expedient way to collect, save, and evaluate system information. The Microsoft Assessment and Planning (MAP) toolkit is a free download that you can use to inventory, assess, and report on your environment. You can use MAP to search your network in a secure, agentless manner and create a detailed inventory of computing resources. Running from a single network-attached system, MAP leverages Active Directory, WMI, the Remote Registry Service, and/or Simple Network Management Protocol (SNMP) to collect data. MAP can collect data from systems running the following supported versions of Windows:

◆ Windows 7

◆ Windows Vista

◆ Windows XP Professional

◆ Windows Server 2008 or Windows Server 2008 R2

◆ Windows Server 2003 or Windows Server 2003 R2

◆ Windows 2000 Professional or Windows 2000 Server

The latest version of MAP (4.0) can also inventory non-Microsoft virtualization platforms:

◆ VMware ESX

◆ VMware ESXi

◆ VMware Server

Future MAP toolkit capabilities will enable data collection from even more non-Microsoft platforms.

You can find MAP on the Microsoft website at www.microsoft.com/map. The data and analysis provided by this toolkit can significantly simplify your planning process for migrating physical hosts and applications.

MAP includes features for gathering performance metrics from computers you're considering for migration. You can generate reports on your existing virtual environment as well as analysis of recommended placement for new VMs. The assessment performed includes an analysis of device-driver availability and recommendations for hardware upgrades that may be required.

NOTE The Microsoft Assessment and Planning toolkit does much more than collect configuration information and evaluate physical servers for migration to Hyper-V. It's a comprehensive analysis tool that you can use to document and evaluate your environment to prepare for migration to Windows 7, Office 2007, and beyond. You can use it to assess system-security settings and readiness for virtualization tools like SoftGrid (now called AppV). We won't be concerned with all that right now, but you should investigate MAP's other capabilities for your organization.

INSTALLING MAP

You can install the toolkit on Windows XP SP2 or later (as well as Windows Vista, Windows 7, Windows Server 2003, and Windows Server 2008 and R2). It leverages Microsoft Office for report creation, so it does have a number of software prerequisites, including the following:

- ◆ .NET Framework v3.5SP1 (3.5.30729.01)

- ◆ Windows Installer v4.5

- ◆ Microsoft Word 2007 or Microsoft Word 2003 SP2

- ◆ Microsoft Excel 2007 or Microsoft Excel 2003 SP2

- ◆ Microsoft Office Primary Interop Assemblies

- ◆ Any available updates for the operating system and Microsoft Office

- ◆ SQL Server 2008 Express, SQL Server 2008, or SQL Server 2005

Don't be too concerned if you don't have all of the prerequisites installed before you install MAP. Even earlier versions of MAP (like version 3.0 shown in this chapter) will check for missing dependencies and provide clickable links to the required components (see Figure 6.1).

FIGURE 6.1
MAP installation
dependencies

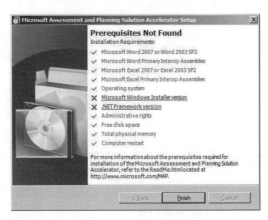

NOTE MAP will download and install SQL Server 2008 Express Edition during setup. You can use Microsoft SQL Server 2005 or Microsoft SQL Server 2008 and an instance named MAPS will be created.

USING MAP

The welcome screen shown in Figure 6.2 includes links and options to perform a variety of actions.

FIGURE 6.2
MAP welcome
screen

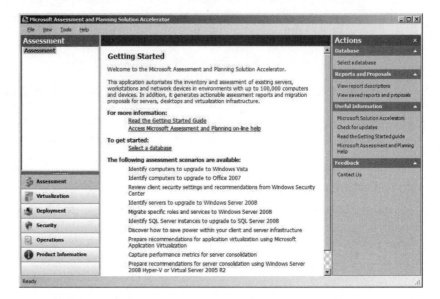

As mentioned, the MAP toolkit application performs inventory, assessment, and reporting tasks. It also serves as a portal for migration and virtualization topics. Clicking Virtualization on the left side of the screen switches to a listing of useful virtualization resources and information accessible from MAP (see Figure 6.3).

FIGURE 6.3
Virtualization
resources

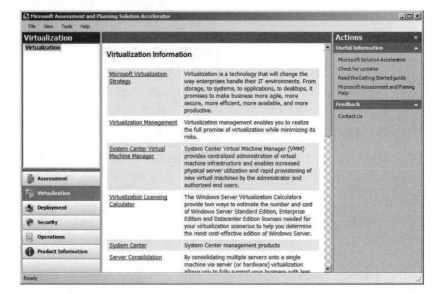

As nice as these resources are, they don't in and of themselves accomplish the inventory and assessment tasks required for a migration (your goal when using MAP). Navigating back to the Assessment area lets you prepare for data collection. But before you can begin, you must select a database from the Actions pane on the left side of the screen while in assessment mode that will function as a repository for collected information (see Figure 6.4). You can specify your own name or use an existing database.

FIGURE 6.4
MAP database
definition

After you create the repository, you can collect performance and inventory data. You can gather performance data over time to help develop an accurate picture of server load, including historical measurements for the utilization of processor, network, and disk. On the other hand, you can collect inventory data all at once, including information about a system's hardware and software configuration. A detailed inventory of all assessed systems is generated in Microsoft Excel format, and it can include hardware device details like those shown in Figure 6.5 as well as summaries of installed software.

FIGURE 6.5
MAP hardware
device details

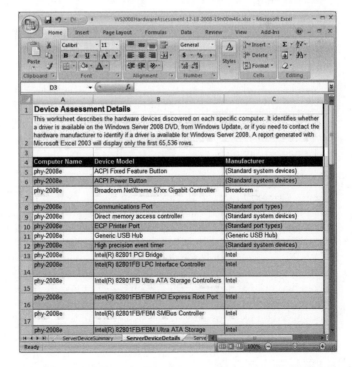

The Excel worksheets are a convenient format for reviewing system-configuration information and provide a wealth of useful information for other purposes in your environment.

Preparing a System for Migration

Some system settings are best altered before you capture the system image. Removing hardware-specific management components (hardware monitoring, audio-management tools, and legacy virtual enlightenments for V2V migrations) will save you time and frustration later. Some application installers won't run if supported hardware isn't detected on a system. Removing such tools after a migration can be difficult.

Pre-staging information and tools on the physical disk can also be a time-saver. Saving collected configuration information to the local physical disk makes it easy to find inside the VM after the migration (for example, you can save static IP settings by directing the output of IPConfig/all to a text file).

Capturing and Deploying Disk Images

After you've collected system-configuration information and evaluated a migration candidate's suitability for conversion to a VM, it's time to capture the actual files used by the system. You can collect images of the attached disks using traditional disk-imaging tools; backup and recovery products; or dedicated, automated P2V tools like the new (and no-cost) Disk2VHD.

Manual Migration with Image-Capture Tools

You can manually capture and deploy disk images a number of ways—each of which involves booting the source system into a separate operating system and capturing an image of the attached disks. For many years, administrators have used Ghost disk imaging (along with other, less-well-known products). Microsoft introduced the Windows Imaging Format (WIM) and related tools to improve operating system deployments.

WIM is an integral part of Windows Vista and Windows Server 2008 installation and deployment (and of course moving forward with Windows 7 and Windows Server 2008 R2!). Like Ghost image files, WIM files can contain deployable disk images. The WIM format supports single-instance storage of disk images, meaning that you can efficiently store multiple disk images from different systems together in one file. You can mount WIM files on a system as a drive letter to manipulate their contents.

ImageX is the no-cost command-line tool for accessing and manipulating WIM files. You can use ImageX to capture and apply disk images to and from WIM files, as well as to perform other WIM management-related tasks. ImageX is available as part of the Windows Automated Installation Kit (WAIK), which you can download from Microsoft. You can use WAIK to generate a bootable Windows Pre-installation Environment (WinPE) CD that includes ImageX.

WinPE is a lightweight version of Windows intended for installing, troubleshooting, and deploying systems. Starting a system from WinPE lets you access a system's physical resources through a command-line interface. You can boot WinPE from a CD, an ISO image (if supported), or even a USB thumb drive. A well-built WinPE image has the advantage over older tools (like those based on DOS) of providing access to attached USB devices as well as networking support. This chapter includes a walkthrough of how to create a simple WinPE CD, as well as a manual P2V migration using WinPE and ImageX.

Other imaging and pre-installation tools exist that you can use for image capture. Disk-imaging tools are available from Acronis, Symatec, and others; and pre-installation environments and tools include BartPE, WinBuilder, and VistaPE.

It's useful to know about all of these imaging options for many reasons, but for the manual P2V migration of contemporary Windows systems they have been made largely obsolete. The Microsoft Sysinternals team created the Disk2VHD image capture tool, which captures a system configuration and saves it directly into VHD format. It is available for download from `http://technet.microsoft.com/en-us/sysinternals/default.aspx` and is my favorite method for the capture of disk images. While it was not originally intended to be a P2V tool, it works well for this purpose in many situations.

Using Traditional Backup and Recovery Tools: SCVMM and Windows Home Server

The backup and recovery tools you (we hope) use every day can often be leveraged to perform a P2V migration. Capturing a full system backup and restoring it into a VM can be just as effective as a manual P2V migration with disk-imaging tools. You may encounter issues around the hardware abstraction layer (HAL), system activation, drivers, and network configuration. Using traditional backup and recovery tools isn't a supported P2V migration method, but then neither is the use of manual tools mentioned earlier (like Disk2VHD). Using System Center Virtual Machine Manager (SCVMM) is the best approach for physical-to-virtual migration; SCVMM was designed with Windows P2V migration scenarios in mind, and it's Microsoft's supported method for P2V migration to Hyper-V.

Microsoft's System Center Data Protection Manager does a fantastic job of backing up physical and virtual systems and could be a cost-effective way to recover a system into a VM. System Center Data Protection Manager (DPM) is covered in Chapter 12. Rather than go over ground we will walk on again, let's use another (wicked simple) backup and recovery tool to demonstrate this concept.

In 2007, Microsoft introduced a file server for home use called Windows Home Server. You can use this file server to provide centralized backup and recovery for systems. Windows Home Server includes a recovery ISO image that allows for the quick and easy recovery of backed-up systems.

NOTE Using Windows Home Server to back up any version of Windows Server isn't supported; nor is it a supported P2V method. But it works pretty well for simple systems, and it can be used to illustrate the process for a manual, backup-based P2V migration.

Acquiring or building a Windows Home Server appliance can be more cost-effective and time-efficient than other manual P2V solutions.

Installing the Home Server agent on a physical host is a simple process, and you can do so in a few minutes. Windows Home Server takes advantage of single-instance storage of files and stores backups in a space-efficient manner. Recovering into a VM is a simple process of booting the Windows Home Server ISO image in a properly configured VM.

NOTE Network drivers for the Hyper-V synthetic NIC aren't included in any pre-configured recovery or Pre-installation Environment (PE) CD that I have used. The initial configuration of VMs to be imaged over a network link should include a Legacy Network Adapter.

Similar to some backup and recovery tools, Windows Home Server won't restore a disk image to a disk that's smaller than the original source disk, regardless of the volume of data. If you use Windows Home Server (or another backup/recovery tool), be certain that you create VHD files with sufficient capacity to successfully restore the system.

Booting a newly created VM from the provided recovery CD (like the one that comes with Windows Home Server) starts the network-aware recovery console for Windows Home Server. Stepping though the recovery process allows you to connect to your Windows Home Server, select a machine backup set to recover, initialize the target disk, and begin a restore over the network, as shown in Figure 6.6.

FIGURE 6.6
Windows Home
Server Restore
console

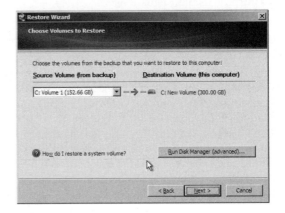

The result of the successful restore is shown in Figure 6.7.

FIGURE 6.7
Windows Home
Server restore
into a VM

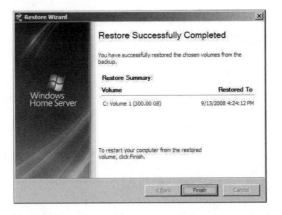

After the restore process is complete, you can address common configuration opportunities within the VM (HAL re-detection, installation of integration components, addition of a synthetic NIC, removal of a legacy NIC, and so on).

Common Dedicated P2V Tools

You can use dedicated tools to perform P2V migration. Some of these tools are produced and supported by Microsoft. We'll also mention some third-party tools.

MICROSOFT-PROVIDED TOOLS

You may be getting tired of hearing about the System Center family of products. They're central to Microsoft's strategy for systems management for both physical and virtual systems. System Center Virtual Machine Manger 2008 is the automated and supported way to perform P2V Windows migrations. SCVMM does a great job and is discussed in Chapter 11.

Microsoft also released the Virtual Server Migration Toolkit (VSMT) to automate migrations to Virtual Server 2005. The VSMT is a free download and relies on Automated Deployment Services (ADS). ADS is a tool for the rapid deployment of Windows Servers (using Windows Server 2003) that has since been superseded by better deployment tools. VSMT used lots of scripting to assess, capture, and deploy images. Although the price was right (free), a P2V migration using VSMT was somewhat clunky. VSMT did support the migration of Windows NT 4.0 Server systems to Virtual Server 2005. VSMT and ADS are still available from Microsoft (as is Virtual Server 2005).

Beyond SCVMM and VSMT, the Sysinternals team at Microsoft created a tool to convert the data in a running, physical system into VHD format files—Disk2VHD. The tool was created to simplify troubleshooting of physical systems by capturing a system image for virtualized diagnosis. Disk2VHD leverages shadow copies to obtain consistent images of volumes of a contemporary Windows system. Since Disk2VHD enables on-line export of volumes into VHD format, it makes for a great, low-cost P2V tool!

Note that SCVMM also creates an image of a running system (unlike most manual imaging methods), but is superior to Disk2VHD because it handles other configuration transposition tasks.

THIRD-PARTY TOOLS

Other companies, including Acronis, PlateSpin, and Vizioncore, provide automated P2V solutions that work with Hyper-V. If you've worked with third-party P2V tools for VMware migrations, you may notice that many of these same companies offer P2V solutions for other virtualization platforms, including Hyper-V.

Updating Images

Updating a captured disk image to accommodate hardware changes is inevitable in nearly any P2V migration. You should remove unnecessary software components before you capture an image. Uninstall hardware-specific system-management tools (such as HP System Insight Manager and Dell OpenManage tools) and other unnecessary components for a virtualized system (audio-management tools, video control panels, some NIC teaming software, and so on).

You can make other changes before the initial boot of the VM, such as pre-staging drivers or virtualization-management tools for later installation. For supported Windows-based VMs moving to Hyper-V, you can usually add required drivers after startup by inserting the Integration Services Setup Disk using the Actions menu from the Hyper-V Virtual Machine Connection screen.

Generally speaking, modern versions of Windows do a good job of detecting new hardware components, and many changes to the operating system can be made automatically. Changes to the number of processors (cores) or processor type shouldn't present a problem for currently supported versions of Windows. If you do encounter a problem at startup, the Repair option available with the original Windows installation media (within the recovery option when the media is inserted) can correct many startup anomalies, including those related to storage changes. Other than obtaining application software to manage missing hardware, you shouldn't encounter insurmountable migration issues with Windows XP, Windows Server 2003, Windows Vista, Windows 7, Windows Server 2008, and Windows Server 2008 R2.

For older operating systems, plug-and-play may not be available to help your new VM get over the shock of a system migration. Altering system software for changes in support of Advanced Configuration and Power Interface (ACPI) or uni/multiprocessor capabilities can be challenging. For Windows 2000, you may need to reinstall the operating system over the existing installation (as per Microsoft Support Knowledge Base article KB246236, accessible on the Microsoft Support website at `http://support.microsoft.com/kb/246236`) or take other actions (as described in KB249694). Automated migration tools can detect and address many troublesome migration issues more easily than you or I might.

The last step in making your migrated server feel at home is the installation of enlightenments.

ENLIGHTENMENTS, INTEGRATION SERVICES, AND INTEGRATION COMPONENTS (ICS) ARE PRETTY MUCH THE SAME THING

Software that makes a child or guest operating system run better while virtualized or "aware" that it is not actually running on physical hardware is referred to as an *enlightenment*, *integration service*, *Integration Component*, or *IC*.

For Hyper-V based VMs, this means the Integration Components that you can install via the Hyper-V Console or `VMConnect.exe`.

Walking through a Physical-to-Virtual Migration

As explained in earlier sections, you can manually capture and deploy disk images a number of ways. All methods involve booting the source system into a separate operating system and capturing an image of the attached disk. We'll provide two walkthroughs:

◆ A traditional manual image capture using a WinPE boot disk and leveraging `ImageX`, which can be used with nearly any physical Windows system

◆ A simpler Disk2VHD capture for Windows XP/Windows Server 2003 or newer—give this a try first!

We'll start with the more labor-intensive traditional imaging process. With both of these examples, remember that some of the "heavy lifting" of updating a captured VM is left to you. Using an automated tool designed for P2V migration may be a better choice.

Traditional Imaging: Collecting and Creating Your Imaging Toolkit

Assembling the right tools to accomplish a manual migration can take some time if you don't normally perform disk-imaging tasks. For server administrators in larger organizations, a fantastic time-saver can be to borrow a preconfigured WinPE CD from another team that handles desktop deployment.

TIP   Remember that WinPE CDs are generated from a specific version of Windows (XP, Vista, Windows 7) and often include drivers and capabilities specific to that version.

Desktop teams often have prebuilt tools for capturing and deploying images to physical systems. A usable WinPE CD at minimum needs to include compatible storage drivers for the source system and ImageX to capture disk images. The WinPE image can also include compatible network drivers for the source and target (VM). If you don't have access to a suitable prebuilt WinPE disk, you can create your own using the WAIK.

WHY WOULD YOU USE WINPE?

I mentioned that there's a simpler way to manually capture a disk image (Disk2VHD—I'll show you that in a minute). If there's an easier way, why would you ever want to go through the hassle of a manual image capture using traditional imaging tools? Disk2VHD only works with versions of Windows that support the Volume Shadow Copy Service (VSS). That means that it will not work on Windows 2000 or older systems. For older versions of Windows, as well as other more fringe requirements (large volumes or an investment in existing imaging repository using some other tool like ImageX or Ghost), you may still want to try to use traditional imaging.

DOWNLOADING AND INSTALLING THE WAIK

The Windows Automated Installation Kit (WAIK) is designed to help corporate IT professionals customize and deploy Windows operation systems. It can help you perform unattended Windows installs, capture Windows images with ImageX, and create Windows PE images. You can download the WAIK from Microsoft in the form of an ISO image file.

NOTE   Several different versions of the WAIK are available for download. The version I had handy when this chapter was written was 6001.18000.080118-1840-kb3aik1_en.iso for Vista SP1 and Windows Server 2008. It's always advisable to use the latest version of the WAIK, and an updated version is available for Windows 7/Windows Server 2008 R2.

You can install the WAIK on a physical Windows system by creating a DVD from the downloaded ISO file and auto-starting the disk. However, mounting the ISO directly in a VM may be easier! The installation is straightforward: click Windows AIK Setup on the Welcome screen (see Figure 6.8).

Walking through the installation installs the WAIK in the default location. The documentation included with the WAIK is useful and extensive; the included *Windows Pre-installation Environment (WinPE) User's Guide* details the processes you can follow to create and customize WinPE. (The options for customizing WinPE are extensive and not entirely applicable here for your image capturing and deployment purposes.) The following steps to create a WinPE ISO image are adapted from this user guide.

FIGURE 6.8
WAIK Welcome
screen

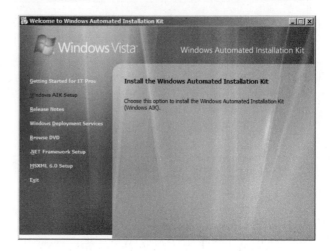

CREATING A SIMPLE WINPE CD WITH THE WAIK

With the WAIK installed, you can quickly create a simple WinPE disk of your own that includes ImageX for image capture and deployment. Follow these steps:

1. Click Start, navigate to Microsoft Windows AIK, and then select Windows PE Tools Command Prompt (called the "Deployment Tools Command Prompt" in the Windows 7 version of the Windows AIK). Doing so opens a command window with the environment prepared for you to create your own WinPE CD, as shown in Figure 6.9.

FIGURE 6.9
WinPE tools
prompt

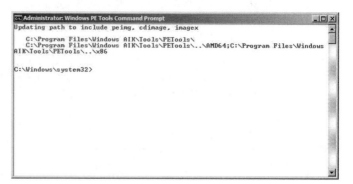

You don't need to concern yourself with lots of configuration options (unless you want to). You simply want to generate a bootable WinPE ISO image that includes ImageX. To do this, you'll run through several commands in the window.

2. Copy the necessary files for your selected processor architecture to a new directory, c:\MyWinPE:

```
copype.cmd x86 c:\MyWinPE
```

3. Copy `ImageX` to the appropriate spot in the newly created directory structure so that it will be part of the ISO image you create:

```
copy "c:\program files\windows aik\tools\x86\imagex.exe" c:\MyWinPE\iso
```

4. Create a small imaging-related configuration file named `wimscript.ini`, which will smooth the imaging process.

```
[ExclusionList]
ntfs.log
hiberfil.sys
pagefile.sys
"System Volume Information"
RECYCLER
Windows\CSC

[CompressionExclusionList]
*.mp3
*.zip
*.cab
\WINDOWS\inf\*.pnf
```

5. Place the file in the same directory as `ImageX` (by saving from your editor or by copying).

6. Copy the base image (`Winpe.wim`) to the `\Winpe_x86\ISO\sources` folder and rename the file to `Boot.wim`.

```
copy c:\MyWinPE_x86\winpe.wim c:\MyWinPE_x86\ISO\sources\boot.wim
```

7. After the files are in place, create the ISO file using the following command line:

```
oscdimg -n -bc:\MyWinPE\etfsboot.com c:\MyWinPE\ISO c:\MyWinPE\MyWinPE.iso
```

This process creates `c:\MyWinPE\MyWinPE.iso`, which includes `ImageX.exe`. You can then burn the file to a writable CD using standard CD-burning software. (For example, the free `CDBurn.exe` is part of the Windows Server 2003 Resource Kit.)

That's it! You're now armed with what some might consider the start of a simple P2V toolkit that will work with many physical systems. Unfortunately, not all hardware drivers are included in your new WinPE CD, including drivers for new or less common storage and network controllers. You can integrate original equipment manufacturer (OEM)–supplied driver packages, but adding drivers to WinPE can be a cumbersome process using the WAIK. You can use the Microsoft Deployment Toolkit to simplify the integration of required storage or network drivers.

ADDING DRIVERS WITH MICROSOFT DEPLOYMENT TOOLKIT

Microsoft Deployment Toolkit (MDT) connects the tools and processes required for deployment. It includes a collection of guidance (whitepaper-type material) for deployment, and it functions as a wrapper for other Microsoft tools and technologies, including the WAIK. Although MDT can help you automate countless deployment tasks, the benefit to you is the simplified process for generating a customized WinPE CD. You can use MDT (leveraging the WAIK) to add specialized storage and network drivers, as well as other tools, to a customized WinPE image.

TIP You don't need MDT to create WinPE images or to integrate drivers. However, it can be useful, and that's why it's mentioned here.

MDT is a tiny download compared to the WAIK. After it's downloaded and installed, you can use it to integrate driver packages from OEMs by using the Out-Of-Box-Drivers option highlighted in Figure 6.10.

FIGURE 6.10
Deployment Work-bench's Out-Of-Box Drivers option

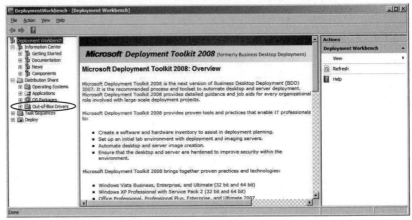

CAPTURING THE IMAGE WITH WINPE/IMAGEX

Before you capture your disk image, it's a good idea to save key information onto the disk. Useful information such as the IP configuration or the MAC addresses of network interfaces might be required for later use. You could use one or both of the following commands:

```
IPCONFIG /ALL >c:\Net.txt
WMIC NIC GET >> c:\Net.txt
```

For the walkthrough, you'll save an image to an attached USB drive. Follow these steps:

1. Connect the USB drive.

2. Restart the system, booting from the WinPE image.

3. Assuming you have the proper storage drivers integrated, you can access the system's attached storage for imaging. To locate the drives on the system, use the diskpart command:

```
diskpart
list disk
list vol
exit
```

4. The example system has only one volume to capture. The following command works to capture an image of the C: drive and write the file sata.img on an attached USB device (E:):

```
imagex /capture c: e:\sata.img "vista"
```

5. After the image is completely captured, turn off the source host, remove the WinPE CD, and detach the USB drive.

NOTE   Because WinPE provides network support, you have the option of saving images to a network drive instead of an attached USB device. This can work well for you as long as your WinPE CD has the drivers for both the physical and virtual network cards in your environment. If you use more exotic physical network cards, you can build a custom WinPE CD which includes drivers for these devices.

Defining the Virtual Machine

Creating the VM configuration is a straightforward process of mimicking the configuration of the physical system. Define a VM within the Hyper-V manager that corresponds to your desired configuration, taking into account RAM, processor, disk, and networking requirements. If necessary, you can use the MAC address(es) of a source system within the VM.

TIP   It may make sense to include a Legacy Network Adapter to provide network access until you can add ICs. By default, VMs are typically created within the Hyper-V Manager using the high-performance synthetic NIC. Remove this NIC and add a Legacy Network Adapter (within the VM settings selecting "Add Hardware") if you need Win PE to access network resources during the imaging process. Drivers for the Legacy Network Adapter should be available in newer WinPE disks and most supported versions of Windows. Note that an x64 driver for Windows XP and Windows Server 2003 was never released, so x64 versions of these operating systems won't work with this adapter.

Deploying the Image with WinPE / ImageX

With the image captured to a WIM file, you can now deploy it as a VM. After defining the VM, you must make the image accessible for deployment. You can use the pass-through disk feature of Hyper-V to expose the image file to the VM. The process is the same for Windows Server 2008 or R2:

1. Attach the USB drive to the Hyper-V host, and offline the disk in the Disk Management task of Computer Management on the physical system (see Figure 6.11). To take a disk off-line, right click on the grey square showing the disk # identifier and select Off-line.

Offlining the USB disk containing the WIM image allows the newly defined VM to mount the disk as an additional drive via pass-through, as shown in the Hyper-V settings in Figure 6.12. The option to present a physical disk to a virtual machine will be inaccessible (greyed out) otherwise.

2. Boot the WinPE disk inside the new Hyper-V–based VM, and identify the source and target volumes. If the VHD file is new, you'll need to prepare it before the image can be applied. You should use diskpart to identify and (possibly) prepare your VHD for the image:

```
diskpart
list disk
select disk 1
create part primary
```

```
list vol
exit
format e: /fs:ntfs /q
```

These commands assume that you didn't pre-create a partition on disk 1 (the VHD file). After the partition was created by this process, it was assigned drive E:, which was then formatted.

FIGURE 6.11
Offline USB disk in Windows Server 2008

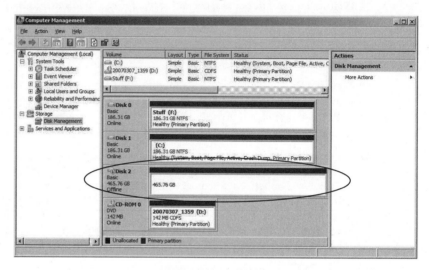

FIGURE 6.12
Settings to access pass-through

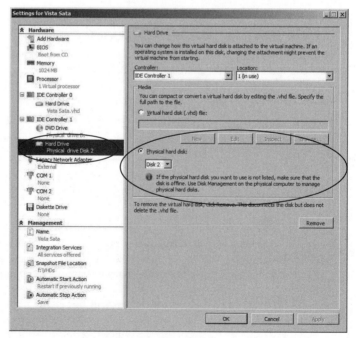

3. When the drive is formatted, you can apply the image to E: using ImageX:

```
imagex /apply c:\sata.img "vista" e:\
```

After you apply the image, the VM reboots, and the newly formatted drive appears as C:.

If you pre-created the VHD file with a partition and file system, the drive probably would show up as C: from the beginning of the process in WinPE. Figure 6.13 shows this entire process with a VHD that was preconfigured before imaging.

FIGURE 6.13
Checking the disk and applying the image

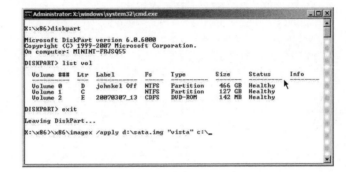

Applying the image to the VHD can take some time. The overall imaging speed is fast, but it depends on the size of the image to be applied as well as the speed of storage. A successful image application is shown in Figure 6.14.

FIGURE 6.14
Successful imaging

4. After you apply the image, shut down the VM, remove the pass-through disk, dismount the captured CD, and restart the VM. The VM should boot the captured operating-system instance.

NOTE In some circumstances, the volume may not have been properly initialized. This can happen if, for instance, you use a WinPE image that isn't based on the same version of Windows that you're deploying. The simplest way to correct this condition is to re-create the volume (in the VHD) using the install media for the operating system in question. If you're working with a Vista image, start the installation of Vista to the VHD, and re-create the volume. After the installation begins, shut down the VM and apply the image again.

> ### WIM2VHD as an Imaging Tool
>
> Another traditional imaging tool is WIM2VHD—a command-line tool that allows you to create SysPrepped VHD images from any Windows 7 installation source. You can find the latest information about WIM2VHD at http://code.msdn.microsoft.com/wim2vhd.

Easy Image Capture: Disk2VHD

You could go through all the hassle of the traditional image capture process, or you can simply go to the Microsoft website and download and run Disk2VHD. As its name implies, Disk2VHD creates VHD versions of physical disks in a single step process. It is different from the WinPE/ImageX process shown previously because it can be executed on a system that is running. Disk2VHD leverages the Volume Shadow Copy Service (VSS) to make a point-in-time image of volumes attached to the physical system. It works on Windows systems running Windows XP SP2/Windows Server 2003 SP1 or newer (Windows 2000 and older do not include VSS).

Follow these steps to use Disk2VHD:

1. Download Disk2VHD from the Sysinternals site:

   http://download.sysinternals.com/Files/Disk2vhd.zip

2. Unzip the tool.

3. On the system you are capturing, shut down common applications and application services.

   Remember that you are capturing an image of a live, running system that will continue to be updated during the process. Taking this step will reduce the chance that updates will not be taken on the physical system and lost to the image.

4. Run the tool. Ensure that volumes you wish to capture are selected and the VHDs to be created are pointed to a disk you are not converting. (See Figure 6.15.)

FIGURE 6.15
Starting Disk2VHD

After the process is kicked off, Disk2VHD will request that a VSS snapshot be created of the source disks, and a VHD file will be created and populated.

Firing Up: Performing System Updates

Similar to a character in a horror movie, the newly created VM may go into a state of shock when it starts up and finds itself living in a new body. The system may not have expected to have its hardware drastically altered. Now it must either adjust or die. Contemporary versions of Windows do a good job of detecting system changes and adjusting where possible. Minor changes can be accommodated after startup within the normal operations, like those shown in Figure 6.16.

FIGURE 6.16
Successful startup

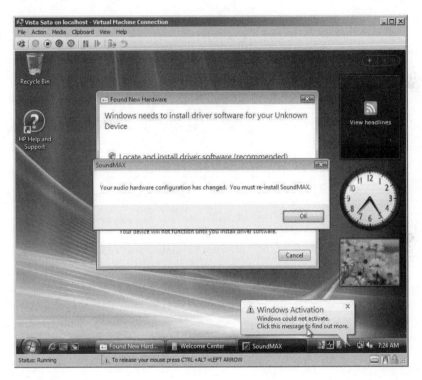

Figure 6.16 shows that Windows Vista has found new hardware that requires drivers. It has also detected the loss of sound support. The drastic change in hardware has also triggered the Windows activation process.

In some cases, you can trigger hardware change detection. You can kick off (for example) a HAL redetection on Windows Vista and Windows Server 2008 by running MSConfig, selecting the Boot tab, and selecting Detect HAL (see Figure 6.17).

Not all hardware changes can be easily addressed within Windows. Changes to the underlying storage can cause the operating system to fail, as shown in Figure 6.18.

FIGURE 6.17
Detect HAL

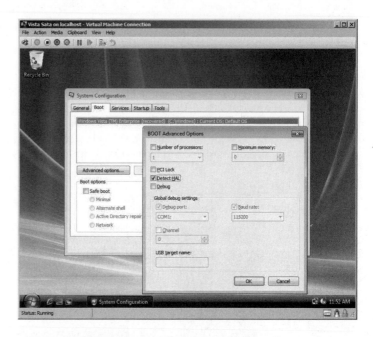

FIGURE 6.18
Nasty startup error

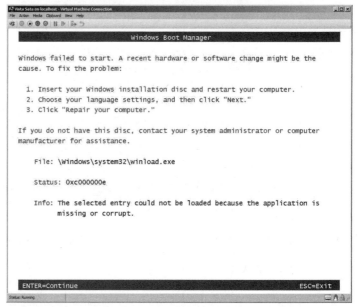

In this case, the source system depended on SATA for the system volume. You can rectify this error condition with the original installation media for the operating system. For this example, boot the VM with the proper Windows Vista installation DVD, and select the Repair Your Computer option on the startup screen (see Figure 6.19) to correct the issue (see Figure 6.20).

FIGURE 6.19
Vista Welcome
screen

FIGURE 6.20
Vista repair

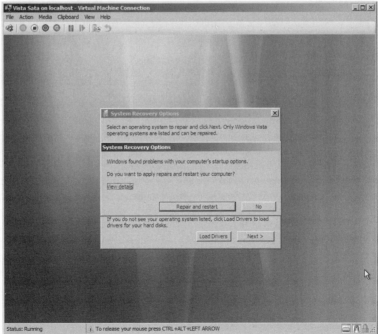

Storage-related issues may be your biggest headache for manual P2V migrations. The variety and complexity of storage available for server hardware can make manual P2V migrations too complicated for some hardware and operating-system configurations. You should use automated and supported P2V tools (such as SCVMM) in these cases.

After your VM is running, you'll also want to install the Hyper-V Integration Components in order to use the higher-performance synthetic NIC, improved mouse integration, and other performance enhancements.

NOTE   Occasionally, you may encounter an error message while installing the Integration Components in Windows Vista, indicating that the ICs require "a newer version of Windows." Applying SP1 to Vista will allow you to install the ICs successfully.

Exporting and Importing in Hyper-V

V2V migrations between different virtualization platforms require steps similar to those in the P2V examples shown earlier. However, you can move VMs between Hyper-V hosts without all these steps by leveraging the built-in export and import functionality. You can export to local disk, or over the network.

NOTE   Export and import aren't truly V2V processes, but they allow you to move VMs from one Hyper-V host to another, and they fit well into a chapter focused on migration.

You can also use failover cluster to migrate a VM from one host to another. This requires you to configure clustering on similar hosts.

SCVMM has the capability to move VMs from one host to another without export and import. (SCVMM is covered in Chapter 11.)

Exporting a Virtual Machine Locally

The Hyper-V Console enables you to export and completely duplicate the configuration of a stopped or saved VM. This capability lets you move or copy an entire VM and configuration (more than simply copying a VHD file). Remember that a virtual machine is made up of a disk (typically attached to the VM in the form of VHD files) and its configuration (XML description of the virtual machine's settings). All these files must be properly permissioned and positioned on the Hyper-V host to ensure secure operation. The export and import processes ensure virtual machines are ready to run properly and securely on a Hyper-V host.

To export, select the VM in the console, and choose Action ➤ Export (see Figure 6.21). Remember that the virtual machine cannot be in a running state to export. It must either be stopped or saved.

You can also right-click a VM and select Export, or select Export from the actions listed for the selected VM on the right side of the console. Any of these techniques will open the Export dialog, allowing you to select a directory location for the data (see Figure 6.22).

TIP   The destination of the export must be accessible to the parent system. A locally attached volume (including an iSCSI attached disk) is usually your simplest bet. The parent partition won't typically have access to a network share unless you first configure permissions on the file server and network share (covered later in the "Exporting Over The Network" section of this chapter).

FIGURE 6.21
Export option

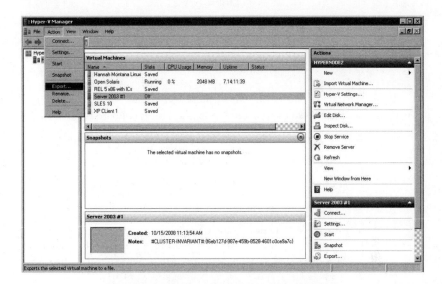

FIGURE 6.22
Selecting the
export location

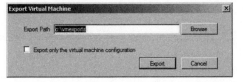

The export process runs in the background, duplicating the VM configuration information, memory contents (if the VM is saved), and disks (VHD and AVHD snapshot files). If you choose, you can export only the VM configuration by selecting the Export Only The Virtual Machine Configuration check box in the dialog box shown in Figure 6.22. This can be useful if you back up the VM disk files using another process, like those described in Chapter 7.

You can view the progress of the export in the Hyper-V Console (see Figure 6.23).

FIGURE 6.23
Export progress

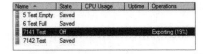

After you complete the export, you can copy or move the entire export directory hierarchy and contents to a local disk on the target Hyper-V host.

NOTE The folder created during the export process *under* the specified export directory is the repository of the VM's information. The folder is named the same as the display name of the VM. This is the folder hierarchy to move or copy to a target host. The folder contains all the information necessary to import the VM on a new host.

Exporting Over the Network

In order to export a VM to a network share (often to the Hyper-V target host), a network share must be created with the appropriate rights granted to the *exporting* Hyper-V host.

This may not be entirely intuitive, since you as the administrator are actually initiating the export. Since the parent partition is performing the export (at your request), it needs rights to the remote share, not you. To demonstrate the process for setting appropriate permissions, I have two Hyper-V systems configured in my lab:

◆ Hypernode1—File Server (target Hyper-V host)

◆ Hypernode2—source (exporting) Hyper-V host

Below are the detailed steps to set appropriate permissions:

1. Create a share on Hypernode1

I shared out C:\VMs, creating the \\Hypernode1\VMs share.

2. Grant rights on the share to the Hypernode2 (source) system.

This can be a little tricky, since the "Select Users, Computers, Service Accounts, or Groups" dialog defaults to searching for computers. You have to remember to search for Computers in the Object Types dialog box rather than selecting the typical Users or Groups. (See Figure 6.24.)

FIGURE 6.24
Selecting Computers in the Object Types dialog box

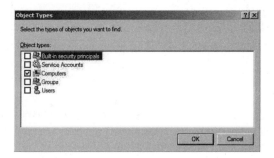

3. After "Object Types" are squared away, you can enter your host name in the From This Location field, and enter the source share in the Enter The Object Name(s) To Select field (see Figure 6.25).

FIGURE 6.25
Specifying the host and source share

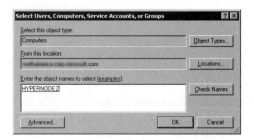

4. In the Permissions dialog box, grant Full Control, Change, and Read share permissions to the host (see Figure 6.26).

FIGURE 6.26

Setting Share
Permissions

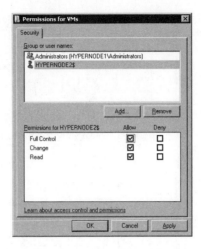

5. In the Properties dialog box you will also need to ensure the exporting host has proper NTFS permissions. The permissions I use are shown in Figure 6.27:

FIGURE 6.27

Setting NTFS
Permissions

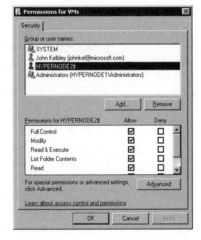

Once the share is created and rights are properly set, VMs from `Hypernode2` can be exported over the network to the `\\Hypernode1\VMs` share.

Importing a Virtual Machine

You import the VM in the reverse order that you export it (see Figure 6.28). The import process takes very little time.

FIGURE 6.28
Starting an import

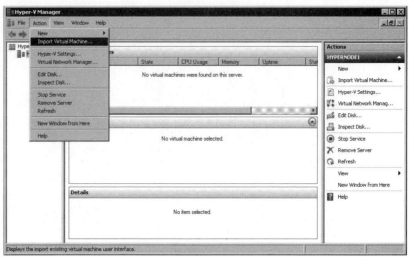

Selecting the Import action on the target host reads in the configuration data from the unique directory containing the exported VM. If the VM is unique to your environment, you can choose to reuse the VM's existing identification information (see Figure 6.29).

FIGURE 6.29
Selecting an
import

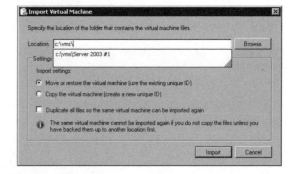

The import process reads the information and creates the VM configuration on the target host. Keep in mind that with Windows Server 2008 you can do an import only once, unless you save the export folder and file hierarchy elsewhere. R2 added an option to the Import Virtual Machine dialog box to duplicate all files so that the same virtual machine can be imported again (great for SysPrepped VMs). You should also consider that the location of the VM you specify during this import will be the final resting place for the VM. The VM will run from this directory after import, so you should be certain your exported VM is in the right location before importing.

You must remember to make the same resources available to the imported VM that it had on the source system. Be sure you define identically named virtual networks and that mounted ISO files registered when exported are available on the new physical host. Missing resources (networks and ISO files) will result in warning messages or cause imports to fail (see Figure 6.30).

FIGURE 6.30
Import warning

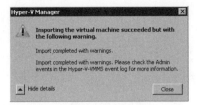

An import warning due to a virtual network switch name mismatch can be easily resolved by selecting the desired virtual network and connecting it to a VM's NIC in the Virtual Machines Settings screen.

FIGURE 6.31
Correcting Network Settings

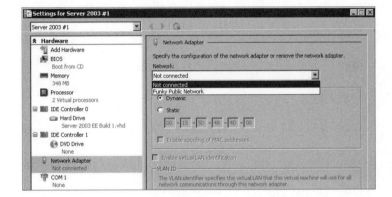

Summary

Migrating existing physical systems to VMs is a necessary part of moving to a virtual environment. You can convert systems manually, but you need the right tools, expertise, and time. Fully automated methods for migrating physical systems and existing VMs to Hyper-V VMs exist. SCVMM is the recommended and supported means for P2V and V2V migration; it's covered in Chapter 11.

Chapter 7

Backing Up and Recovering VMs

Companies often move to virtualization in order to separate a server-based application from *at-risk* physical hardware and thus guard against failure. When you migrate "that scary server in the corner that we don't have the install CDs for anymore" to a virtual machine, you can perpetuate a key business function well into the future.

When you encapsulate virtual machine (VM) information inside one or more virtual hard disks (VHDs), you can easily back up, migrate, and restore server-based services and applications—something you can't always easily accomplish with a physical server. A coordinated *save* or *shutdown* of a VM hosting an application without backup awareness allows an otherwise impossible recovery in the event of a failure. The great news is that everything you need to back up and restore Hyper-V VMs is included in Windows Server!

With all of its promise, virtualization introduces huge disruptions to traditional operational procedures and processes. How is it possible to quickly back up a dozen running VMs, each of which uses tens of gigabytes of VHD files? Where will you store these backups to make them quickly recoverable? How will you recover the configurations for each VM, as well as critical configuration data for the physical host, in a timely manner?

The aim of this chapter is to explore important considerations for backing up and recovering VMs as well as common backup and recovery approaches. In the latter part of the chapter, we'll walk you through two approaches for host-based backup that don't require additional third-party software licensing.

This chapter will cover the following areas:

◆ Virtual machine backup considerations

◆ Host-based backup approaches

◆ Child backup: backing up from within

◆ Manually backing up and recovering a virtual machine

Virtual Machine Backup Considerations

For any administrator, the goal of a backup is to allow computer-based data or services to be easily restored. Your organization may be driven by different requirements, including compliance, business continuity, disaster recovery, application development, and testing. Data volumes, timing, network bandwidth, security, heritage backup solutions, and budget concerns can influence how your company implements a backup solution.

The considerations that drive plans and solutions for backing up VMs and their host systems are the same as for traditional server backups. The benefits of virtualization (abstracting software from hardware and encapsulating storage in VHDs) give you new options for rapid backup and recovery.

You can often replicate the bulk of VM data by copying associated VHD files to a new location or host. But remember that a VM is defined by more than the data contained in VHDs. The VM's configuration also contains critical information necessary for the smooth and rapid recovery of a virtual operating system instance. Virtual networks are defined on the Hyper-V host system—outside of VM configurations—and may also be required in many recovery scenarios. You must consider backup and recovery for multiple components of an entire virtualization environment (more than simply the VHDs) when you develop backup and recovery solutions.

ADDITIONAL CONSIDERATIONS FOR BACKUP AND RECOVERY OF CLUSTERED VIRTUAL MACHINES

We will not dive deeply into the backup and recovery of clusters in this chapter, since we're covering manual (less sophisticated) backup and recovery techniques here. For details on the backup and recovery of VMs using failover-clustering technology (quick migration, live migration, and cluster-shared volumes), go to Chapter 8, "High Availability," and Chapter 12, "Protecting Virtualized Environments with System Center Data Protection Manager."

You can't, of course, physically connect a tape drive to a VM, but you can use other traditional backup and recovery processes with VMs. In the following sections you'll find common, tested, network-based backup approaches that often install agents that back up and restore data on physical and virtual machines. As noted earlier, virtualization may disrupt the rhythm of existing backup and recovery processes if you don't take its impact into account.

Using the Volume Shadow Copy Services

Before Microsoft introduced the Volume Shadow Copy Services (VSS), administrators often had to shut down a service or application before performing application backup operations on Windows Server systems. Not all backup processes required service interruption, but a shutdown allowed administrators to ensure that file input/output activity ceased and that files were duplicated reliably for later recovery.

Microsoft introduced VSS as part of Windows Server 2003. VSS lets you coordinate necessary actions to create a consistent point-in-time copy (also known as a *shadow copy* or *snapshot*) of data for backup purposes. You can copy these shadow copies to separate disk or tape-based storage without affecting data files used by an active application or service.

Four key components must be present for a service or application to take advantage of VSS:

◆ *VSS writer*: An application-aware software component (usually from an application vendor) that ensures the consistency of the data being backed up

◆ *VSS requester*: A backup tool or command asking for a snapshot to be created

◆ *VSS provider*: A tool that manages the shadow copies after they're created (a software provider comes with Windows Server, but hardware-specific providers can also come from a storage subsystem vendor with integrated snapshot capability)

◆ *VSS coordination service*: A part of the operating system that coordinates the cooperation of all necessary VSS components

For a VSS-enabled backup to work properly, the following steps occur:

1. The VSS requester asks for a backup set to be created.

2. The VSS writer responds by coordinating the queuing of disk writes for the associated application (*quiesces* the application).

3. This action of halting disk writes to related files allows the VSS provider to create a point-in-time shadow copy of the files used by the application.

4. After the shadow copy is created, the VSS writer (application) is informed that I/O operations can proceed as normal.

5. When I/O operations are restored to normal, the VSS requester (backup software) has access to the snapshot and can proceed with creating a consistent backup copy of the application's data (see Figure 7.1).

FIGURE 7.1

VSS shadow-copy process

1. Requestor asks VSS for writer details and to prepare for shadow-copy creation.
2. Writer creates a description of the components and the restore method.
3. Writer prepares for shadow-copy creation (completes transactions, flushes caches).
4. Writer tells VSS it's ready.
5. VSS tells the writer to quiesce data (a maximum of 60 seconds) and then flushes and freezes the filesystem.
6. VSS tells the provider to create the shadow copy (a maximum of 10 seconds).
7. VSS thaws the filesystem and releases the writer from quiesce.
8. VSS verifies that I/O was held and that the shadow copy was created.
9. If the copy was successful, VSS tells the requestor where to find the data, and the backup can proceed.

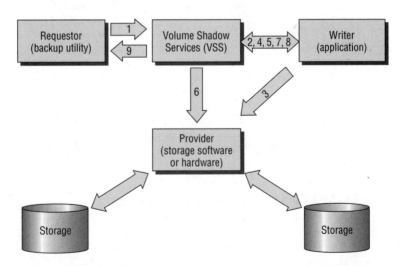

Windows Server 2008 and Windows Server 2008 R2 include a VSS writer for many of the applications and services that come with the platform, including file services, Internet Information Services (IIS), Background Intelligent Transfer Service (BITS), and Hyper-V. The Hyper-V VSS writer lets you back up properly enlightened VMs while they're running. You can also do rapid backup of unenlightened VMs (those without installed integration components; more on this in the "Using VSS Backups and Saving State" section later in this chapter).

Successfully completing a VSS-aware backup is complex and must be done relatively quickly to limit the effect on VSS-aware applications—I/O can't be held indefinitely. If underlying disk performance is slow or is under high load, the VSS snapshot process may take longer than allowable, and the shadow-creation process may fail. A VSS request from a physical host to an enlightened VM needs to not only hold I/O between the VM and the VHD but also ask VSS-aware applications within the VM to quiesce writes (see Figure 7.2). This longer chain of VSS coordination further complicates the VSS process.

FIGURE 7.2

VSS process with a virtual machine

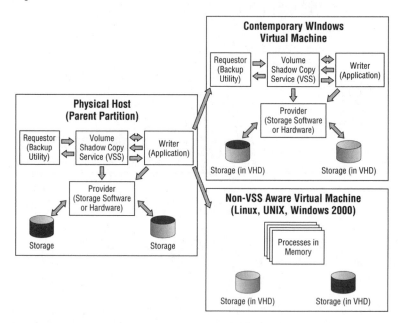

Even with the complicated orchestration necessary for VSS-integrated backups, they vastly improve backup and recoverability of Windows-based applications and services, including Hyper-V–based VMs. VSS gives software developers and administrators tools to reduce system downtime and meet recovery objectives.

Using VSS Backups and Saving State

When you integrate VSS, it allows you to back up Windows VMs that have installed integration components (ICs) without interruption. What happens to non-Windows VMs or those without ICs? Rather than pass the VSS request through the ICs to coordinate the queuing of disk writes, the VSS writer for Hyper-V saves the state of a nonenlightened VM (like those running Linux or UNIX).

NOTE   The Integration Components for Linux do not support VSS integration, since Linux doesn't have VSS! All Linux or UNIX virtual machines will have their state saved during a host-based backup. Currently the Linux Integration Components provide only synthetic driver support for disk (IDE and SCSI) and networking, with more capabilities coming in the future.

Saving state temporarily halts processing in the VM and writes the contents of memory for the VM to disk during VSS processing. The interruption of processing in the VM helps ensure that you create a valid backup. Any running VM that either does not include VSS support or does not have "backup" integration services installed and enabled will be backed up in this way.

NOTE   Running Linux and UNIX in Hyper-V makes sense for many environments, since many Linux and UNIX systems often serve only one function in a primarily Windows environment. If you have only a few Linux systems, being able to take advantage of your Windows Server backup infrastructure to provide recovery services for them can save you the expense and headache of implementing a separate backup infrastructure.

You can use *saving state* to back up VMs with applications that don't support VSS (no properly functioning VSS writer), even if they have all ICs/integration services installed and enabled. You can force the saving of state during a host-based VSS backup by disabling the Backup integration service in the VM settings, accessible via the Hyper-V Manager (see Figure 7.3).

FIGURE 7.3

Virtual machine settings—disabling the Backup integration service

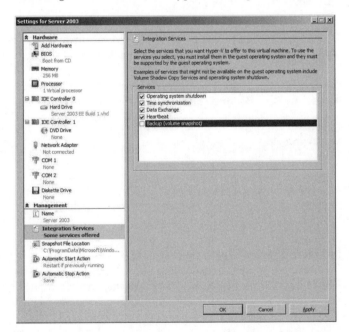

Note that all integration services are enabled by default, including the Backup integration service. This isn't true for all child operating systems, because some enlightened operating systems (all flavors of Linux and Windows 2000) do not include support for VSS.

The huge benefit of backing up a VM using saved state is the VM's restore state. Restoring a backup of a VM in the Saved state means the VM will still be in that state when recovered. You can return the VM to the Running state from Saved and almost instantly begin processing. In contrast, a VM that uses the Backup integration service and VSS integration won't be recovered to Saved state; it will be restored as Off and will need to boot up to restore services—taking longer than moving from the Saved state to the Running state.

> **NOTE** Disabling the Backup IC capability can be a great way to improve the end-to-end recovery time for some VMs, because the VM may not require startup. It can cause issues for some replicated services (like Active Directory, for instance) if you restore an VM that is not "in sync" with its partners. It is always best to use VSS and the backup integration service for those services that support VSS.

You must consider the interruption in processing during backup, VM recovery state, and data consistency when you employ VSS for VM backup and recovery. Review Table 7.1 to see how VSS the Backup integration service is applied.

TABLE 7.1:   Volume Shadow Copy Services Backup Integration

BACKUP INTEGRATION SERVICE STATUS	VM STATE DURING BACKUP	SERVICE INTERRUPTION DURING BACKUP?	VM STATE UPON RESTORE
Enabled	Running	No	Off
Missing/Disabled	Saved	Yes	Saved

Hyper-V Snapshots Are Not Backups!

With Hyper-V, you can use VSS to make snapshots of running VMs to which a VM's state can be reverted in the future. You can make snapshots from the Hyper-V Manager console or via scripts and programs using the appropriate Windows Management Interface (WMI) APIs. You can repeatedly capture the running state of a VM and quickly roll back to a known state. Snapshots can facilitate common testing scenarios, such as repeated installation or reconfiguration of software. The integrated snapshot capability has only limited production value, however, because it doesn't in itself provide the backup and recovery of a VM, the VM configuration, or the configuration of the physical host. You can back up snapshots via common physical host-based backup solutions and restore them with a VM backup.

> **NOTE** Be sure to make backups of all your virtual machines, do not rely on snapshots for backup and recovery, and do not use snapshots in your production environment!

Host-Based Backup Approaches

You can take advantage of the benefits of virtualization by creating backups on a Hyper-V physical host. Numerous approaches let you create recoverable images of VMs, including the following:

◆ Export/import

◆ Physical to virtual image capture

◆ Manual VHD backup

◆ Windows Server Backup (WSB)

◆ Third-party backup and recovery tools

◆ System Center Data Protection Manager (DPM)

Each approach has benefits and drawbacks that you should consider when you select a solution. Table 7.2 summarizes high-level considerations and issues for each of the backup approaches mentioned.

TABLE 7.2: Subjective Comparison of Backup and Recovery Approaches

	SOFTWARE COST	NETWORK UTILIZATION	STORAGE UTILIZATION	RECOVERY FLEXIBILITY	ADMIN EXPERTISE REQUIRED	OVERALL COST/ VALUE
Export/import	☺	☺	☹	☺	😐	😐
P2V	😐	😐	☹	☺	☹	☹
Manual backup	☺	😐	☺	☺	☹	😐
Windows Server Backup	☺	😐	😐	😐	☹	😐
Third-party tools	☹	😐	😐	☺	☺	😐
Data Protection Manager	😐	☺	☺	☺	☺	☺

Export/Import

Using the Hyper-V Manager console or WMI APIs to export a VM is a simple, cost-effective way to create a backup instance. Export duplicates the configuration data and associated VHD files for a VM. The process also makes the output transportable so that you can import the VM and start it on a separate Hyper-V host.

You should understand certain drawbacks of the export process:

◆ The export process doesn't work on running VMs. A VM's state must be Off or Saved to initiate an export, limiting the usefulness of export for backup and recovery when VM uptime is required.

◆ During the export process, you typically write VM information to locally attached storage—not to a file share. You can export a virtual machine to a file share, but appropriate security rights must be configured on the share as outlined in Chapter 6, "Migrating Physical Machines."

◆ Internet SCSI (iSCSI)–attached volumes and removable disks (such as USB) can provide flexible export and backup destinations for Hyper-V.

◆ During recovery of an export, the storage location housing the export is used to host the VM files. This means if you attach a USB drive to a Hyper-V host and import a previously exported VM, the VHDs will execute going forward from the USB drive.

◆ A new feature of Windows Server 2008 R2 allows multiple reimports of an exported VM by duplicating VM files, if desired (see Chapter 6 for more details).

If you export a VM using removable storage (USB drive) you will want to copy the entire export directory to dedicated storage on a physical recovery host before importing it.

NOTE Make sure when you export to an attached USB drive that it is formatted NTFS. You may encounter a failure while exporting to FAT- or FAT32-formatted volumes because of the size of the VHD files. Export and import are discussed in Chapter 6.

Physical to Virtual Conversion

Some administrators consider using *physical to virtual* conversion for the backup and recovery of physical hosts. If you regularly schedule conversions, you can use a *physical to virtual* (P2V) image of a physical server for recovery services on a virtualization host in the event of a failure. This is an important strategy for physical systems enabled by virtualization. System Center Virtual Machine Manager (SCVMM) can create a VHD of a running physical system, as can the Disk2VHD utility mentioned in Chapter 6. You can, in many cases, use P2V tools and processes for the backup and recovery of an existing VM as well. The process of capturing a VM in this manner is known as a *virtual to virtual* (V2V) conversion or migration.

You can use P2V and V2V conversion for backup and recovery, but each has limited applicability for VM backup and recovery. With much of the VM information already encapsulated in VHD files, the conversion process is largely unnecessary. For VMs that use pass-through disk or iSCSI-mounted volumes, V2V may be a viable and valuable option to provide backup outside of a child-based (inside the VM) solution.

Manual VHD Backup and Recovery

Because the configuration information for a VM is contained in files, you can move and recover a VM via an entirely manual process. You can duplicate VM data files (VHD), configuration files (XML), and memory files (VSV) and restore them manually and with a high degree of flexibility.

We'll review a sample manual backup and recovery process later in the chapter in the "Performing a Manual Backup" section.

Windows Server Backup

Windows Server 2008 and Windows Server 2008 R2 include WSB as a replacement for NTBackup, which is no longer available. Like NTBackup, you can access WSB via a graphical interface or through command-line options for the automation of repeatable backup and recovery options.

Similar to other Windows Server 2008 and Windows Server 2008 R2 backup solutions, WSB is fully VSS-aware and, when properly configured, can minimize VM downtime during the backup process. You'll learn how to use WSB and walk through WSB backup and recovery later in this chapter in the "Performing a Windows Server Backup" section.

Enterprise Backup Tools and Solutions

Most enterprises have invested in backup and recovery processes and may rely on dedicated third-party tools. Enterprise-wide, dedicated backup and recovery tools promise to provide the highest level of operational consistency by reducing inconsistent user interfaces for administrators and centralizing hardware and media (tape and disk).

Many traditional enterprise backup solutions do a poor job of exploiting virtualization for better disaster recovery and business continuity. These solutions may be inadequate because of monolithic architectures, components, or vendor-driven economic models. Backup solutions that understand and integrate with storage enhancements such as shadow copies and allow for fast, low-cost disk-based backup or include tight Hyper-V integration and awareness will provide you the most benefit. System Center Data Protection Manager (DPM) is one such tool that will be discussed in detail in Chapter 12.

Agent Multiplexing

Some organizations may need a single system or technology, for compliance reasons, to include all system backups or application data of a certain type. The costs for certain solutions can be driven by expensive backup agents or clients that are application-specific. Enterprises with an investment in existing, monolithic backup architectures that don't support Hyper-V, or for which the cost of a Hyper-V agent may be prohibitive, can often still use Hyper-V backup through the process of backup multiplexing (see Figure 7.4).

Using Windows Server Backup or a manual backup process to create static, restorable file sets of Hyper-V, VMs can often enable more flexible backup and recovery scenarios with other backup and recovery technologies. Centralizing backups to a single file share or storage device using WSB, a custom manual process, or a cost-effective commercial solution such as DPM can reduce the per-server or per-agent licensing expense for other backup and recovery solutions.

Backup Encapsulation Benefits

Traditional server backup tools support the backup and recovery of physical systems running Hyper-V, because Hyper-V is a Windows Server 2008 role. By virtue of their support for file-based backup and integration with VSS, they can easily provide the same backup and recovery features to filesystem-based components of a Hyper-V physical host. Note that specific backup and recovery services vary between backup tools, and you should confirm supported scenarios with the particular solution vendor and through testing.

FIGURE 7.4
Backup
multiplexing

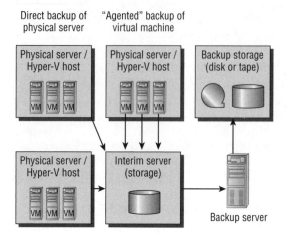

A key benefit of physical host-based backup in a virtual environment is derived from the *encapsulation* of VM data in VHD files. Applications residing within a VM may not be *backup aware*—they may not be able to integrate with common backup and recovery tools. You can essentially ignore application- or platform-specific backup awareness if you properly manage and replicate a VM's configuration, state, and storage data (save the state of the VM, snapshot the "in-flight" configuration and associated VHDs, restart the VM, and replicate snapshots to remote storage). By virtue of their installation within VMs, these applications or services can be made more operationally stable. Parent partition backups of VMs may also reduce licensing costs for certain enterprise backup tools, because they facilitate backup and recovery without the need for certain platform- or application-specific agents in a VM instance.

Beware of Bloat in Host Backups

Encapsulation vastly simplifies the backup and recovery of VMs, but it has a downside. Many traditional backup and recovery tools manage recoverable objects at a file level. Performing daily host backup of a VM means that all associated VHD files would require replication.

Prior to virtualization, you might have set up a physical file server with a nightly incremental backup schedule. With 100GB of files and (for the sake of argument) a 2 percent nightly change, the incremental backup volume might have been 2GB. After virtualization, a host-based backup of the same virtual file server with 100GB of associated VHD would generate 50 times the backup traffic, because the entire virtual hard disk would be replicated every time.

Without any planning, the increased backup traffic that can result from host-based backups can negatively impact not only the enterprise network but also disk and tape drives and media for backups, and it can expand required backup-timing windows. Enterprise backup and recovery tools optimized for virtualization technology, such as System Center Data Protection Manager (discussed in Chapter 12), alleviate the detrimental effect of encapsulation. These tools identify and replicate only changed fractions of storage (VHD) files. Additionally, you can complete incremental backup processes within the VM to reduce backup volume, but doing so eliminates the encapsulation benefit of virtualization.

Figure 7.5 shows common backup scenarios for use with Hyper-V, including the use of backup processing from within a VM.

FIGURE 7.5
Common backup
scenarios

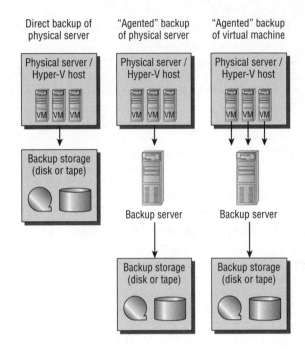

Child Backup: Backing Up from Within

Many backup solutions call for you to initiate a backup process on a computer via an agent and replicate data to a backup infrastructure (a recoverable file set on either disk or tape). Initiating a backup *within* a VM is a valid approach to back up and recover data, and in some instances a child-based backup is necessary. Common scenarios that may mandate a child-based backup include the following:

◆ Use of pass-through disk

◆ iSCSI storage mounted within a VM

◆ Certain applications running within an enlightened VM

◆ Failover clustering using Cluster Shared Volumes (CSV)

VM Backup Driven by Storage

Accessing storage within a VM using a pass-through disk or via iSCSI (using the iSCSI initiator in the VM to mount a remote volume) means that some data won't be encapsulated within a VHD for a parent partition-based backup. Because the data isn't in a VHD hosted by (or accessible to) the parent, it may not be easily backed up from the physical host. Although you may be able to use storage-area network (SAN) hardware snapshot technology to replicate the data on these volumes, the simplest solution for backing up data accessible to a VM is to use backup or replication software from within the VM.

VM Backup Driven by Applications

VSS integration/awareness within a VM is important, because a backup process in the parent partition or physical host can make a VSS request that affects a running child VM. Some applications may not be VSS aware or may not properly integrate with a VSS request that comes through the ICs installed in a VM from a physical host. It may seem that you created a good backup of a VM; however, without proper end-to-end VSS coordination between the parent partition and applications inside the VM, backup quality can't be guaranteed.

You can perform child-based backups essentially the same way you have always done physical host backups. Common third-party backup tools rely on the installation of an agent component on a backup client system that transmits data to a central backup server. Installing a backup agent within a network-connected VM enables these existing backup solutions—assuming, of course, that the backup software is supported in the VM.

Cluster-Shared Volumes and Backup

With Windows Server 2008 R2, Microsoft introduced a cluster volume manager to simplify storage provisioning and management for highly available virtual machines. CSV technology enables you to house multiple virtual machines on a single logical disk and let each VM run on a separate failover-cluster node. Windows Server 2008 failover clustering required that all VMs housed on a logical disk execute (and fail over) as a single unit (on a single physical cluster node). Failover clustering (and CSV) will be covered in more depth in Chapter 8.

What you need to know is that although CSV leverages the NTFS filesystem, *encapsulated backup and recovery of VMs is vastly more complicated with CSV because of the manner in which the storage is managed and presented to cluster nodes.* The strategies for VM backup and recovery discussed in this chapter are not compatible with CSV. System Center Data Protection Manager (covered in Chapter 12) and other enterprise-class backup and recovery tools can provide complete VM backup and recovery. An "inside the VM" backup strategy may be your best bet if you do not have DPM or another enterprise-level, CSV-aware tool.

Manually Backing Up and Recovering a Virtual Machine

You can accomplish backup and recovery a number of ways. We'll devote the remainder of the chapter to walking you through two low-cost options for parent-based/host-based backup and recovery using Windows Server Backup (WSB) and a manual process using VSS via the Diskshadow command.

Performing a Windows Server Backup

As noted earlier, WSB is the backup and recovery tool integrated into Windows Server 2008 and Windows Server 2008 R2. You can easily use WSB to back up and recover Hyper-V hosts and child VMs. WSB requires that you back up all volumes associated with Hyper-V to facilitate a recovery. The WSB requirement to capture lots of data can substantially increase the overall time and storage to complete a backup. However, WSB does offer a simple backup and recovery experience, and its inclusion in Windows Server 2008 and Windows Server 2008 R2 makes it a great option to consider for backup and recovery.

INSTALLING AND CONFIGURING WINDOWS SERVER BACKUP

WSB is an installable feature of Windows Server 2008 R2. To add WSB, select Features in the bar on the left side of the Server Manager console, and then select Add Features to start the Add Features Wizard (see Figure 7.6).

FIGURE 7.6
Add Features
Wizard

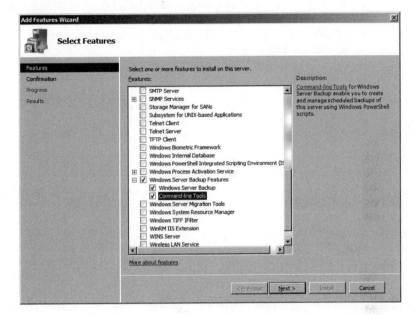

NOTE The command-line tools aren't installed by default when you install WSB. To install these tools, expand the Windows Server Backup Features selection, and select Command-Line Tools, as shown in Figure 7.6.

You can also install WSB from the command line using OCSetup:

```
OCSETUP WindowsServerBackup
```

WSB is VSS aware, but Hyper-V doesn't by default register its associated VSS writer with WSB. Without knowledge of the Hyper-V VSS writer (or other application-aware VSS writers), WSB may be unable to successfully complete a VSS snapshot operation for running VMs during a backup. To register the Hyper-V VSS writer with WSB, add the appropriate registry keys by executing the following two commands:

```
reg add "HKLM\Software\Microsoft\windows nt\currentversion\↵
WindowsServerBackup\Application Support\{66841CD4-6DED-4F4B-8F17-FD23F8DDC3DE}"
reg add "HKLM\Software\Microsoft\windows nt\currentversion\↵
WindowsServerBackup\Application Support\{66841CD4-6DED-4F4B-8F17-FD23F8DDC3DE}"↵
/v "Application Identifier" /t REG_SZ /d Hyper-v
```

This registry update is necessary for both Windows Server 2008 *and* Windows Server 2008 R2. After you complete the registry changes, you can review them using a graphical registry tool such as the Registry Editor (RegEdt32), as shown in Figure 7.7.

FIGURE 7.7
Registry entries

You can also check the entry by querying the registry:

```
reg query "HKLM\Software\Microsoft\windows nt\currentversion\↵
WindowsServerBackup\Application Support\{66841CD4-6DED-4F4B-8F17-FD23F8DDC3DE}"↵
/sWindows Server Backup Graphical Interface
```

NOTE Microsoft Support has a simpler way to make this change. You can run the Fix It application found in the following Knowledge Base article: http://support.microsoft.com/ kb/958662. It will tidy up the registry and make WSB aware of the Hyper-V VSS writer.

You can access WSB through the Administrative Tools program group on the Start menu (Start ➢ Administrative Tools ➢ Windows Server Backup). The WSB console is a fairly typical MMC snap-in and should look familiar. You can access administrative actions either from the menu bar at the top or via the Actions pane on the right (see Figure 7.8).

You can configure two types of backup processes through the graphical user interface: a *Backup Once* process and a *Backup Schedule*. R2 has been enhanced to allow the Backup Schedule action to use a locally attached disk or a network share as the backup destination. The Backup Once action has options similar to those of Backup Schedule.

FIGURE 7.8
Windows Server
Backup console

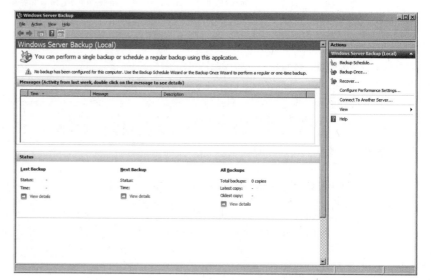

USING iSCSI WITH BACKUP SCHEDULE IN WINDOWS SERVER 2008

Before Windows Server 2008 R2, the Backup Schedule option in WSB could not use a remote file share or a nondedicated disk as a storage location. A dedicated, locally attached volume was required for a scheduled backup using Windows Server 2008.

We used iSCSI with Windows Server 2008 to bypass this limitation for scheduled WSB backups. ISCSI has changed what may constitute a locally attached disk. Using iSCSI to mount volumes across local-area network (LAN) and even wide-area network (WAN) links as if they were internal to a system lets you easily add remote storage to a system for backup/restore and other needs.

Chapter 8 includes iSCSI command examples (using `iscsicli`) that you can use to attach volumes as part of a scheduled backup and recovery process.

USING THE BACKUP ONCE ACTION

You can start a one-time manual backup by selecting the Backup Once action. The Backup Once Wizard walks you through the configurable options (see Figure 7.9); the first choice is to perform a predefined scheduled backup or to select Different Options.

FIGURE 7.9
Backup
Options page

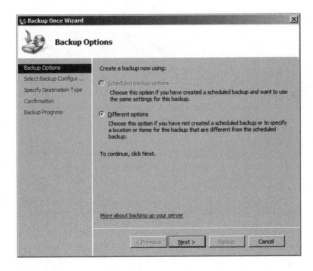

Selecting Different Options lets you create a customized backup set. This may be the only option available if no predefined scheduled backups exist.

As you proceed through the wizard, you can choose either to perform a full system backup or to customize your backup (see Figure 7.10).

The complete Backup Once Wizard within R2 is slightly different than that found in Windows Server 2008. Not only can you reduce the size and time of the backup in R2 by choosing which volumes to include or exclude, but you can select specific directories to exclude from backup processing. Note that no volumes are included in a custom backup by default. You must select items to add using the Add Items button shown in Figure 7.11.

FIGURE 7.10
Select Backup
Configuration page

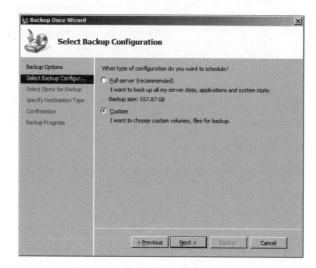

FIGURE 7.11
Empty Select Items
For Backup page

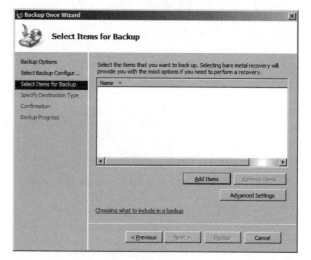

If you plan to use a local volume as the backup destination, you should not include it in the scope of the backup. Remember that all volumes and directories used for Hyper-V VMs must be selected to be within scope of the backup, as must other "system" configurations such as Hyper-V details. Figure 7.12 shows selections that can produce a successful restore when all Hyper-V related files are housed on c: and d:.

As mentioned earlier, a one-time backup may use a network share or nondedicated local volume as a destination (see Figure 7.13).

If you want to use a local volume, you can select eligible volumes from a drop-down menu. You can use removable disks (USB or eSATA) as well as other forms of direct-attached storage (see Figure 7.14).

FIGURE 7.12
Select Items
dialog box

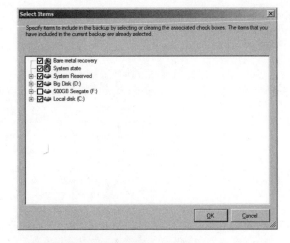

FIGURE 7.13
Specify Destination
Type page

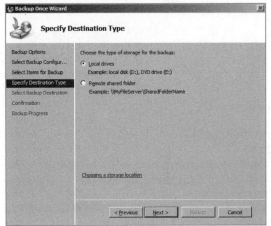

FIGURE 7.14
Select Backup
Destination page

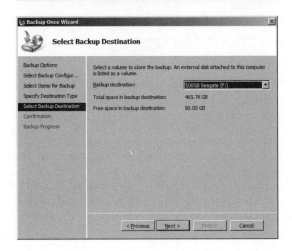

Some application backups let you clear/truncate the transaction log files as part of the backup process. The options on the VSS Settings tab of the Advanced Settings dialog box have no effect on Hyper-V backups, and you can ignore it—select either option (see Figure 7.15).

FIGURE 7.15
VSS Settings tab of the Advanced Settings dialog box

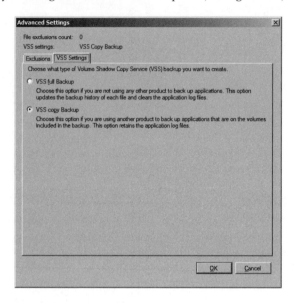

After you choose your configuration options, you must confirm the initiation of a backup (see Figure 7.16).

After the backup begins, its status is reflected in the wizard. You may close the wizard at any time while the backup is executing without affecting the backup's progress (see Figure 7.17).

FIGURE 7.16
Confirmation page

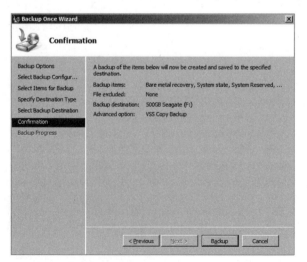

FIGURE 7.17
Backup
Progress page

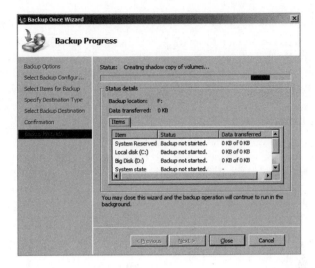

SETTING THE BACKUP SCHEDULE

The process for creating a Backup Schedule is similar to the Backup Once process; we won't include the flow of the schedule wizard here. As the name suggests, this action lets you define backup processes that execute on a regularly scheduled basis—either once a day or more than once a day.

With Windows Server 2008, scheduled backups (unlike one-time backups) require a dedicated volume. WSB reformats the volume you select as the backup destination, and all data contained on the volume is destroyed (see Figure 7.18).

FIGURE 7.18
Scheduled backup
format warning
in Windows
Server 2008

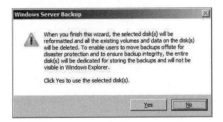

This is not the case with Windows Server 2008 R2. As we mentioned earlier, R2 has been enhanced to allow the Backup Schedule action to use a locally attached disk or a network share as the backup destination. WSB in R2 also allows for greater granularity in selecting (and limiting) what to back up. Before R2, entire drives would be chosen as backup sources, but R2 allows you to select or exclude subdirectories. To more completely understand the differences between versions of WSB, check out the following Microsoft TechNet article: http://technet.microsoft.com/en-us/library/ee344835(WS.10).aspx.

PERFORMING A BACKUP USING THE COMMAND LINE

Extensive command-line support is provided for WSB via the WBadmin command. The command-line tools provide increased flexibility for scheduling and managing backup and recovery processing; we won't cover them here. Documentation of the WSB command-line tools is available online at http://technet.microsoft.com/en-us/library/cc754015.aspx.

RESTORING WITH WSB

Recovering VMs and their configurations is a simple process via the graphical user interface. We won't cover the process to recover the parent partition and physical host, but you can do this easily with WSB. (Often, recovering the physical host isn't required for a VM recovery.)

To begin the recovery of a VM, launch WSB (Start ➤ Administrative Tools ➤ Windows Server Backup), and select Actions ➤ Recover. The Recovery Wizard walks you through the restore process, beginning with the selection of the recovery server (see Figure 7.19).

FIGURE 7.19

Server selection

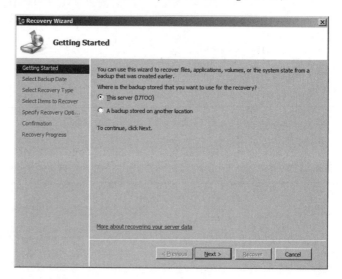

Typically, you'll have multiple backup sets available from which to restore. Available backup sets are displayed with a calendar to help you choose (see Figure 7.20). Note that the most recent backup is selected by default.

You can also choose the type of recovery. You can restore individual files, entire volumes, or applications using WSB. For a Hyper-V recovery, select Applications (see Figure 7.21).

Often, Hyper-V is the only application listed for recovery (see Figure 7.22), because other applications typically aren't loaded in the parent partition.

The names (in this case, the GUID) of VMs and the initial store for the Hyper-V configuration are listed as application components to be restored (see Figure 7.23). Note that *all* VMs that are part of a backup are restored; WSB can't restore individual VMs backed up from the same volume.

FIGURE 7.20
Select Backup
Date page

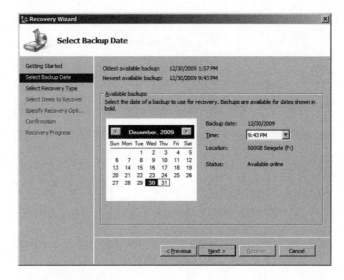

FIGURE 7.21
Select Recovery
Type page

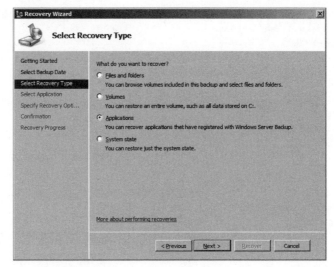

You have two options for the restore location of recovered application data. You can direct the recovery of VM-related files to the original source location or to another location (see Figure 7.24).

After you select all your options, the Recovery Wizard's Confirmation page appears, and the restore proceeds (see Figure 7.25).

Similar to the backup process, you can watch the recovery progress in the wizard (see Figure 7.26). The wizard's progress bar shows the completion percentage for each item you selected for recovery.

FIGURE 7.22
Select Application page

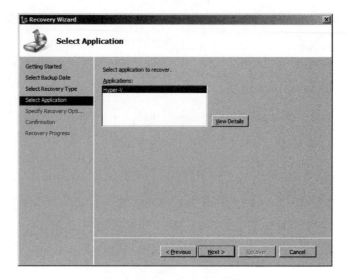

FIGURE 7.23
Application Components list

FIGURE 7.24
Specify Recovery Options page

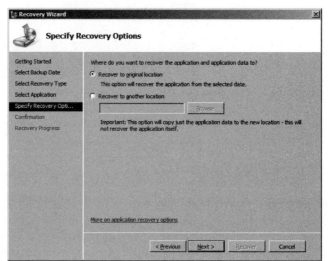

FIGURE 7.25
Confirmation
of backup and
restore options

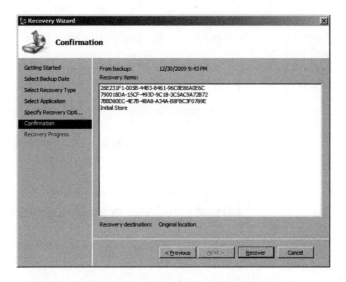

FIGURE 7.26
Recovery
Progress page

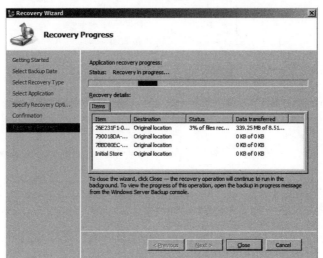

I mentioned earlier that you can close the progress dialog boxes without impacting the backup or restore process. The status of the WSB process is displayed in the main console (see Figure 7.27).

You can reopen the detailed status of an executing job through the console. Figure 7.28 shows the Progress dialog box.

Performing a Manual Backup

We mentioned earlier in the chapter that you can successfully craft and execute a manual backup and restore of Hyper-V VMs and their configurations. Such a process can take advantage of the VSS in a manner similar to WSB. Creating such a process requires substantial testing and tinkering and lacks the vendor support of a more mainstream backup process. To develop and automate this kind of manual backup and restore, you must understand the command line, batch files, scripting, and the relatively new `Diskshadow` command, and you must have a thorough grasp of Hyper-V. A manual process isn't well suited for all recovery scenarios, and the example we'll explore here won't apply to many situations.

FIGURE 7.27
WSB console status

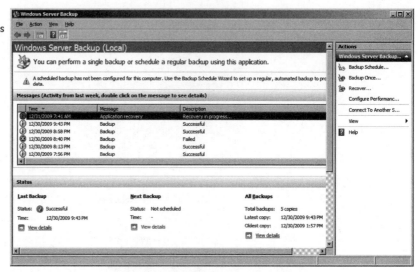

FIGURE 7.28
Recovery job status

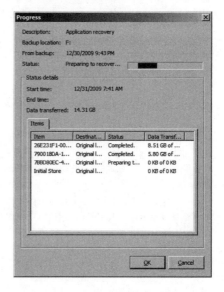

The backup and recovery method outlined in the next section makes numerous unstated assumptions about underlying infrastructure—including hardware performance, software patch levels, and other critical considerations that full-featured, supported backup solutions may more easily and completely address. This process doesn't, for example, back up or recover virtual network switch information defined on the physical host, which would be necessary for proper VM operation. Understanding this process is important in developing a complete understanding of backup and recovery for Hyper-V, but the batch files and scripts aren't supported in any fashion.

USING THE DISKSHADOW COMMAND

Diskshadow is a command-line tool included in Windows Server 2008 and Windows Server 2008 R2 that exposes the functions of VSS. It lets you interact with VSS directly in an interactive mode or automate VSS-related tasks via prewritten scripts.

A fantastically useful function of Diskshadow is the ability to request a VSS snapshot and expose the resulting point-in-time copy as a drive letter. This gives you read access to a consistent snapshot for backup purposes. You can automate the coordinating VSS snapshot for required Hyper-V volumes, expose these volumes to the operating system, and copy required files for a recovery of VMs, all from within Diskshadow.

To access Diskshadow, type **Diskshadow** from the command line. Because Diskshadow is its own command shell, you can also start it from the search bar. You can access available commands and options through Help by typing **/?** in the Diskshadow command shell. From within the shell, you can list VSS writers, requestors, and providers; set a variety of VSS-related options; control backup processes; create, expose, and delete shadow copies; and perform other VSS-related tasks.

You can run a prewritten script with Diskshadow by launching the command with the **-s** parameter and specifying the name of the text-based script file:

```
diskshadow -s HyperVBackup.txt
```

The script file should contain the sequence of Diskshadow commands and options to be executed. Follow these high-level steps to automate a Hyper-V backup:

1. Identify the volumes to back up.

2. Verify that the Hyper-V Writer is available and ready.

3. Create shadow copies.

4. Expose the shadow copies for backup.

5. Copy the files.

6. Unexpose the shadow copies.

For the purposes of this example, we'll assume that all required files for backup are housed on two core volumes, c: and d:. All VM configurations and VHDs are stored in d:\VMs, and required pointers to VM configuration files remain in c:\ProgramData\Microsoft\Windows\ Hyper-V\. You need to coordinate a VSS snapshot of both c: and d: to successfully recover VMs in this case. Here is an example Diskshadow script fragment to accomplish this process:

```
begin backup
        add volume C: alias ConfigVolume
        add volume D: alias VHDVolume
        writer verify {66841cd4-6ded-4f4b-8f17-fd23f8ddc3de}
```

```
        create
        EXPOSE %VHDVolume% X:
        EXPOSE %ConfigVolume% Y:
EXEC c:\HypervBackup.bat
        UNEXPOSE X:
        UNEXPOSE Y:
end backup
```

Additional housekeeping commands and options are required to successfully complete the backup process (shown later, in the complete listing). Note the EXEC command in the script segment, which invokes a batch file. It is called after the system volume (c:) and the VHD volume (d:) are snapped to create a shadow copy and exposed as new drive letters. For this system, only drive d: needs to be exposed to copy off data (as drive x:). The y: drive is exposed to make the script more flexible—it could be easily modified for a single (or multiple) volume configuration or allow you to back up files from the c: drive. For this two-volume configuration, the directory c:\ProgramData\Microsoft\Windows\Hyper-V\ actually only contains links to the VM configurations (found on the d: drive). Note that it is necessary to include the c: drive in the script to properly capture and subsequently restore the VMs. The necessary information to restore the links is captured by Diskshadow into a .cab file you will see later. The batch file invoked (HypervBackup.bat) accomplishes the critical task of copying required files to secure storage (a USB drive in this case). You can easily accomplish this task using xcopy. The following is an example command to copy the required data exposed on drive x: to a local g: drive.

```
Xcopy x:\VMs\*.* g:\HyperVBackup\VHDs\*.* ↵
    /e /s /y /F /O /X /R /H /B
```

A complete VM backup process may require multiple component batch files with robust error checking, a scheduler, and one or more Diskshadow scripts. Ensuring the complete backup of a Hyper-V physical host, all settings, and VM data requires much more than is shown here; Figure 7.29 shows the components of a complete (and entirely unsupported) backup process for VMs.

FIGURE 7.29
Example Disk-
shadow backup
process flow

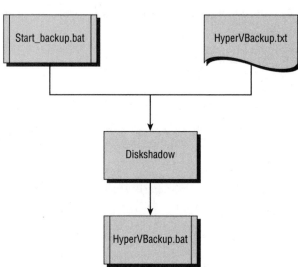

EXAMPLES: DISKSHADOW FOR BACKUP AND RESTORE

We've covered using Diskshadow for Hyper-V backup here as well:

```
http://blogs.technet.com/enterprise_admin/
```

The example scenario there is for a single-drive system. The single-drive (c:) backup samples is here:

```
http://blogs.technet.com/enterprise_admin/archive/2009/11/19/diskshadow-xcopy-
backup-of-hyper-v.aspx
```

You can find the restore here:

```
http://blogs.technet.com/enterprise_admin/archive/2009/11/20/diskshadow-xcopy-
restore-of-hyper-v.aspx
```

The commented batch and script files supporting this process appear in Listing 7.1, Listing 7.2, and Listing 7.3. You can start the example backup process by launching Start_backup.bat, which calls Diskshadow using a prewritten script file: HyperVBackup.txt. The script file in turn calls HyperVBackup.bat to replicate (using xcopy) the necessary files for a subsequent recovery of the VMs.

LISTING 7.1   Start_backup.bat

```
@echo off

cls

REM Calls Diskshadow to backup running Hyper-V Virtual Machines

REM

REM This example process assumes all virtual machine files

REM are homed on the F: drive and located in F:\VHDs

REM This includes VM related configuration files

REM

REM Also captures contents of

REM C:\HyperVBackup\ProgramData\Microsoft\Windows\Hyper-V\

REM

REM note the -S option which allows for the use of a pre-configured script
```

```
REM

Echo Beginning backup process...

diskshadow -s HyperVBackup.txt > c:\HyperVBackup.log

Echo Completed backup process. Check c:\HyperVBackup.log for results
```

LISTING 7.2   HyperVBackup.txt

```
set context persistent

set metadata C:\backup.cab

set verbose on

begin backup

        add volume C: alias ConfigVolume

        add volume D: alias VHDVolume

        #The GUID of the Hyper-V Writer is below

        writer verify {66841cd4-6ded-4f4b-8f17-fd23f8ddc3de}

        create

        EXPOSE %VHDVolume% X:

        EXPOSE %ConfigVolume% Y:

EXEC c:\HypervBackup.bat

        UNEXPOSE X:

        UNEXPOSE Y:

end backup
```

LISTING 7.3   HyperVBackup.bat

```
@Echo off

REM Note that backup could be to any accessible storage local
```

```
REM or over the network

REM

REM Also note that running this copy process more than once

REM to the same destination can result in unnecessary files being retained.

REM

REM

REM The destination should be cleared or perhaps renamed before each copy.

REM Renaming the destination folder to reflect a particular backup generation

REM (rename g:\HyperBackup to g:\HyperBackup-OLD for example).

REM

g:

cd \

if exist g:\HyperVBackup-OLD (

     rmdir g:\HyperVBackup-OLD /s /q

)

pause

if exist g:\HyperVBackup (

     rename HyperVBackup HyperVBackup-OLD

)

pause


REM copy centralized VHD files to locally attached USB Drive

Xcopy x:\VHDs\*.* g:\HyperVBackup\VHDs\*.* /e /s /y /F /O /X /R /H

pause
```

NOTE The first edition of the book showed a process that required the backup and restore of the contents of the `c:\HyperVBackup\ProgramData\Microsoft\Windows\Hyper-V\` directory. This process is not optimal, since the restore actually replaced the symbolic link in the directory to the configuration with the actual configuration file. We've redefined the backup and restore process in this second edition to include a simpler (and more reliable) Diskshadow restore.

NOTE You can copy files captured in this manner to the appropriate locations in the directory hierarchy of a preexisting VM export. Landing VHD, VSV, XML, BIN, and other files in the correct locations with proper security is a complicated process. Swapping files into exported VM configurations is simplified if the VM exported and backup files are all generated while the VM is in an Off state.

RECOVERING FROM A MANUAL BACKUP

The basic purpose of recovering from a manual backup is to put copies of all necessary files back where they were before, which is not as simple as it sounds. The information and files required to recover a Hyper-V host and dependent VMs can be spread widely, with some information residing in the registry, on the operating system volume, on other local volumes, and across network links.

Many files have critical security attributes (file ownership, for example) that must be preserved as part of the backup and recovery process. Again, using a backup tool engineered specifically for the backup and recovery of Hyper-V may be simpler and more effective in most scenarios than a manual backup process. Recovery of VMs in the following scenario assumes that the Hyper-V physical host didn't fail or that it has already been recovered up to the point where VMs require restore. It also assumes that all VMs will be recovered from the same backup and that existing VMs configured on the host may be overwritten.

The `RestoreVMs.bat` batch file in Listing 7.4 controls the restore process from the previously automated backup—essentially the reverse of the backup process. There really is very little to it—it confirms you would like to perform a restore and then calls `diskshadow -s c:\HyperVRestore.txt`. Listing 7.5 shows the contents of `HyperVrestore.txt` (the `Diskshadow` script file managing the restore), which in turn calls a batch file (`HyperVRestore.bat`), shown in Listing 7.6.

LISTING 7.4 `RestoreVMs.bat`

```
REM

REM Restore requires that all VMs be off

REM - safest bet is shut down Hyper-V on the host

REM

@echo off

cls
```

```
echo NOTE THIS RESTORE WILL OVERWRITE THE ENTIRE SERVER's HYPER-V CONFIGURATION

pause

Echo .

echo Are you REALLY sure?

echo        ******

pause

REM call diskshadow to restore configuration

REM from backup and invoke Xcopy to restore VM files

REM

Diskshadow -s HyperVrestore.txt

REM

Echo Hyper-V configuration and virtual machine backups should now be restored!

Echo You may now restart your virtual machines
```

LISTING 7.5   HyperVrestore.txt

```
set context persistent

#the backup.cab file mentioned below is the one created during backup.

load metadata G:\Hypervbackup\backup.cab

set verbose on

begin restore

exec C:\HypervRestore.bat

end restore
```

LISTING 7.6   HyperVRestore.bat

```
Xcopy g:\HyperVBackup\VMs\*.* D:\VMs\*.* /e /s /y /F /O /X /R /H
```

COMMENTS ON THE MANUAL RECOVERY PROCESS

The majority of required recovery data resides in the VHD files for each VM. Without proper recovery of the XML configuration files, as well as shortcuts to these files (both external to the VHDs), the VMs won't start. Security information tied to these files must be preserved for full recovery of VMs (which is why so many parameters appear at the end of the xcopy commands).

You can successfully recover individual VMs using this manual backup process. Virtual machines may even be restored to alternate hosts, but success may require additional manual configuration.

Summary

Modern enterprises depend on successful backup and recovery of applications, services, and systems. The encapsulation of software within VMs gives you new scenarios you can use to back up, migrate, and restore server-based services and applications. Virtualization does create disruptions to traditional operational procedures and processes. But with planning and testing, you can exploit these disruptions and use the benefits of virtualization to investigate, construct, and adopt more efficient backup and recovery processes.

Chapter 8

High Availability

Failover clusters typically protect against hardware failure. Overall system failures (times of system unavailability) often aren't the result of server failures but are more commonly caused by power outages, network stoppages, security issues, or misconfiguration. A redundant server generally won't protect against an unplanned outage such as lightning striking a power substation, a backhoe cutting a data link, an administrator inadvertently deleting a machine or service account, or the misapplication of a zoning update in a Fibre Channel SAN fabric.

Failover clustering protects against certain hardware failures but against few of the typical causes of system instability or unavailability. With that being said, many organizations look to failover clustering to improve system availability.

Virtualized operating system instances can help with the goal of improved availability. In this chapter, we'll show you how to leverage Windows failover clustering of physical Hyper-V systems, using Quick Migration and Live Migration (introduced in Windows Server R2). We will also discuss Windows failover clustering within virtual machines (application-level clusters inside VMs are sometimes referred to as *guest clustering*).

This chapter will cover the following topics:

◆ Windows Server 2008 R2 failover clustering

◆ Storage considerations for clustering

◆ Building a failover cluster for Hyper-V

◆ Clustered virtual machine management

Windows Server 2008 Failover Clustering

A *failover cluster* is a group of similar computers (referred to as *nodes*) working in a coordinated fashion to increase the availability of specific services or applications. You typically employ failover clusters to increase availability by protecting against the loss of a single physical server from an unanticipated hardware failure or by proactively maintaining a single physical system. Clustering protects against planned downtime as well as unplanned because the proactive maintenance of hardware usually takes down the system and results in system unavailability.

If you've worked with a failover cluster via Microsoft Cluster Service (MSCS) using Windows NT Server, Windows 2000 Server, or Windows Server 2003, you already understand the basics of failover clustering in Windows Server 2008. Like those earlier Windows Server clustering technologies, failover clustering in Windows Server 2008 uses shared disks in a *shared-nothing* model to provide multiple servers one-at-a-time volume access.

But failover clustering in Windows Server 2008 and R2 differs from those implementations in several notable ways. Changes introduced for Windows Server 2008 focus on simplifying, securing, and stabilizing failover-clustering installations. Updates include the networking enhancements, a new quorum model, removal of support for parallel SCSI, and the elimination of the cluster service account. Additional enhancements were made in Windows Server 2008 R2, with the most noteworthy being the additions of Live Migration and Cluster Shared Volume support, which we'll discuss shortly.

The most significant difference for administrators is the vastly simplified setup process supported by cluster validation, which we take you through step-by-step in "Building a Failover Cluster for Hyper-V" later in this chapter. The cluster-validation process helps ensure a better cluster experience by identifying and eliminating configuration issues up front. During the validation process, you can check requirements for creating a cluster. The automated validation process includes discrete sections and tests that do the following:

◆ Inventory the hardware, software, and configuration of each individual node

◆ Check network-configuration items such as TCP/IP settings and firewall configuration and validate communication

◆ Investigate the storage infrastructure by listing disks, identifying "clusterable" storage, and validating failover capability

◆ Examine the configuration, installed software, and settings across systems to ensure a uniform configuration

After successful validation, you can quickly set up nodes to form a failover cluster. You can automate failover configuration for services and applications when you use the High Availability Wizard for common application failover scenarios. This wizard contains more than a dozen preconfigured application and service selections that set up failover capabilities homed on a failover cluster (see Figure 8.1). After a cluster is validated and created, you can select this action for an application or service and test its suitability for clustering. If the application is appropriate, the wizard automatically configures it for high availability (HA).

FIGURE 8.1
Some HA-ready services and applications

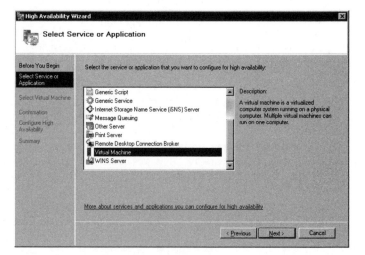

The setup and validation changes in Windows Server 2008 and Windows Server 2008 R2 enable server generalists (rather than clustering specialists) to quickly and efficiently configure a cluster. Determining whether your cluster configuration meets support requirements no longer requires checking the Microsoft Hardware Compatibility List (HCL) or Server Catalog for the exact hardware setup.

The specific support requirements for creating a failover cluster are as follows (as per Microsoft):

◆ Successfully passing the Validate test in the Failover Cluster Management snap-in.

◆ All hardware and software components must meet the qualifications to receive a "Certified for Windows Server 2008 R2" logo.

You can build a simple failover cluster with two servers, networking infrastructure, and shared storage, as shown in Figure 8.2. With the appropriate physical servers, enough network cards, cables, and suitable shared storage, you can set up and configure a Windows Server 2008 or Windows Server 2008 R2–based failover cluster in a matter of hours.

FIGURE 8.2
A simple cluster of
Hyper-V hosts

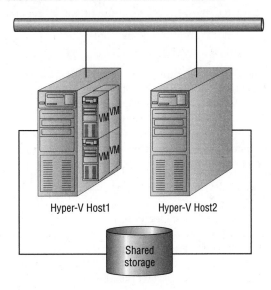

For more information on identifying tested and validated hardware configurations for high availability, check with the Microsoft Failover Cluster Configuration Program at the following URL:

`www.microsoft.com/windowsserver2008/en/us/failover-clustering-program-overview.aspx`

Failover Clustering Basics

When you consolidate systems through virtualization, you raise the potential business impact of a single physical-server failure. Failover clustering can help protect against this risk. Using failover clustering to protect virtual machines (VMs) with Windows Server 2008 has been dubbed

Quick Migration by Microsoft. An additional option to increase VM availability was introduced in Windows Server 2008 R2 called *Live Migration*. Both Live Migration and Quick Migration may be used in Windows Server 2008 R2 failover clusters.

QUICK MIGRATION

Quick Migration enables VMs to execute on multiple physical Hyper-V nodes with the ability to failover (or migrate) between nodes with a brief processing interruption. At a high level, Quick Migration performs the following actions for VMs that are part of a VM group requested to move to another node:

1. Saves the VM state: stops execution and writes the contents of RAM into the associated .vsv file on shared storage

2. Unregisters the VM configuration on the current node

3. "Transfers" storage from the source node to the target node

4. Registers the VM configuration on the target node

5. Resumes the VM: reads the contents of the associated .vsv file into RAM and resumes execution

More is going on behind the scenes to facilitate the movement of services (managing access to storage, for example), but this is the basic process as it pertains to the VMs. The VMs are essentially frozen on one system, passed to another system, and thawed. The amount of time the services on a moved VM are unavailable depends on the amount of RAM allocated to and used by the VM (the more RAM involved, the longer it will take to save and reload the VM on a different cluster node). Because the VM isn't executing at that point, the workload deployed in the VM has no influence on the migration times.

LIVE MIGRATION

Windows Server 2008 R2 includes Live Migration, which migrates running VMs between failover cluster nodes without the processing interruption associated with Quick Migration. Live Migration enables a more rapid relocation of a virtual machine by transferring memory contents from one physical host directly to another over the network while a VM is running. The Live Migration process works like this:

1. All pages of memory for a running VM are transferred from the source node to the target node.

2. Memory pages for the VM that were changed during the initial transfer are transferred again.

3. Storage is "transferred" from the source node to the target node.

4. The VM configuration is registered on the target node.

For more details on the nuts and bolts of Live Migration, go to www.microsoft.com/virtualization and search for *Live Migration Overview & Architecture*.

NOTE Microsoft Hyper-V Server (the free downloadable product that includes Hyper-V) was enhanced in the R2 release to include the same availability features for hosted VMs found in Windows Server 2008 R2. Hyper-V Server 2008 R2 can be used in a failover cluster for Quick Migration or Live Migration and supports the use of Cluster Shared Volumes that we'll talk about in "Clustered Shared Volumes in R2" later in this chapter.

Quick Migration vs. Live Migration

So if Live Migration can provide more uptime, why would you ever use Quick Migration?

Live Migration can place a significant burden on networking resources between nodes to accomplish the VM move. Because of this, only one VM may be migrated at a time using Live Migration. For some implementations, there may not be sufficient bandwidth to support a successful Live Migration of a virtual machine.

Quick Migration saves the memory state of VMs to be moved to shared disk without all the memory monitoring overhead. It allows you to move multiple VMs from one node to another at the same time. Yes, virtual machines migrated using Quick Migration may be "frozen" for short time, but this can be an acceptable trade-off if you must accomplish a mass migration of VMs in a short period of time.

Configuring a Cluster

Configuring Quick Migration or Live Migration involves validating and creating a failover cluster and then successfully configuring one or more VMs for HA. Clustering is configured within the parent partitions on multiple Hyper-V–capable systems and can protect configured child partitions. Beyond the consolidation benefits you can achieve through Hyper-V, running on top of a failover cluster makes services that aren't cluster-aware highly available by clustering the servers hosting VMs.

After you set up the cluster, it will allow for nearly continuous operation of VMs during planned maintenance of the underlying hardware as well as automated recovery (VM restart) in the event of unplanned node failures. For planned maintenance, you can move VM(s) to another node from within the Failover Cluster Management console (or by using enterprise management software such as System Center Virtual Machine Manager).

Protecting the VM vs. Protecting the Application

As mentioned earlier, with Quick Migration or Live Migration, failover clustering of physical Hyper-V systems can make VMs (child partitions) highly available. It *may* make sense to create failover clusters *between* VMs—making cluster-aware applications or services inside multiple VMs highly available. By clustering between child VMs, you can consolidate multiple application failover clusters on a single physical server or a group of servers, which can help you meet consolidation and availability goals.

One consideration for clustering within VMs is the lack of access to common types of shared storage from within a VM. VMs don't have direct access to physically attached shared storage, via Fibre Channel host bus adapters (HBAs) or serial-attached SCSI (SAS) controllers, and pass-through disk isn't supported for clustering applications and services within VMs. For these reasons, you must use storage presented via the network, such as Internet SCSI (iSCSI), to meet shared storage requirements, as shown in Figure 8.3.

FIGURE 8.3
Clustering within/
between VMs

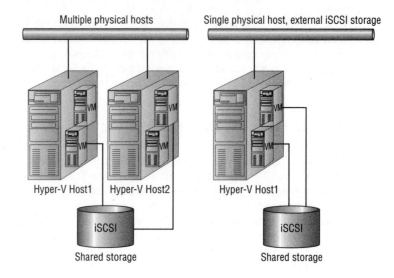

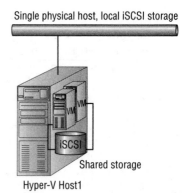

Another key consideration is the *cluster awareness* of a particular workload. File services, printing, Domain Name Service (DNS), Dynamic Host Configuration Protocol (DHCP), Windows Internet Naming Service (WINS), Internet Storage Name Service (iSNS), and other common services are failover cluster–aware out of the box in Windows Server 2008 or Windows Server 2008 R2. Other applications and services lend themselves to different HA approaches, including using the Network Load Balancing (NLB) feature in Windows Server 2008 and R2. NLB enables two or more servers (VM or physical) to combine into a single virtual application cluster, typically for the delivery of stateless services such as web or FTP applications.

Required Components for Failover Clustering

We'll focus on creating clusters specifically for use with Hyper-V without diving deeply into less common clustering scenarios. Common components are required for successful cluster deployments, including appropriate hardware and the correct software.

SERVER HARDWARE

The same basic hardware is required to cluster Hyper-V as to run Hyper-V on a stand-alone system, but failover clustering has additional requirements.

Before you go wiring all your systems together into a failover cluster, you should strive to ensure you use similar systems for all nodes in a cluster. The systems in your cluster (the nodes) should be as identical in configuration as possible.

Why must your cluster nodes be the same? The more dissimilar a cluster node is from other systems in a cluster, the less likely it is to successfully assume the operation of an application or service.

A simple example is a two-node cluster of servers that are identical except for RAM. What could happen if the active node has 64 GB of RAM and the passive, backup server has only 32 GB of RAM? If most of the RAM (50 GB) on the active node is in use by VMs, how can the passive node take over operations? It can't—and in the event of a failover, some of the VMs will go offline. Your hardware should be identical, from the amount of RAM down to the settings and firmware revisions of interface cards.

The Cluster Validation Wizard does many checks to ensure that you'll have a stable, reliable cluster. It evaluates the CPU (manufacturer and version), BIOS settings, network configuration, network interface card (NIC) settings, storage configuration, and security; in short, the wizard checks a vast array of settings and system parameters to validate that the servers you want to cluster will work together.

This extensive checking is fantastic. But sometimes you may not want or need all the automated testing. For example, perhaps you'd like to create a simple cluster for training or testing. In such cases, the Cluster Validation Wizard lets you create failover clusters that aren't optimal, such as if you want to use a single NIC rather than multiple NICs for separate networking functions (iSCSI access, cluster intercommunication, application services, general networking, and so on). Although you can ignore the warnings of the Cluster Validation Wizard, doing so introduces known risk to your configuration, as noted by the generated validation report, and is not recommended.

CPUs

Normally the CPUs in your cluster should be identical. Why not use a mix of Intel and AMD processors in your cluster? CPUs differ in their capabilities and characteristics, even if they're from the same manufacturer. How memory is managed and what instructions are available varies by processor family and minor revision. These variations in CPUs become significant in failover clustering because VMs are migrated *in flight* from one node to another.

As noted earlier, the process of proactively migrating VMs from one node to another with Quick Migration is similar to hibernating a running laptop, removing the stopped hard drive, installing the drive in another identical laptop, and starting it again in the other laptop. Hardware for cluster nodes should be as similar as possible because Hyper-V nodes with different hardware are less likely to support the stateful migration of VMs.

NETWORK

Networking is a core function of a failover cluster. It's the manifestation of uptime to other systems, and it lets nodes communicate status and access storage (in the case of iSCSI). Each network interface should be dedicated to a single purpose (management, storage access, applications/VMs, and so on) to ensure adequate performance, security, and availability of network resources.

PROCESSOR COMPATIBILITY MODE

Windows Server 2008 R2 includes a new Processor Compatibility mode that can be set on a VM-by-VM basis. It allows Hyper-V to expose only the common CPU features to a VM, which allows you to mix CPUs from a given manufacturer. For example, you can migrate a VM from a host using Intel Core i7 CPUs to a host using a Pentium 4 VT processor (processors that support Intel VT). You can learn more about this feature in the article "Tech Ed: Windows Server 2008 R2 Hyper-V News!" on the Virtualization Team Blog:

```
http://blogs.technet.com/virtualization/archive/2009/05/12/
tech-ed-windows-server-2008-r2-hyper-v-news.aspx
```

Remember that Live Migration transmits the memory contents of a running VM over a physical network connection (rather than committing it to disk, the way Quick Migration does). The throughput of cluster internode network connections is therefore even more important when using Live Migration. Using Gigabit Ethernet for cluster heartbeat (and all other connections) is our minimum recommendation; 10 Gigabit Ethernet is commonly used in some environments, because it can reduce the time required for an individual VM's Live Migration process.

SHARED STORAGE

Beyond having multiple networks attached and physical systems to run Hyper-V, you also need shared locations on which to store VMs and their configurations. Failover cluster nodes have traditionally accessed disk volumes presented to the cooperating systems via a Fibre Channel storage area network (SAN) or other shared storage subsystem. iSCSI-attached storage is increasingly used in addition to traditional Fibre Channel SANs for block-level access. iSCSI can often be installed and managed at a lower cost and with less complexity.

It is also technically possible to host VMs on traditional Windows file shares (CIFS-based) with additional security and configuration. There is no support at this time for hosting VMs via network-attached storage (NAS) using either the CIFS or NFS protocol.

MAJORITIES, QUORUMS, AND VOTING

Shared storage provides another important function beyond storing the VMs: it can act as a witness in determining which node controls shared resources (the volumes used for data). Although a disk-based witness (also referred to as a *quorum disk*) isn't required for a cluster, this witness functionality enables a cluster of two nodes to clearly identify which system has access to storage and thus control of the running applications or services (VMs). In the event of a single node failure, the remaining node can vote with the witness to restart a failed application or service.

Without a witness in a two-node Hyper-V cluster, Quick Migration or Live Migration could still function, but restarting a failed VM resulting from a down physical node would require intervention. This *node and disk majority* model included in Windows Server 2008 or R2 failover clustering is an enhancement over earlier Windows-based availability clusters: it doesn't require a dedicated disk volume, and it enables the cluster to continue to function even if the disk witness is unavailable (the nodes can vote without the witness to take action).

Traditional block-level storage requires the following elements for cluster volumes:

◆ The style of partitions can be master boot record (MBR) if they're less than 2 TB in size or GUID Partition Table (GPT) if they're larger

◆ Basic disk (not dynamic)

◆ Witness disk (*quorum*) formatted NTFS

A similar quorum configuration can rely on a file share as a witness in Windows Server 2008, rather than traditional block-level storage; this model is called *node and file share majority*.

SOFTWARE

Failover clustering for Windows Server 2008 R2 requires either Windows Server 2008 R2 Enterprise edition or Datacenter edition on the Hyper-V host systems or requires Hyper-V Server 2008 R2. Although it may be possible to configure nodes with different editions of Windows Server 2008 within a cluster (Enterprise edition, Datacenter edition, or Hyper-V Server), doing so isn't suggested. You can use Server Core or the full installation of Windows Server 2008 R2 for cluster creation, but you can't configure a mixture of nodes using Server Core and a full Window Server 2008 R2 installation.

NOTE   It is possible to create a cluster using various Windows Server 2008 R2 Core installations and Hyper-V Server 2008 R2. But remember that these versions of the software are different. We do not recommend mixing Windows editions or versions in a failover cluster. Keep your installation versions the same, if at all possible.

Storage Considerations for Clustering

At the heart of every failover cluster is some type of shared storage to host the application or service being shared between nodes. Failover clustering with Hyper-V is no different from other failover cluster solutions in its reliance on storage; however, considerations for clustering VMs are different than for other applications or services.

Using Pass-Through Disk to Improve Performance

Virtual machines typically access disk-based information in the form of a virtual hard disk (VHD) file, which contains all the data for a given virtual disk. VHD files, in conjunction with a VM's configuration, define the VM. The portability and versatility of the VHD file enable simplified disaster recovery and facilitate the failover functionality. But in some cases, the VHD file presents limitations that can negatively affect the performance and scalability of a given VM (as noted in Chapter 3, "Configuring Hyper-V").

Storage performance enhancements were made between Windows Server 2008 and Windows Server 2008 R2 to reduce the I/O performance penalty encountered using VHD files. In Windows Server 2008 R2, the performance of dynamic VHDs (which expand as needed) is nearly equivalent to that of predefined static sized VHDs, and the performance of all VHD file access is close to (but perhaps still slower than) that of native disk access.

To alleviate disk-related performance bottlenecks from VHD files, you may configure pass-through disk for disks used by highly available VMs. Configuring highly available VMs to use pass-through disk provides enhanced I/O performance as well as access to disk volumes larger than 2 TB. Using pass-through disk eliminates the VHD-related benefits of virtualization (simplified backup and recovery, snapshot capability, and more). Combining VHDs with pass-through disk can also be valuable: housing a VM's boot disk within a VHD while accessing an additional pass-through volume for data may provide an appropriate mix of system performance and recoverability (see Figure 8.4).

FIGURE 8.4
Virtual machines with highly available pass-through disk

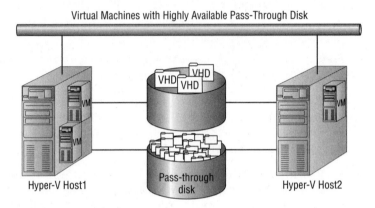

Virtual Machines with Highly Available Pass-Through Disk

Hyper-V Host1 Pass-through disk Hyper-V Host2

Clustering with GUIDs and Mount Points

It's possible (and in some situations advisable) to use volumes without assigning drive letters—mounting and using volumes via their GUIDs or as mount points within folders. You may want to use these two methods of accessing volumes (without drive letters) when you require large numbers of volumes and have insufficient drive letters available. Mounting volumes via GUIDs or mount points is supported for failover clusters, but either approach adds a great deal of complexity to the overall configuration.

Configuring Multiple VMs on a Single Physical Volume

Included in Windows Server 2008 R2 is an update for Windows Server 2008 (KB951308) that increases functionality in the Windows Server 2008 Failover Cluster Manager for Hyper-V. One key enhancement lets you configure and manage multiple VMs on a single shared disk from within the cluster-management console. This capability simplifies storage provisioning and management as well as the VM configuration process. Because this update is already included in Windows Server 2008 R2, there is no need to download and apply the update from Microsoft.

Before the release of this update (and Windows Server 2008 R2), you had to manually configure resources and dependencies to host multiple VMs in this manner. Dedicating a volume for each highly available VM was a common recommended practice. You can move each VM between nodes independently if it's hosted on a dedicated disk/logical unit number (LUN). By hosting multiple VMs on a single disk, the unit of migration (or failure) becomes the disk, meaning that any migration of services or applications from one node to another requires all VMs hosted on that disk to move. In the case of Hyper-V, this increases the overall migration time for

VMs hosted on the disk, because multiple VMs must be saved before the disk can be accessed by the target cluster node. You must weigh the cost of labor for storage provision and management against the increased migration time of highly available consolidated VMs.

Using a clustered file system (CFS) provides an alternative to "one VM per disk" while still allowing individual VM movement between nodes. A CFS lets systems lock resources at a level other than the disk level. This enables failover cluster nodes to access files on the same volume at the same time. Sanbolic's Melio FS is an example of an existing cluster file system that works with Windows Server 2008 and Hyper-V. Windows Server 2008 R2 includes Cluster Shared Volume support, which can simplify storage provisioning for Hyper-V failover clusters.

Clustered Shared Volumes in R2

A Clustered Shared Volume (CSV) is a standard, shared NTFS volume in a Hyper-V failover cluster that is enabled for concurrent access by multiple nodes. VMs homed on a CSV can run on separate cluster nodes and may be migrated between nodes independently. Using the CSV feature eliminates the requirement to migrate all VMs homed on a volume as a failover unit. Each VM has the freedom to migrate between execution nodes independently, as if the VM were housed on its own dedicated volume or LUN.

Once CSV support is enabled (through the Failover Clustering Management console or via the command line), LUNs exposed to the cluster can be added the CSV pool. CSVs are then accessible via the C:\ClusterStorage directory (unless you use a different letter for your system volume). Each CSV appears as a separate subdirectory on every member of the Hyper-V failover cluster— similar to a mount point. We'll walk you through a configuration example later.

WARNING CSVs are only for use with Hyper-V! You may be tempted to use a CSV for other than Hyper-V–related files (VM configuration information and VHDs), but that's not supported! You should not copy other files to a CSV or attempt to use it with other failover cluster–aware services or applications.

Using CSVs can reduce the number of LUNs presented to a cluster while still enabling individual VM migration. In some environments, the CSV feature also simplifies host configurations by reducing the need for drive letters (or separate mount points) for each LUN.

CSV works by carefully coordinating the I/O operations of all cluster nodes on one of cluster members. One node actually "owns" a CSV volume and is the coordinator of I/O for all nodes in the cluster. The coordinator decides the best path to the storage for all nodes.

Backup and Recovery of a VM's Host CSV

The host-based backup of CSVs is more complicated because the underlying LUN is owned by a single cluster node. A request to make a VSS snapshot on an execution node that is hosting a VM on a CSV coordinated by another node does not have the same access to storage as it might if the LUN were owned locally (for details of how VSS enables host-based backup and recovery, see Chapter 7, "Backing Up and Recovering VMs"). It is possible to tie the CSV volume to the physical cluster node where a VM is executing for the duration of a VSS snapshot and backup, but this can be complicated. Enterprise backup and recovery tools can handle this level of coordination, including System Center Data Protection Manger 2010 and NetApp SnapManager for Hyper-V. They are the best options for host-based backup and recovery of CSV-based VMs.

> **USING A HARDWARE VSS PROVIDER IS RECOMMENDED FOR SNAPSHOTS OF CSV CLUSTERS**
>
> Because back-end storage can off-load the burden of creating a point-in-time copy of a LUN, using a hardware VSS provider (rather than the software provider included in Windows Server 2008 R2) is recommended. A hardware provider can substantially reduce the amount of time required to create and back up an CSV LUN, reducing the time that a particular cluster node must be the CSV coordinator. For more details, check out the DPM Insider blog, in particular the post titled "Snapshot Provider Considerations while backing up a CSV Cluster":
>
> http://blogs.technet.com/asim_mitra/archive/2009/12/11/snapshot-provider-considerations-while-backing-up-a-csv-cluster.aspx

If you don't want to dive into the complexities of host-based backups of VMs leveraging CSVs, you can always rely on a backup *inside* the VM. An agented backup process inside the VM should work the same way it would with a physical system. Many administrators continue to use traditional backup tools inside VMs for compliance or for other reasons, as mentioned in Chapter 7.

> **LIVE MIGRATION DOESN'T REQUIRE CSV**
>
> Failover clustering in Windows Server 2008 R2 can use a cluster file system (Like Sanbolic's Melio FS), CSV, or dedicated LUNs for each VM group. The nearly transparent migration of VMs from one node to another supported in Windows Server 2008 R2 works best with some sort of cluster file or volume access. The CSV included with Windows Server 2008 R2 is only for use with Hyper-V. You may want to consider a CFS for more complicated clustering or data-sharing applications. You can also implement Live Migration without any sort of CFS or CSV, but you may find storage provisioning to be a bigger chore.

Building a Failover Cluster for Hyper-V

As noted earlier, building a failover cluster for Hyper-V Quick Migration or Live Migration is a straightforward process of configuring multiple, similar physical servers with shared networking, shared storage, and Windows Server 2008 R2. At a high level, you follow these steps to build a failover cluster for Hyper-V like the one shown in Figure 8.5:

1. Configure the network infrastructure.

2. Install required roles, features, and updates.

3. Provision storage, and prepare the disk.

4. Validate the cluster.

5. Create the cluster.

6. Enable CSV (if desired).

7. Configure the service or application.

FIGURE 8.5
Example cluster
configuration

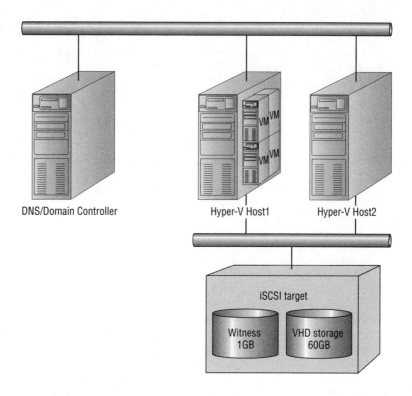

DNS/Domain Controller   Hyper-V Host1   Hyper-V Host2

iSCSI target

Witness
1GB

VHD storage
60GB

Setting Up a Failover Cluster

In the remainder of this chapter, we'll walk you through these high-level steps and the details behind them required to configure a typical two-node Hyper-V failover cluster. We'll also include tips to help you develop insight into the overall process. The entire procedure used here should take less than one workday, including all the required tasks from unpacking and installing hardware through installing and configuring failover clustering. We will first walk through creating a failover cluster on full (non-Core) installations of Windows Server 2008 R2. Then we'll touch on some key points you should know for using Hyper-V Server 2008 R2 and Server Core.

CONFIGURING THE NETWORK INFRASTRUCTURE

Not to sound casual about infrastructure requirements, but failover clustering requires pretty much the same security and networking infrastructure as most other contemporary Microsoft technologies. If you're reading this, you're probably already aware of the requirements—the cluster nodes need to be attached to a network with DNS, an AD domain in which each node has a valid machine account, an accessible domain controller (DC), and an account that has administrator rights on the nodes (it can be a domain user account that has been added to the local administrator group on each system). Note that the account needs the right to create computer objects in the domain. Other networking requirements, dependencies, and recommended practices are involved in creating a failover cluster for Hyper-V (multiple network interface cards, for instance), but the foundation of stable DNS, AD, and the proper administrative access are fundamental requirements that you can't overlook.

INSTALLING ROLES, FEATURES, AND UPDATES

To install and configure failover clustering, you must install specific roles and features (see Table 8.1). For Windows Server 2008, don't forget the release to manufacturing (RTM) update (KB950050) of Hyper-V (install the update first and then add the role). You also need to install the Failover Clustering feature and (depending on your storage requirements) the Multipath I/O feature.

TABLE 8.1:   Typical Features and Roles Installed for Quick Migration on Physical Nodes

ROLE/FEATURE	NAME
Role	Hyper-V
Feature	Failover Clustering
Feature	Multi-Path I/O

You install features in a manner similar to that used for server roles: start Server Manager, select Features, and choose Action ➢ Add Features. Remember that an important update for failover clustering for Windows Server 2008 (KB951308) increases the functionality when you work with Hyper-V. (This update is not required if you have R2.) Take care to check for additional Microsoft updates for failover clustering and Windows Server that should be installed. Many key (non-security-related) updates aren't distributed via the automated update processes. The best option to locate and obtain noncritical updates for Microsoft products is via http://support .microsoft.com, where you can search by product, topic, or KB article.

PROVISIONING STORAGE WITH iSCSI

Attaching storage via iSCSI can be a simpler overall process than connecting to storage via traditional Fibre Channel. Regardless of your storage infrastructure, you should confirm with the manufacturer that it's compatible with failover clustering in Windows Server 2008 and Windows Server 2008 R2. A wide variety of iSCSI-capable storage devices (called *targets*) are available on the market, including Windows Server–based Unified Data Storage Server (WUDSS) systems that can present block-level storage to other systems. We won't show the process of provisioning storage on the iSCSI target system, but we'll demonstrate a minimal configuration of the client systems (initiators) common to any iSCSI-based cluster setup. Two volumes have been preconfigured on the iSCSI target for presentation to the demonstration cluster: a 1 GB witness and a larger volume as a VM store.

Open the Control Panel on one of the installed Hyper-V nodes, and double-click the iSCSI Initiator service.

NOTE   If you're accessing the iSCSI Initiator service for the first time, you'll be prompted to start the Microsoft iSCSI service (it's off by default) and to enable exceptions in the Windows Firewall.

On the iSCSI Initiator Properties page, you can enter information and configure behavior to locate, log in to, and access iSCSI storage devices. Each iSCSI device (initiator or target) is typically assigned an iSCSI qualified name (IQN) that identifies the devices. An IQN is automatically generated for the initiator in the format iqn.*yyyy-mm.<reversed domain name>*. You do have the option to change the IQN, but typically this isn't required.

You locate iSCSI-based storage for your initiator by adding target portal information to the Discovery tab or by configuring an Internet Storage Name Service (iSNS) on your network. You can proceed by entering the IP address of the iSCSI target as a target portal, which discovers preconfigured iSCSI targets to which access has been granted.

Switching to the Targets tab shows iSCSI targets that have been preconfigured for use. Click the Log On button to see the Log On To Target dialog box. This screen provides configurable options for access to the iSCSI target, including future logon behavior and multipath support.

NOTE   If you've used earlier versions of the iSCSI initiator, you may notice and appreciate that it has been updated in Windows Server 2008 R2 to remove some of the clutter, making it easier to navigate and to configure.

After the node is logged onto the target, you must configure the volumes to be used (in this case, we'll assume they're preconfigured for you). Clicking the Autoconfigure button causes the iSCSI Initiator service to automatically configure the devices for use.

When the iSCSI Initiator configuration is complete, you can access the disks; they should be visible in the Disk Management section of Server Manager (although they aren't yet accessible as online, formatted volumes).

You can also use the command line to complete all actions required to configure the iSCSI Initiator. The command line is necessary when using Server Core or Hyper-V Server, since they have no graphical user interface (GUI). We don't want to go too far astray from the process of creating a cluster right now. We'll show you the commands as well as a sample batch file that automates attaching an iSCSI disk to a Hyper-V Server 2008 R2 system later in the chapter in the "Hyper-V Server 2008 R2 and Server Core" section.

PREPARING THE DISK

After you complete the storage connectivity work for each node, you must configure the individual disks for use (bring them online, initialize them as MBR or GPT, create volumes, and format). You can accomplish all these tasks by running Server Manager or Computer Management and accessing Storage\Disk Management *on one of the nodes* sharing the storage (see Figure 8.6).

Right-click each of the new, offline volumes (in the gray Disk block), and bring each disk online. You must also initialize each disk as either MBR or GPT (GPT allows for volumes larger than 2 TB) by right-clicking in the same area of the display. After you initialize the disks with drive letters assigned, create new, simple volumes on each device, and format them with the NTFS file system. Assign drive letters to your cluster storage that make sense. For this demonstration, the witness is labeled *Witness* and has the drive letter W:, and the VM store is drive V: and is named *VMs*, as shown in Figure 8.7.

Remember that assigning drive letters isn't required for failover clustering, and in some cases, as with large number of volumes, it's impractical.

After you complete the storage configuration on the first node, log into the other node, and access the disk configuration. Because the volumes have already been initialized and formatted, you should only need to *online* each disk (that is, right-click each of the new, offline volumes, and bring it online) and change the assigned drive letters to match those of the other node.

FIGURE 8.6
Shared disk before
configuration

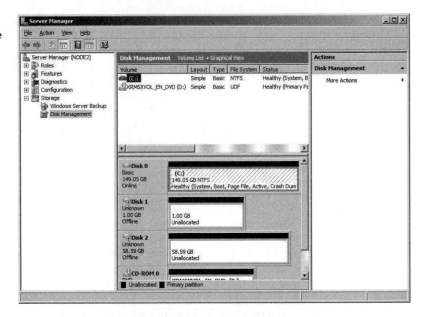

FIGURE 8.7
Shared disk after
configuration

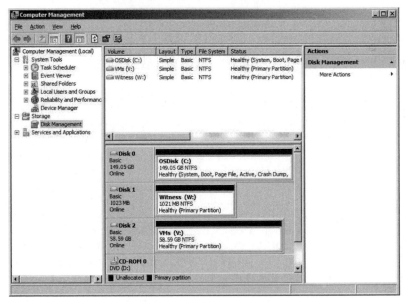

VALIDATING THE CLUSTER

The servers are ready, the features and roles are installed, and the storage is configured. The next step in creating your failover cluster is to jump in and validate your configuration using the Failover Cluster Manager, which you can access via Administrative Tools (see Figure 8.8). In the console, click Validate A Configuration.

FIGURE 8.8
Failover Cluster
Manager

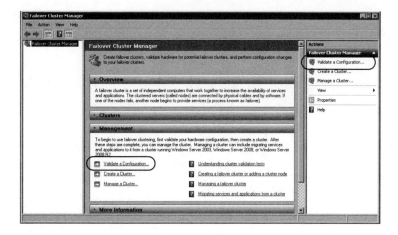

As stated earlier, the cluster validation process eliminates much of the guesswork and manual configuration required by previous implementations of failover clustering, and it's a vast enhancement to the overall cluster setup process. To validate a cluster configuration, enter the names of the nodes to be tested (see Figure 8.9), and click Next.

FIGURE 8.9
Validate A
Configuration
Wizard: selecting
systems

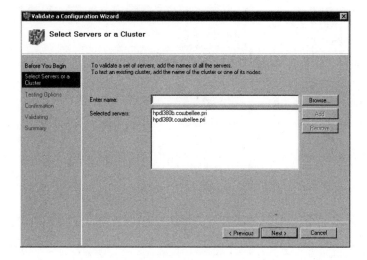

If the report you receive after validation doesn't show any issues (and your hardware is certified for Windows Server 2008 R2), you have a supportable configuration.

You can scroll through the detailed validation report until you see a warning or error, using the familiar and intuitive "green means go, red means stop" paradigm. For the run shown in Figure 8.10, the nodes were found to have a few inconsistencies related to networking and storage.

Clicking the Storage link displays more detailed reporting information that you can act on, as shown in Figure 8.11 (you can see an issue related to MPIO and can drill down further to see how best to resolve it).

FIGURE 8.10

Failover Cluster Validation Report: system configuration sections

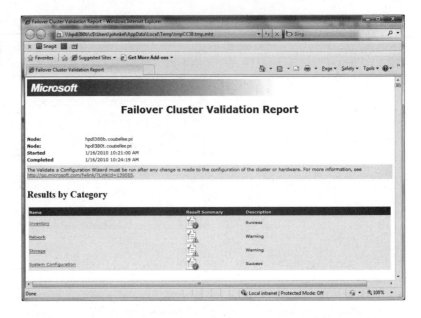

FIGURE 8.11

Failover cluster validation report detail

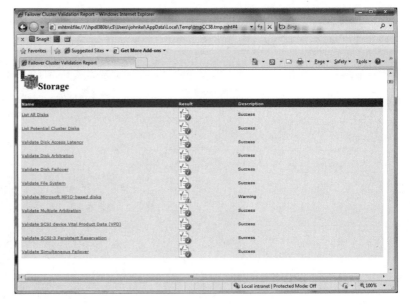

CREATING THE CLUSTER

After you successfully validate your proposed cluster configuration, you're ready to create your cluster. Referring to Figure 8.8, you'll see that underneath Validate A Configuration in the middle of the Failover Cluster Manager is the option Create A Cluster. Creating a cluster is just as simple as validating one. At the completion of the cluster-creation process, the nodes are ready to protect cluster-aware applications or services, including Hyper-V. The name of the new cluster is displayed in the left pane of the Failover Cluster Manager, and configured services are in the center. The new cluster shown in Figure 8.12 does not have any configured services added yet.

FIGURE 8.12
Cluster ready
for work

Enabling CSV and Adding CSVs

The cluster nodes may now be aware of each other, but they still don't know what applications or services you would like them to protect. We're focused on failover clustering for Hyper-V virtual machines, but we haven't yet told the cluster that. The failover cluster also doesn't know if you would like to use CSVs for hosting virtual machines.

If you want to use the CSV feature, you need to enable the capability within the cluster and dedicate shared storage for this purpose. To enable CSV for the cluster, select Enable Cluster Shared Volumes within the Failover Cluster Manager. You will be reminded that the CSV feature should be used only with Hyper-V (see Figure 8.13).

FIGURE 8.13
CSV Hyper-V
reminder

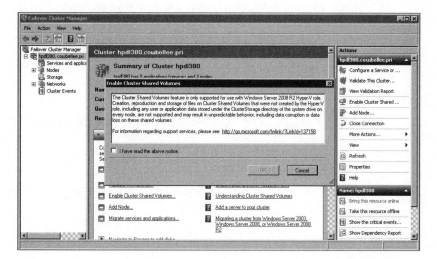

Existing shared storage attached to the cluster can be made to behave as a CSV by selecting CSVs and choosing Add Storage. Eligible storage will be displayed and can be added to the CSV pool. Figure 8.14 shows one CSV added to the pool.

FIGURE 8.14
Summary of storage added to a CSV

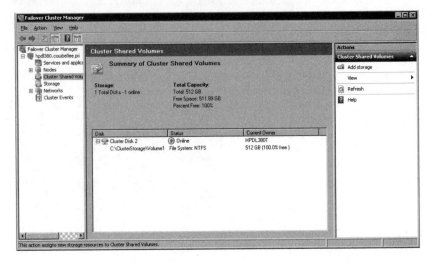

You will be able to access CSVs via the `C:\ClusterStorage` path (assuming that `C:` is your system drive). The first CSV added would be `C:\ClusterStorage\Volume1` with subsequent CSVs being accessible with a higher-numbered directory name.

Updating the Hyper-V Configuration

Before you make your VMs highly available, you should make the Hyper-V configuration on each node consistent and ready to use the configured shared storage. Ensure that all node-specific settings are identical in the Hyper-V Manager. (As noted in earlier chapters, you can access the Hyper-V Manager by expanding the Hyper-V role in Server Manager or via the Start menu as part of Administrative Tools.) Include the names for all defined virtual networks and default file locations. The Hyper-V role should already be installed on each of the cluster nodes (if you forgot to add the Hyper-V role before, now would be a good time to add it!).

In the Hyper-V Manager, review the existing virtual networks defined on each node (select a Hyper-V server at far left, and choose Action ➤ Virtual Network Manager). Ensure that all defined networks that will be used by clustered VMs exist and are identical on all physical Hyper-V nodes.

TIP Consistent naming of virtual networks on all Hyper-V hosts in an environment can save you from unnecessary hassles—just like properly labeling physical network cables and switches. Some administrators consider it to be a best practice to properly define and configure your virtual network switches before creating your cluster.

For this cluster, we'll define two virtual networks on each node, as shown in Table 8.2.

TABLE 8.2:   Sample Cluster Defined Virtual Networks

NAME	DESCRIPTION	CONNECTION TYPE
External	Bound to physical NIC	External
Internal	Access between VMs and host	Internal only

Changing the default file locations for clustered Hyper-V nodes is also a good practice, but it's not necessary. VM configuration data and VHD files must be stored on shared storage, but this isn't the default setting in Hyper-V. Changing the default on cluster nodes helps ensure that the configuration for new VMs and their associated VHD files will be created on shared volumes. If you select the appropriate shared storage location each time you provision a new VM, the default settings are irrelevant.

Select a Hyper-V server on the left of Hyper-V Manager, and choose Action ➤ Hyper-V Settings. For this cluster, you'll change the default path for both VHDs and VMs to C:\ClusterStorage\Volume1 (assuming a CSV has been added to the cluster). Note that if you are not using CSV, only one Windows Server at a time has access to a shared volume, and the Hyper-V Manager validates access to the paths entered into these fields. To successfully change these settings without a CSV, the node must be provided exclusive access to the volume. You can accomplish this by a series of reboots of the nodes, save this task for later, or forgo making the change indefinitely after the Hyper-V cluster configuration is complete and VM services (and the volume) can be moved to the node.

NODE-SPECIFIC RESOURCES

You must review one final node-specific resource: each VM's CD/DVD capture setting. Locally captured CD/DVD drives and ISO images can cause a moved VM to fail to resume, because those resources are typically node-specific (an ISO file located on one node on the D: drive won't be accessible on another node after the VM is moved). Be sure that no CD/DVD resources are captured on VMs residing on failover clusters except when in use.

CREATING A VIRTUAL MACHINE

The last step before you complete the cluster configuration is to create a VM to make highly available. You still create (or place and import) VMs using the Hyper-V Manager. Create and configure a VM on the attached shared storage through Hyper-V Manager using the node that has ownership of the shared storage volume. For CSVs, locate your virtual machine files in one of the Volume subdirectories under C:\ClusterStorage.

To import a VM, copy the export to the shared volume, and import it using the Hyper-V Manager. For this cluster example, I've copied three previously exported virtual machines to C:\ClusterStorage\Volume1. Using the Hyper-V Manager connected to one of the nodes (HPDL380B), I imported each of the VMs and updated their configurations to conform to the local configuration (adjusted the NIC configurations to match defined virtual networks).

NOTE For Windows Server 2008, you should change the Automatic Start Action setting to Nothing, because the state of the VMs will be managed via the cluster service going forward. You can find the Automatic Start Action setting in the Management section of each VM's settings. This does not apply to Windows Server 2008 R2, because failover clustering has been enhanced to respect the changes of state made through the Hyper-V Manager.

CONFIGURING FAILOVER FOR A VIRTUAL MACHINE

After the VMs are created or imported successfully, you can make them highly available. Return to the Failover Cluster Manager, select the configured cluster at left, and expand it by clicking the + next to the cluster name.

Choose Action ➤ Configure A Service Or Application; alternatively, right-click Services And Applications and choose Configure A Service Or Application. Doing so starts the High Availability Wizard, which automates the configuration of HA services for common applications, including Hyper-V.

Figure 8.1 earlier in this chapter showed the initial screen of the wizard. Scroll down the list of services and applications, choose Virtual Machine, and click Next. The three virtual machines added to the cluster nodes earlier are shown as eligible to be made highly available in Figure 8.15.

FIGURE 8.15
Virtual machines ready for HA

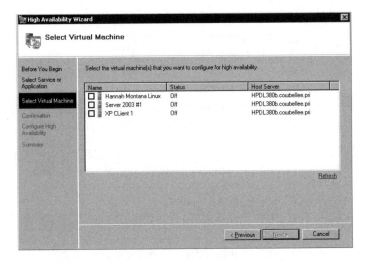

Select the VM to be made highly available (we chose an instance of Hannah Montana Linux for fun). After you complete the wizard, you will be notified if the VM was successfully configured to be highly available. If so, it can execute on any of the configured cluster nodes (see Figure 8.16).

All virtual machines that are configured for high availability will be displayed within the Failover Clustering console. You can see (and manage) all of the cluster's VMs on a service-by-service basis by looking at the services and applications. You can also see the virtual machines owned by a particular cluster node by navigating through the nodes, as shown in Figure 8.17.

FIGURE 8.16
High availability
successfully
configured

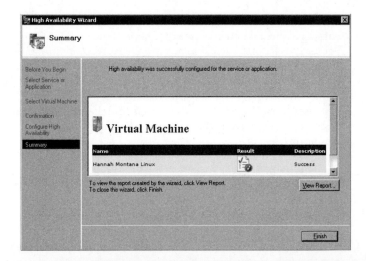

FIGURE 8.17
VMs on Node
HPDL380B

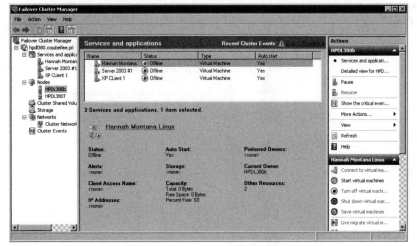

Hyper-V Server 2008 R2 and Server Core

We showed you earlier how you can use the iSCSI command line (iscsicli) to update the iSCSI storage configuration of a system, but we didn't go deep into the configuration steps or why you might want to use the command line. Windows Server 2008 R2 includes an installation option for a lighter-weight, command-line-only Server Core configuration. There is also a similar, no-cost version of Hyper-V available as a stand-alone product that also has no GUI. Hyper-V Server 2008 R2 is available for download from Microsoft and looks and feels a great deal like a Server Core installation of Windows Server 2008 R2.

However, there are a few noteworthy differences between Server Core and Hyper-V Server 2008 R2. For example, Hyper-V Server 2008 R2 does not include the licensing entitlements that are included with Windows Server 2008 R2. For example, Windows Server 2008 R2 Enterprise edition includes the entitlement to run up to four Windows-based server VMs. A detailed discussion of virtualization licensing is beyond the scope of the book, so we'll just say that Hyper-V Server 2008 R2 gives you similar virtualization capabilities to a Server Core installation of Windows Server 2008 R2 Enterprise edition without the licensing entitlements. If you have an investment in an older Windows Server version (2000, 2003, 2008) or other operating system (Linux or x86 Unix), you can still virtualize them on Hyper-V Server without additional license expenses from Microsoft (we can't speak for other platforms you may virtualize). Contact your Microsoft sales team, or check out the licensing information on the Microsoft website for more details on licensing.

As we mentioned, Hyper-V Server 2008 R2 is similar in capability to a Server Core installation of Windows Server 2008 R2 Enterprise editions. It includes failover clustering support with both Quick Migration and Live Migration. Hyper-V Server also has a few other interesting twists, including the smaller size of the installation ISO image. Also, it installs out of the box with the Hyper-V role already enabled. It has a friendly, text-based menu to simplify those common configuration tasks you might ordinarily accomplish via the Windows GUI.

Once you build a Hyper-V Server and log in, you will be greeted with a menu similar to the one shown in Figure 8.18.

FIGURE 8.18
Hyper-V
Server menu

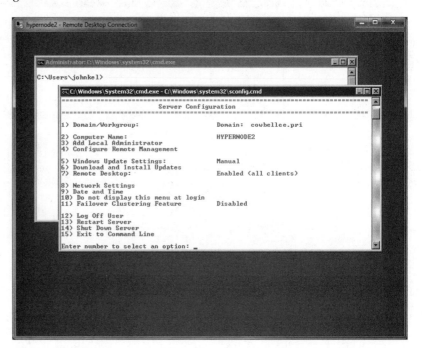

Common configuration tasks such as joining the system to an Active Directory domain, enabling remote management, changing the networking configuration, and enabling failover clustering can all be accomplished using the included menus, so you can avoid the more difficult to remember command-line tools. After installing Hyper-V Server, joining it to a domain, adding an account to the local administrator's group, and enabling remote management, you can accomplish many common management tasks from another system with a full graphical interface. You can do tasks such as bring disks online or manage services and security remotely (see Figure 8.19).

FIGURE 8.19
Managing a Hyper-V Server via the Computer Management console

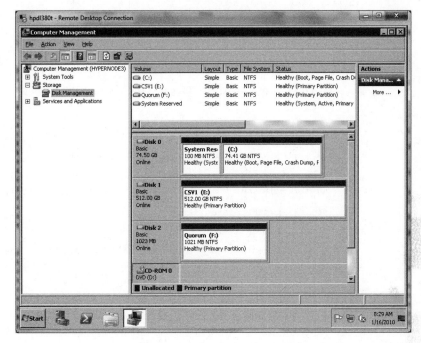

Configuring iSCSI from the Command Line

One task in configuring a Hyper-V Server failover cluster that can be challenging is attaching and configuring iSCSI storage. Two of the disks shown in Figure 8.19 are actually remote to the system and presented by an HP/LeftHand iSCSI subsystem. We could not use the iSCSI Initiator configuration tool in the Control Panel on Hyper-V Server, because we don't have a Control Panel!

The following are example commands that show how to enable and configure the iSCSI Initiator using the command line. First you must enable the state of the iSCSI Initiator service and start the service using the SC command:

1. Set the iSCSI Initiator service to start automatically:

```
sc \\localhost config msiscsi start= auto
```

2. Start the iSCSI Initiator service:

```
sc start msiscsi
```

3. Complete the remaining tasks using the iSCSI command-line interface (iscsicli):

A. Add the target portal:

```
iscsicli QAddTargetPortal <IP address of Portal>
```

B. Add the target:

```
iscsicli QAddTarget <iqn address of target>
```

C. Log in to the target:

```
iscsicli QloginTarget <iqn address of target>
```

D. Make login persistent:

```
iscsicli PersistentLoginTarget <iqn address of target> ↵
T * * * * * * * * * * * * * * * 0
```

E. Bind all persistent volumes:

```
iscsicli BindPersistentVolumes
```

4. Confirm some critical settings by using these two command lines:

```
iscsicli ListPersistentTargets
iscsicli ReportTargetMappings
```

It may be more useful to show you exactly what we did to attach iSCSI disk to our Hyper-V Server instances. We ran the following batch file to connect the two disks to a Hyper-V Server instance in a lab (similar to the disks attached to the cluster shown earlier):

```
REM Let Hyper-V Server node know about iSCSI subsystem
iscsicli QAddTargetPortal 192.168.0.99

REM Add first LUN (CSV)
iscsicli QAddTarget iqn.2003-10.com.lefthandnetworks:lhfarm:19:csv1
iscsicli QloginTarget iqn.2003-10.com.lefthandnetworks:lhfarm:19:csv1
iscsicli PersistentLoginTarget iqn.2003-10.com.lefthandnetworks:lhfarm:19:csv1↵
T * * * * * * * * * * * * * * * 0

REM Add second LUN (Quorum)
iscsicli QAddTarget iqn.2003-10.com.lefthandnetworks:lhfarm:21:quorum
iscsicli QloginTarget iqn.2003-10.com.lefthandnetworks:lhfarm:21:quorum
iscsicli PersistentLoginTarget iqn.2003-10.com.lefthandnetworks:lhfarm:21:quorum↵
T * * * * * * * * * * * * * * * 0

REM Check it all worked
iscsicli BindPersistentVolumes
iscsicli ListPersistentTargets
```

Figure 8.20 shows the results of running the previous commands and successfully attaching to the storage.

FIGURE 8.20
Attached
iSCSI disk

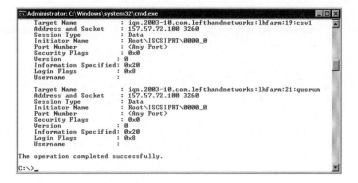

Clustered Virtual Machine Management

After you make a VM highly available, you can proactively move it between nodes by accessing the Failover Cluster Management console, selecting the appropriate VM instance below Services And Applications, and moving it to another node via either Live Migration or Quick Migration. Before the VMs can perform any useful work, however, you must turn them on.

To start a VM, expand Services And Applications, and click the VM instance to be started. Select the VM to be managed in the center pane, right-click, and select Start Virtual Machines (see Figure 8.21).

FIGURE 8.21
Available actions
for a stopped VM

Although the Failover Cluster Manager is fully integrated with the Hyper-V Manager (in that you can start, stop, and otherwise manage VMs from the Cluster MMC), the reverse is not true. The Hyper-V Manager isn't integrated with or aware of failover clustering. The Hyper-V Manager doesn't communicate with the cluster service to coordinate the state or status of a VM. To illustrate this point, try using the Hyper-V Manager to save state for a clustered VM on Windows Server 2008.

NOTE Failover clustering in Windows Server 2008 R2 respects control requests from the Hyper-V Manager and does not "interfere" with state change requests you might make, unlike in Windows Server 2008.

When the cluster service in Windows 2008 (not R2) detects that the VM isn't running, it will try to restart the VM. Depending on timing and other factors, it may restart the VM, mark it as "failed" with a restart attempt later (the default in Server 2008 is up to 15 minutes), or attempt to move the VM to another node in the cluster.

In Windows Server 2008, you should make VM state changes (Save, Shutdown, Turn Off) from within the Failover Cluster Manager to ensure proper cluster service integration. To change the state of a VM, select the appropriate VM instance below Services And Applications, highlight the VM you want to modify, and choose the appropriate action.

For both Windows Server 2008 and Windows Server 2008 R2, VM configuration changes other than state are still commonly accomplished via the Hyper-V Manager, which you can launch from within the Failover Cluster Manager. Select the appropriate VM instance below Services And Applications, and choose the action Manage VM.

NOTE System Center Virtual Machine Manager 2008 (see Chapter 11, "Using System Center Virtual Machine Manager") is tightly integrated with failover clustering and provides a virtualization management infrastructure and a console that you can use to manage VM configuration, state, and cluster capacity.

Summary

The configuration of highly available VMs has been vastly simplified by carefully constructed automation via the failover clustering feature integrated into Windows Server 2008 and Windows Server 2008 R2. You can create a simple failover cluster of Hyper-V–ready hosts in a matter of hours with proper preparation; doing so can help you meet the ever-increasing demands for robust computing infrastructure. With additional planning and testing, you can also create complex configurations with varied availability requirements, but such configurations will probably require a higher investment in properly trained people, good processes, and the right technology to meet availability goals.

Chapter 9

Understanding WMI, Scripting, and Hyper-V

It's fortunate that the technology underpinnings exist in Windows and Hyper-V to customize access to virtual machines for users, easily automate processes, and collect information about a virtualization environment. You can use command-line tools, batch files, and scripting languages to tailor solutions in Windows Server 2008 and Hyper-V to meet nearly any virtualization requirements.

This chapter examines many of the scenarios you may encounter that require more than standard tools and looks at some of the automation techniques you can use with Hyper-V. We'll look at the role of Windows Management Instrumentation (WMI) for managing Hyper-V and how you can use WMI from both VBScript and Windows PowerShell. Only a basic understanding of programming concepts is expected, and the chapter introduces PowerShell. Detailed scripting examples are shown in Chapter 10, "Automating Tasks."

We'll cover the following topics in this chapter:

- Common management tasks
- WMI overview
- Scripting technology overview
- PowerShell for newcomers
- Common elements of WMI scripts
- WMI Virtualization classes

Common Management Tasks

Virtualization administrators everywhere perform similar tasks in their environments that can be categorized into common groups:

- Provisioning
- Configuration management
- Access management
- Migration
- Backup and recovery
- Data collection and monitoring

You can use interactive tools such as the Hyper-V Manager, Task Manager, Task Scheduler, and System Center Virtual Machine Manager (SCVMM) for these administrative tasks. Interacting directly with these tools provides flexibility, but not always the highest efficiency.

System provisioning provides a great example of flexibility with sometimes lower efficiency. Many organizations have a mature process for acquiring, installing, and operating new systems. In these enterprises, an end user may need to complete an electronic form to request a new server. In the past, this request would trigger the purchase of a new physical system that might be online and available weeks or months later. With the advent of virtualization, you can create a new virtual machine (VM) in a matter of minutes, provided sufficient capacity exists in the environment. With VM provisioning, you can set up an automated system where users can submit a request for a new VM; a server is then created without an administrator intervening.

Data-collection tasks demonstrate the value of automation as well. You can display the individual Media Access Control (MAC) address of each virtual network adapter in the Hyper-V Manager by viewing each VM's settings individually (see Figure 9.1).

FIGURE 9.1
MAC address in the
Hyper-V Manager

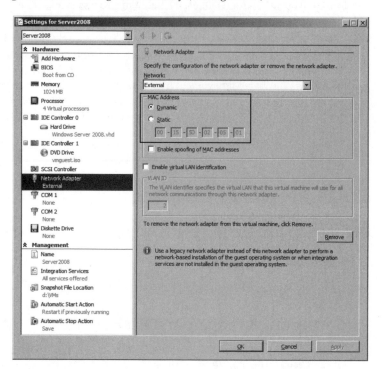

What if you need an audit of MAC addresses and their associated virtual local area networks (VLANs)? Clicking though the settings for each network interface card (NIC) on each VM and recording the addresses manually can take a lot of time and may not provide an accurate accounting due to errors or bad handwriting. You can more easily retrieve this information through a script-based query of the parent partition (see Figure 9.2), so why not create a time-saving automated report that you can use repeatedly?

FIGURE 9.2
MAC address listing using PowerShell Library

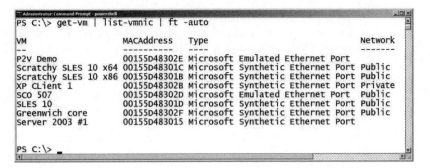

```
PS C:\> get-vm | list-vmnic | ft -auto

VM                    MACAddress    Type                               Network
--                    ----------    ----                               -------
P2V Demo              00155D48302E  Microsoft Emulated Ethernet Port
Scratchy SLES 10 x64  00155D48301C  Microsoft Synthetic Ethernet Port  Public
Scratchy SLES 10 x86  00155D48301B  Microsoft Synthetic Ethernet Port  Public
XP Client 1           00155D48302B  Microsoft Synthetic Ethernet Port  Private
SCO 507               00155D48302D  Microsoft Emulated Ethernet Port   Public
SLES 10               00155D48301D  Microsoft Synthetic Ethernet Port  Public
Greenwich core        00155D48302F  Microsoft Synthetic Ethernet Port  Public
Server 2003 #1        00155D483015  Microsoft Synthetic Ethernet Port


PS C:\> _
```

Not every task can be accomplished out of the box with Hyper-V—the useful information in Figure 9.2 actually requires an additional scripting library (we'll get to that!). The point is that time and quality pressures commonly drive administrators to automate tasks. You can follow two basic paths to automation and reporting with Hyper-V: customized scripts and commercial management tools.

Hyper-V was designed for optimal integration with Microsoft management tools (as well as third-party tools). Microsoft System Center Operations Manager (SCOM) and SCVMM together provide a fantastic management infrastructure to automate and collect data for physical and virtual systems that isn't available with the Hyper-V console alone. SCVMM includes capabilities for virtualization automation beyond what is available from custom scripts, including the following:

◆ Virtualization-specific task orientation

◆ Specialized PowerShell *cmdlets* (pronounced "commandlets") for virtualization management

◆ Script generation

◆ Heterogeneous virtualization platform management (Hyper-V, Virtual Server, and VMware ESX)

System Center tools allow you to meet enterprise response metrics for all aspects of system management. To maximize value, all enterprises using Windows should aim to use System Center tools.

In some situations, System Center tools are unavailable. In such cases, you may need other tools or custom scripts. Hyper-V has a rich interface through a virtualization WMI provider, accessible via scripts and numerous tools. This provider lets you control and monitor VMs and the physical host on which they run. Creating custom scripts via the WMI provider can give you more flexibility and portability than SCVMM. However, custom scripts are often more complex and lack the detailed error handling and high-quality code that comes with commercial software tools.

WMI Overview

The preferred method of administering Hyper-V programmatically is by leveraging the WMI-based APIs provided. The Hyper-V Manager, System Center Virtual Machine Manger, and nearly every other tool for manipulating Hyper-V leverages these APIs. WMI is Microsoft's implementation of an industry-wide initiative called Web-Based Enterprise Management (WBEM) that involves accessing and managing systems in an enterprise environment. WMI uses the Common Information Model (CIM) standard to represent system components. The CIM is maintained by the Distributed Management Task Force (DMTF), of which Microsoft is a member.

Some administrators consider WMI to be Microsoft's primary management-enabling technology for Windows. WMI enables access to many system components—from hardware all the way up to installed applications. You can use WMI to access event logs, operating system attributes, processes, installed applications, and much more. You can use it to easily start or stop processes on local or remote systems, reboot a system, inventory installed applications and patches, and even check the internal temperature of a server. Nearly everything you need to manage Hyper-V is available through WMI. More complex HyperCall APIs let developers implement integration components between VMs and the host OS, for example, but they aren't intended for use by administrators.

Nearly all Windows development tools and scripting languages can access WMI and use it to simplify the creation of tools and code for managing Hyper-V. Common scripting languages that you can use include Windows PowerShell, VBScript, JScript, and Perl. You can also use C/C++, C#, Visual Basic, and other compilable programming languages to create WMI-based tools. You can even access WMI from the command line using the WMI command-line interface (WMIC), which is included in Windows XP, Windows Server 2003, Windows Vista, Windows 7, Windows Server 2008, and Windows Server 2008 R2 (see Figure 9.3). WMI namespaces may be accessed remotely, enabling remote data-collection management.

FIGURE 9.3
Using WMIC to access Hyper-V from Windows XP

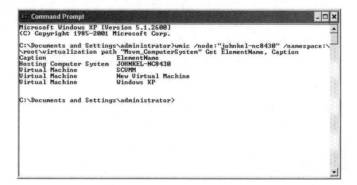

NOTE Because WMI has been an integral part of Windows for many years, you can create tools and scripts to manage Hyper-V that you can execute from earlier versions of Windows. It's possible for WMI-based Hyper-V management scripts to run from Windows 2000 and newer systems to manage remote Hyper-V hosts.

The hypervisor is managed by a service running in the parent partition and has no other connection to the outside world. This virtualization provider is the service that is the target for WMI calls for anything wanting to give instructions to the hypervisor (see Figure 9.4). The hypervisor itself has no access to network services and no understanding of user accounts—it's the management service that validates that the user is trying to perform a task.

FIGURE 9.4
WMI virtualization provider

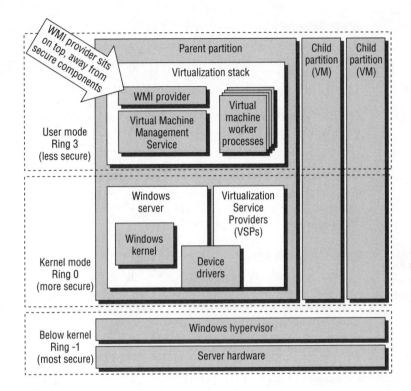

Accessing WMI

The key to unlocking the value of WMI is to understand where relevant information may lie. Windows offers more than 100 providers to access system components, including the event log, the Registry, performance counters, and so on. Software developers—including Microsoft—can add new providers, and that is what has been done for Hyper-V. The virtualization WMI provider exposes a rich interface that lets you monitor and control Hyper-V and the virtual environment.

WMI organizes information on a given computer into namespaces. Information about the computer's hard disk, operating system, hotfixes, and so on, are found in the `root\cimV2` namespace. Hyper-V uses the `root\virtualization` namespace.

Properties of objects that are accessible through WMI (like a VM name) are organized into groups called *classes*. Hotfixes have a class, processors have a class, and VMs have a class named `MSVM_ComputerSystem`. There may be one or more instances of an object class. For example, on a system with four VMs, there are four instances of the `MSVM_ComputerSystem` object, one for each VM (and a fifth for the parent partition).

WMI classes for a provider are commonly accessed via the corresponding namespace. The namespace that corresponds to the classes made available by the virtualization provider is `\root\virtualization`. Scripting tools access WMI through a WMI scripting library. The WMI scripting library provides the set of script-enabling objects to access the WMI infrastructure.

WMI Security

WMI uses Windows security to validate logon information on local computers and for remote access. WMI enforces security for resources at the level of individual namespaces. For the purposes of all WMI-related examples in this book, it's assumed that you'll execute them with full administrative access to the parent partition and the underlying WMI namespaces.

NOTE The security check for WMI occurs only when a user logs in. Changes to user access (including access revocation) take effect the next time a user logs in.

Accessing the Virtualization Namespace

You use similar syntax to access the virtualization namespace for nearly any tool or language. Establishing a connection to the namespace is the first step and generally requires referencing or selecting \root\virtualization.

WMI Scripting Tools and Resources

By knowing what tools and resources are available, you can simplify the process of creating custom scripts and tools with WMI. The first and most important resource is the online Microsoft TechNet Script Center (http://www.microsoft.com/technet/scriptcenter/). The Script Center contains valuable samples and guides for Microsoft-focused administrative scripting in a variety of scripting languages, including Windows PowerShell and VBScript.

If you have little scripting experience, you can access online scripting tutorials. The Script Center also has several tools that can speed the creation of WMI-centric scripts and tools. Scriptomatic 2.0, PowerShell Scriptomatic, and WMI Code Creator let you browse available WMI namespaces and generate simple code examples to access data and execute methods.

Browsing the Virtualization Namespace

Accessing and browsing the elements of the virtualization namespace is an excellent hands-on approach to understanding how to use it. You can use the WMI Code Creator for this purpose. It's available from Microsoft TechNet at http://technet.microsoft.com/ (search for "WMI Code Creator"). Follow these steps:

1. To access the namespace, first download, unpack, and run the tool WMICodeCreator.exe. The WMI Code Creator provides several capabilities, including the ability to generate code that you can use to do the following:

    ◆ Query for WMI data

    ◆ Execute a method in WMI

    ◆ Receive an event

    ◆ Browse WMI namespaces

2. When the WMI Code Creator starts, it enumerates available WMI namespaces and classes on the local computer. By default, it starts on the Query For Data From A WMI Class tab, displaying the commonly used namespace root\CIMV2 (see Figure 9.5).

FIGURE 9.5
WMI Code Creator
default screen

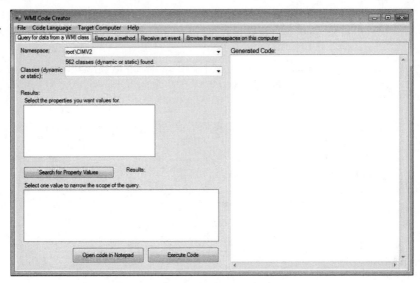

TIP The WMI namespace root\CIMV2 is a fantastically useful namespace that enables access to a host of system properties worthy of additional investigation.

3. You can access available WMI namespaces in WMI Code Creator using the Namespace pull-down menu. Select the root\virtualization namespace and choose the Msvm_ ComputerSystem class in the pull-down menu to display the properties of the class (see Figure 9.6).

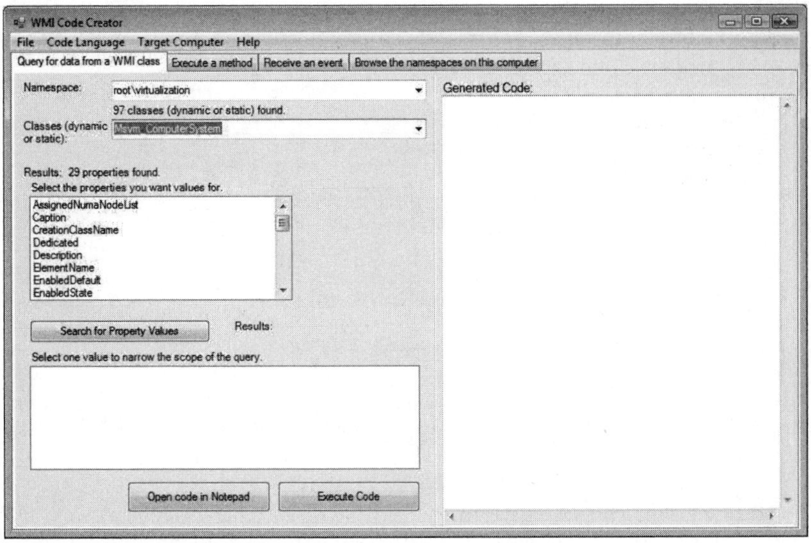

FIGURE 9.6
Virtualization
provider and
the Msvm_
ComputerSystem
class

Msvm_ComputerSystem represents the parent partition/hosting Hyper-V system in the namespace. Using this class, you can discover and alter general information about VMs, such as their name and state.

4. To show the friendly name for a VM (for example), select ElementName in the Results box, and click the Search For Property Values button. The names of each VM on the local system are displayed (see Figure 9.7).

FIGURE 9.7
ElementName =
friendly virtual
machine name

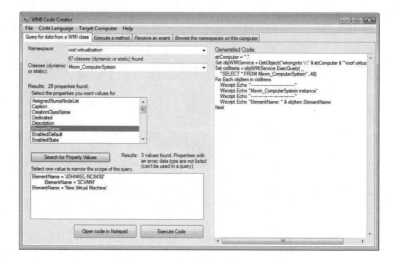

Note that the parent partition (JOHNKEL-NC8430) is also listed as a VM. This is because it runs on top of the hypervisor just as other VMs do (remember that the parent partition is a special class of VM). Changing the selection of properties to include both ElementName and Caption shows both sets of values (you can multiselect by holding the Ctrl key while clicking additional properties, as shown in Figure 9.8).

FIGURE 9.8
Caption and
ElementName

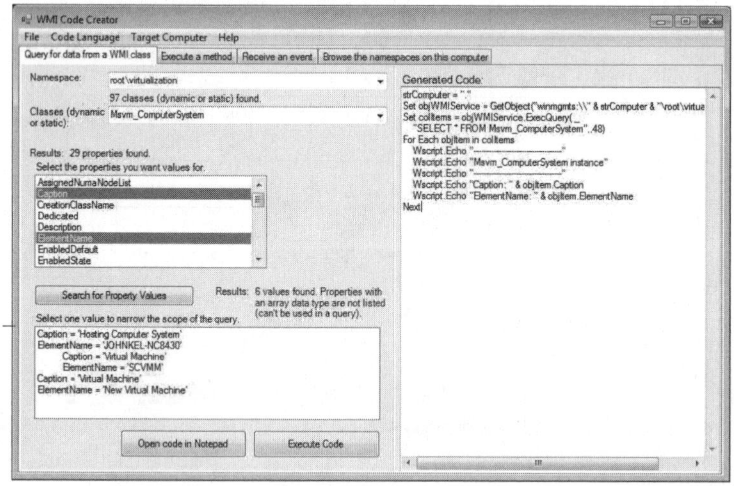

Browsing the WMI virtualization namespace can help you develop an understanding of which classes and elements contain useful information, but WMI Code Creator does a great deal more. On the right side of the screen, you can see example generated code, which you can save and use to create more complicated scripts or tools that use the properties you select. Here's an example:

```
strComputer = "."
Set objWMIService = GetObject _
    ("winmgmts:\\" & strComputer & "\root\virtualization")
Set colItems = objWMIService.ExecQuery( _
    "SELECT * FROM Msvm_ComputerSystem",,48)
For Each objItem in colItems
    Wscript.Echo "---------------------------------"
    Wscript.Echo "Msvm_ComputerSystem instance"
    Wscript.Echo "---------------------------------"
    Wscript.Echo "Caption: " & objItem.Caption
    Wscript.Echo "ElementName: " & objItem.ElementName
Next
```

Clicking the Execute Code button executes the sample code (in this case, VBScript) using the Windows Script Host. The code outputs the display name (`ElementName`) and type (`Caption`) of each virtualized system on the local Hyper-V host. The results of executing the code above are shown in Figure 9.9.

FIGURE 9.9
Sample script output

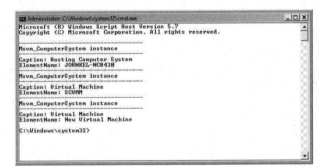

WMI Code Creator can generate example code for VBScript, Visual Basic .NET, and C#. As noted, it has additional capabilities that we won't discuss further. To generate sample code for other languages, you can use Scriptomatic 2.0 from the TechNet site. Scriptomatic has similar WMI code-generating capabilities for VBScript, Perl, Jscript, and Python. The PowerShell Scriptomatic has similar capabilities and generates code in Windows PowerShell. The Scriptomatic tools lack element search/browsing as well as method execution and event handling found in the WMI Code Creator.

Scripting Technology Overview

Before diving further into what you can accomplish with scripting, let's take a step back and review scripting in general. A *scripting language* is a programming language used to control applications or other system components. In this way, scripts are different from other programs: they're sets of instructions to a computer that run tasks implemented in other programs. Scripting languages have many of the features found in full-scale programming languages—storing results in variables, running commands only if conditions are met, and so on.

Windows administrators commonly use batch files (.BAT or .CMD) to string together commands that can be entered at the command prompt. VBScript or other Windows Script Host (WSH) dependant scripting languages have been available for years to perform complex administrative automation that can more flexibly interact with systems and applications.

Microsoft released Windows PowerShell in 2006 to provide a more extensible and scriptable command-line shell for administrators. Windows PowerShell includes integration with the Microsoft .NET Framework. Although older scripting technologies may not include all the bells and whistles of PowerShell, they're still useful for automating tasks with Hyper-V. Following are some of the common scripting languages for Windows.

Visual Basic Script

Microsoft launched Visual Basic Script (also called VBScript or VBS) in the mid-1990s. It initially targeted web developers for *Active Scripting* (formerly known as *Active-X* scripting) along with JScript and third-party Active Scripting tools. It lets you automate routine tasks using the WSH. VBScript examples for administration are common and relatively easy to find on the Internet. New versions of VBScript and other Active Scripting tools aren't planned. Contemporary tools that use the .NET Framework (PowerShell and Visual Basic .NET) will replace VBScript and other WSH-dependant languages.

NOTE   VBScript, JScript, Perl, and other scripting tools without a dependency on the .NET Framework still have value. A Server Core installation of Windows Server 2008 doesn't include the .NET Framework, and thus PowerShell is unavailable for automation tasks. The great news is that this changed with Server Core for Windows Server 2008 R2! You can install and use PowerShell in Server Core for R2, as well as in Hyper-V Server 2008 R2. Active Scripting tools continue to be used because of their portability and widespread compatibility. VBScript and PowerShell automation scripts are the focus of Chapter 10, "Automating Tasks."

JScript

JScript is the Microsoft dialect of ECMAScript (originally JavaScript). It uses the WSH in the same fashion as VBScript, and you can use it in a similar way to automate administrative tasks. JScript seems to be used less frequently by administrators than VBScript, and scripting examples for Hyper-V automation aren't included in this book. If you desire, you should be able to adapt WMI-intensive VBScript code samples easily to JScript.

Perl, Python, and Others

The WSH can use scripting engines other than VBScript and JScript—including Perl and Python. It's not uncommon to see administrators taking advantage of Active State Perl for automation; but again, we won't cover WSH samples other than VBScript.

Command-Line Tools

Sadly, few traditional command-line tools ship with Hyper-V to automate common administrative tasks. You can use WMIC to interrogate and affect Hyper-V. A brief WMIC command-line example with functionality similar to that of the WMI Code Creator sample case is shown here, and the results appear in Figure 9.10 (this is similar to Figure 9.2, but should make more sense now):

FIGURE 9.10

WMIC accessing Hyper-V information

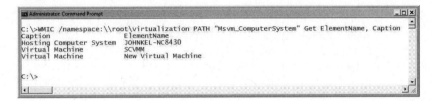

```
C:\>WMIC /namespace:\\root\virtualization PATH "Msvm_ComputerSystem" Get ElementName, Caption
Caption                          ElementName
Hosting Computer System          JOHNKEL-NC8430
Virtual Machine                  SCVMM
Virtual Machine                  New Virtual Machine

C:\>
```

```
WMIC /namespace:\\root\virtualization PATH "Msvm_ComputerSystem"↵
   Get ElementName, Caption
```

WMIC includes an interactive shell that you can invoke by typing **WMIC** from a command prompt. You can access integrated help for WMIC by typing **/?** from within the shell. WMIC doesn't have the flexibility of other scripting tools, but it does enable command-line access to Hyper-V via WMI. Combined with batch files (a form of scripting), WMIC can provide the required WMI connection to Hyper-V and automation support.

TIP   WMIC is the predecessor to PowerShell, and it's an underutilized administrative tool included in Windows XP through Windows Server 2008—including Server Core. WMIC defaults to the root\CIMV2 namespace, which includes access to all manner of system information.

Windows PowerShell

Windows PowerShell is a scripting language and interactive shell designed especially for system administration. Introduced by Microsoft in 2006, it's customizable with complete access to the .NET Framework. Task-focused *cmdlets* allow you to manage systems from the command line as well as access key data stores, including the Registry and WMI, using a single, consistent syntax.

You can manage event logs, services, processes, and applications with PowerShell. The extensible interface lets you create integrated custom tools and utilities, such as the powerful virtualization-management cmdlets included with SCVMM 2008 (covered in Chapter 11, "System Center Virtual Machine Manager").

PowerShell 2.0 is installed by default in Windows Server 2008 R2 and Windows 7. PowerShell 1.0 is an installable feature that's included in Windows Server 2008. PowerShell 2.0 is also available as a separate download for Windows XP (SP2 or later), Windows Server 2003 (SP1 or later), and Windows Vista.

PowerShell for Newcomers

Windows PowerShell 1.0 was part of an effort to provide a comprehensive and rational command-line environment for administration within Microsoft Windows. It can be argued that the command shell within Windows (cmd.exe) has changed little since the introduction of DOS. Although cmd.exe has in fact progressed, it still lacks features common to advanced shells in UNIX, Linux, and other operating systems.

PowerShell addresses many of the shortcomings of the "heritage" Windows command shell while maintaining a reasonable level of consistency and compatibility with it. You can execute existing, familiar stand-alone programs (chkdsk.exe, ping.exe, regedt32.exe, shutdown.exe, and others) from within Windows PowerShell; this command compatibility means you can largely abandon the Windows cmd.exe shell and use Windows PowerShell instead.

> **NOTE**   PowerShell uses the term *command* to mean any single instruction—which can include cmdlets, script files, blocks of script stored as functions, aliases, external programs, or combinations of these grouped together into a pipeline using the vertical bar or pipe character (|).

Windows PowerShell includes new *cmdlets* (pronounced "commandlets"). Cmdlets are small commands named in a consistent way that you can string together into pipelines to create more complex commands that produce customized results. These modular cmdlets with their pipeline "glue" are the real value of PowerShell to you. Cmdlet pipelines can be short and simple or long and complex, depending on the results desired. Saving complex collections of cmdlets as scripts to execute from the command line is common (similar to saving collections of cmd.exe commands in a .BAT or .CMD file). Windows PowerShell scripts are typically named with a .PS1 extension.

This section of the chapter is an effort to shed light on the basic items you need to be a functional administrator in an increasingly PowerShell world. PowerShell's flexibility gives you multiple ways to perform the same task (as you may notice). We won't present different approaches to using PowerShell in many cases—we'll leave alternate (and sometimes more concise) coding examples to more comprehensive PowerShell resources outside of this book. Our goal in this section is to enable you to be functional, not to strive for mastery. If you're already familiar with Windows PowerShell, you can skip ahead to the "Common Elements of WMI Scripts" section of the chapter.

PowerShell Installation and Setup

PowerShell ships in the box with Windows Server 2008 and can be added as a feature through Server Manager. You install features in a similar manner to server roles by starting Server Manager, selecting Features, and selecting the Add Features option from the Action menu (see Figure 9.11).

After you install PowerShell in Windows Server 2008, you can start it either by opening a command window and typing **PowerShell** or by selecting Windows PowerShell from the Start menu. In Windows Server 2008 R2, PowerShell can also be started using the "QuickLaunch" icon on the taskbar.

> **NOTE**   Windows PowerShell 2.0 is installed by default in Windows Server 2008 R2 and Windows. You can download and install PowerShell 2.0 for older versions of Windows as well. Remember that all versions require the .NET Framework version 2.0, but some features of PowerShell 2.0 rely on the .NET Framework 3.0, including the Graphical PowerShell feature and the Out-GridView cmdlet. PowerShell 1.0 scripts should run unmodified in Version 2.0.

FIGURE 9.11
Selecting
PowerShell in
Server Manager

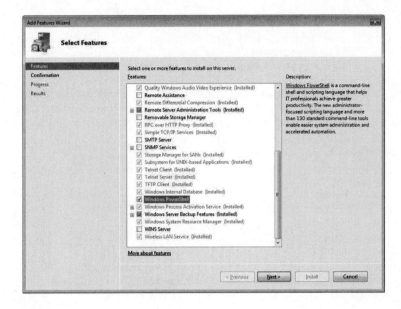

PowerShell is integrated with Windows security features included in Windows Server 2008/R2 and Windows Vista/7, including User Account Control (UAC). UAC is intended to improve system security by limiting the privileges of applications. If you enable UAC, you may find that when you run PowerShell (or the `cmd.exe` shell) you don't have sufficient rights to complete many common tasks. Disabling UAC eliminates this security block but isn't advisable in many environments. You can disable UAC through the Control Panel by clicking the User Accounts icon (see Figure 9.12). Note that turning UAC on or off requires a system reboot.

FIGURE 9.12
Disabling UAC

NOTE User Account Control has been enhanced in Windows Server 2008 R2 and Windows 7 to provide increased granularity. The UAC controls in Windows Server 2008 R2 include a slider to select your desired level of "annoyance," rather than the Boolean on or off choices shown in Figure 9.12 from Windows Server 2008.

An alternative to disabling UAC is to start PowerShell with elevated privileges. To do so, right-click the Windows PowerShell selection on the Start menu (or the Quick Start icon) to reveal additional startup options, including Run As Administrator (see Figure 9.13).

FIGURE 9.13
Right-clicking
to Run As
Administrator

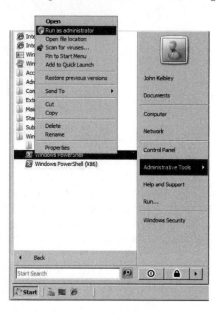

After you start PowerShell, you're greeted with a DOS-like window with a slightly altered prompt that starts with PS (see Figure 9.14).

FIGURE 9.14
PowerShell upon
starting

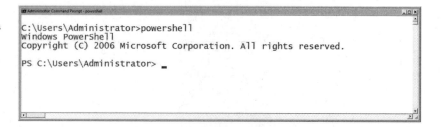

```
C:\Users\Administrator>powershell
Windows PowerShell
Copyright (C) 2006 Microsoft Corporation. All rights reserved.

PS C:\Users\Administrator> _
```

Numerous startup options are available for PowerShell, including parameters to display help (PowerShell Help), suppress the logo, specify the data input and output formats, and other options.

Integration with UAC is only one example of the secure design of PowerShell. The execution of stand-alone scripts is blocked as part of the initial installation (see Figure 9.15).

FIGURE 9.15

Restricted execution of scripts

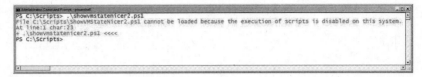

To enable scripts, you must change the execution policy using the Set-ExecutionPolicy cmdlet:

```
Set-ExecutionPolicy -ExecutionPolicy "RemoteSigned"
```

This cmdlet allows saved scripts (.PS1 files) to be executed without having been digitally signed. Note that unless you are running PowerShell as Administrator (or have disabled UAC), you may be prevented from changing the execution policy.

NOTE The default installation of PowerShell V2 in Windows Server 2008 R2 is handy, but may not meet all of your needs since it does not include the Integrated Scripting Environment features. Some cool capabilities (like Active Directory integration, graphical script editing, and the useful Out-Gridview cmdlet) can be accessed by using the Add Feature Wizard to install the Windows PowerShell Integrated Scripting Environment (ISE).

Finding Your Way Around PowerShell

PowerShell is installed, rights are escalated, scripts can run, the shell is up and ready to go—now what? Understanding how to investigate the secrets of PowerShell and use cmdlets is the core of being a functional PowerShell user.

Verb-Noun Format for Cmdlets

The names of cmdlets native to PowerShell are constructed using an easy-to-remember verb-noun format. A cmdlet that retrieves information commonly starts with the word *get* and a dash, and ends with a description of the information desired. Typing **get-process** returns information about running processes, and **get-service** returns information about configured services. For Hyper-V, **get-WMIObject** is critical because it retrieves information using WMI. Commonly used PowerShell verbs include add, clear, convert, export, format get, import, invoke, join, measure, move, new, out, remove, select, set, start, update, where, and write.

Asking PowerShell for Help

PowerShell has integrated, flexible help that you can access by using the same verb-noun format and typing **get-help**. Typing **get-help** by itself displays general help information for using PowerShell. Following the cmdlet with another cmdlet (get-help get-WMIObject, for example) displays help information specific to that cmdlet (see Figure 9.16).

Detailed examples for how to use each cmdlet are available by specifying the -examples parameter with get-help (for example, get-help get-WMIObject -examples). You can retrieve more information by using other parameters or by following a cmdlet with -? (for example, get-WMIobject -?).

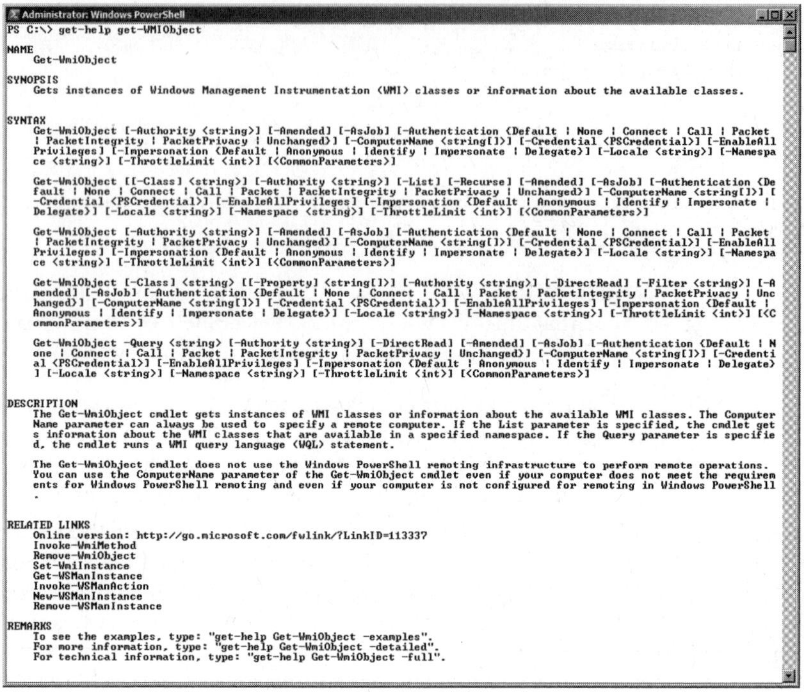

FIGURE 9.16 Output of `get-help get-WMIObject`

NOTE This is an example of PowerShell's consistency. All cmdlets use `-?` to provide help information. There is no question of whether to use `/H`, `-help`, or `-?`.

Often, help information is too extensive to fit on a single screen. Following a request for help with a pipe to `more` can make information more usable (`get-WMIobject -? | more` or `get-help get-WMIobject -full | more`). The `help` function is available and equivalent to `get-help`, except it already includes logic for paging. Typing **`help`** followed by a cmdlet name pages through help information (`help get-WMIobject` is the same as `Get-Help Get-WMIObject | more`).

The integrated help is extensive and not limited to individual cmdlets. To access a list of help topics, type **`get-help about*`**. (Note that there is no space between `about` and `*`.)

NOTE Hang on! Didn't we say PowerShell uses a verb-noun format? What about `help` and `more`? They don't use that format. PowerShell uses aliases (and some functions like `more`) to let you use commands that are familiar in CMD or UNIX shells. The `Set-Location` cmdlet has an alias of CD. `More` is slightly more complicated.

Finding Commands, Aliases, and Members

The consistent verb-noun format isn't always enough magic to help you find or remember the right cmdlet to complete a task. Finding cmdlets is simplified with the `get-command` cmdlet. Available cmdlets can be filtered, listed, and sorted in a number of convenient ways including by verb, noun, command type, and other criteria. Perhaps you need to understand all the cmdlets available for manipulating services. Typing **`get-command -noun service`** creates such a list (see Figure 9.17).

FIGURE 9.17
Cmdlets for
services

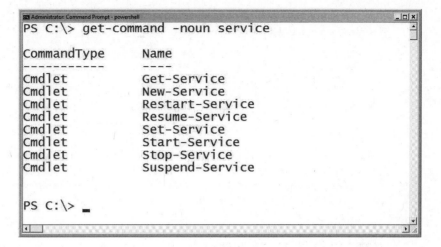

```
PS C:\> get-command -noun service

CommandType        Name
-----------        ----
Cmdlet             Get-Service
Cmdlet             New-Service
Cmdlet             Restart-Service
Cmdlet             Resume-Service
Cmdlet             Set-Service
Cmdlet             Start-Service
Cmdlet             Stop-Service
Cmdlet             Suspend-Service


PS C:\> _
```

But knowing the proper cmdlets isn't enough: Understanding the information they expose is key as well. Everything passed to or returned by any PowerShell command is an object. With CMD, if you store text in an environment variable, the text is all there is. In PowerShell, if you store text, it's a .NET string object with a collection of properties such as `length` and methods such as `PadRight()`. You can expose the information accessible through a cmdlet or other object by using `get-member`. Piping any cmdlet to `get-member` lists the component information available. Typing **`get-service | get-member`** shows the methods and properties associated with the cmdlet.

Aliases are abbreviations or alternate names for running cmdlets in PowerShell to save typing. The `sort-object` cmdlet, for example, has the `sort` alias defined. `GWMI` is an alias for `Get-WMIObject`, which is used extensively to manage Hyper-V. You can generate a listing of aliases by typing **`get-alias`** or **`get-command -commandtype alias`**.

NOTE   Aliases can reduce typing, but PowerShell also includes a tab-completion feature so you can avoid typing long cmdlet names and parameters. For example, typing **`get-h`** followed by the Tab key completes the typing of **`get-help`**.

Making Things Work in PowerShell

PowerShell includes commands and functions to perform all the familiar programming tasks: accepting input, creating output, evaluating information, looping, and navigating through data stores (including file systems, the Registry, variables, and more). Keep in mind while you're using PowerShell that it's insensitive to case (unless you ask it to differentiate)—uppercase and lowercase are treated the same.

RUNNING EXISTING COMMANDS

As noted earlier, you can execute existing Windows commands from within PowerShell. You can enter multiple independent commands on the same line if you separate them with a semi-colon (`;`). With `cmd.exe`, individual commands you type into the same shell windows can also be entered on the same line but are separated by an ampersand (&). This means that typing commands one after the other like this

```
C:
cd \logs
Dir
```

has the same result in PowerShell as the following:

```
C:; cd \logs; dir
```

WARNING   Caution! Some Windows commands have been "replaced" in PowerShell by roughly equivalent aliases or cmdlets. In PowerShell, Del, for example, is an alias for the Remove-Item cmdlet, which does a great deal more than delete files and behaves differently (including deleting directories, Registry items, certificates, and other objects).

Common Cmdlet Parameters

Different cmdlets are intended to perform different functions, but the standard syntax for PowerShell cmdlets means they often have common options. Parameters common to all cmdlets are listed in Table 9.1.

TABLE 9.1:   Some Common PowerShell Cmdlet Parameters

PARAMETER	DESCRIPTION*
-Verbose	Asks the cmdlet for more detailed execution information than the default provides
-Debug	Asks the cmdlet to provide debugging information
-ErrorAction	Specifies how to handle errors: Continue (default), Stop, SilentlyContinue, Inquire
-ErrorVariable	Specifies the variable to contain error information (beyond the standard $error)
-OutVariable	Specifies the variable that contains output
-OutBuffer	Specifies the number of objects to buffer before calling the next cmdlet in a pipeline
-WhatIf	Shows what happens if the cmdlet is executed, without actually executing the cmdlet (only for cmdlets that alter system state)
-Confirm	Prompts you before the cmdlet executes (only for cmdlets that alter system state)

*For more information enter **Get-Help about_CommonParameters** in PowerShell*

Not all common parameters affect all cmdlets. `-WhatIf` and `-Confirm` are useful only for cmdlets that make changes to a system. `-Verbose` works only for cmdlets that support increased details.

PIPELINES

A *pipeline* is a string of cmdlets executed in sequence where objects are passed for processing. Objects resulting from the execution of the first command in the pipeline become the input for the next command. Nearly every useful task completed in PowerShell uses pipelines. As mentioned earlier, commands in the pipeline are separate by a vertical bar (|) also sometimes referred to as a *pipe*.

Pipes are also used in the `cmd.exe` shell (type **`<filename> | more`** to display a file one screen at a time), but they're less useful. Piping output in the **`cmd.exe`** shell is limited to text and doesn't include the benefits of an object model as with PowerShell. `get-service | get-member`, mentioned earlier, helps to illustrate this point. `get-service` has specific member components that are part of a model that `get-member` understands and can consume. By calling `get-service` and passing the object created by the call to `get-member` as input, `get-member` can consume information that is part of the object.

FILTERING WITH *WHERE-OBJECT*

Administrative tasks commonly require that the cmdlet process only a subset of the information returned. You may need to apply filtering to tasks such as starting or stopping particular services or finding processes that use large amounts of RAM. The `where-object` cmdlet enables filtering of information. Including `where-object` as part of a pipeline can create useful filters by testing the values of objects. For example, you can use `get-service` to list all services on a system. Adding a filter for services that include "Hyper-V" in the display name yields a much shorter list (see Figure 9.18):

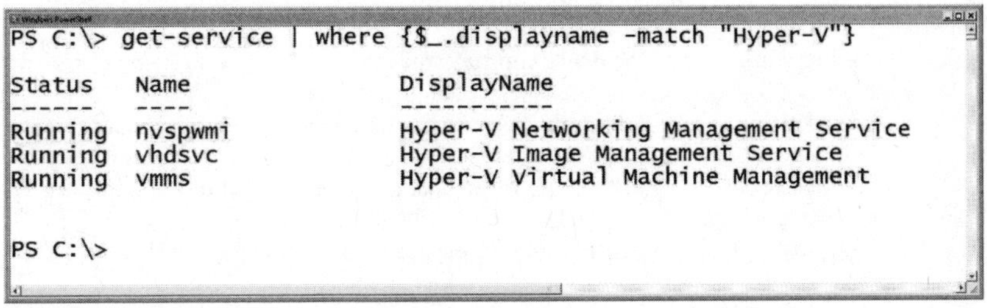

FIGURE 9.18
Services found via filter

```
PS C:\> get-service | where {$_.displayname -match "Hyper-V"}

Status    Name              DisplayName
------    ----              -----------
Running   nvspwmi           Hyper-V Networking Management Service
Running   vhdsvc            Hyper-V Image Management Service
Running   vmms              Hyper-V Virtual Machine Management


PS C:\>
```

```
get-service | where-object {$_.displayname -match "Hyper-V"}
```

TIP Where-Object has an alias of Where; they can be used interchangeably.

NOTE `$_` is a variable that represents the current pipeline object. It's commonly seen and used for filtering with `where-object`, looping with `foreach-object`, and making decisions with `switch`.

Showing filtered information from a cmdlet is only part of what you may need to accomplish. You can pass filtered output to yet another cmdlet for action to be taken. You can make the previous example more functional by extending the pipeline:

```
get-service |
where {$_.displayname -match "Hyper-V"} | Start-Service
```

NOTE   As mentioned earlier, `Where` is the associated alias for the `Where-Object` cmdlet and can be used to shorten filter statements.

The numerous comparison operators you can use with `Where` and `Where-Object` are listed in Table 9.2.

TABLE 9.2   Some Comparison Operators in PowerShell

OPERATOR	DESCRIPTION*	EXAMPLE	RESULT
-eq	Equal	10 -eq 10	True
-ne	Not equal	10 -ne 10	False
-gt	Greater than	10 -gt 10	False
-ge	Greater than or equal to	10 -ge 10	True
-lt	Less than	10 -lt 10	False
-le	Less than or equal to	10 -le 10	True
-like	Wildcard comparison	"one" -like "o*"	True
-notlike	Wildcard comparison	"one" -notlike "o*"	False
-match	Regular expression comparison	"book" -match "oo"	True
-notmatch	Regular expression comparison	"book" -notmatch "oo"	False
-contains	Includes identical value	"mooo" -contains "moo"	True
-notcontains	Does not include identical value	"mooo" -notcontains "oink"	True
-replace	Changes specified elements	"Moo Moo" -replace "Moo", "Oink"	Oink Oink

*For more information enter `Get-help about_comparison_operators` in PowerShell

NOTE   Remember that PowerShell isn't case sensitive, so comparison by default disregards case. Adding the letter **c** to the front of a comparison operator (`-cmatch` instead of `-match`) enforces case sensitivity.

DECISION MAKING

PowerShell includes common comparison tools like if and switch (case statement). You can use comparison operators (already shown) with if. Later in the chapter, we'll cover the numeric codes representing the execution state of a VM. Following is an example of how to evaluate state using if:

```
if ($state_num -ne 2)
{
    Write-Host "Virtual Machine is not in the Running State"
}
else
{
    Write-Host " Virtual Machine is running"
}
```

More than one VM execution state exists; and although you can nest if statements, the code may be hard to read. You can use switch to simplify decision-making:

```
switch ($state_num)
{
            2           {$State_text = "Running"}
            3           {$State_text = "PowerOff"}
            4           {$State_text = "ShuttingDown"}
            10          {$State_text = "Reset"}
            32768       {$State_text = "Paused"}
            32769       {$State_text = "Saved"}
            32770       {$State_text = "Starting"}
            32771       {$State_text = "SnapshotInProgress"}
            32772       {$State_text = "Migrating"}
            32773       {$State_text = "Saving"}
            32774       {$State_text = "Stopping"}
            32776       {$State_text = "Pausing"}
            32777       {$State_text = "Resuming"}
            Default     {$State_text = "Unknown"}

}
```

USING VARIABLES

PowerShell allows for the use of variables like other languages. Variables are preceded by the dollar sign ($), and you can assign values using the familiar equal sign (=):

```
$i = 1
```

A variable can contain a simple object—1 in the previous example is an integer—or complex objects. A single property of an object can be assigned to a variable, and multiple objects—the output from a cmdlet, for example—can be stored in a single variable. You can assign a list of the processes on a system (for instance) and access it later:

```
$Processes = Get-Process
```

Cmdlets commonly return a collection, or *array*, of objects. The variable $Processes holds multiple entries—one for each process returned by Get-Process (and accessible by an array index or subscript):

```
write-host $Processes[0]
```

NOTE The write-host cmdlet isn't necessary here, but we include it to make a point. You can also display the contents of the variable simply by typing **$Processes[0]**.

Each instance of a process within $Processes contains accessible member properties. You can access these elements by using the member name, as shown in Figure 9.19, which displays the service name of one instance:

```
write-host $Processes[0].Name
```

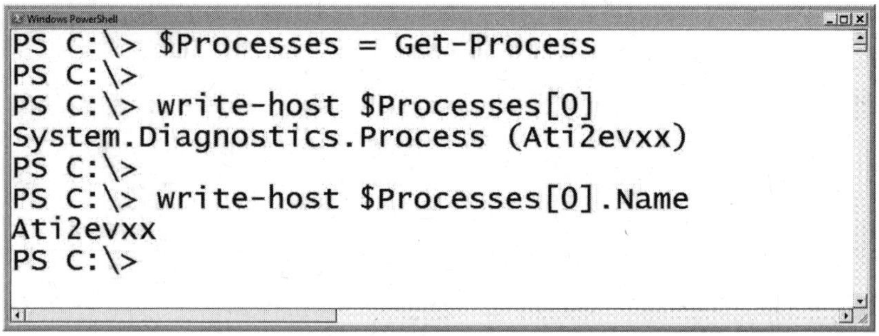

FIGURE 9.19
Accessing Information in a collection

```
PS C:\> $Processes = Get-Process
PS C:\>
PS C:\> write-host $Processes[0]
System.Diagnostics.Process (Ati2evxx)
PS C:\>
PS C:\> write-host $Processes[0].Name
Ati2evxx
PS C:\>
```

PowerShell sets numerous important predefined variables. You can find information for these by typing **help about_automatic_variables** in the shell. One valuable predefined variable, mentioned previously, is $_,which represents the current pipeline object. $_ is often used in pipelines or other code with where-object, switch, and foreach-object, as in this example (shown previously):

```
get-service | where-object {$_.displayname -match "Hyper-V"}
```

LOOPING

As in other coding languages, the cmdlets for, foreach, while and do/while let you iterate through data or repeat an operation until a condition is met:

For *Loop*

You use for to create a loop that runs commands in a script block while a specified condition evaluates to true. The format of a for loop is as follows:

```
for (<init>; <condition>; <repeat>) {<script_block>}
```

The following sample shows a simple for loop that prints out a sequence of numbers:

```
for ($i = 10; $i -ge 0; $i--)
```

```
{
    write-host "Countdown: $i"
}
```

Foreach *Loop*

The `foreach` statement provides `for` loop functionality for stepping through a series of values in a collection of items (array). `Foreach` can be more useful than `for` in PowerShell given its object-focused nature. Looping through a collection that is assigned to a variable is common and made simple by `foreach`:

```
foreach ($<item> in $<collection>){<command_block>}
```

Examples later in the chapter demonstrate how to use `foreach` to change the state of VMs. The following sample is adapted from that code:

```
$VMs = Get-WMIObject -Namespace root\virtualization ↵
-Class Msvm_ComputerSystem
foreach ($VM in $VMs)
{
    write-host "VM Name:"    $VM.ElementName
}
```

In this example, the output of the `Get-WMIObject` cmdlet is assigned to `$VMs`, which becomes the set of information to be processed. You don't need to first assign the output of a cmdlet to a variable in order to use `foreach`. The collection or array to be processed may be included as part of the `foreach` statement:

```
foreach ($VM in Get-WMIObject -Namespace root\virtualization ↵
-Class Msvm_ComputerSystem)
{
    write-host "VM Name:"    $VM.ElementName
}
```

In either case, the output is identical.

NOTE   There is also a `foreach-object` cmdlet (with an associated `foreach` alias) that is different from the `foreach` statement. `foreach-object` allows you to loop through each instance of an object as part of a pipeline. You can learn more about `foreach-object` on your own, or check out the examples in Chapter 10.

While *and* do/while

`While` and do/while are loops that execute while a condition is true. The difference between them is the point at which the condition is evaluated. `While` checks a condition before entering the loop and may not enter the loop:

```
while (<condition>){<command_block>}
```

do/while executes the loop first and then evaluates the condition. A do/while loop always executes at least once:

```
do {<command_block>} while (<condition>)
```

You can see the difference between while and do/while in the following sample code. In each case, the variable $i is initialized to 10 before entering the loop. Because the value of $i is already 10, the while loop doesn't execute:

```
$i = 10
while($i -lt 10) {
    write-host "The value is " $i
    $i++
}
```

The check for the do loop is at the end, so the loop is executed once, even though the condition is false:

```
$i = 10
do {
    write-host "The value is " $i
    $i++
} while($i -lt 10)
```

While and do/while can be useful in managing various aspects of VM configuration (waiting for the VM to be in a specific state, for instance).

CREATING FUNCTIONS

You can group pieces of PowerShell code into blocks as functions. You call functions similarly to cmdlets by typing the name of the function. Functions can accept input as arguments or values passed through a pipeline. Unlike functions in other languages, PowerShell functions return all output to the caller of the function (VBScript and C programmers may expect only specifically designated values to be returned). Functions must be defined before being called, so they're typically first in PowerShell script files.

To create a function, you wrap and name a block of code as follows:

```
Function Say_Hi
{
    write-host "Hello World"
}
```

You can then call the function Say_Hi from within PowerShell (see Figure 9.20).

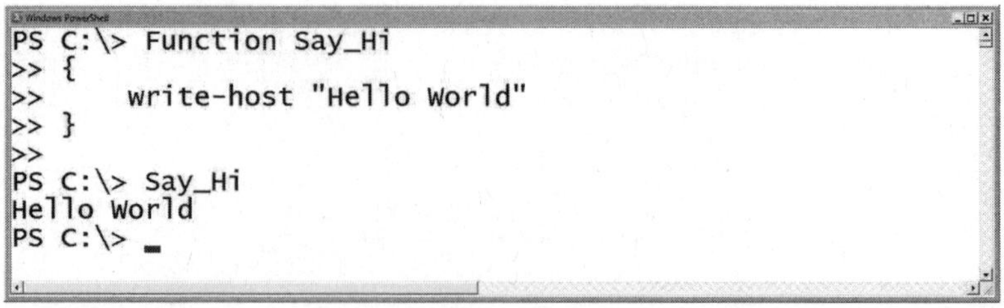

FIGURE 9.20
Calling a pre-defined script function

```
PS C:\> Function Say_Hi
>> {
>>     write-host "Hello World"
>> }
>>
PS C:\> Say_Hi
Hello World
PS C:\>
```

A more useful (Hyper-V related) example creates a function to show the state of VMs running on the local system (it's based on a code example shown later in the chapter):

```
Function Show-VM
{
write-host ""
write-host "Name                    Description↵
                  State"
write-host "-------------------- -----------↵
---------------------- -------------"
foreach ($VM in Gwmi -Namespace root\virtualization ↵

-Query "Select * from Msvm_ComputerSystem")
{   $name = $VM.Elementname.PadRight(19," ")
    $desc = $VM.Description.PadRight(33," ")
    $state_num = $VM.EnabledState
    switch ($state_num)
    {
            2        {$State_text = "Running"}
            3        {$State_text = "PowerOff"}
            4        {$State_text = "ShuttingDown"}
            10       {$State_text = "Reset"}
            32768    {$State_text = "Paused"}
            32769    {$State_text = "Saved"}
            32770    {$State_text = "Starting"}
            32771    {$State_text = "SnapshotInProgress"}
            32773    {$State_text = "Saving"}
            32774    {$State_text = "Stopping"}
            32776    {$State_text = "Pausing"}
            32777    {$State_text = "Resuming"}
            default  {$State_text = "Unknown"}
    }
    Write-host "$name $desc $State_text ($State_num)"
}write-host ""
}
```

After the function is loaded, you can type **Show_VM** in PowerShell to list the friendly name, description, and state of each VM (see Figure 9.21).

FIGURE 9.21
Calling a useful function

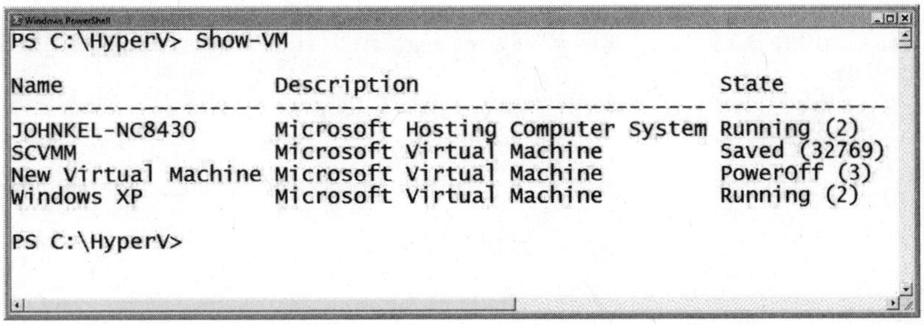

LOADING SCRIPTS AND FUNCTION LIBRARIES

You can save predefined groups of commands in script files for later use. (The preceding function example was loaded from a file and executed.) As mentioned earlier, PowerShell code is typically saved in files with a .PS1 extension. The call to load and run a prewritten script file must include the explicit path to the file, or it won't execute.

NOTE PowerShell searches for files in directories listed in the Path environment variable; but unlike in CMD, the current folder isn't considered for such searches.

Typing just the name of the script file generates an error, as shown in Figure 9.22.

FIGURE 9.22
Calling a script incorrectly

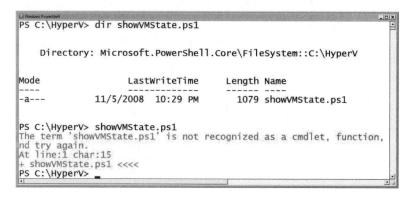

```
PS C:\HyperV> dir showVMState.ps1


    Directory: Microsoft.PowerShell.Core\FileSystem::C:\HyperV


Mode                LastWriteTime     Length Name
----                -------------     ------ ----
-a---        11/5/2008  10:29 PM       1079 showVMState.ps1


PS C:\HyperV> showVMState.ps1
The term 'showVMState.ps1' is not recognized as a cmdlet, function,
nd try again.
At line:1 char:15
+ showVMState.ps1 <<<<
PS C:\HyperV>
```

As mentioned, you can execute a script using the full path (see Figure 9.23).

FIGURE 9.23
Successfully calling a script

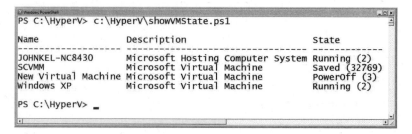

```
PS C:\HyperV> c:\HyperV\showVMState.ps1

Name                   Description                          State
----                   -----------                          -----
JOHNKEL-NC8430         Microsoft Hosting Computer System   Running (2)
SCVMM                  Microsoft Virtual Machine           Saved (32769)
New Virtual Machine    Microsoft Virtual Machine           PowerOff (3)
Windows XP             Microsoft Virtual Machine           Running (2)

PS C:\HyperV>
```

To execute a script from the current directory, precede its name with a period and a backslash (.\ or <period><backslash>, as shown in Figure 9.24).

FIGURE 9.24
Calling a script in the current directory

```
PS C:\HyperV> .\showVMState.ps1

Name                   Description                          State
----                   -----------                          -----
JOHNKEL-NC8430         Microsoft Hosting Computer System   Running (2)
SCVMM                  Microsoft Virtual Machine           Saved (32769)
New Virtual Machine    Microsoft Virtual Machine           PowerOff (3)
Windows XP             Microsoft Virtual Machine           Running (2)

PS C:\HyperV>
```

You can also save prewritten libraries of functions in .PS1 files and load them for use in PowerShell. Loading a library of functions is similar to running a script (using the path), except that the call to the library must be by preceded by an additional period and space before the path (see Figure 9.25).

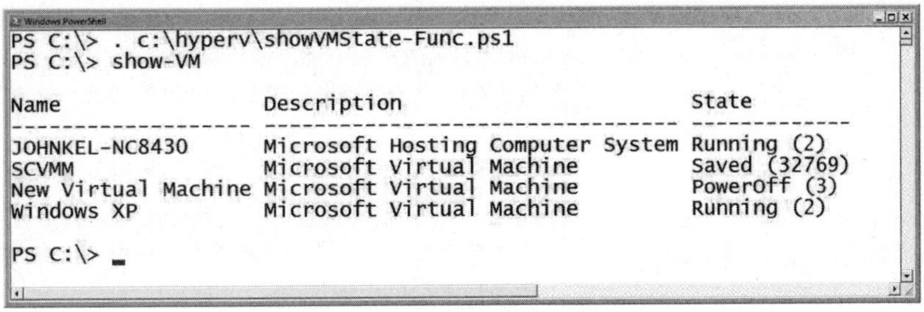

FIGURE 9.25
Loading a library
of functions

```
Windows PowerShell                                                        _□x
PS C:\> . c:\hyperv\showVMState-Func.ps1
PS C:\> show-VM

Name                  Description                        State
-------------------   --------------------------------   ------------
JOHNKEL-NC8430        Microsoft Hosting Computer System  Running (2)
SCVMM                 Microsoft Virtual Machine          Saved (32769)
New Virtual Machine   Microsoft Virtual Machine          PowerOff (3)
Windows XP            Microsoft Virtual Machine          Running (2)

PS C:\> _
```

TIP Remember that the execution of unsigned scripts is blocked by default in PowerShell. You can use the set-executionpolicy cmdlet to allow for the execution of scripts.

Common Elements of WMI Scripts

WMI scripts have some common elements regardless of the language used. Short scripts (like the one generated in the previous section) frequently have three core sections:

◆ Connect: Access WMI

◆ Collect: Request and receive WMI data

◆ Project: Act on or display the WMI data

A brief walkthrough demonstrating the basics of accessing the WMI virtualization namespace using VBScript and PowerShell follows. This walkthrough provides a foundation only; you'll find more advanced information about automation and scripting in Chapter 10.

WMI and VBScript

A listing of the VBScript created earlier by the WMI Code Creator is shown in Figure 9.26, divided into its three core sections.

Walking through the sample script provides examples of each of the required elements of WMI scripting. The first step in any WMI script is to connect to the WMI Service on the intended target computer. The first two lines of the script accomplish this by specifying the moniker for the WMI scripting library (winmgmts), the local system, and the WMI namespace. An object reference is returned, which enables access to WMI on the target system. A simplified one-line version of this VBScript code is as follows:

```
Set objWMIService = GetObject("winmgmts:\\.\root\virtualization")
```

As noted earlier, you can access WMI from a remote computer. Replacing the . in the strComputer variable (or the . between the slashes in the simplified example) with the resolvable name of a remote system returns an object reference for WMI on the remote system.

FIGURE 9.26

VBScript sample, in sections

Connect

```
strComputer = "."
Set objWMIService = GetObject("winmgmts:\\" & strComputer & "\root\virtualization")
```

Collect

```
Set colItems = objWMIService.ExecQuery(
    "SELECT * FROM Msvm_ComputerSystem",,48)
```

Project

```
For Each objItem in colItems
    Wscript.Echo "---------------------------------"
    Wscript.Echo "Msvm_ComputerSystem instance"
    Wscript.Echo "---------------------------------"
    Wscript.Echo "Caption: " & objItem.Caption
    Wscript.Echo "ElementName: " & objItem.ElementName
Next
```

After you establish a connection to WMI, the cmdlet typically retrieves information. In the example, all resource instances that are exposed as part of MSVM_ComputerSystem are requested and (we hope) returned. The resources in this case are VM instances:

```
Set colItems = objWMIService.ExecQuery _
("SELECT * FROM Msvm_ComputerSystem",,48)
```

NOTE   The SELECT verb may appear familiar. Windows Management Instrumentation Query Language (WQL) is a great deal like Structured Query Language (SQL) and lets you query the CIM repository using similar syntax.

The information returned by this query is in the form of a collection (colItems), which is a group of related objects (VMs). You can access the collection using a simple for loop to display the desired information for each VM. A simpler version of the sample code is shown here:

```
For Each objItem in colItems
    Wscript.Echo "-----------------------------------"
    Wscript.Echo "VM Name:" & objItem.ElementName
    Wscript.Echo "   Type:" & objItem.Caption
Next
```

The complete, simplified VBScript is as follows, and the improved output is shown in Figure 9.27:

```
Set objWMIService = GetObject _
  ("winmgmts:\\.\root\virtualization")

Set colItems = objWMIService.ExecQuery _
  ("SELECT * FROM Msvm_ComputerSystem",,48)

For Each objItem in colItems
      Wscript.Echo "---------------------------------"
    Wscript.Echo "VM Name:" & objItem.ElementName
    Wscript.Echo "   Type:" & objItem.Caption
Next
```

FIGURE 9.27
Improved sample
script output

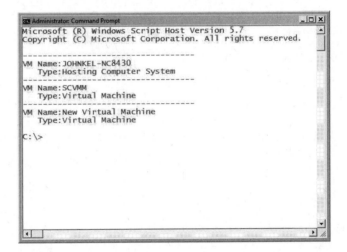

TIP   WSH runs VBScript (.VBS) using WScript as the default host. Setting the default script host tells Windows how to handle the output of scripts you run. With WScript as the default, output from a VBScript creates a pop-up message box every time it writes output to the screen, unless it was called directly using CScript (from the command prompt—cscript <script.vbs>). Using CScript, output is displayed in a command-prompt window. You can change the default script host to avoid this situation by typing **cscript //h:cscript** at a command prompt.

WMI and PowerShell

PowerShell's task-focused design simplifies the process of connecting to WMI, retrieving data from Hyper-V, and putting that data to use. The PowerShell code snippet necessary to access the same information from Hyper-V as the VBScript sample is much shorter while generating similar output (see Figure 9.28):

```
Get-WMIObject -namespace root\virtualization -class Msvm_ComputerSystem |
Format-Table ElementName, Caption -autosize
```

FIGURE 9.28
PowerShell output

PowerShell 1.0 can't remotely access other systems. That being said, Get-WMIObject is unlike other cmdlets in that you can use it to target remote systems because it relies on WMI. In a way similar to the VBScript sample, you can specify a remote system by adding an option to specify the target:

```
Get-WMIObject -computername node1 -namespace root\virtualization ↵
-class Msvm_ComputerSystem | Format-Table ElementName, Caption
```

Aliases, which we mentioned earlier, illustrate PowerShell's task-focused design. Shortcuts for commonly typed cmdlets are built in, including one for the Get-WMIObject cmdlet: gwmi. Using gwmi and other aliases shortens the input:

```
gwmi -namespace root\virtualization -class Msvm_ComputerSystem |
ft ElementName, Caption
```

Virtualization Classes

The virtualization provider includes more than 100 associated classes for managing and monitoring Hyper-V. These classes are well documented on Microsoft's MSDN website (http://msdn.microsoft.com/en-us/library/cc136992(VS.85).aspx or search for "Virtualization WMI Provider"). The MSDN reference provides great insight for scripting access to Hyper-V, including limited scripting examples.

NOTE   The number of classes associated with the virtualization provider is much larger than 100. Some classes aren't specific to the provider/namespace or aren't intended for common use. These classes typically aren't accessed for script-based automation, but they may be visible, depending on the tools used to access the provider/namespace.

Useful WMI Virtualization Classes to Know

Each class (and its associated methods) was created with at least one purpose in mind. You may not find each class as useful for day-to-day automation tasks. Classes that have been found useful repeatedly for automation are listed in Table 9.3, including brief descriptions.

TABLE 9.3:   Frequently Used WMI Virtualization Classes

FUNCTIONAL GROUP	VIRTUALIZATION CLASS	PROPERTY COUNT	COMMENT/DESCRIPTION
Virtual System	Msvm_ComputerSystem	29	Parent or child computer system (VM); core to many automations
Virtual System	Msvm_VirtualSystemGlobalSettingData	13	Global settings for a VM
Virtual System	Msvm_VirtualSystemSettingData	21	Virtualization-specific settings for a VM
Management	Msvm_VirtualSystemManagementService	21	Virtualization service on the parent (host)
Management	Msvm_VirtualSystemManagementServiceSettingData	12	Setting for the virtualization service on the parent (host)
Resource Mgmt	Msvm_AllocationCapabilities	11	Means by which a client can discover the valid range of default settings for a virtual resource; useful for adding storage resources
Resource Mgmt	Msvm_ResourceAllocationSettingData	21	Current and recorded allocation states of a virtual resource; useful for storage-related tasks
Integration	Msvm_KvpExchangeComponent	34	State of the key/value pair exchange component that enables data exchange between child and parent (shutdown, timesync, other); dependant on ICs
Integration	Msvm_ShutdownComponent	32	State of the shutdown component; enables request for a clean shutdown; dependent in ICs
Processor	Msvm_Processor	47	Virtual processor in a VM
Processor	Msvm_ProcessorPool	19	Aggregation of processor resources allocated to a VM
Processor	Msvm_ProcessorSettingData	28	Virtual processor settings for a VM
Memory	Msvm_Memory	66	Memory allocated to a VM
Memory	Msvm_MemorySettingData	24	Configured state of memory on a VM
Storage	Msvm_DiskDrive	56	Hard disk inside a VM

TABLE 9.3: Frequently Used WMI Virtualization Classes *(CONTINUED)*

FUNCTIONAL GROUP	VIRTUALIZATION CLASS	PROPERTY COUNT	COMMENT/DESCRIPTION
Storage	Msvm_DVDDrive	56	DVD drive inside a VM
Storage	Msvm_IDEController	36	IDE controller attached to a VM
Storage	Msvm_ImageManagementService	21	Virtual media controller for a VM (.vhd, .iso, and .vfd files)
Storage	Msvm_MountedStorageImage	15	Details for manually mounted storage image
Storage	Msvm_StorageJob	39	Image operation created by Image Management Service
Storage	Msvm_VirtualHardDiskInfo	6	Details about the existing VHD image (.vhd file)
Network	Msvm_EmulatedEthernetPort	53	Emulated Ethernet adapter (legacy network adapter)
Network	Msvm_EmulatedEthernetPortSettingData	22	Configured state of an emulated Ethernet adapter (legacy network adapter)
Network	Msvm_ExternalEthernetPort	54	External Ethernet port (physical network adapter on the parent)
Network	Msvm_InternalEthernetPort	53	Internal Ethernet port (internal network adapter on the parent)
Network	Msvm_SwitchLANEndpoint	30	LAN endpoint connected to an Ethernet port (internal or external)
Network	Msvm_SwitchPort	24	Port on a virtual network switch
Network	Msvm_SyntheticEthernetPort	53	Synthetic Ethernet adapter
Network	Msvm_SyntheticEthernetPortSettingData	23	Configured state of a synthetic Ethernet adapter
Network	Msvm_VirtualSwitch	27	Virtual network switch
Network	Msvm_VirtualSwitchManagementService	21	Controller for global networking resources including switches, switch ports, and internal Ethernet ports

Understanding how these classes interrelate to automate common tasks is important. Walking through some examples should help you begin to develop value-added automation tools.

The *Msvm_ComputerSystem* Class

Global/general settings and information for VMs are accessible using the various virtual system classes. Msvm_ComputerSystem was used for the earlier sample code examples because it's central to many automation tasks. Looping through a collection of VMs is one of the most fundamentally useful management or data-collection tasks. As demonstrated, Msvm_ComputerSystem supplies a list of all VMs (including the parent partition) as well as general information about each VM. Important properties of the class include those listed in Table 9.4.

TABLE 9.4: Important Properties of Msvm_ComputerSystem

PROPERTY NAME	COMMENT
ElementName	Display name of a VM (friendly)
Name	Unique name of a VM object (unfriendly, but useful)
Caption	Instance type: VM or host
Description	Instance type: VM or host (verbose)
EnabledState	VM state: turned off, running, or in between
HealthState	Heath indicator: 5=healthy, 25=critical error
InstallDate	Installation date and time (valuable for sprawl control)
TimeOfLastConfigurationChange	Configuration-change date and time
TimeOfLastStateChange	State-change date and time

Properties exposed in Msvm_ComputerSystem are the key to coordinated data collection and system-wide management. For example, if you want to save the state of all running VMs on a given host, you can use Msvm_ComputerSystem. You may need to save (for example) the state of all VMs in order to restart the physical system for maintenance. To accomplish this task, you check the state of each child partition and, if necessary, make a request to change the state to Saved:

```
foreach ($VM in gwmi -Namespace root\virtualization -Query ↵
  "Select * from Msvm_ComputerSystem ↵
Where Description='Microsoft Virtual Machine'")
{
    # request state change if appropriate
    if (($VM.EnabledState -eq 2) -or ($VM.EnabledState -eq 32768))
    {
```

```
        write-host "Saving ",$VM.Elementname
        $RequestReturn = $VM.RequestStateChange(32769)
    }
}
```

You can accomplish the same result using the following single-line example:

```
gwmi -namespace root\virtualization -query ↵
  "Select * from MSVM_computerSystem where ↵
((Caption like 'Virtual%') and ↵
(enabledState=2) or (enabledState=32768))" | ↵
foreach {$_.requestStateChange(32769) }
```

The enabledState property contains a numeric value that describes the execution state of each machine. The requestStateChange method understands these same values for changing the state of a VM. The known values are shown in Table 9.5.

TABLE 9.5:   Virtual Machine States

STATE DESCRIPTION	STATE CODE
Unknown	0
Enabled (Running)	2
Disabled (PowerOff)	3
Shutting Down	4
Paused	32768
Suspended (Saved)	32769
Starting	32770
Snapshotting	32771
Migrating	32772
Saving	32773
Stopping	32774
Deleted	32775
Pausing	32776
Resuming	32777

The ability to both decode and request state codes is important. Adding the status descriptions to screen output and diagnostic logs is handy and relatively simple with a switch (case) statement. Output from a function containing the PowerShell code sample below can be seen in Figure 9.29:

```
write-host ""
write-host "Name                Descriptioni
                     State"
write-host "------------------- -----------↵
---------------------- -------------"
foreach ($VM in gwmi -Namespace root\virtualization ↵
-query "Select * from MSVM_Computersystem")
{   $name = $VM.Elementname.PadRight(19," ")
    $desc = $VM.Description.PadRight(33," ")
    $state_num = $VM.EnabledState
    switch ($state_num)
    {
            2         {$State_text = "Running"}
            3         {$State_text = "PowerOff"}
            4         {$State_text = "ShuttingDown"}
            10        {$State_text = "Reset"}
            32768     {$State_text = "Paused"}
            32769     {$State_text = "Saved"}
            32770     {$State_text = "Starting"}
            32771     {$State_text = "SnapshotInProgress"}
            32772     {$State_text = "Migrating"}
            32773     {$State_text = "Saving"}
            32774     {$State_text = "Stopping"}
            32776     {$State_text = "Pausing"}
            32777     {$State_text = "Resuming"}
            Default   {$State_text = "Unknown"}
    }
    write-host "$name $desc $State_text ($State_num)"
}write-host ""
```

FIGURE 9.29
Friendly show-state output

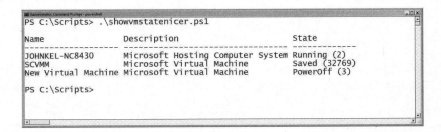

Knowing the VM state is critical for some operations. Many resources can't be added or altered while a VM is running, saved, or paused, including memory, disk, CPU, and network cards.

VM system state is one example of critical information required to successfully automate Hyper-V, which you can access and alter through `Msvm_ComputerSystem`. `Msvm_ComputerSystem` is also the home for the display name for VMs. Querying WMI for an individual VM by the friendly name is a simple process, using the `ElementName` property:

```
$VM = gwmi -namespace root\virtualization -query ↵
"select * from Msvm_ComputerSystem where ElementName='Windows XP'"
```

`$VM` is assigned an object describing the VM "Windows XP," which includes the less friendly Name element (see Figure 9.30).

FIGURE 9.30
Elements of "Windows XP"

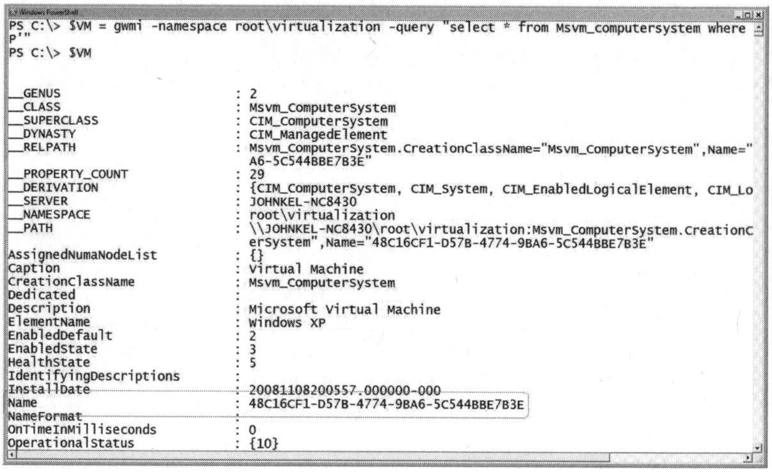

The `Name` element is the common thread tying much of the information about a VM together between the various virtualization classes. `Name` contains the unique identifier for a VM. Unlike the friendly `ElementName`, this unique name is maintained (and searchable) in almost all the virtualization classes containing information and resources about a VM and its components. Amazingly, it isn't exposed in the Hyper-V Manager console. Expanding the use of classes is simple when you understand this relationship. For example, the amount of RAM assigned to a VM isn't accessible via `Msvm_ComputerSystem` but is exposed by `Msvm_Memory`. You can find the unfriendly (but useful) `Name` first and use it to request information about RAM from `Msvm_Memory` (see Figure 9.31):

FIGURE 9.31
Using Name to access other classes

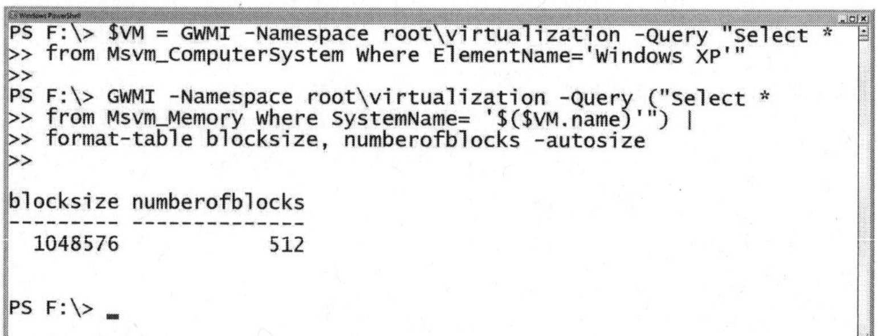

NOTE Nothing is returned by Msvm_Memory if the VM isn't running, because no memory is allocated.

```
$VM = GWMI -Namespace root\virtualization -Query ↩
"Select * from Msvm_ComputerSystem Where ElementName='Windows XP'"
GWMI -Namespace root\virtualization -Query ↩
("Select * from Msvm_Memory Where SystemName= '$($VM.name)'") | ↩
format-table blocksize, numberofblocks -autosize
```

The VM name isn't always accessible as a stand-alone element. For some operations, you must search for it as part of a larger element—such as instanceID in the following example, where you change the amount of RAM allocated to a VM:

NOTE Allocated memory can't be changed for a running VM (at this time with current versions of Hyper-V).

```
$VM = GWMI -Namespace root\virtualization -Query ↩
"Select * from Msvm_ComputerSystem Where ElementName='Windows XP'"

$MemoryDesired = 348
$Memory=GWMI -NameSpace "root\virtualization" -Query ↩
"select * from Msvm_MemorySettingData where ↩
instanceId Like 'Microsoft:$($vm.name)%'"
$Memory.Limit           =    $MemoryDesired
$Memory.Reservation     =    $MemoryDesired
$Memory.VirtualQuantity =    $MemoryDesired
$SettingArguments=@($VM.__Path, @($Memory.psbase.GetTexti
([System.Management.TextFormat]::WmiDtd20)) , $null)

$ManagementData = GWMI -NameSpace "root\virtualization" ↩
-Class "MsVM_virtualSystemManagementService"
$ManagementData.psbase.invokeMethod(i
"ModifyVirtualSystemResources",$SettingArguments)
```

Many unforeseen circumstances can affect the execution of scripts. For efficient production use of your scripts, you should incorporate effective error handling to address common scenarios.

Summary

The virtualization WMI provider is a flexible and useful tool for manipulating and interrogating Hyper-V. Much as a chisel would be useless without a hammer or the hands of a craftsman, the provider requires additional tools and expertise to demonstrate value. You can access the virtualization namespace through tools including the command line (WMIC), flexible scripting languages (VBScript, PowerShell, and others), and WMI browsers and code generators. WMI lets you manage Hyper-V from platforms that can't accommodate the Hyper-V Manager, including Server Core and older versions of Windows. Windows PowerShell provides a consistent syntax and command model for Hyper-V automation that we'll explore in greater detail in Chapter 10.

Chapter 10

Automating Tasks

In Chapter 9, "Understanding WMI, Scripting, and Hyper-V," you were introduced to Windows Management Instrumentation (WMI) and scripting concepts that are important to understanding when effectively automating Hyper-V administrative tasks. The chapter used some relatively simple automation tasks and code examples.

The focus of this chapter is to show you how to accomplish more complex automation tasks for managing a Hyper-V virtualization environment. The examples in this chapter are exclusive to Hyper-V, unlike the Windows PowerShell code generated by (and used with) System Center Virtual Machine Manager (SCVMM) discussed in Chapter 11, "Using System Center Virtual Machine Manager 2008."

This chapter will discuss common administrative areas as well as automation and scripting examples. Scripting samples are primarily written in Windows PowerShell and rely heavily on a prewritten library of functions available on the Internet.

Common administrative tasks are often categorized in the following groups, which are the topics we'll cover in this chapter:

◆ Building on the work of others

◆ Provisioning

◆ Configuration management

◆ Managing access

◆ Migration

◆ Backup and recovery

◆ Collecting and monitoring data

Building on the Work of Others

Chapter 9 introduced the Hyper-V WMI provider and namespace. The script examples in Chapter 9 were fairly simple. Although they're useful, they don't accomplish much. Writing useful scripts can take a great deal of time and effort. Developing an understanding of the right WMI classes to access and how best to use them can be laborious. Using the insights of others and building on their efforts is therefore an attractive approach to efficient Hyper-V automation. SCVMM (covered in Chapter 12, "Protecting Virtualized Environments with System Center Data Protection Manager") is the best way to benefit from the expertise of others, but you can also use other approaches.

Many of the examples in this chapter use an evolving, prewritten library of Windows PowerShell Hyper-V functions. The library was created by James O'Neill and is available from CodePlex (`www.codeplex.com`).

TIP O'Neill has a wonderful blog at `http://blogs.technet.com/jamesone/` where he goes into great detail about Windows, virtualization, motor racing, and other topics.

CodePlex is Microsoft's website for open source project hosting, and it's home to numerous useful development projects. You can find code for other Hyper-V–focused initiatives on CodePlex, but James' library is among the most complete currently available anywhere; it's used widely for Hyper-V automation. His `HyperV.PS1` management library uses all the same WMI calls discussed in Chapter 9. The difference is that the calls in the library are surrounded by carefully written Windows PowerShell code. You can access the library for Hyper-V by navigating to `www.codeplex.com/PSHyperv`.

Original Hyper-V Library

There are multiple versions of the library, with some dating back to mid-2008. Each version is bundled in a `.zip` file that you can find by clicking the page's Downloads tab (there may also be separate documentation available). An older iteration of the library, 0.95a Beta, released in August 2008, is available as a single `.ps1` function library via this link:

```
http://pshyperv.codeplex.com/releases/view/16422
```

NOTE You may wonder why we would show you a vintage version of the library. We still often use this older version of the library when we work with customers, because it is compatible with PowerShell 1.0, it's simple to load using the conventions we use every day, and it's all contained in one `.ps1` file. Nearly every function or filter in the library includes helpful examples within the source code to demonstrate its value. Browsing through the source can provide you with a wealth of ideas about how to use the library, as well as fantastic examples of how to write great Windows PowerShell code.

Inside the `.zip` file for the August 2008 version, you'll find `HyperV.PS1`, which is the library of functions O'Neill has created for Windows Server 2008, PowerShell 1.0, and Hyper-V.

Loading the `HyperV.PS1` library of functions is straightforward, assuming the execution policy is set and you follow proper calling conventions (see Figure 10.1).

FIGURE 10.1
Calling the library

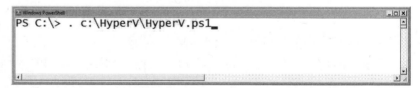

NOTE Remember that you load prewritten Windows PowerShell libraries of functions in a similar way to running a script (specifying the path), except that the call to the library must be proceeded by an additional period. Also recall that you must set the execution policy in Windows PowerShell to allow for scripts to execute. See Chapter 9 for more information.

When the library loads, it lists the functions available for use (see Figure 10.2).

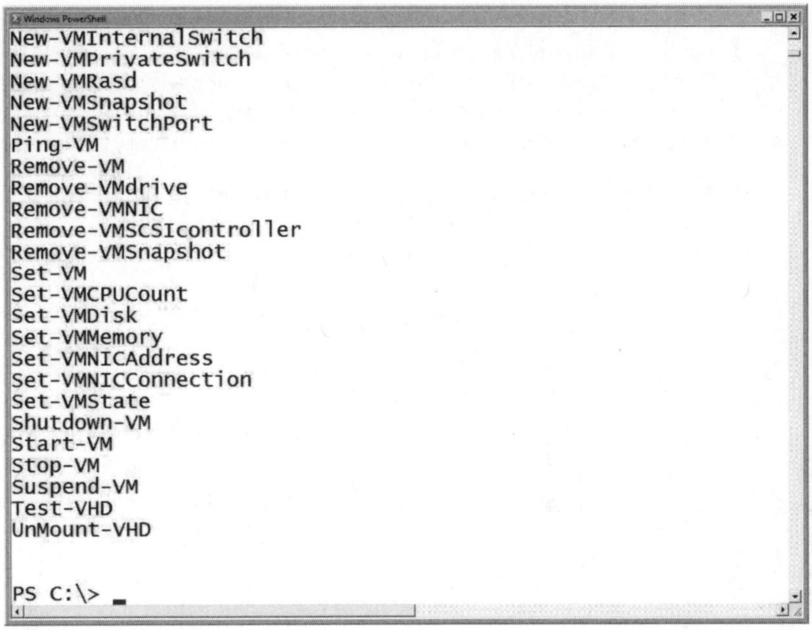

FIGURE 10.2

Functions in the 0.95a Beta library

```
Windows PowerShell
New-VMInternalSwitch
New-VMPrivateSwitch
New-VMRasd
New-VMSnapshot
New-VMSwitchPort
Ping-VM
Remove-VM
Remove-VMdrive
Remove-VMNIC
Remove-VMSCSIcontroller
Remove-VMSnapshot
Set-VM
Set-VMCPUCount
Set-VMDisk
Set-VMMemory
Set-VMNICAddress
Set-VMNICConnection
Set-VMState
Shutdown-VM
Start-VM
Stop-VM
Suspend-VM
Test-VHD
UnMount-VHD

PS C:\> _
```

New R2 Library

Newer versions of the library have been revised to work exclusively with PowerShell 2.0. They include numerous fixes and additional functionality. We'll work through the chapter using the latest available library ("R2 Gold" from January 18, 2010) available here:

```
http://pshyperv.codeplex.com/releases/view/38769
```

Newer versions of the library don't load the same way as the early releases. O'Neill has chopped up the library into smaller files that now can be loaded as modules. Unzipping the contents of the install .zip file into a directory reveals a large collection of files rather than a single .ps1 file (see Figure 10.3). Don't let all these files scare you! They're (mostly) there to make things easier.

FIGURE 10.3

Files in ZIP download

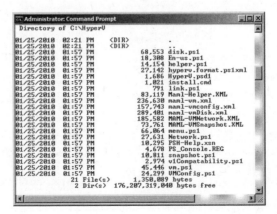

To load the library, start PowerShell, and be certain you have administrative rights and that the Execution Policy is set (we often execute a `set-executionpolicy -executionpolicy "Unrestricted"` command to be certain we do not have any issues!). Loading the library can be as simple as typing **import-module .\HyperV** (see Figure 10.4). Note that we ran the `import-module` command while our PowerShell session was in the directory containing the library files.

FIGURE 10.4

Loading the HyperV module

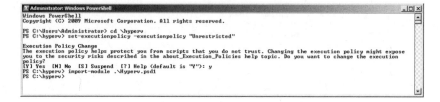

> **NOTE** Even with the `Unrestricted` option, you may encounter security warning prompts that need to be answered for each `.ps1` and `.ps1xml` file in the module. If these prompts are not answered with R, then the modules do not get imported, and the subsequent commands may fail. To prevent this, use Windows Explorer to access the properties of each file in the library, and choose to "unblock" access.

Using a newer version of the library has advantages, such as the integrated help you can get with a fully developed, imported PowerShell module. Unlike older versions of the library, you can access a list of cmdlets using `get-command` and specifying `-module HyperV`. The `help` and `get-help` cmdlets also work with the newer libraries, so documentation is always handy. You can even combine it with other fancy PowerShell cmdlets (assuming you have installed the Windows PowerShell Integrated Scripting Environment [ISE] feature) like `out-gridview` to generate a sortable, filterable module help reference, as shown in Figure 10.5.

```
get-command -module HyperV | get-help | select-object -property name, synopsis | out-gridview
```

FIGURE 10.5

`out-gridView` list of functions

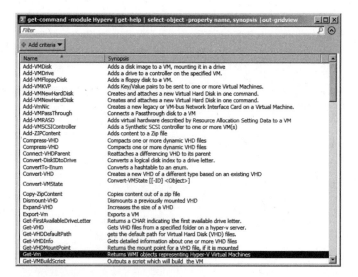

OTHER WAYS TO LOAD THE LIBRARY

The library is fantastic, but the documentation and some of the tools (like the `install.cmd` file) may not be 100 percent accurate or applicable to your environment. You may want to run (and investigate) the `install.cmd` file that comes in the package in some situations to update the registry as well as to enable PowerShell. We've chosen not to use this file and instead import the library as demonstrated here.

Loading the library as show earlier in this section is the easiest way we've found to get started, but feel free to experiment. After the installation is smoothed out, we often create a shortcut on the desktop of our Hyper-V hosts (if the library is set up) to start PowerShell and load the library automatically. We typically use the following command line (in a `.bat` file):

```
start powershell -noexit -command "import-module c:\hyperv\hyperv"
```

You can add the parameters to a PowerShell shortcut on your desktop instead of using a batch file without the `start` command. Note that this particular command-line example assumes that the library files have all been unzipped to the `C:\HyperV` directory.

Regardless of the version of the library you use and how you load it, the predefined Windows PowerShell functions included in the library are the underpinning of *all* the useful scripts in this chapter. The library is going to save you lots of time and effort if you want to automate Hyper-V–related tasks without the burden of other, more costly tools. We'll now show how to automate the creation of virtual machines.

Provisioning

Creating new virtual machine (VM) instances is the first big, useful automation task to conquer. With a good VM provisioning process, you can quickly and reliably create new VMs in minutes.

Creating a Bare-Bones VM

We'll use the VM provisioning process to help make the point that using O'Neill's library of functions simplifies creating your own scripts. The following Windows PowerShell code creates a new VM instance on the local server with the display name of New VM:

```
# Set the display name of the VM
$New_VM_Name = "New VM"
$VM_Service = GWMI -namespace root\virtualization ↵
Msvm_VirtualSystemManagementService
$NewVM = $VM_Service.DefineVirtualSystem()

# Parse the result and find the created VM
$resultID = $NewVM.DefinedSystem.Split('=')[2]
$resultID = $resultid.split('"')[1]
$VM = GWMI -namespace root\virtualization Msvm_ComputerSystem |
  where {$_.Name -match "$resultID"}

$VMSettingData = GWMI -namespace root\virtualization ↵
```

```
Msvm_VirtualSystemSettingData -filter "SystemName = `'$($VM.Name)`'"

# Set the display name of the VM
$VMSettingData.ElementName = $New_VM_Name
$VM_Service.ModifyVirtualSystem($VM.__PATH, $VMSettingData.psbase.getText(1))
```

Not all that much code is shown, but then again, it doesn't do much. You create a new VM on the local physical system and give it the intended display name. By contrast, the following single line of code accomplishes the same task using any version of the library:

```
$myVM = (New-VM "New VM")
```

Using the library vastly simplifies VM management tasks by reducing the amount of code you need to write. In either case, you set defaults for the number of processors (one) and the amount of RAM (512 MB), but you do little else. The VM defined at this point is similar to a bare-bones PC kit (see Figure 10.6). It has only a virtual case, a power supply, a motherboard, limited RAM, and a single processor. The VM has no hard disks, no CD/DVD, and no network interface cards (NICs). You must attach and configure all these resources before you can use the VM.

FIGURE 10.6
Virtual settings after creating a basic VM

Defining a usable VM means more effort. You must write additional code to perform the following actions:

◆ Change the amount of RAM

◆ Alter the number of virtual CPUs

◆ Add NICs

- ◆ Connect NICs to a particular virtual switch

- ◆ Create a virtual hard disk (VHD) file

- ◆ Add hard drive(s) attached to VHD file(s) or pass-through disk

- ◆ Add CD/DVD drive(s)

- ◆ Mount CD/DVD(s)

- ◆ All other provisioning tasks (you get the point—changing startup actions, BIOS boot order, and so on)

Each of these actions requires you to weave more code into the basic provisioning process. The complexity of a script that must be handcrafted and maintained to handle all provisioning processes can be substantial. Writing a script of this magnitude is similar to running a marathon—not everyone has the capacity or even wants the challenge (especially if a free ride is available, like O'Neill's library!).

The following Windows PowerShell sample (using any version of the library) completes the common VM provisioning tasks mentioned and starts the new VM, with the execution shown in Figure 10.7:

```
$New_VM_Name  = "New VM"
$New_VHD_Name = "c:\VHDs\$($New_VM_Name).VHD"

$myVM = (New-VM $New_VM_Name)
Set-VMMemory    $myVM 1024MB
Set-VMCPUCount  $myVM 2
Add-VMDrive     $myVM 0 0
New-VHD         $New_VHD_Name 20GB -wait
Add-VMDisk      $myVM 0 0 $New_VHD_Name
Add-VMDrive     $myVM 1 0 -dvd
Add-VMDisk      $myVM 1 0 "C:\ISOs\2008R2.iso" -dvd
Add-VMNIC       $myVM -virtualSwitch "Public"

Start-VM $myVM
```

You can immediately see the results of this compact and complete script in the Hyper-V console. Each customized element of the VM's settings are reflected in the settings (see Figure 10.8).

NOTE   All the code examples shown have been tested with the latest versions of the library. Most of the code shown will work with either version of the library that we introduced earlier in the chapter. Everything shown was specifically tested with the newer R2 Gold library from January 18, 2010, using PowerShell 2.0.

Setting BIOS Options, Startup/Shutdown, and Additional Elements

You can set BIOS options (such as boot order) and startup/shutdown actions for a VM using the set-VM function:

```
set-vm $myVM -bootorder @(3,2,0,1)
```

FIGURE 10.7
Script execution

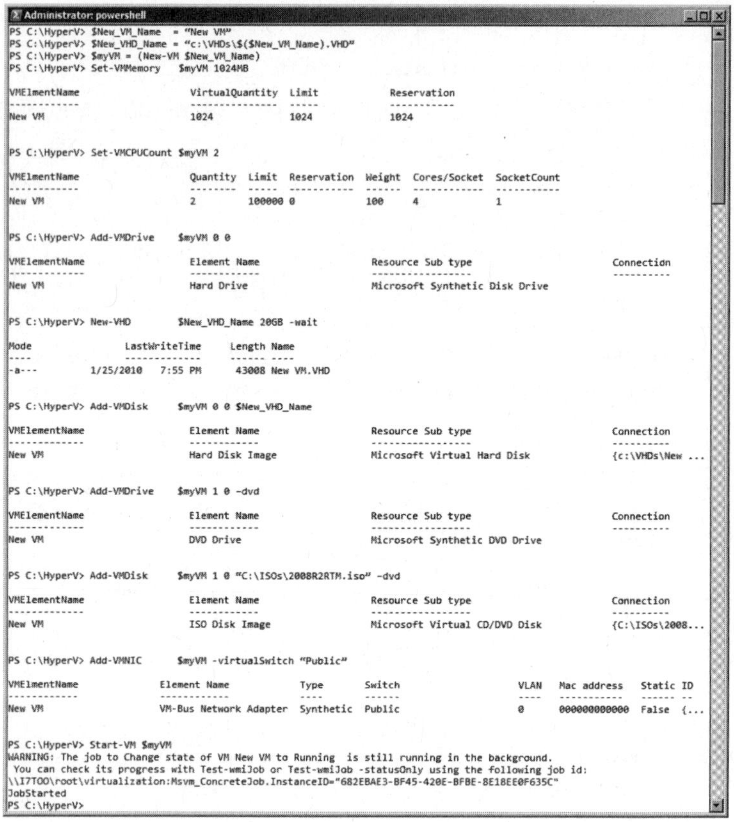

You can find friendly names for boot media (rather than numbers) in the definition of the $BootMedia global variable, as shown in Figure 10.9.

Additional global variables exist to clarify the codes behind the VM state as well as startup, shutdown, and recovery actions. To set the default startup action for a VM to always start, use either of the following lines (note that this code works only with the R2 Gold library):

```
set-vm -VM $myVM -AutoStartup $StartupAction["AlwaysStartup"]
set-vm -VM $myVM -autoStartup 2
```

You can add error handling and management to the earlier basic provisioning script (checks to ensure the ISO file exists, disk space is sufficient, the Public network switch is defined, and each step of the process completes successfully), but it may not be necessary in all situations.

NOTE   You may notice that we call all the useful tools in the library functions, when in actuality many of them are defined as filters. Functions and filters are essentially the same thing (filters are a subset of functions). They're both blocks of code that process data. The difference is in how they process data that is piped into them from other functions. Through the evolution of the library, many functions have been converted to filters to add support for piped input, and some filters have changed to functions. Rather than split hairs and keep track, we'll continue to call everything a *function*.

FIGURE 10.8
VM settings
after creating a
complete VM

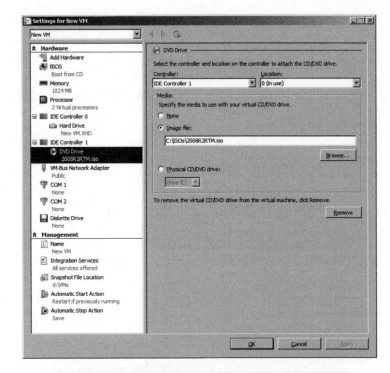

FIGURE 10.9
Script execution

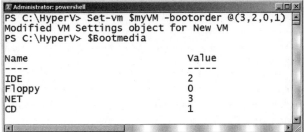

Remote Virtual Machine Provisioning

We haven't explicitly mentioned this in the chapter yet, but most functions in the library have been constructed to be executed against a remote server by specifying the `-server <hostname>` argument. Remotely managing servers is key, because Windows PowerShell doesn't run on the more compact Core installations of Windows Server 2008 (but of course PowerShell does run on Core for R2 as well as Hyper-V Server 2008 R2). Calling the `new-VM` function and specifying a remote host (if successful) populates `$myVM` with information about a new VM created on that remote host:

```
$New_VM_Name  = "New VM"
$myVM = (New-VM $New_VM_Name -server "RemoteHost")
```

You can see the results of successful remote calls to a system named hypernode2 in Figure 10.10. Any code in the examples that use $myVM to set VM settings (set-VMmemory, set-VMCPUcount), add resources (add-VMdrive, add-VMdisk, add-VMNIC), or in other ways affect the VM (start-VM) should work properly remotely.

FIGURE 10.10

Call to

remote server

NOTE When a variable containing the description of a VM is passed to any of the functions that affect the VM, the function automatically contacts the remote server. If no VM parameter is passed to a function or if convenience dictates that you access the VM by name, you need to specify the −server parameter.

Some functions, such as new-VHD (called to create a new VHD to be later attached to the VM), don't rely on the VM information found in $myVM. Calls to these functions must also include the -server argument:

```
$New_VM_Name  = "New VM"
$New_VHD_Name = "c:\VHDs\$($New_VM_Name).VHD"
$Target_Host = "RemoteHost"


$myVM = (New-VM $New_VM_Name -server $Target_Host)
Set-VMMemory    $myVM 1024MB
Set-VMCPUCount  $myVM 2
Add-VMDrive     $myVM 0 0
New-VHD         $New_VHD_Name 20GB -wait -Server $Target_Host
Add-VMDisk      $myVM 0 0 $New_VHD_Name
Add-VMDrive     $myVM 1 0 -dvd
Add-VMDisk      $myVM 1 0 "C:\ISOs\XP_Pro.iso" -dvd
Add-VMNIC       $myVM -virtualSwitch "Public"

Start-VM $myVM
```

Precreating Generic VHDs

In the previous provisioning example, the VM created has an ISO image file *inserted* in its virtual CD/DVD drive from which you can install Windows Server 2008 R2. Automating the insertion of an installation disc for a vanilla operating system is a convenient way to build VMs, but installation still requires considerable time and manual intervention (clicking through).

Creating a generic VM for a given operating system instance is a more efficient way to create multiple VMs. Installing a particular operating system version/edition once completely (the x64 full installation of Windows Server 2008 R2 Enterprise Edition, for instance), followed by properly executing SysPrep.exe, can save time and effort for repeated installations. SysPrep.exe is Microsoft's system preparation utility, which you can use to *depersonalize* a configured operating system instance for widespread deployment (commonly using an imaging tool such as ImageX and/or an automated deployment tool like Windows Deployment Services). When you correctly execute the command, you reset key system elements so that you can configure them again in setup to ensure uniqueness and the appropriate personalization in your environment.

TIP SysPrep.exe is specific to each edition of Windows. For Windows Vista, Windows 7, Windows Server 2008, and Windows Server 2008 R2, it ships with the product and can be found in the C:\Windows\system32\sysprep directory.

You can run SysPrep.exe either by passing it various command-line arguments to guide behavior (see Figure 10.11) or by using a graphical interface (see Figure 10.12).

FIGURE 10.11
SysPrep.exe
arguments

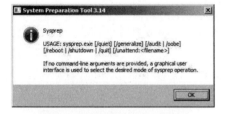

FIGURE 10.12
SysPrep.exe
graphical interface

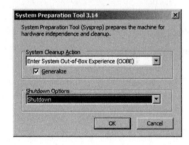

You should keep in mind that not all software can be preinstalled and configured before you run SysPrep.exe. The following list includes tasks you can perform before executing SysPrep.exe:

◆ Installing updated integration components (ICs), if not already included in the installation media

◆ Setting the time zone

◆ Configuring the patching option

◆ Applying patches from Windows Update

◆ Adding common features (PowerShell, for example)

The manual installation of Windows Server 2008 R2 Enterprise edition typically takes almost an hour when you apply patches and complete common configuration tasks. Duplicating a VHD file that has been Sysprepped and repersonalizing should take a small fraction of this time (80 to 90 percent less time is common, depending on system performance).

Automated installation (using answer files and scripts) can further reduce the install effort by automating domain joining, system renaming, and license activation, as well as the installation and configuration of application software and server roles.

TIP You can find detailed information and guidance about how to automate these tasks using SysPrep.exe online at http://technet.microsoft.com and other websites.

Here's a modified version of the VM provisioning script, including code to copy and register a preconfigured VHD file without an installation ISO or a new, blank VHD:

```
$New_VM_Name  = "New VM"
$New_VHD_Name = "c:\VHDs\$($New_VM_Name).VHD"
Copy "c:\SYSPREPed\Windows Server 2008R2.VHD" $New_VHD_Name

$myVM = (New-VM $New_VM_Name)
Set-VMMemory   $myVM 1024MB
Set-VMCPUCount $myVM 2
Add-VMDrive    $myVM 0 0
Add-VMDisk     $myVM 0 0 $New_VHD_Name
Add-VMDrive    $myVM 1 0 -dvd
Add-VMNIC      $myVM -virtualSwitch "Public"

Start-VM $myVM
```

Deprovisioning

You can automate the removal of VMs as well. You may think twice about creating scripts to remove VMs, because (operationally) simplifying the deletion of a VM presents risks. As with the Hyper-V Manager, removing a VM programmatically requires that the VM not be in a running state (in other words, it must be stopped or saved). Only the configuration of the VM is removed; associated VHD files are left behind and may also need to be deleted. You can remove a VM with one line of code that uses the function library:

```
Remove-VM "New VM"
```

You may also remove resources attached to a VM using functions from the library. Table 10.1 lists these destructive functions.

TABLE 10.1: Hyper-V Library Remove Functions

FUNCTION NAME	DESCRIPTION
remove-VM	Deletes the VM configuration
remove-VMdrive	Detaches a disk (VHD or pass-through)
remove-VMfloppydisk	Removes a floppy disk
remove-VMKVP	Removes key/value pair

TABLE 10.1:   Hyper-V Library Remove Functions *(CONTINUED)*

FUNCTION NAME	DESCRIPTION
remove-VMNIC	Removes a virtual NIC
remove-VMSCSIcontroller	Removes a virtual SCSI controller
remove-VMRASD	Removes virtual hardware described by Resource Allocation Setting Data
remove-VMsnapshot	Deletes snapshot
remove-VMswitch	Deletes virtual switch
remove-VMswitchNIC	Removes the parent (physical) NIC associated to a virtual switch

Physical Server Setup

Jumping ahead to show basic VM creation (as we did here) may seem like putting the cart before the horse. You want to ensure that the physical server is ready to accommodate VMs before you set up VMs. You have some common tasks to perform on a physical host, all of which you can automate for consistency. There is more value in automating some configuration tasks than others. For example, changing the default path for new VHDs and configuration files can be important but may not be entirely useful. If you configure failover clustering on a series of hosts, defaulting the settings to a particular volume may be useless, because these settings are typically ignored (VM configuration information and VHDs are often on unique shared storage unless a common file share, CSVs, or a cluster file system is used). Automating the creation of virtual network switches may be more important in a clustered environment, because virtual network switches across cluster nodes must be named consistently to ensure smooth operation.

Functions are available to create each of the three kinds of virtual network switches: *private*, *internal*, and *external*. Creating private and internal virtual switches programmatically is a relatively straightforward process:

```
New-VMInternalSwitch "VM and Host Network"
New-VMPrivateSwitch "VM ONLY Network"
```

Creating a virtual switch with external connectivity is a bit more complicated, because you must specify a physical network card:

```
New-VMExternalSwitch -virtualSwitchName "Wired Network" -ExternalEthernet
"Intel(R) PRO/1000 MT Desktop Adapter"
```

Knowing the name ahead of time for the desired physical NIC is important but not always practical. To simplify virtual switch creation, use the choose-VMexternalethernet function. This function queries the host operating system to discover Ethernet connections not already in use by Hyper-V. If more than one connection is found, you're prompted to select one, which is returned as the result:

```
choose-VMExternalEthernet |
New-VMExternalSwitch -virtualSwitchName "Wired Network""
```

Configuration Management

Discovering, managing, and maintaining the configurations of systems are core tasks in any well-managed infrastructure. Locating virtual hosts and VMs is a first step. Accessing and decoding configuration information for hosts and VMs is key to sustaining the health of the overall environment.

Discovery

The ease with which you can create VMs is both a blessing and a curse. The ability to create entire new virtual system instances with a few lines of code or clicks of a mouse means the traditional barriers to server deployment have dramatically changed. No longer do you need to purchase a new server for each new project. Now, a primary goal of server virtualization is often to reduce costs through server consolidation.

Once users begin to understand the speed with which you can create new servers, expectations for new servers increase. As you realize the promise of virtualization, enterprising users will create their own VMs in their own ways. Sometimes they will create systems without triggering processes to ensure that appropriate software licenses are ordered, backup capacity is reserved, or security audits are performed. The impact and cost implications of an unmanaged virtual environment can be enormous.

NOTE More than once, innovative users have built their own virtual test infrastructures, exposing (for example) Dynamic Host Configuration Protocol (DHCP) servers to production networks and interrupting business. (Let's just say we know a guy who did something really bad, and we'll leave it at that!)

DETECTING VIRTUALIZATION HOSTS

You can locate installed Hyper-V hosts in a number of ways, including searching servers for running services (vhdsvc, nvspwmi, vmms), scanning volumes for files (including .vhd and .vsv), enumerating WMI namespaces, and using the power and efficiency of Active Directory (AD). You may not know that properly configured virtualization servers (those running Hyper-V and Virtual Server 2005) publish their binding information in AD as service connection point (SCP) objects.

TIP For more information about service connection points, go to the Service Publication page on the MSDN website at http://msdn.microsoft.com/en-us/library/ms677950(VS.85).aspx.

Querying AD for Hyper-V hosts is a great starting point for gathering a bounty of information about virtualization in an enterprise environment. The following sample VBScript generates a list and a count of Hyper-V hosts from the current domain:

```
' Adapted from Alex A. Kibkalo —
' (his is more complete) available from
' http://blogs.technet.com/vm/attachment/3048135.ashx

Set objSystemInfo = CreateObject("ADSystemInfo")
Set objRootDSE = GetObject("LDAP://rootDSE")
szDomainShortName = objSystemInfo.DomainShortName
szDomainDN = objRootDSE.Get("defaultNamingContext")
```

```
Set oConnection = CreateObject("ADODB.Connection")
Set oCommand = CreateObject("ADODB.Command")
oConnection.Provider = ("ADsDSOObject")
oConnection.Open "Ads Provider"
oCommand.ActiveConnection = oConnection
oCommand.Properties("Page Size") = 99
oCommand.Properties("Searchscope") = &H2 'ADS_SCOPE_SUBTREE
oCommand.Properties("Chase Referrals") = &H60 'ADS_CHASE_REFERRALS_ALWAYS
oCommand.CommandText = "select distinguishedName from 'LDAP://" _
  & szDomainDN & "' " & _
  "where objectCategory='serviceConnectionPoint' and cn='Microsoft Hyper-V'"
Set oRecordSet = oCommand.Execute
oRecordSet.MoveFirst
Do Until oRecordSet.EOF
    szNodeName = oRecordSet.Fields("distinguishedName")
    ' Trim "CN=<szSCP>,CN="
    szNodeName = Mid(szNodeName, InStr(szNodeName, ",CN=") + 4)
    ' Trim the domain DN
    szNodeName = Left(szNodeName, InStr(szNodeName, ",") - 1)
    wscript.echo szNodeName
    oRecordSet.MoveNext
Loop
wscript.echo  "Domain: " & szDomainShortName & _
": " & oRecordSet.RecordCount & " hosts"
```

TIP   John Howard posted a similar script on his virtualization blog at http://blogs.technet .com/jhoward/. The entry is dated June 30, 2008, and entitled "Hyper-V: Locate Hyper-V Enabled Servers In Your Domain."

Once again, O'Neill's library demonstrates its value by simplifying the task of searching AD for Hyper-V hosts. Using the get-VMhost function returns a list of registered Hyper-V servers in the current domain.

ENUMERATING VIRTUAL MACHINES

Creating a list of VMs on a particular host is a relatively simple process, as shown in Chapter 9. Creating such a list is even simpler using the functions included in the library (see Figure 10.13):

```
get-vm | format-table elementname
```

You can access all the externally viewable properties of a VM via the information available from the command get-vm | FL *.

Wrapping a call to get-vm with a loop that can access a list of virtualization hosts provides a useful building block for later automation. A simple text file with the name of each server on a single line can be the input (perhaps created from a query of Active Directory). For our purposes, we've created a file named serverlist.txt, which contains two server names:

```
HPDL380t
HPDL380b
```

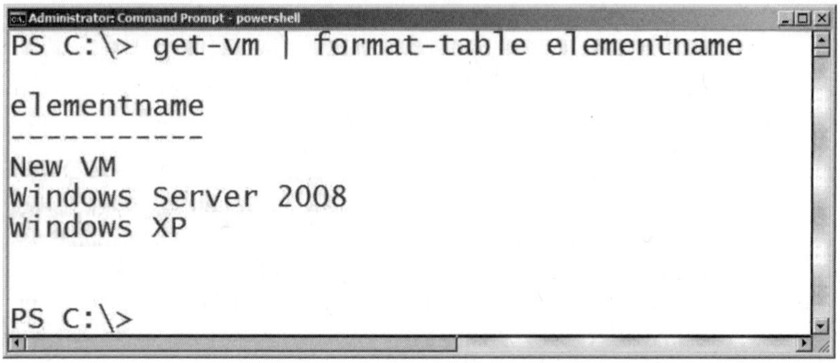

FIGURE 10.13
List of local VMs

FIGURE 10.13
List of local VMs

CUSTOMIZING THE OUTPUT OF LIBRARY COMMANDS

PowerShell allows you to use an XML file to set the default output format for different classes of objects. The early versions of the library didn't use this facility, so `get-VM` (for example) output a list of all the object properties, and the companion function `list-VM` provided formatted output. The newer versions of the library have an associated `Hyperv.Format.PS1XML` file that defines the default output format. In some cases, the XML file processes a property of an object and displays something that isn't available as a property—for example, it translates the value 2 in the `EnabledState` property to the text "running."

With the newer versions, if you want to see all the available properties from `get-VM`, you can pipe its output into `Format-List -Property *`; this can be shortened to `FL *`.

If you want to display output that is different from the default, you can either pipe the output of the function into `Format-Table` (which can be abbreviated to FT) or customize the PS1.XML file.

Iterating through the text file using `get-content` and `foreach-object` can generate a list of configured VMs (see Figure 10.14):

```
get-content .\serverlist.txt |
foreach-object {get-VM -server $_ |
format-table __SERVER, elementname, enabledstate -auto}
```

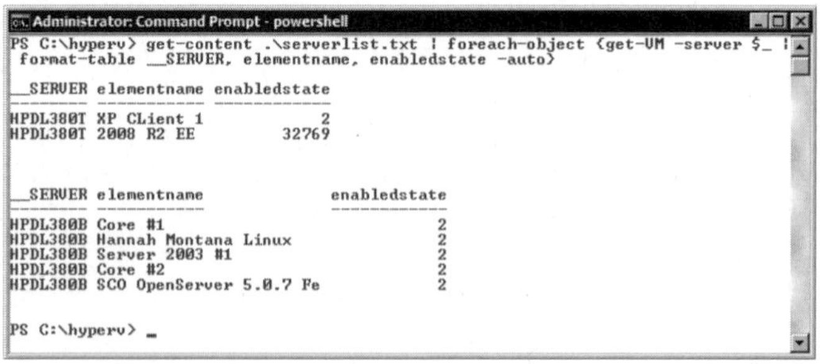

FIGURE 10.14
List of VMs using
host input

NOTE   Yes, you could pipeline the output from get-VMhost to foreach-object, but not all Hyper-V hosts may be online or accessible to you. In that case, exceptions are generated and/or additional error handling is required. You could also call get-VM and pass it all the host names (get-VM -server hypernode1, hypernode2 HPDL380B | FT __SERVER, elementname, enabledstate -auto) to achieve a similar result, but that may be more difficult to automate using a generated list of hosts.

You can extend or alter this basic *host loop* to gather additional useful information beyond those pieces of data exposed by get-VM (which uses the MSVM_ComputerSystem class shown in Chapter 9). Other VM interrogation functions such as get-VMstate can access additional information and handle common formatting tasks (see Figure 10.15).

```
get-content .\serverlist.txt | foreach-object {get-VMState -server $_}
```

FIGURE 10.15
Using get-VMstate with a host input file

get-VMstate decodes the numeric VM state and displays it in a more understandable manner. The function also can access the fully qualified domain name (FQDN) of running VMs with installed ICs (which is super useful!). Fully *enlightened* VMs (those with installed ICs) *that are running* can communicate key information about the installed operating system to the parent partition via the ICs. The get-VMKVP function exposes more of these available attributes. Figure 10.16 shows the output from the August 2008 version of the library.

```
get-vmkvp "Core #1"
```

FIGURE 10.16
The get-VMKVP output from the 0.95a Beta version of HyperV.PS1

```
PS C:\Hyperv> get-vmkvp "Windows XP"


VMElementName              : Windows XP
FullyQualifiedDomainName   : XPVM
OSName                     : Microsoft Windows XP
OSVersion                  : 5.1.2600
CSDVersion                 : Service Pack 3
OSMajorVersion             : 5
OSMinorVersion             : 1
OSBuildNumber              : 2600
OSPlatformId               : 2
ServicePackMajor           : 3
ServicePackMinor           : 0
SuiteMask                  : 256
ProductType                : 1
ProcessorArchitecture      : 0
Descriptions               : {x86, Workstation, Si
```

The R2 Gold version of the library returns more information, as shown in Figure 10.17.

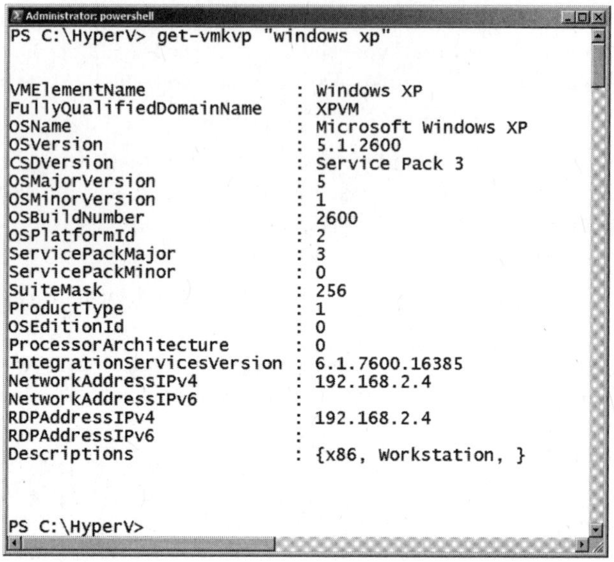

FIGURE 10.17
The get-VMKVP
output from the R2
Gold version of the
Hyper-V library

```
Administrator: powershell                                    _ □ ×
PS C:\HyperV> get-vmkvp "windows xp"


VMElementName                : Windows XP
FullyQualifiedDomainName      : XPVM
OSName                       : Microsoft Windows XP
OSVersion                    : 5.1.2600
CSDVersion                   : Service Pack 3
OSMajorVersion               : 5
OSMinorVersion               : 1
OSBuildNumber                : 2600
OSPlatformId                 : 2
ServicePackMajor             : 3
ServicePackMinor             : 0
SuiteMask                    : 256
ProductType                  : 1
OSEditionId                  : 0
ProcessorArchitecture        : 0
IntegrationServicesVersion   : 6.1.7600.16385
NetworkAddressIPv4           : 192.168.2.4
NetworkAddressIPv6           :
RDPAddressIPv4               : 192.168.2.4
RDPAddressIPv6               :
Descriptions                 : {x86, Workstation, }



PS C:\HyperV>
```

TIP This Hyper-V PowerShell library is a work in progress and continues to evolve. To get the most value from the library, remember to periodically check www.codeplex.com for updates.

Collecting information such as the operating system version, service pack level, and FQDN without directly accessing a VM can be valuable when you're troubleshooting or auditing your environment. Combining the server loop with get-vmkvp is fairly straightforward (see Figure 10.18):

```
get-content .\serverlist.txt |
foreach-object {get-VM -server $_ | get-VMKVP} |
format-table FullyQualifiedDomainName, OSName, CSDVersion -auto
```

Windows PowerShell allows you to create output in a great many formats besides standard text, including comma-separated (CSV) and XML. Altering the format of your output can make the information easier for other tools and applications to use. You can create a CSV file of the information shown in Figure 10.18 by calling the export-CSV cmdlet:

```
get-content .\serverlist.txt |
foreach-object {get-VM -server $_ | get-VMKVP} |
export-csv -path c:\VMInfo.csv
```

CSV and XML files are handy formats for producing output to pass to other applications. Windows PowerShell version 2 includes a useful out-gridview cmdlet that you can use to view and manipulate data interactively (remember you have to install the Windows PowerShell

Integrated Scripting Environment [ISE] feature). The graphical interface lets you sort, search, and group data. Figure 10.19 shows output similar to Figure 10.18, but sent to out-gridview and grouped by operating system name. The full command would be something like this:

```
get-content .\serverlist.txt | foreach-object {get-VM -server $_ | get-VMKVP} |
out-gridview
```

FIGURE 10.18

Looping with
Get-VMKVP

FIGURE 10.19

get-VMKVM set to
out-gridview

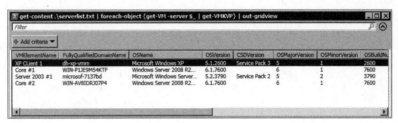

COLLECTING OTHER VIRTUAL MACHINE DETAILS

The library includes numerous get functions (and one list function). Table 10.2 provides a complete list of these functions and their results.

TABLE 10.2:   get Functions

FUNCTION NAME	DESCRIPTION
get-firstavailabledriveletter	Gets the drive letter of the first available drive letter on the host
get-VHD	Retrieves VHD file information from a directory
get-Vhddefaultpath	Retrieves the default VHD path (parent specific)
get-VHDinfo	Retrieves information about a VHD file
get-VHDmountpoint	Returns a mount point of a VHD (if mounted)
get-VM	Accesses general VM information
get-VMByMACaddress	Retrieves VM information by Media Access Control (MAC) address
get-VMclustergroup	Shows the cluster group for a VM

TABLE 10.2:   get Functions *(CONTINUED)*

FUNCTION NAME	DESCRIPTION
get-VMCPUcount	Retrieves the CPU count
get-VMdisk	Displays VM disk controller and drive information
get-VMdiskbydrive	Accesses a VM disk by drive
get-VMdiskcontroller	Accesses a VM disk by controller
get-VMdrivebycontroller	Accesses a VM drive by controller
get-VMfloppydisk	Displays VM floppy disks
get-VMhost	Queries AD for Hyper-V hosts
get-VMintegrationcomponent	Returns IC data for a VM
get-VMKVP	Returns key/value pairs for running VMs
get-VMlivemigrationnetwork	Gets the list of cluster networks
get-VMmemory	Displays the RAM allocated to a VM
get-VMNIC	Retrieves NIC information for a VM
get-VMNICport	Accesses network port information
get-VMNICswitch	Shows the switch connected to a virtual NIC
get-VMNICVLAN	Retrieves the VLAN ID for a NIC
get-VMprocessor	Returns CPU information for each VM
get-VMserialport	Retrieves VM serial port information
get-VMsettingdata	Gets active settings for a VM (BIOS, asset tag, other)
get-VMsnapshot	Accesses VM snapshot information
get-VMsnapshottree	Accesses VM snapshot information and shows it as a tree
get-VMstate	Alias for get-VMsummary
get-VMsummary	Retrieves/decodes the VM state and FQDN
get-VMswitch	Gets virtual switch information
get-VMthumbnail	Retrieves a JPEG image of a VM display (replace get-VMJPEG)
get-ZIPcontent	Returns information about the contents of a ZIP file

Get to know these functions. Experiment with them and read the examples included, and you'll gain a wealth of configuration knowledge.

TIP Real-life, useful examples abound for the get functions. For example, only one VM at a time can access a physical CD/DVD resource. A stopped VM may expect access to a drive when it starts and will fail to start if the drive is already being used. Adding a filter to the get-VMdisk function can help you find VMs that are using the physical CD/DVD: get-VMdisk * | where {$_.diskpath -match "^IDE"} | select VMElementname.

Creating Simple Reports

Windows PowerShell enables nearly limitless options for report generation. You may not have time or the PowerShell savvy to construct the ideal report. The supplied get functions do a fantastic job of exposing the components of Hyper-V and VMs, but sometimes the output is missing important information. The get-VMNIC cmdlet provides a great example of this point; it retrieves a list of configured VMs and their corresponding NICs with MAC address and the connected virtual network switch (see Figure 10.20):

```
get-vmnic
```

FIGURE 10.20

get-VMNIC output

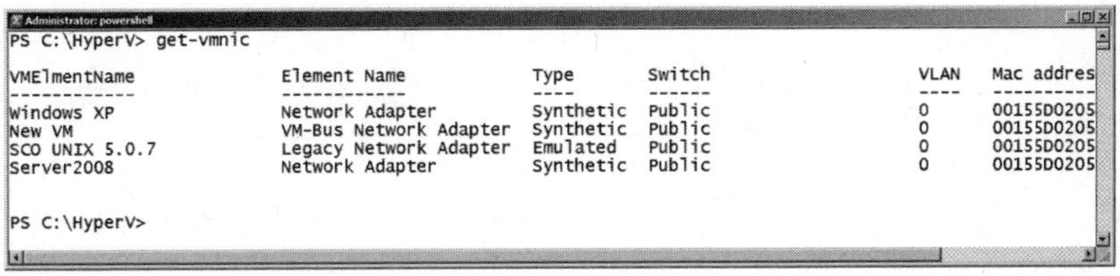

This function can be useful for collecting the MAC addresses for all VMs in your environment, but the default output lacks the name of the physical host. The server (host) name is available; you just have to ask for it, as in Figure 10.21.

```
get-vmnic | ft __Server, VMElementName, ResourceSubType, SwitchName, Address -Auto
```

Remember that you can use the -server parameter to pass multiple server names to most of the functions in the library (as shown in Figure 10.22). This lets you see information on multiple hosts at once.

FIGURE 10.21

get-VMNIC
including server
(host) name

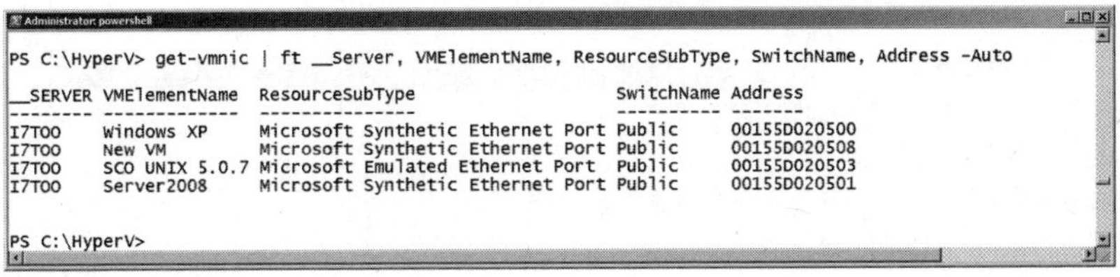

FIGURE 10.22
get-VMNIC output including two servers

```
Administrator: Command Prompt - powershell
PS C:\hyperv> get-vmnic -server hpdl380t, hpdl380b | ft __Server, VMelementname, ResourceSubType, Sw
itchname, Address -auto

__SERVER VMElementName               ResourceSubType                 SwitchName Address
-------- -------------               ---------------                 ---------- -------
HPDL380T XP CLient 1                 Microsoft Synthetic Ethernet Port Public   00155D483703
HPDL380T 2008 R2 EE                  Microsoft Synthetic Ethernet Port Public   00155D483700
HPDL380B Core #1                     Microsoft Synthetic Ethernet Port Public   00155D484C04
HPDL380B Hannah Montana Linux        Microsoft Emulated Ethernet Port  Public   00155D484C08
HPDL380B Hannah Montana Linux        Microsoft Synthetic Ethernet Port Public   00155D484C09
HPDL380B Server 2003 #1              Microsoft Synthetic Ethernet Port Public   00155D484C07
HPDL380B Core #2                     Microsoft Synthetic Ethernet Port Public   00155D484C0A
HPDL380B SCO OpenServer 5.0.7 Fe     Microsoft Emulated Ethernet Port  Public   00155D484C06

PS C:\hyperv> _
```

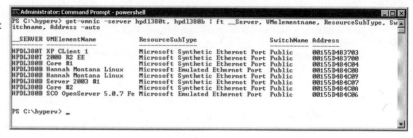

It may not always be easy to pass all the server names into a function at once. It might be more convenient for you to use a list of servers contained in a file (as shown in the "Enumerating Virtual Machines" section earlier). Using `get-content` and `foreach-object` can help you collect information from a larger number of targets, as shown in Figure 10.23, without too much extra code.

FIGURE 10.23
get-VMNIC using loop

```
Administrator: Command Prompt - powershell
PS C:\hyperv> get-content .\serverlist.txt | foreach-object { $Server = $_; get-vmnic -server $Serve
r | ft __Server, VMelementname, ResourceSubType, Switchname, Address -auto}

__SERVER VMElementName ResourceSubType                   SwitchName Address
-------- ------------- ---------------                   ---------- -------
HPDL380T XP CLient 1   Microsoft Synthetic Ethernet Port Public     00155D483703
HPDL380T 2008 R2 EE    Microsoft Synthetic Ethernet Port Public     00155D483700


__SERVER VMElementName               ResourceSubType                   SwitchName Address
-------- -------------               ---------------                   ---------- -------
HPDL380B Core #1                     Microsoft Synthetic Ethernet Port Public     00155D484C04
HPDL380B Hannah Montana Linux        Microsoft Emulated Ethernet Port  Public     00155D484C08
HPDL380B Hannah Montana Linux        Microsoft Synthetic Ethernet Port Public     00155D484C09
HPDL380B Server 2003 #1              Microsoft Synthetic Ethernet Port Public     00155D484C07
HPDL380B Core #2                     Microsoft Synthetic Ethernet Port Public     00155D484C0A
HPDL380B SCO OpenServer 5.0.7 Fe     Microsoft Emulated Ethernet Port  Public     00155D484C06

PS C:\hyperv> _
```

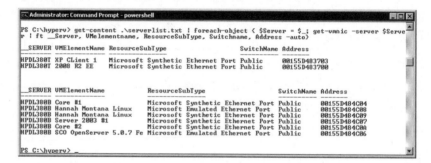

You may have noticed that the output isn't presented in the most easy-to-read format. By calling `get-vmnic` multiple times, you get multiple tables of information returned (one for each host). A better way to use `get-content` is within the `get-vmnic`, rather than the other way around:

```
get-vmnic -server (get-content .\serverlist.txt)
```

This actually outputs a single table, as shown in Figure 10.24. You can add extra code to select just the columns you want, similar to the output in Figure 10.21, earlier in this chapter.

```
get-vmnic -server (get-content .\serverlist.txt) |
ft __Server, VMElementName, ResourceSubType,
SwitchName, Address -Auto
```

FIGURE 10.24
get-VMNIC output presented as a single table

```
Administrator: Command Prompt - powershell
PS C:\hyperv> get-vmnic -server (get-content .\serverlist.txt)
WARNING: 2 columns do not fit into the display and were removed.
VMElmentName              Element Name            Type      Switch           VLAN  Mac a
                                                                                   ddres
                                                                                   s
------------              ------------            ----      ------           ----  -----
XP CLient 1               Ethernet Port           Synthetic Public                 00...
2008 R2 EE                Network Adapter         Synthetic Public                 00...
Core #1                   Network Adapter         Synthetic Public           0     00...
Hannah Montana Linux      Legacy Network Adapter  Emulated  Public           0     00...
Hannah Montana Linux      Network Adapter         Synthetic Public           0     00...
Server 2003 #1            Network Adapter         Synthetic Public           0     00...
Core #2                   Network Adapter         Synthetic Public           0     00...
SCO OpenServer 5.0.7 Fe   Legacy Network Adapter  Emulated  Public           0     00...
```

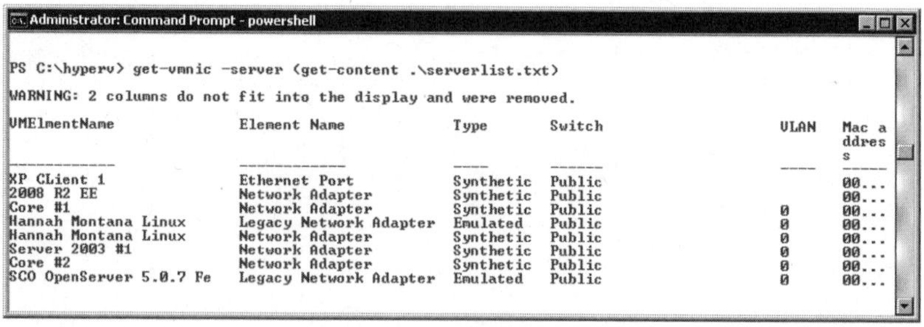

We like to simply dump the output to `out-gridview` and select the data we're interested in by "selecting columns" in the GUI (Figure 10.25 shows the output):

```
get-vmnic -server (get-content .\serverlist.txt) |
select * | out-gridview
```

FIGURE 10.25
get-VMNIC information sent to `out-gridview`

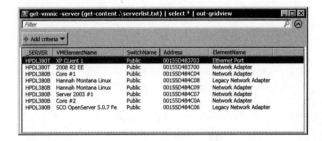

Regardless of your approach for creating usable scripts and reports, using the HyperV library will save you the time and effort of creating custom code. To make this point again, the following is the Windows PowerShell code that is roughly equivalent to the previous loop but does *not* use O'Neill's functions:

```
foreach ($s in (gc c:\serverlist.txt)) {
  $vms=gwmi -computer $s -namespace "root\virtualization" ↵
msvm_computersystem -filter "name <> '$s'"
  foreach ($vm in $vms) {
    gwmi -computer $s -NameSpace "root\virtualization" ↵
-query "Select * From MsVM_EmulatedEthernetPortSettingData ↵
Where instanceId Like 'Microsoft:$($vm.name)%'"|
    select-object ↵
@{name="VM";expression={$vm.elementname}}, ↵
@{name="MACAddress";expression={$_.address}}, ↵
@{name="Server";expression={$_.__SERVER}}, ↵
@{name="Type";expression={$_.ResourceSubType}}, ↵
@{name="Network";expression={(gwmi -computer $s ↵
-NameSpace "root\virtualization" -Query "ASSOCIATORS OF ↵
{$(gwmi -computer $s -NameSpace ""root\virtualization"" ↵
-Query ""Select * From Msvm_SwitchPort where ↵
__Path='$($_.connection[0].replace("""\""","""\\"""))'"")} ↵
where resultclass = Msvm_VirtualSwitch").elementname}}
    gwmi -computer $s -NameSpace "root\virtualization" ↵
-query "Select * From MsVM_SyntheticEthernetPortSettingData ↵
Where instanceId Like 'Microsoft:$($vm.name)%'"|select-object
@{name="VM";expression={$vm.elementname}}, ↵
@{name="MACAddress";expression={$_.address}}, ↵
@{name="Server";expression={$_.__SERVER}}, ↵
@{name="Type";expression={$_.ResourceSubType}}, ↵
@{name="Network";expression={(gwmi -computer $s ↵
```

```
    -NameSpace "root\virtualization" -Query "ASSOCIATORS OF ↵
    {$(gwmi -computer $s -NameSpace ""root\virtualization"" ↵
    -Query ""Select * From Msvm_SwitchPort where
    __Path='$($_.connection[0].replace("""""\""""","""""\\"""")'"")} ↵
    where resultclass = Msvm_VirtualSwitch").elementname}}
      }
}
```

Managing the Virtual Environment

Creating VMs and collecting configuration information about your environment are only the first steps. Managing your virtual environment is critical to realizing the benefits of virtualization. You should strive to use enterprise system management tools if at all possible. The Microsoft System Center family of products provides comprehensive tools to manage physical and virtual environments and is covered in Chapters 11 through 13.

System management can mean many different things, such as managing system configuration, provisioning, performance, security policies, hardware configuration, storage, and even the power state of a system. For our purposes, we'll only discuss managing the system state (power state) for VMs and the management tasks for VHD files. The scripts shown earlier for provisioning VMs demonstrated how to alter the configuration of a VM (add/set resources). We'll review additional VM configuration tasks later, in the "Maintaining Virtual Systems" section of this chapter.

MANAGING STATE

Chapter 9 included verbose examples of how to show and alter the system state of VMs. In this chapter, Figures 10.14 and 10.15 illustrate accessing and viewing the state of all VMs on a group of hosts to demonstrate information discovery. The system/power state of a VM is represented by an integer value, discussed and shown in Table 9.5 in Chapter 9. You may not need to care much about this table, because the Hyper-V library discussed in this chapter understands the friendly names of these states. The codes and decodes are contained in the $VMState global variable, found near the beginning of the library. Calling get-VMsummary (or get-VMstate, which is the same) returns the state information of all VMs on the local host (see Figure 10.26):

```
get-vmsummary | ft Host, VMelementname,
CPUcount, EnabledState, Heartbeat, FQDN -auto
```

FIGURE 10.26
get-VMsummary
output

```
PS C:\HyperV> get-vmsummary | ft Host, VMelementname, CPUcount, EnabledState, Heartbeat, FQDN -auto

Host   VMElementName   CPUCount EnabledState Heartbeat FQDN
----   -------------   -------- ------------ --------- ----
I7TOO  Windows XP         2      Running            OK XPVM
I7TOO  New VM             2      Running No_Contact
I7TOO  SCO UNIX 5.0.7     1      Running No_Contact
I7TOO  Server2008         4      Running            OK 2008VM

PS C:\HyperV> _
```

To access the state of a single VM, use the get-VMsummary function and specify the friendly name of the VM (see Figure 10.27):

```
Get-VMSummary "New VM"
```

FIGURE 10.27

get-VMstate
output for one VM

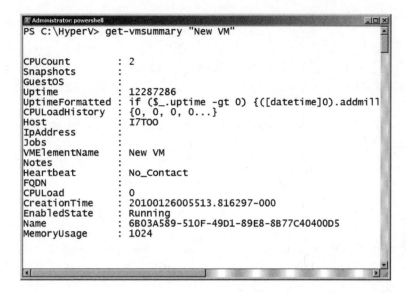

FIGURE 10.27

get-VMstate
output for one VM

NOTE   In the beta version of the library, when you run get-VMsummary or get-VMstate, you'll
see an error if a paused VM is found. A fix for this and other enhancements are in the R2 Gold
version of the library.

Changing the state of a VM is just as simple as retrieving it. Table 10.3 shows state
management functions.

TABLE 10.3:   Hyper-V Library State Management Functions

FUNCTION NAME	DESCRIPTION
get-VMstate or get-VMsummary	Shows the state of VMs
start-VM	Turns on/resumes VMs
stop-VM	Turns off VMs
suspend-VM	Suspends VMs (pause)
shutdown-VM	Shuts down VMs via ICs
set-VMState	Specifies the desired VM state

You use start-VM, stop-VM, suspend-VM, and shutdown-VM the same way. To call each of
these functions, specify the name of the target VM:

```
Start-VM "New VM"
```

As with many functions in the library, you may also specify a remote physical host:

```
Start-VM "New VM" -server HyperNode1
```

It's important to know the state a VM is in before you make a change request. For example, you can't transition from a saved (suspended) state to a paused state. If a VM is already running, a request to start it will fail (see Figure 10.28).

Administrator: powershell
PS C:\HyperV> start-vm "New VM"
Test-WMIResult : Failed to change state of VM New VM to: RunningInvalidStateForOperation
At C:\hyperv\VM.ps1:709 char:65
+ $VM.RequestStateChange($State) | Test-wmiResult <<<< -wait:$wait -JobWaitT
-f $State, $Vm.elementName)
+ CategoryInfo : NotSpecified: (:) [Write-Error], WriteErrorException
+ FullyQualifiedErrorId : Microsoft.PowerShell.Commands.WriteErrorException,Test-WMIResult
Failed
PS C:\HyperV>

FIGURE 10.28
Trying to start a running VM

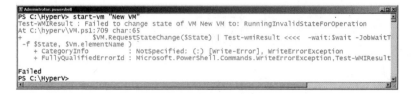

You can change the state of all VMs on a host at once. For example, it could be valuable to put all VMs on a given host into a saved state for backup or while you perform maintenance on the physical system. Using an asterisk instead of the individual VM name with `suspend-VM` saves the state of all running or paused VMs (see Figure 10.29):

```
suspend-vm *
```

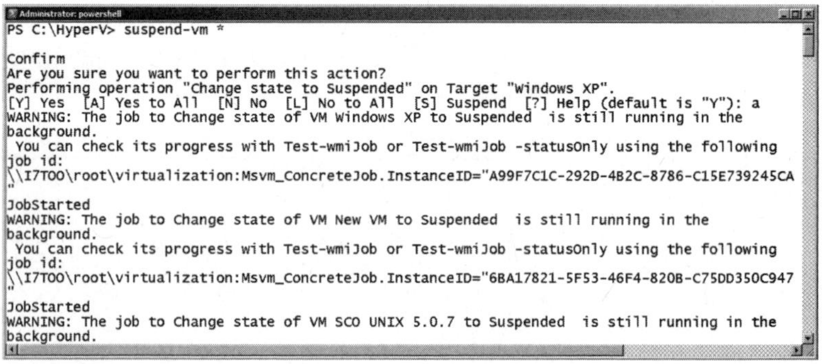
Administrator: powershell
PS C:\HyperV> suspend-vm *
Confirm
Are you sure you want to perform this action?
Performing operation "Change state to Suspended" on Target "Windows XP".
[Y] Yes [A] Yes to All [N] No [L] No to All [S] Suspend [?] Help (default is "Y"): a
WARNING: The job to Change state of VM Windows XP to Suspended is still running in the background.
You can check its progress with Test-wmiJob or Test-wmiJob -statusOnly using the following job id:
\\I7TOO\root\virtualization:Msvm_ConcreteJob.InstanceID="A99F7C1C-292D-4B2C-8786-C15E739245CA"
JobStarted
WARNING: The job to Change state of VM New VM to Suspended is still running in the background.
You can check its progress with Test-wmiJob or Test-wmiJob -statusOnly using the following job id:
\\I7TOO\root\virtualization:Msvm_ConcreteJob.InstanceID="6BA17821-5F53-46F4-820B-C75DD350C947"
JobStarted
WARNING: The job to Change state of VM SCO UNIX 5.0.7 to Suspended is still running in the background.

FIGURE 10.29
Suspending all running VMs

Understanding the role of ICs is also important. They allow for a coordinated shutdown of a VM. You can facilitate an orderly power-down of a VM with installed ICs by using `shutdown-VM` (see Figure 10.30):

```
shutdown-VM "Windows XP"
```

Administrator: powershell
PS C:\HyperV> shutdown-VM "Windows XP"
Waiting for heartbeat
Windows XP
Stopping

FIGURE 10.30
Shutting down a VM with ICs

A VM without installed and running ICs can't take advantage of shutdown integration. An unenlightened VM must be shut down from within the VM or via another means (perhaps simply turned off). Currently, only supported versions of Windows with installed ICs support integrated shutdown. For the example in Figure 10.31, new-VM is a VM with no operating system (or ICs) installed. Attempting to shut down this VM using the HyperV library fails.

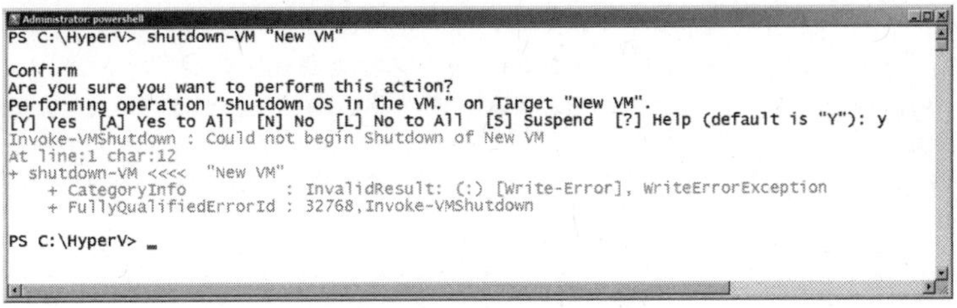

FIGURE 10.31

Failed shutdown request

```
Administrator: powershell
PS C:\HyperV> shutdown-VM "New VM"

Confirm
Are you sure you want to perform this action?
Performing operation "Shutdown OS in the VM." on Target "New VM".
[Y] Yes  [A] Yes to All  [N] No  [L] No to All  [S] Suspend  [?] Help (default is "Y"): y
Invoke-VMShutdown : Could not begin Shutdown of New VM
At line:1 char:12
+ shutdown-VM <<<<  "New VM"
    + CategoryInfo          : InvalidResult: (:) [Write-Error], WriteErrorException
    + FullyQualifiedErrorId : 32768,Invoke-VMShutdown

PS C:\HyperV> _
```

You also can't shut down VMs with ICs if the ICs aren't available. For example, if VMs are in a saved (suspended) state, the ICs are unavailable (see Figure 10.32).

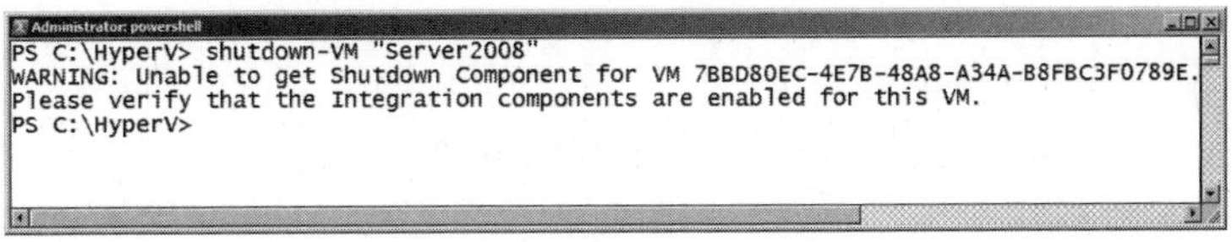

FIGURE 10.32

Failed shutdown—all VMs are suspended

```
Administrator: powershell
PS C:\HyperV> shutdown-VM "Server2008"
WARNING: Unable to get Shutdown Component for VM 7BBD80EC-4E7B-48A8-A34A-B8FBC3F0789E.
Please verify that the Integration components are enabled for this VM.
PS C:\HyperV>
```

MANAGING VHDS

The common container for storing a VM-accessible disk is the VHD file. You can create, change, test, and compact these disks while they aren't in use by a VM. Table 10.4 lists common VHD management functions.

TABLE 10.4:   Common Storage Management Functions in the Hyper-V Library

FUNCTION NAME	DESCRIPTION
new-VHD	Creates a new VHD file
compress-VHD	Compacts a VHD file
convert-VHD	Changes to/from fixed or dynamic; creates new VHD
expand-VHD	Increases the size of a VHD
get-VHDInfo	Retrieves information about a VHD
merge-VHD	Merges a child with a parent disk (untested at time of writing)
mount-VHD	Mounts a VHD on a host for access
unmount-VHD	Unmounts a VHD from a host
test-VHD	Validates the integrity of a VHD file

You learned how to create a new VHD file using new-VHD as part of VM provisioning (see "Creating a Bare-Bones VM" earlier in this chapter). As you're likely aware, you can create VHD files with either a static (fixed) or dynamic size; dynamic is the default. To create a new VHD file, you must supply a name and the desired size (see Figure 10.33) in the default directory for virtual hard disks. The following code creates a dynamic VHD named tiny with a size of 2 GB:

```
new-vhd tiny 2gb
```

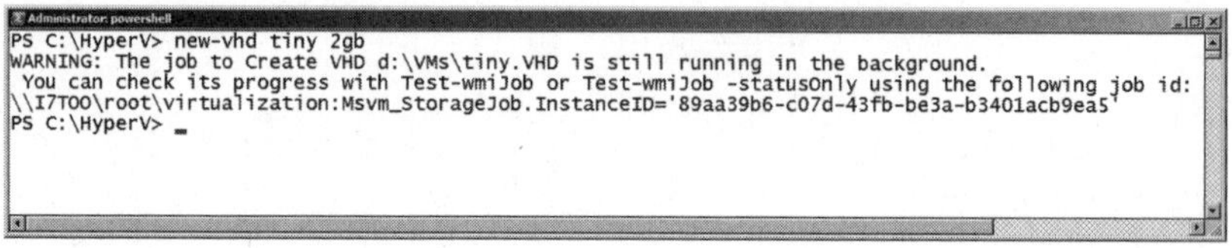

FIGURE 10.33

Using the new-VHD function

You may notice that the call to new-VHD spawns a job that runs in the background. Some Hyper-V administrative tasks (like VHD creation) can take a long time. In the case of new-VHD, you can opt to have your script wait for the task to complete by using the -wait parameter:

```
New-VHD "big" 20GB -fixed -wait
```

You can periodically check the status of the WMI job by using the included test-WMIjob function (see Figure 10.34):

```
new-vhd BIGDisk 200gb -Fixed
Test-WMIJob $Diskjob
```

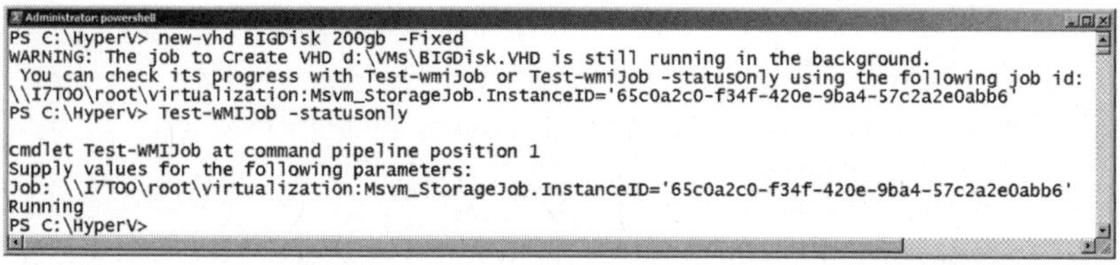

FIGURE 10.34

Using the test-WMIjob function

get-VHDinfo can provide basic information about a VHD file, including the actual file size, the maximum internal size, the type, and whether it's in use at a given time (see Figure 10.35):

```
get-vhdinfo "Windows XP"
```

Just like new-VHD, get-VHDinfo defaults to the Hyper-V virtual hard disk directory.

Monitoring storage used by VHDs can be a critical management function, particularly when you're using dynamic VHDs. Unexpected VHD growth on a shared physical disk can lead to performance issues for all VMs homed there. You can create a tiny and useful VHD storage report like the one in Figure 10.36:

```
get-vhdinfo *| out-gridview
```

FIGURE 10.35
get-VHDinfo
retrieves basic
information.

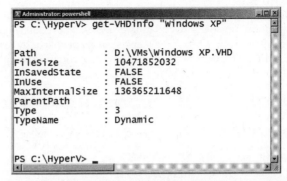

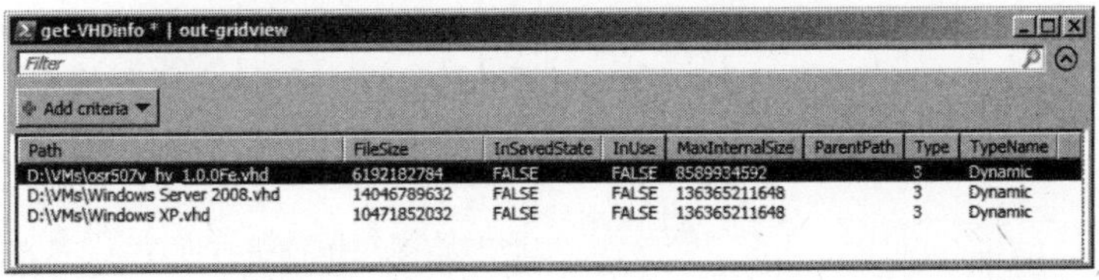

FIGURE 10.36
VHD size report

If your VHDs reside somewhere other than in the default virtual hard disk directory, you can get a similar report by stringing together the path and additional formatting information:

```
dir "d:\VMs\*.vhd" | get-vhdinfo *| out-gridview
```

It's useful to access the contents of a VHD file from the virtualization host as if it were a locally attached drive. Being able to add files to or remove files from a VHD without starting a VM can save you time and can facilitate offline maintenance. You can use mount-VHD and unmount-VHD to simplify the mounting of local VHD files:

```
Mount-VHD HUGE
```

The mount-VHD function doesn't return much useful information in the PowerShell user interface, but you can see the VHD listed as a volume within Server Manager's Disk Management (Figure 10.37).

FIGURE 10.37
Mounted VHD in
Server Manager

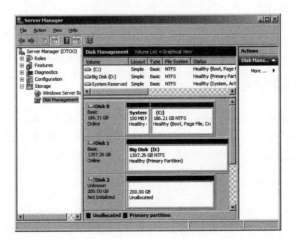

This mounted VHD wasn't formatted as part of the creation process (it hadn't yet been exposed to an operating system installation process). After mounting, you can locate the VHD on the host either by using the Computer Management console or by using the diskpart command (see Figure 10.38). Once you identify the volume, you can then perform additional storage tasks from the host.

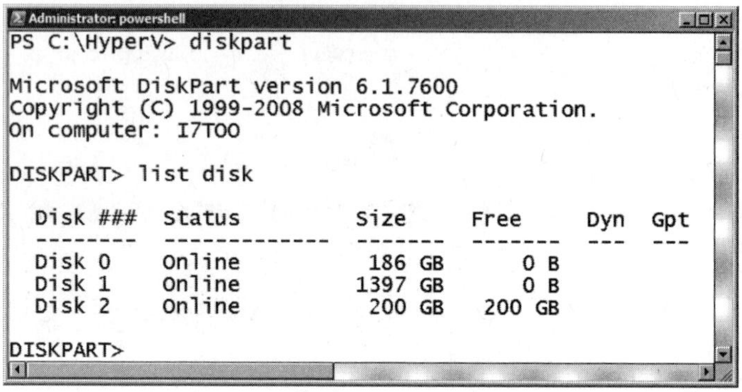

FIGURE 10.38

Using diskpart to see information about a mounted VHD

```
Administrator: powershell                                        _ □ x
PS C:\HyperV> diskpart

Microsoft DiskPart version 6.1.7600
Copyright (C) 1999-2008 Microsoft Corporation.
On computer: I7TOO

DISKPART> list disk

  Disk ###  Status          Size     Free    Dyn  Gpt
  --------  -------------   -------  -------  ---  ---
  Disk 0    Online           186 GB     0 B
  Disk 1    Online          1397 GB     0 B
  Disk 2    Online           200 GB   200 GB

DISKPART>
```

NOTE The capability to mount a VHD within the parent partition is so useful that it was added to Server Manager in Windows Server 2008 R2. The functions dismount-VHD, compress-VHD, convert-VHD, expand-VHD, test-VHD, and merge-VHD all help you manage and alter your VHDs in ways consistent with their names. For more information about how to use them, you can review the examples contained in the Hyper-V library.

Maintaining Virtual Systems

Your virtual systems depend on you to keep them properly maintained. Automating required configuration changes, installing software updates, and sometimes rolling back changes are all tasks necessary to keep physical systems and VMs running efficiently.

CONFIGURATION CHANGES

Business and technical pressures may require you to alter the configurations of existing VMs. Perhaps the applications on a given VM require more RAM or CPU resources. Maybe a physical NIC is experiencing a high network load, and some VM traffic must be offloaded to a new interface. Earlier in the chapter, we reviewed functions for automating configuration changes for VMs. Table 10.5 lists functions commonly used from the library to define or alter the configuration of a VM.

TABLE 10.5:   HyperV Library VM Configuration Management Functions

FUNCTION NAME	DESCRIPTION
add-VMdisk	Adds a disk (VHD or ISO) to a defined drive
add-VMdrive	Adds a drive to a defined controller

TABLE 10.5: HyperV Library VM Configuration Management Functions *(CONTINUED)*

FUNCTION NAME	DESCRIPTION
add-VMKVP	Adds key/value pairs to be sent to a VM
add-VMfloppydisk	Adds a floppy disk
add-VMnewharddisk	Creates a new VHD and attaches it to a VM
add-VMNIC	Adds a NIC to a VM
add-VMpassthrough	Connects pass-through disk to a VM
add-VMRASD	Adds hardware described by virtual Resource Allocation Setting Data
add-VMSCSIcontroller	Adds a synthetic SCSI controller
add-ZIPcontent	Adds content to a ZIP file (extra bonus!)
new-VFD	Creates a new virtual floppy drive
new-VHD	Creates a new VHD file
new-VM	Creates a new VM
new-VMswitchport	Creates a new virtual switch port
set-VM	Sets the BIOS boot order and startup/shutdown actions
set-VMCPUcount	Sets the CPU count (1–4)
set-VMdisk	Changes the configuration of an existing disk
set-VMintegrationcomponent	Enables/disables ICs for one or more VMs
set-VMmemory	Sets the amount of RAM
set-VMNICaddress	Sets the MAC address for a virtual NIC
set-VMNICswitch	Connects a NIC to a virtual switch
set-VMNICVLAN	Sets VLAN ID for a NIC
set-VMRASD	Changes virtual hardware described by Resource Allocation Setting Data to a VM
set-VMSerialPort	Connects serial port to a named pipe
set-VMNICSwitch	Connects NIC to a virtual switch

PATCHING

You can update the software components of a running VM the same way you do for a physical system. You can also patch VMs while they're offline using the Offline Virtual Machine Servicing Tool, discussed briefly in Chapter 4, "Utilizing Virtualization Best Practices." You can use mount-VHD to access the disk for offline VMs and prestage software for later installation.

SNAPSHOTS

Hyper-V can create point-in-time VM snapshots. You can use retained snapshot information to revert a VM to a known state in the past. Table 10.6 lists the snapshot-related functions found in the library.

TABLE 10.6: HyperV Library Snapshot Management Functions

FUNCTION NAME	DESCRIPTION
merge-VHD	Merges VHDs from snapshots
restore-VMsnapshot	Reverts to a previous snapshot
choose-VMsnapshot	Selects a snapshot
get-VMsnapshot	Accesses VM snapshot information
get-VMsnapshottree	Accesses VM snapshot information and shows it as a tree
new-VMsnapshot	Creates a new snapshot
remove-VMsnapshot	Deletes a snapshot
rename-VMsnapshot	Changes the name of an existing snapshot
update-VMsnapshot	Creates a new snapshot using an existing name

NOTE Snapshots aren't backups. We hate snapshots! They are very useful for development and testing purposes (to roll back changes), but they aren't suitable for all situations and should never ever be used in production scenarios.

Creating a snapshot is a straightforward process of calling new-VMsnaphot and specifying or passing the target VMs to be snapped (see Figure 10.39):

```
new-vmsnapshot "SCO UNIX 5.0.7" -wait
```

A more useful function for creating new snapshots may be update-VMsnapshot. This function creates a new snapshot and alters the displayed name to something of your choosing (see Figure 10.40 and Figure 10.41):

```
Update-VMSnapshot "SCO UNIX 5.0.7" "Before Scary Update"
```

FIGURE 10.39
New snapshot

```
PS C:\HyperV> new-vmsnapshot "SCO UNIX 5.0.7" -wait

Confirm
Are you sure you want to perform this action?
Performing operation "Create Snapshot " on Target "SCO UNIX 5.0.7".
[Y] Yes  [A] Yes to All  [N] No  [L] No to All  [S] Suspend  [?] Help (default is "Y"): y

Desc.   VMElementName                    Boot order              Created        Notes
-----   -------------                    ----------              -------        -----
Snapshot SCO UNIX 5.0.7 - (1/31/2010 -... {CD, IDE, NET, Floppy}  1/31/2010 9:1...


PS C:\HyperV> _
```

FIGURE 10.40
New snapshot with
specified name

```
PS C:\HyperV> update-VMSnapshot "SCO UNIX 5.0.7" "Before Scary Update"

Confirm
Are you sure you want to perform this action?
Performing operation "Create Snapshot " on Target "SCO UNIX 5.0.7".
[Y] Yes  [A] Yes to All  [N] No  [L] No to All  [S] Suspend  [?] Help (default is "Y"): y

Confirm
Are you sure you want to perform this action?
Performing operation "Modify VM Settings object" on Target "SCO UNIX 5.0.7".
[Y] Yes  [A] Yes to All  [N] No  [L] No to All  [S] Suspend  [?] Help (default is "Y"): y
Modified VM Settings object for SCO UNIX 5.0.7
PS C:\HyperV> _
```

FIGURE 10.41
New snapshot In
Hyper-V GUI

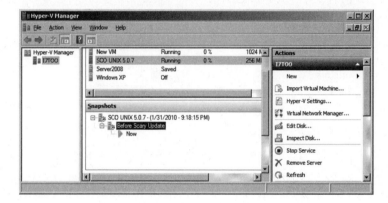

Reverting and applying snapshots is also simplified with the library when you use
`select-VMsnapshot` in conjunction with `restore-VMsnapshot` (see Figure 10.42):

```
select-vmsnapshot "SCO UNIX 5.0.7" | Restore-VMSnapshot
```

FIGURE 10.42
Restoring and
applying snapshots

```
PS C:\HyperV> select-vmsnapshot "SCO UNIX 5.0.7" | restore-vmsnapshot
0   +SCO UNIX 5.0.7 - (1/31/2010 - 9:18:15 PM)
1   | +Before Scary Update
2   | |--After Scary Update
Which one ?: 1
WARNING: VM SCO UNIX 5.0.7 is currently Running and needs to be stopped

Confirm
Are you sure you want to perform this action?
Performing operation "Change state to Stopped" on Target "SCO UNIX 5.0.7".
[Y] Yes  [A] Yes to All  [N] No  [L] No to All  [S] Suspend  [?] Help (default is "Y"): y
OK

Confirm
Are you sure you want to perform this action?
Performing operation "Restore SnapShot " on Target "SCO UNIX 5.0.7".
[Y] Yes  [A] Yes to All  [N] No  [L] No to All  [S] Suspend  [?] Help (default is "Y"): y
PS C:\HyperV>
```

Managing Access

Controlling access to VMs is an important task for IT managers. When you encapsulate an entire system into a single file, you run into new security challenges. Poorly secured network links to a physical host or shaky backup processes can quickly bypass locked data-center doors. If you have bad security practices, entire virtual systems can be pilfered without detection.

Virtualization enables a new mechanism for system access: remote desktop interaction. You can remotely view and interact with the console of a VM. Before virtualization, server consoles could be secured in a data center or computer room unless remote-access tools (IP-based keyboard/ video/mouse [KVM] or lights-out/remote console hardware) were employed. Virtualization can create a security opportunity for these formerly inaccessible system consoles.

Securing access to VM consoles is just as important as other means of securing virtual systems. Virtual hosting of desktops also requires careful access control management for VMs. Chapter 5, "Securing Hyper-V," discusses access management for individual VMs. After you set up proper security for users or administrative access, you can start remote display sessions to a particular VM by calling VMConnect.exe. The VMConnect client is typically found in C:\Program Files\ Hyper-V, and it has its own set of command-line options, which are shown in Figure 10.43.

FIGURE 10.43
VMConnect
parameters

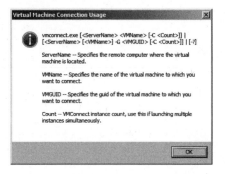

You can create a remote access session without calling VMConnect.exe directly by using the new-VMconnectsession function.

Migration

In many situations, you need to migrate a VM from one physical server to another. Hardware failures, capacity limitations, and maintenance are all reasons to relocate a VM. You can automate the move of a VM between systems in a number of ways. Common methods include importing/exporting (discussed in Chapter 6, "Migrating Virtual Machines"), using failover clustering (covered in Chapter 8, "High Availability)," performing a simple file copy, or undertaking a virtual to virtual (V2V) migration. SCVMM 2008 and SCVMM 2008 R2 support the automation of VM migration better than any other solution; we'll cover it in Chapter 11.

Simple File Copy

VM information lives in files. Why not copy or move the files that define a VM from one host to another? Finding all the necessary files and ensuring they're properly migrated can be a complicated task. Guaranteeing the VM is in a movable state (off or saved) is important, as is handling host-specific dependencies such as the migration of virtual network resources and security settings.

Copying all the files from one host to another doesn't work without careful coordination. The export and import capabilities exposed through the Hyper-V Manager handle these checks fairly well, and they're a supported way to migrate VMs. SCVMM also has a supported move process as well as V2V capability.

Still, you may choose to move a VM using an entirely unsupported copy process. For more information about how to do this, review the diskshadow backup and recovery process detailed in Chapter 7, "Backing Up and Recovering VMs." Using xcopy parameters can address the specifics of file security issues, but you're still likely to run into issues.

Export/Import

Exporting a VM from one host and importing it on another is perhaps the simplest and cleanest migration method to automate without SCVMM. Exporting requires that a VM be either off or in a saved state. The HyperV library supports the exporting and importing of VMs by using the export-VM and import-VM functions. Calling export-VM requires a reference to the VM to be exported as well as the export path, with optional parameters that include the name of the physical server, whether to export state (VHDs), and the ability to wait for the process to complete:

```
export-VM "New VM" c:\exports -server localhost -copystate -wait
```

The import-VM function only requires the path to the exported VM as a parameter, with optional parameters similar to those of export-VM:

```
import-VM "C:\exports\New VM" -wait
```

SCVMM's ability to move VMs between hosts masks the storage and security dependency of Hyper-V export and is a more suitable approach for automating migrations in many environments.

Failover Clustering

Failover clustering facilitates the migration of VMs from one physical host to another with limited or no perceptible downtime, but it requires preconfiguration. Hyper-V clusters are presented in Chapter 8. Hyper-V failover clustering (Quick Migration and Live Migration) requires identically configured physical hosts as well as shared storage. You typically automate cluster management tasks—creation, configuration, and workload migration—using cluster.exe or via PowerShell. Clustering tasks can also be performed using the failover-clustering WMI provider (root\MSCluster). SCVMM provides cluster management capabilities for Hyper-V that you can automate using its set of Windows PowerShell cmdlets.

The R2 Gold version of the library includes failover cluster management functions, such as get-VMclustergroup, get-VMlivemigrationnetwork, move-VM, select-clustersharedvolume, select-VMlivemigrationnetwork, and sync-VMclusterconfig. A simple, real-world example of the cluster management functions is the common requirement to migrate all VMs from a failover cluster node. In our test cluster, we have one VM still running on a system (HPDL380T) that we need to migrate in order to perform hardware maintenance. The following command migrates all clustered VMs from HPDL380T to the other node in the cluster (HPDL380B), as shown in Figure 10.44:

```
Get-VM -server HPDL380T | move-vm -Destination HPDL380B
```

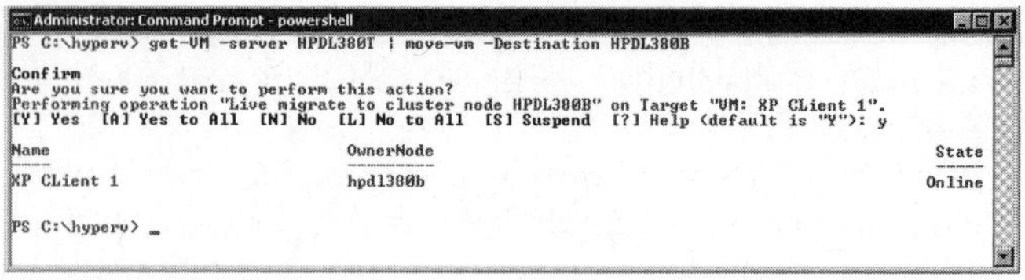

FIGURE 10.44
Moving all VMs
from a node

```
Administrator: Command Prompt - powershell                                    _ □ X
PS C:\hyperv> get-VM -server HPDL380T | move-vm -Destination HPDL380B

Confirm
Are you sure you want to perform this action?
Performing operation "Live migrate to cluster node HPDL380B" on Target "VM: XP CLient 1".
[Y] Yes  [A] Yes to All  [N] No  [L] No to All  [S] Suspend  [?] Help (default is "Y"): y

Name                           OwnerNode                              State
----                           ---------                              -----
XP CLient 1                    hpdl380b                               Online

PS C:\hyperv> _
```

Virtual to Virtual Migration

Virtual to virtual (V2V) migrations are similar to physical to virtual (P2V) migrations; they're discussed in Chapter 6. Automating V2V migrations is a tricky process and is largely unnecessary if you're moving a VM from one host to another. You can also automate V2V migrations with SCVMM cmdlets.

Backup and Recovery

In Chapter 7, we covered backup and recovery without the use of enterprise tools. System Center Data Protection Manager (DPM) is the best option for enterprise-class backup with Hyper-V; we discuss that process in Chapter 12.

Earlier versions of the library included a `diskshadow` script-generating function (`get-VMbackupscript`). Calling the function generated a `diskshadow` script similar to the one used in Chapter 7. It has been removed from the R2 Gold version of the library, so you should look to the processes in Chapter 7 or Chapter 12 for more sustainable backup and recovery processes.

Collecting and Monitoring Data

Monitoring how your virtual environment performs is key to ensuring smooth operation. You've seen how to locate virtual hosts, enumerate their child VMs, and access configuration information. Visibility into the health and performance of each VM is also important.

Enterprise tools like those found in the Microsoft System Center family are the best solution for collecting, analyzing, and monitoring health and performance. System Center Operations Manager (SCOM), which can be connected to SCVMM, can serve as a repository for historical performance data for your entire Microsoft-centric computing environment. SCOM 2007 R2 also has the capability to monitor systems running common Linux and UNIX operating systems, so monitoring non-Microsoft-centric VMs is also possible. It is challenging to do comprehensive monitoring if you don't have access to System Center tools.

Viewing the Desktop

Before you go too far down the path of data collection, you have to please corporate management. Data centers and operations rooms often have banks of monitors filled with color images including graphs, charts, maps, and system consoles. A dirty little secret of many of these rooms is that certain screens are simply for show—some of the big, blinking displays exist only to create the appearance of a well-monitored environment.

Another truth of large data centers is that operators (personnel who work regularly in the computer room) often need to see what is on the screen of a particular system. It's also a reality that these employees aren't always trusted to interact with these same systems for regulatory reasons or by management mandate.

The virtualization provider allows you to request a JPEG picture of a VM's desktop. You can capture and display these images in any number of ways, and they can be useful to operators and administrators for auditing/monitoring purposes (or handy to show on a large display). The get-VMthumbnail function creates a JPEG file of a running VM with a name based on the VM's display (element) name and writes it to the current directory (as shown in Figure 10.45):

```
Get-VM | Get-VMThumbnail
```

FIGURE 10.45
Using
get-VMthumbnail
to create images of
VM desktops

You can post the generated image files to a website, save them into SharePoint, or easily view them using Windows Explorer. Regularly capturing an image of the desktop can be useful for troubleshooting or compliance purposes.

Testing for Service

Ping is often the first monitoring tool most administrators use to check the health of a system. It's not a comprehensive test, but it can show that a particular system's TCP/IP stack is accessible under normal circumstances, as well as point out environmental issues on a network (name resolution, routing, firewall settings, or latency challenges). The ping-VM function makes it convenient to ping configured VMs (see Figure 10.46):

```
get-vm | ping-VM |
FT VMElementName, FullyQualifiedDomainName, Status -auto
```

FIGURE 10.46
Using ping-VM to
check the status of
configured VMss

> **TIP** Firewall status for contemporary versions of Microsoft Windows may not allow a response from Ping, so this function may not provide much value in a secure environment.

You can also use test-VMheartbeat and get-VMKVP to verify that a VM is running and functioning (get-VMKVP was discussed earlier in the chapter). You can think of test-VMheartbeat as a sort of a ping to the ICs running in a VM. If the heartbeat component included in the ICs is functioning, the test is successful. O'Neill has included a timeout parameter for managing the startup sequence of VMs. Using `test-VMheartbeat`, you can stagger an environment's power-up until key network services are ready:

```
start-vm "TestDC"
Test-vmheartBeat "TestDC" -Timeout 300
start-vm "TestExchange"
```

TIP Staggering/delaying the startup of a VM is such a common need that O'Neill recently added more options to the `start-VM` function. You can alternately use `start-VM "Test-DC" - wait -Heartbeat  300` to achieve the same result.

Accessing Processor Performance Data

You may have noticed that the memory used by VMs is reflected on the Windows Task Manager's Performance tab. Every time you start a VM, the amount of memory used by the physical system increases, which is reflected by the Windows Task Manager. This isn't true for processor (CPU) utilization: the CPU load of child VMs isn't reflected in the Windows Task Manager of the host/parent. Figure 10.47 shows the CPU and memory usage history of a quad-core system.

FIGURE 10.47

Host's Task
Manager: low load

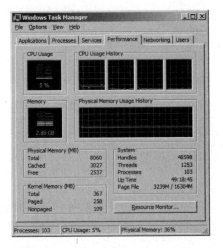

The Task Manager reflects relatively low CPU usage. But the system is the host for a two-processor Server 2003 VM running at more than 90 percent processor load (Figure 10.48 is the Task Manager from within the VM).

You could query each individual VM remotely to access and retrieve the CPU load, but that wouldn't give you an accurate view of the actual load on the host. It would also require network access to the VM as well as an appropriate level of security.

You can access information about the performance of individual VM virtual processors through the parent using the virtualization provider and the `MSVM_Processor` class, as reflected by the WMI query in Figure 10.49:

```
GWMI -Class MSVM_Processor -Namespace root\virtualization |
   ft SystemName,LoadPercentage -auto
```

FIGURE 10.48

VM: high CPU load

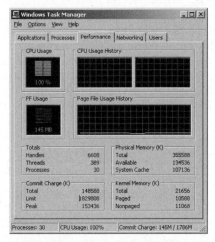

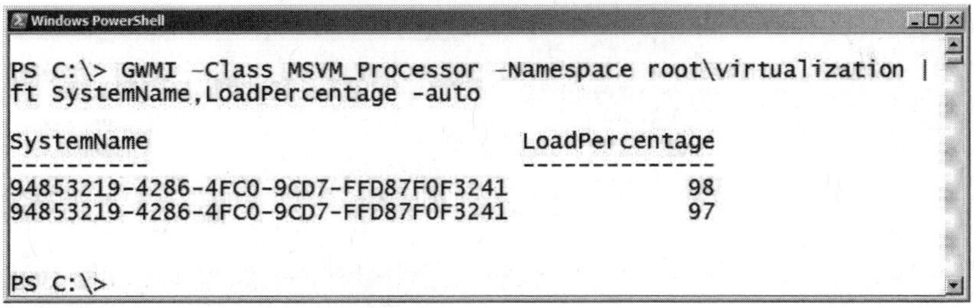

FIGURE 10.49

CPU load-
percentage query

```
PS C:\> GWMI -Class MSVM_Processor -Namespace root\virtualization |
ft SystemName,LoadPercentage -auto

SystemName                              LoadPercentage
----------                              --------------
94853219-4286-4FC0-9CD7-FFD87F0F3241                98
94853219-4286-4FC0-9CD7-FFD87F0F3241                97

PS C:\>
```

The query shows the CPU load percentage and the unfriendly name of the associated VM. HyperV.PS1 didn't include any processor performance-related functions, but O'Neill has enhanced newer versions of the library with the get-VMprocessor function (we'll show you that later). The following is a sample Windows PowerShell function that collects the virtual processor information from a local host and ties in the VM name:

```
function List-VMCPULoad
{Param ($server=".")
   $Procs= GWMI -computerName $server -Namespace ↵
root\virtualization -Class MSVM_Processor
   foreach ($Proc in $Procs) {
      GWMI -computerName $server -Namespace ↵
root\virtualization -Query ↵
"Select * From MSVM_ComputerSystem Where Name = '$($Proc.SystemName)'" |
      add-member -passthru noteproperty "Load%" $Proc.LoadPercentage |
      add-member -passthru noteproperty "CPUID" $Proc.deviceid.split("\")[-1]
   }
}

list-vmcpuload | ft elementname, CPUID, Load% -auto
```

This function lists all individual running virtual processors on a system, showing each VM name. This may not be entirely useful in developing a clear picture of processor performance, because other processes on the physical host (including other VMs) can reduce the available compute cycles. This interference can artificially reduce the LoadPercentage value retrieved from MSVM_Proccessor. For example, two VMs are listed in Figure 10.50 (one with four cores and one with two) using about as much CPU as they're allowed (the six virtual cores are running on a host with only four cores). The individual LoadPercentage value for each virtual CPU can appear to be low (55 percent for one) because of the sharing of resources. The VMs themselves believe they're running at full steam, but LoadPercentage doesn't clearly reflect this. Adding an additional four-core VM under extreme CPU load makes this point more clearly, as shown in Figure 10.51.

FIGURE 10.50

Nice CPU load percentage query

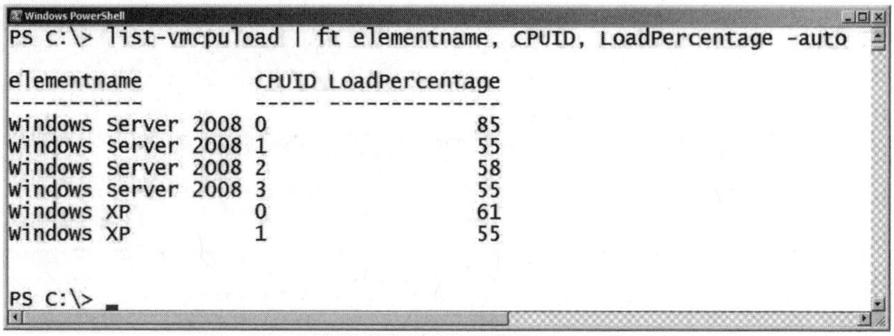

FIGURE 10.51

More load, lower percentage

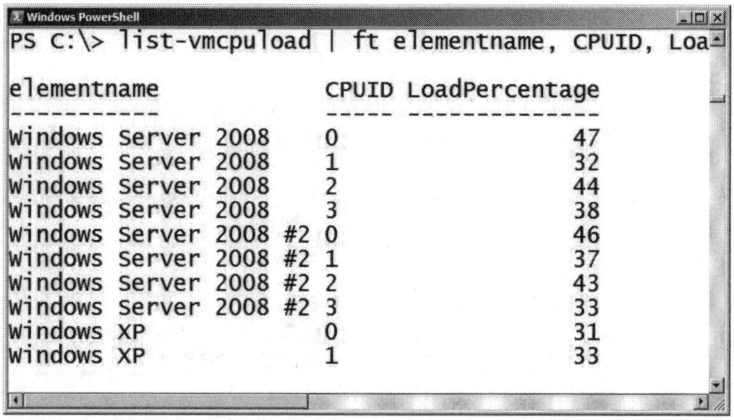

With 10 virtual cores all taxed and competing for the power of the 4 physical cores (along with processes on the parent partition), the LoadPercentage value is reduced. Looking solely at the LoadPercentage of a single VM can mislead you into believing that a VM isn't low on processing power. To get the actual utilization of each physical processor, it's recommended that you don't use the virtualization provider but instead use the tried-and-true Common Information Model (CIM) version 2.

TIP Several good performance resources describe how to access counters and troubleshoot performance issues for Hyper-V, including "Measuring Performance on Hyper-V" (`http://msdn` `.microsoft.com/en-us/library/cc768535.aspx`) and an "All Topics Performance" post titled "How to Get Processor Utilization for Hyper-V via WMI" (`http://blogs.msdn.com/tvoellm/` `archive/2008/07/14/how-to-get-processor-utilization-for-hyper-v-via-wmi` `.aspx`). They're both informative and can help you create a comprehensive and accurate view of CPU utilization. They also have too much math and too many formulas for day-to-day use.

Accessing the WMI CIMv2 class `Win32_PerfRawData_HVStats_` `HyperVHypervisorLogicalProcessor` is the recommended approach, but the formulas to derive processor utilization are a hassle. You can approximate the overall utilization by adding together the `loadPercentage` values from each virtual processor and dividing the total by the number of physical cores. The following function creates a useful CPU utilization report with color coding to connote high CPU load on individual virtual CPUs, as well as on the host system (see Figure 10.52):

```
function Report-VMCPU
{Param ($server=".")
    $LoadSum = 0
    $PCores = 0
    $VProcs= GWMI -computerName $server -Namespace ↵
root\virtualization -Class MSVM_Processor
    write-host "`n                                        CPU  Load"
    write-host "VM Name                                 #    %"
    write-host "----------------------------------- ---- -----"
    foreach ($VProc in $VProcs) {
        $VM = GWMI -computerName $server -Namespace ↵
root\virtualization -Query ↵
"Select * From MSVM_ComputerSystem Where Name = '$($VProc.SystemName)'"
        $VMname = $VM.Elementname.PadRight(39," ")
        $VMCPU  = $VProc.deviceid.split("\")[-1]
        $VMCPULOAD = $VProc.LoadPercentage
        Write-Host "$VMname $VMCPU     "   -nonewline
        if ($VMCPULOAD -lt 30) {
            write-host $VMCPULOAD -backgroundcolor green
        }
        elseif ($VMCPULOAD -gt 80) {
            write-host $VMCPULOAD -backgroundcolor red
        }
        else {write-host $VMCPULOAD}
        $LoadSum = $LoadSum + $VMCPULOAD
    }
    $PProcs= GWMI -computerName $server -Namespace ↵
root\CIMV2 -Class Win32_Processor
    foreach ($PProc in $PProcs) {
        $PCores = $PCores + $PProc.NumberOfCores }
    $VLoad =  $LoadSum / $PCores
    write-host "`n-----------------------------------------"
```

```
Write-Host "Physical Host Virtual CPU Perf Summary" -nonewline
if($Server -ne ".") {
    write-host " for $Server"} else {write-host " "}
Write-Host "`n        Total Physical Cores: " $PCores
Write-Host "Approx. Virt. CPU Utilization: " -nonewline
if ($VLoad -lt 30) {write-host $VLoad -backgroundcolor green}
elseif ($VLoad -gt 80) {write-host $VLoad -backgroundcolor red}
else {write-host $VLoad}
write-host "-------------------------------------------`n"
}
```

FIGURE 10.52

Better CPU
load report

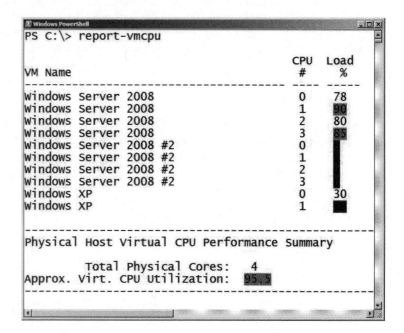

The code may not reflect the acme of Windows PowerShell or mathematics elegance, but you can use the output to clearly show a high CPU load condition.

NOTE   MSVM_Processor also includes LoadPercentageHistory, which is an array of recent measurements of LoadHistory.

As we mentioned earlier, James has included the get-VMprocessor function in later versions of the library, which generates a very similar report. Figure 10.53 shows the output of get-VMprocessor on a different system.

Performance Monitoring and PowerGadgets

The previous code sample produces some usable and ugly output. SoftwareFX sells a great set of inexpensive graphical tools, called PowerGadgets, that connect right into PowerShell. You can use PowerGadgets to quickly and easily create interactive tools using gauges, charts, graphs, and maps; you can then use these tools with Windows PowerShell to monitor and manage Hyper-V. Gadgets you create can even be added to the Vista or Windows 7 Sidebar. You can download an evaluation copy of PowerGadgets from the SoftwareFX website at `www.softwarefx.com`.

FIGURE 10.53

The `get-VMprocessor` output

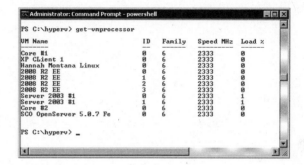

Summary

The WMI provider combined with Windows PowerShell or another scripting language can help you automate virtually any Hyper-V administrative task. Building on the work and insight of others can save you time. The library maintained in `www.codeplex.com` is a useful resource. Learning basic tricks in Windows PowerShell can magnify your capabilities and the value of your Hyper-V environment.

Chapter 11

Using System Center Virtual Machine Manager 2008

Virtualization brings new flexibilities to the IT landscape, such as rapid deployment of systems, server migration, and the ability to deploy systems without regard to the physical server environment.

These virtualization flexibilities have spawned a new area of software dedicated to managing the virtualization environment. *Virtualization management* software is geared completely toward managing the virtualization platform and adding capabilities to a very flexible virtualization environment.

System Center Virtual Machine Manager (SCVMM) 2008 focuses on bridging the gap between physical systems management, virtualization management, and application knowledge. The ability to bring application knowledge into the virtualization management space marries the flexibility of virtualization with the applications running in the virtual machines.

In this chapter, we focus on equipping you with the necessary information to get a SCVMM 2008 deployment going. Although SCVMM 2008 manages various virtualization platforms, the focus of this chapter is specifically on managing the Hyper-V environment. Detailed technical information about using SCVMM 2008 to manage other virtualization platforms is covered in the book *Mastering Virtual Machine Manager 2008 R2* by Michael and Linares (Sybex, 2009).

In this chapter, we cover the following topics:

- ◆ System Center suite overview
- ◆ SCVMM 2008 architecture
- ◆ Installing SCVMM 2008
- ◆ Integrating SCOM 2007 and SCVMM 2008
- ◆ Provisioning virtual machines from the library

System Center Suite Overview

The System Center suite is a cohesive group of products, each targeting specific systems management functionality, directed at managing the IT life cycle. It's important to place the SCVMM 2008 functionality in the context of the broader System Center suite (see Figure 11.1).

Four main software components of the System Center family of products offer management capabilities to the physical and virtual infrastructure. As a virtualization professional, you need to understand the capabilities of each component and how each applies to managing Microsoft and non-Microsoft virtualization platforms.

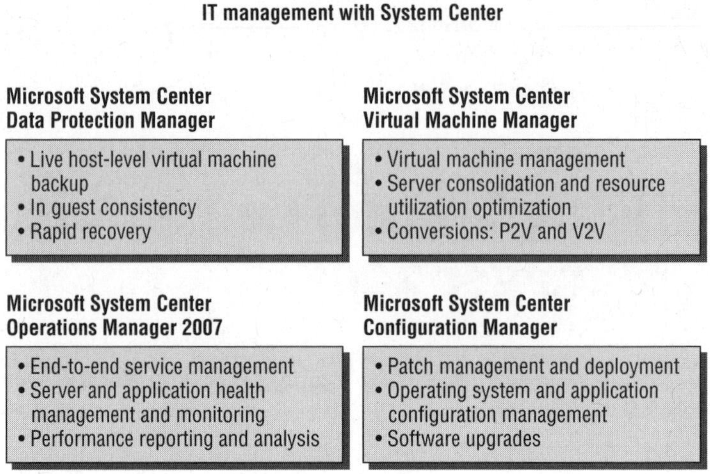

FIGURE 11.1
Functionality within the System Center product family

IT management with System Center

**Microsoft System Center
Data Protection Manager**

- Live host-level virtual machine backup
- In guest consistency
- Rapid recovery

**Microsoft System Center
Virtual Machine Manager**

- Virtual machine management
- Server consolidation and resource utilization optimization
- Conversions: P2V and V2V

**Microsoft System Center
Operations Manager 2007**

- End-to-end service management
- Server and application health management and monitoring
- Performance reporting and analysis

**Microsoft System Center
Configuration Manager**

- Patch management and deployment
- Operating system and application configuration management
- Software upgrades

System Center Virtual Machine Manager 2008

SCVMM lets you perform heterogeneous hypervisor management by managing Virtual Server 2005 R2 SP1, as well as Hyper-V and VMware ESX hypervisors. SCVMM provides you with all the functionality for managing virtualization hosts and guests as well as the framework for enhancing virtualization management with application-level knowledge.

You can integrate Virtual Machine Manager with System Center Operations Manager (SCOM) 2007 to obtain the Performance and Resource Optimization (PRO) functionality. PRO is a feature of SCVMM 2008 that enables the dynamic management of a virtualized infrastructure. Additional functionality in SCVMM includes the following:

- Physical to virtual (P2V) and virtual to virtual (V2V) conversions

- Self-service portal that allows end users to perform VM creation and delegation

- Delegated administration

- Library functionality

- Deep PowerShell integration

- Quick Migration, Live Migration, and VMotion support

- Storage area network (SAN) and N_Port ID Virtualization (NPIV) integration

- Intelligent placement of virtual machines in the managed environment

- Host-capacity management

System Center Operations Manager 2007

System Center Operations Manager provides a health/service model: a real-time alerting, infrastructure-monitoring, and reporting environment that lets you manage physical and virtual environments as well as Microsoft and non-Microsoft platforms. SCOM provides the following functionality:

End-to-end monitoring SCOM lets you look at the health of all virtualization components. For example, the Microsoft virtualization environment generally consists of the following components: Hyper-V, Quick Migration and Live Migration clusters, SCVMM components, and System Center Data Protection Manager (DPM) components for host and virtual machine (VM) recovery. All of these components are important to the health of a Microsoft virtualization infrastructure. SCOM provides management packs, health models, alerts, and reports for each of these components.

Comprehensive views of health states SCOM includes a health model in the management pack for each managed component. Health models include monitors to report on the health of all the components of the system. For example, the SCVMM management pack includes a model that looks at the health of the SCVMM components including the SCVMM server, the SQL database, the self-service portal, and the SCVMM agent. When one component isn't healthy, it affects the health of the entire service.

Rapid response to events for managed systems You can respond to error conditions detected by managed components, or you can set up automated actions/tasks in the management pack.

Application-specific management packs Each management pack is specific to a managed application. The management pack provides specific knowledge about the errors and conditions that determine the health of the application. In addition, the management pack also includes tasks and reports on an application-by-application basis.

Automated tasks per application Each management pack includes tasks that are specific to an application. For instance, you can start or stop services specific to each application.

Comprehensive automated reporting infrastructure The reporting infrastructure built on top of SQL Server Reporting Services provides the infrastructure for reporting. Each managed component comes with a set of reports in the management pack that reports on health, availability, and other related items specific to the service.

Suppose you've developed a custom line-of-business application. Specific error conditions, dependencies between application components, and actions to take to maintain application health are largely stored in your brain. A management pack captures your knowledge in a health model stored in the management pack. As a result, that knowledge can be added to the SCOM infrastructure, and the applications can be detected on servers running in the environment. After the applications are detected, they can be managed immediately with the knowledge captured in the management pack.

The end goal is to bridge application alerting and monitoring into the virtualization management framework. SCVMM and SCOM provide the PRO system connector to share information about managed VMs and applications. This enables VMs that have SCOM agents and PRO packs installed to exchange information with SCVMM 2008.

System Center Data Protection Manager 2007 SP1

DPM is a comprehensive disk-to-disk and disk-to-tape data protection solution. It adds backup, recovery, and disaster-recovery functionality for key applications: Hyper-V, Virtual Server, Exchange, SQL Server, and SharePoint.

DPM uses the Volume Shadow Services (VSS) infrastructure in Windows Server and application-specific VSS writers to take continuous snapshots of data. DPM combined with Hyper-V protects VM and configuration data and, when combined with a DPM agent in the VM, gives you the ability to do granular data recovery for support applications. With DPM-to-DPM server replication of protected applications, you can add disaster recovery of protected VMs.

You now have the flexibility to configure a DPM server in data center A to protect VMs and to configure another DPM server in data center B. You can then use the DPM replication functionality, which you can schedule, throttle, and configure to work over specific network interfaces. You can replicate protected content between data centers so that in the event of data center failure, you can recover DPM-protected content on the server in the surviving data center. Chapter 12, "Protecting Virtualized Environments with System Center Data Protection Manager," provides more information about how DPM works with Hyper-V.

DPM provides the following functionality:

Disk-based protection and recovery DPM protects data by using storage to provide multiple recovery points for critical applications. For instance, VMs can have multiple recovery points that represent different days, are stored on disk, and can be recovered at any time.

Command-line driven via PowerShell All DPM actions in the user interface can be driven by the DPM PowerShell with a set of cmdlets offering flexibility to create event-driven recovery actions.

Tape-based backup and archival solution Some industry-compliance laws require long-term storage of sensitive data. In such cases, DPM can integrate directly with hardware tape-backup solutions.

Encrypted tape backup While protecting sensitive data to tape, DPM can also protect the content by using encryption.

Integration with leading tape solutions Integration with tape hardware solutions lets you move DPM-protected data directly from disk to tape.

Bare-metal disaster recovery Using the VSS services and system-state backup, DPM can recover the system configuration and data of protected applications to a bare-metal server.

Business continuity and continuous data protection DPM allows backups at 15-minute intervals, providing continuous data protection. Combine that functionality with the ability to replicate protected DPM data from one DPM server to another, and you have the components needed to provide a business continuity solution.

System Center Configuration Manager 2007

Systems Center Configuration Manager (SCCM) provides a comprehensive solution for change and configuration management. It functions not only as a delivery infrastructure for software updates of all types but also as a comprehensive reporting solution. SCCM 2007 with SCVMM 2008 provides a solution for ensuring that VMs stored in the SCVMM library can be brought online, scanned for needed patches, and placed back in the library in a completely automated fashion.

SCCM 2007 provides the following functionality:

Operating system deployment SCCM provides the ability to deploy the operating system to bare-metal machines without an operating system. This includes desktop and server operating systems.

Software application deployment   You can deploy custom business applications and off-the-shelf applications to targeted systems in the enterprise.

Deployment of software security updates   SCCM provides the infrastructure for reporting and targeting specific security updates to SCCM-managed systems. This includes reporting on systems that are missing updates and systems that have specific updates.

Assessment of variations from desired configuration   SCCM provides a desired-configuration management tool, which lets you baseline systems and report on configuration changes from the base configuration.

Hardware and software inventory   How often would you like to know the hardware configuration and applications deployed throughout the enterprise? SCCM provides reports on specific configurations' hardware and software. In addition, SCCM can differentiate between virtual and physical machines so you can generate inventory reports by VM.

Offline VM update integration with SCVMM 2008   Offline VMs that are stored in the SCVMM library can be brought online, scanned, patched, and then put back into an offline state using the Offline Virtual Machine Servicing Tool. Doing so gives you the peace of mind that even offline VMs are in an up-to-date patched state. You can find the tool at `http://technet.microsoft.com/en-us/library/cc501231.aspx`.

Application virtualization integration   In keeping with the SCCM software deployment role, SCCM can deploy sequenced application packages from Microsoft Application Virtualization. This lets you use the existing SCCM infrastructure to target specific systems for deploying application virtualization packages.

SCVMM 2008 Architecture Overview

The architecture and components of SCVMM 2008 provide its functionality. In this section, we'll explore the various components of the SCVMM 2008 system.

SCVMM 2008 provides virtualization administration and centralized control of your virtualization environment. It lets you perform rapid provisioning, migrate physical servers, and migrate VMs from other virtualization platforms. One of the core enhancements in SCVMM 2008 is the ability to manage additional virtualization platforms: Microsoft Hyper-V and VMware environments.

A SCVMM 2008 implementation consists of required core components. Other components aren't required but are useful for specific scenarios, such as creating a test and development virtualization environment. Figure 11.2 shows the SCVMM architecture and components.

Table 11.1 lists the ports and protocols used by the SCVMM components as outlined in the architecture diagram in Figure 11.2.

TABLE 11.1:   Ports and Protocols for SCVMM

DATA FLOW BETWEEN SCVMM COMPONENTS	COMMUNICATION TYPE	PORT
SCVMM server to Windows host agent (control)	WinRM	80
SCVMM server to Windows host agent (data)	SMB	445
SCVMM server to remote Microsoft SQL Server database	TDS	1433

TABLE 11.1: Ports and Protocols for SCVMM *(CONTINUED)*

DATA FLOW BETWEEN SCVMM COMPONENTS	COMMUNICATION TYPE	PORT
SCVMM server to P2V source agent	DCOM	135
Administrator console to SCVMM 2008 server	WCF	8100
Self-service portal Web server to SCVMM 2008 server	WCF	8100
Self-service portal to SCVMM 2008 self-service web server	HTTPS	443
Library to hosts	BITS	443
Host-to-host file transfer	BITS	443
VMRC connection to virtual server host	VMRC	5900
VMConnect to Hyper-V hosts	RDP	2179
Remote desktop to VMs	RDP	3389

FIGURE 11.2
SCVMM 2008
architecture

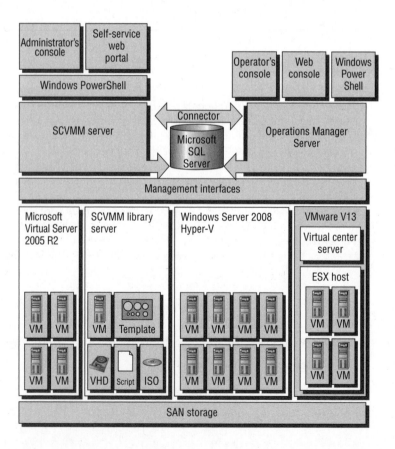

The components central to each SCVMM 2008 installation are as follows:

◆ SCVMM 2008 server

◆ Default library server

◆ SCVMM 2008 database

◆ SCVMM 2008 administrator console

Each SCVMM 2008 component fulfills a specific purpose and adds core virtualization management functionality. Let's look in more detail at the core and secondary components.

SCVMM Server

The SCVMM 2008 server is the central brain of a SCVMM 2008 implementation. Through it, all other components interact and communicate. Because all core and secondary components depend on the SCVMM server, it's the first component installed.

The SCVMM 2008 server runs as a service and is always active regardless of direct user interaction with the system through the supported interfaces. The server is responsible for running commands, transferring files, and controlling communications with other SCVMM 2008 components and with all VM hosts and library servers.

The SCVMM 2008 server has a dependency on the SCVMM database server, as shown in Figure 11.2. The architecture of SCVMM 2008 is stateless with the exception of the SQL Server database, where all configuration information and short-term performance information is stored. This stateless architecture design adds recoverability of the SCVMM system.

By default, the SCVMM 2008 server is also the default library server. You can use the SCVMM 2008 library to store file-based resources such as virtual hard disks (unless attached to a stored VM), templates, ISO images, PowerShell scripts, answer files, and VMs. You can set up additional SCVMM 2008 library servers, which is recommended when you'll be managing a large number of hosts.

SCVMM 2008 Library Server

The SCVMM library provides an inventory of resources to provision various types of VMs (see Figure 11.3). The library can store the following types of resources:

◆ Virtual hard disks: `.vhd` and `.vmdk`

◆ PowerShell scripts and answer files: `.ps1, .inf, .xml`

◆ ISO image files: `.iso`

◆ Virtual floppy disks: `.vfd, .flp`

◆ VMware templates: `.vmtx`

TIP   SCVMM 2008 doesn't synchronize library server contents between library servers. If you need to keep library server content synchronized across many library servers, you can use file replication tools such as Robocopy and Double-Take. SCVMM doesn't support Distributed File System Replication (DFS-R) replication.

FIGURE 11.3
SCVMM library
server view

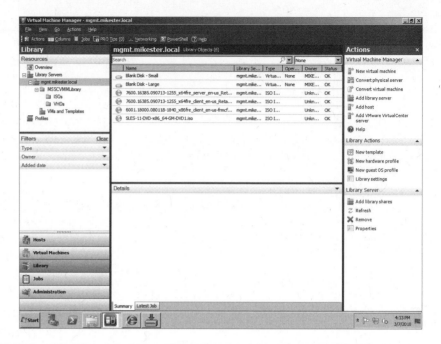

In each SCVMM server installation, the server is the default library server. After you install the SCVMM 2008 server, you can add other computers as library servers. You should take into account the amount of space you'll need to store library objects, and plan the storage capacity to match.

NOTE   You can't delete or move the default library server and library share installed on the SCVMM server. So, be very careful about the amount of content you store in the initial library. A best practice is to create a second library server on at least one managed host right after installing your first SCVMM server.

SCVMM Database

The SCVMM 2008 database stores all SCVMM 2008 configuration information. You interact with the database by using the SCVMM administrator console.

The SCVMM database requires one of the following supported versions of Microsoft SQL Server:

- SQL Server 2005 SP2

- SQL Server 2008

- SQL Server Express 2005 SP2

The database can be local to the SCVMM server, or you can use a remote database server. Because the state of the system is stored in the database, it's a best practice for large installations to either cluster the database or install the SCVMM database instance on a cluster.

NOTE   If you decide to install the SCVMM database on a new cluster, the Enterprise edition of SQL Server is required.

SCVMM Administrator Console

The SCVMM administrator console is one of three methods for interacting with the SCVMM server. You can also use the self-service portal or the PowerShell interface.

The administrator console is built on top of the SCVMM PowerShell interface, so all commands available in the console are also available from PowerShell. This means PowerShell must be installed on each computer on which you plan to install the administrator console.

You can install the administrator console on the following systems:

◆ Windows Server 2008 and Windows Server 2008 R2

◆ Windows Server 2003 and Windows Server 2003 R2

◆ Windows 7

◆ Windows Vista (all editions)

◆ Windows XP SP2 and SP3

All aspects of managing SCVMM 2008 are available from the administrator console (see Figure 11.4). The common actions that you as an administrator will perform include the following:

◆ Creating VMs

◆ Interacting with PRO tips

◆ Managing global configuration settings

◆ Managing hosts and host groups

◆ Implementing intelligent placement settings

We'll cover some of these tasks later in the chapter.

FIGURE 11.4
SCVMM administrator console

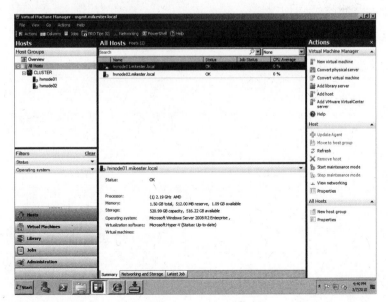

Virtual Machine Host

A *virtual machine host* is a physical computer that can run a SCVMM-supported virtualization platform. When you add a host to be managed by SCVMM (see Figure 11.5) and the virtualization platform hasn't been installed or enabled, you must take the actions outlined in Table 11.2.

TABLE 11.2:   SCVMM Add-Host Actions by Server Operating System

SERVER OPERATING SYSTEM	SCVMM ACTION
Windows Server 2003	Install Virtual Server 2005 R2 SP1 (if not already installed), and add SCVMM agent to host.
Windows Server 2008 (x86)	Install Virtual Server 2005 R2 SP1 (if not already installed), and add SCVMM agent to host.
Windows Server 2008 (x64)	Enable the Hyper-V role (if not already enabled), and add SCVMM agent to host.
Windows Server 2008 R2	Enable the Hyper-V role (if not already enabled), and add SCVMM agent to host.
VMware ESX Server	Add a host, provided VirtualCenter (VC) server was already configured (see Figure 11.5).

FIGURE 11.5

Adding a Hyper-V host to be managed by SCVMM

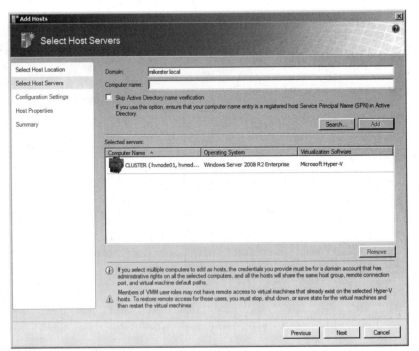

SCVMM supports the following types of hosts:

♦ Windows Server hosts located in an Active Directory (AD) domain that doesn't have two-way trust with the SCVMM 2008 server's AD domain

♦ Windows Server–based hosts located in a demilitarized zone (DMZ)

♦ Windows Server–based hosts that are in a disjointed namespace, where the host's fully qualified domain name (FQDN) resolved from the domain name service (DNS) isn't the same as the name obtained from AD

♦ VMware ESX Server hosts located anywhere in your environment

SCVMM Additional Components

Some components of the SCVMM environment are optional and map to specific environments and use cases. These optional components include the following:

♦ VM self-service portal

♦ PRO

SCVMM SELF-SERVICE WEB PORTAL

The SCVMM 2008 self-service portal is an optional, web-based component that you can install and configure to let users create and manage their own VMs within a controlled environment on a limited group of VM hosts (see Figure 11.6). You create self-service user roles that determine the scope of the users' actions on their own VMs.

You determine the host groups where self-service users can create VMs. When a self-service user creates a VM, the VM is automatically placed in the most suitable host in the host group based on host ratings. The host rating is calculated by SCVMM based on a number of factors, including the overall performance of the host, the capacity available for additional virtual machines, and the I/O subsystem performance. You can set a VM quota in a self-service user role and assign quota points to VM templates to limit the number of VMs that a user or group can deploy.

FIGURE 11.6
SCVMM self-service web portal

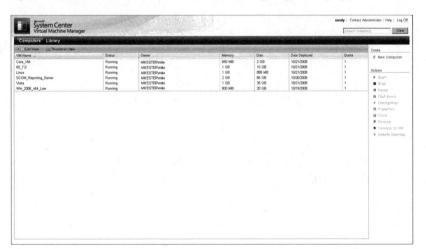

PERFORMANCE AND RESOURCE OPTIMIZATION (PRO)

PRO supports workload- and application-aware resource optimization in a virtualized environment (see Figure 11.7). Based on performance and health data provided by PRO-enabled management packs in SCOM 2007, PRO can automatically or manually implement recommendations for minimizing downtime and accelerating time to resolution.

FIGURE 11.7

PRO view

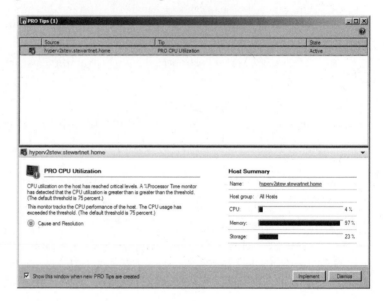

Installing SCVMM 2008

Now that you've learned about the SCVMM 2008 components, the next step is to install SCVMM to manage the Hyper-V environment.

You can install all the SCVMM components on a single server or on multiple servers. For smaller configurations, a single server or even a virtual machine will suffice. Larger installations will want to utilize multiple servers, including a SQL Server (for the database), multiple file servers as library servers, and front-end web servers for the self-service portal functionality. For this example, we'll be installing everything on a single server.

NOTE If you plan on setting up PRO functionality between System Center Operations Manager and System Center Virtual Machine Manager, you must use a full installation of SQL Server for the database store.

SCVMM 2008 Prerequisites

To install SCVMM 2008, the following prerequisites must be present on the target system:

◆ Microsoft .NET Framework 2.0

◆ Microsoft .NET Framework 3.0

- Windows Remote Management (WinRM)
- Microsoft Core XML Services (MSXML) 6.0

In addition to this software, the system must be joined to a Windows Active Directory (AD) domain.

Installing the SCVMM 2008 Server Role

Before installing any SCVMM roles on a server, use the Virtual Machine Manager Configuration Analyzer (VMMCA). This diagnostic tool can spot configuration issues and missing prerequisites before you discover them during the actual installation, thereby saving you time during installations. The VMMCA tool includes a model that checks for predetermined problems and assists in providing best-practice configuration guidance.

You can access the VMMCA tool directly from the SCVMM 2008 setup screen (see Figure 11.8). The link takes you directly to a website where you can download the tool.

FIGURE 11.8
VMMCA link in the SCVMM 2008 installation

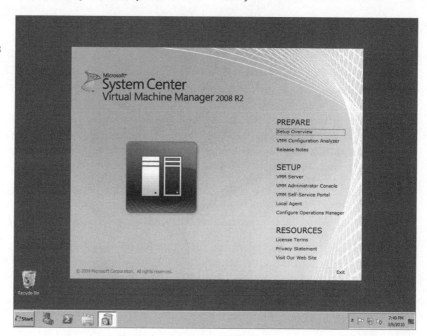

After installing the tool, you can run it directly on the server where you plan to install SCVMM roles or against a remote server. The VMMCA tool checks the server for the following SCVMM server roles (see Figure 11.9):

- SCVMM server
- SCVMM administrator console
- SCVMM self-service portal

FIGURE 11.9
VMMCA tool

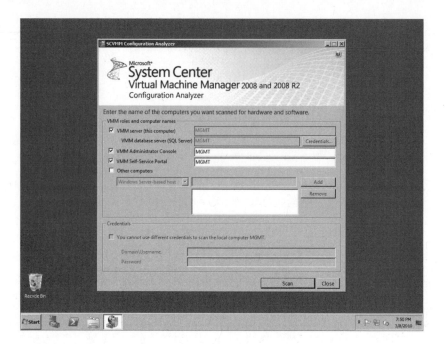

When you've resolved any alerts sent from the VMMCA tool, you're ready to start the SCVMM server installation. To start the installation, launch the SCVMM setup program, and select the VMM Server option under the Setup heading. Some of the most important decisions during the setup are the database configuration and the default library configuration.

NOTE The SCVMM server role can be installed only in Windows Server 2008 x64 or Windows Server 2008 R2. Other roles, like the self-service portal and the administrator console, can be installed on both the x86 and x64 versions of Windows Server 2003 and Windows Server 2008 editions.

Since SCVMM 2008 requires a SQL database to function, administrators have a couple of options for the database functionality. If there's a supported version of SQL Server somewhere in the enterprise, a new instance can be created for SCVMM. For smaller installations, however, the free SQL Server 2005 Express database (which is included with SCVMM 2008) can be used.

The Library Share Settings page dictates where the default library share will be created on the VMM server. Every VMM server has a default library share. It's important to locate the library share on a volume that has enough storage bandwidth. For example, don't place the default library share on a volume that's backed by a single physical disk, especially if multiple virtual machines will be deployed at the same time from the share.

You can accept the default library configuration, which creates a share automatically or uses an existing share. It's important that you specify a disk location that has available storage, because the default library share can't be removed or relocated to another disk location. You can create additional library servers from the SCVMM administrator console at any time.

NOTE You should make it a point to add a second library server on the first set of managed hosts that you add.

Installing the SCVMM 2008 Administrator Console

On any computer where you plan to administer a SCVMM instance, you can install the SCVMM administrator console. Because the administrator console is built on top of the SCVMM PowerShell interface, PowerShell and the .NET Framework version 2.0 are prerequisites. You can install the administrator console on both client and server operating systems, including the following:

◆ Windows XP Service Pack 2 and 3 x86/x64 editions

◆ Windows Vista Service Pack 1 x86/x64 editions

◆ Windows 7 x86/x64 editions

◆ Windows Server 2003 x86/x64 editions

◆ Windows Server 2008 x86/x64 editions

◆ Windows Server 2008 R2

Adding a Managed Host

After installing the SCVMM administrative console, you're ready to start managing your virtualization environment. The first step is to add a host to be managed via SCVMM. When a host is added to SCVMM, an agent is installed on the target system that communicates with the VMM server.

To add a server to be managed by SCVMM, launch the SCVMM administrative console, and select Add Host from the Virtual Machine Manager's Actions pane on the right. Enter your credentials, and click Next, as shown in Figure 11.10.

FIGURE 11.10
Adding a server
to be managed by
SCVMM

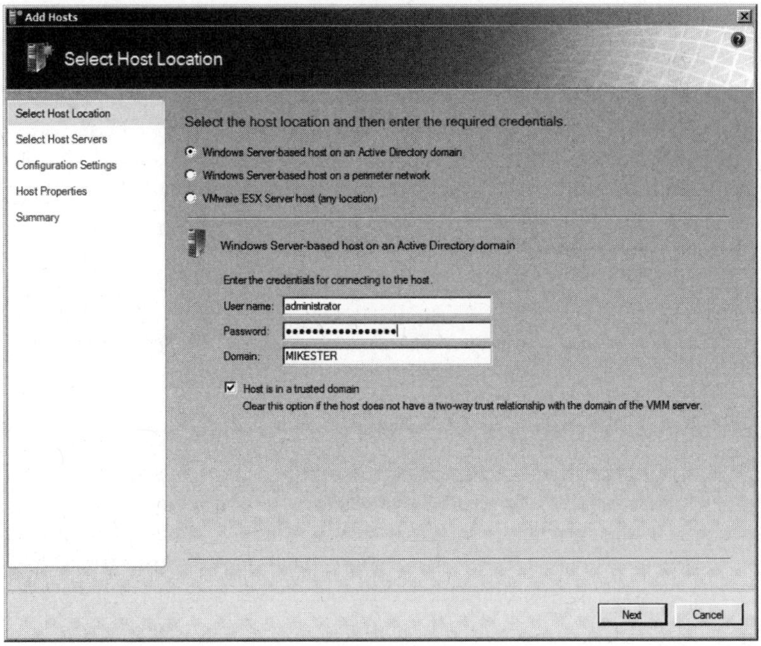

In the Select Host Servers window, enter the name of the machine that you'll be adding in the Computer Name field. This can be either the name of a single machine or the name of a cluster of virtual machines running Hyper-V.

After the name has been entered, the host will appear under Selected Servers, and you will see the version of the operating system on the host and the type of virtualization software that is supported. This will match what is reflected in Table 11.2 earlier in this chapter.

In the Configuration Settings window, you have the option to place the host in a specific host group. A host group is a way to organize your virtual machines—by location, by organization, or by purpose. Because you haven't created any host groups for this example, accept the default selection (All Hosts), and click Next.

Host properties allow you to specify a default virtual machine path, which is where virtual machines will be created. If the host has a specific location where virtual machines reside (for example, on a large volume on a SAN), enter it here to ensure VM deployment doesn't take place on a local disk.

After you review the summary screen and click Add Host, a job will execute that will install the VMM agent on the host and ensure the virtualization platform (Hyper-V or Virtual Server, based on the operating system of the target system) has been added. After the job completes, the host will appear in the administration console (see Figure 11.11).

FIGURE 11.11
The new managed host appears in the administration console.

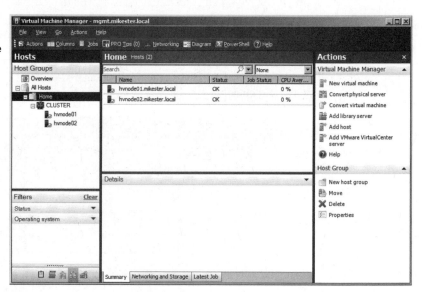

Creating Your First VM in SCVMM

Now that we have a host being managed by SCVMM, we can create a virtual machine to place on a host. Although you can use the stand-alone Hyper-V MMC to do this, using SCVMM gives you access to a couple of useful features.

To start the virtual machine creation process, in the SCVMM administration console, click New Virtual Machine in the Actions pane on the right of the screen. Because we don't have any items in the library, select the last option, Create The New Virtual Machine With A Blank Virtual Hard Disk, and click Next.

The next page allows you to set the name and owner of the virtual machine. SCVMM uses its own instance of the Authorization Manager (as we covered in Chapter 5, "Securing Hyper-V") to set ownership of a specific virtual machine. By default, the owner here will have exclusive access to the virtual machine.

SCVMM provides a rich set of hardware configuration options (see Figure 11.12). Although many of them match up with Hyper-V's inbox tools, a few options deserve special mention:

◆ *Processor*: SCVMM uses the concept of *CPU types*, as well as the number of processors. If you specify a CPU type on the Processor Settings page, SCVMM will adjust the CPU weights and reserves to match the CPU profile selected.

◆ *Availability*: If you select Make This VM Highly Available, SCVMM will restrict the placement of the newly created virtual machine to a clustered host.

◆ *Hardware profile*: The hardware profile definition (including processor count/type, memory, and so on) can be saved. This allows for quick deployments of identically configured virtual machines.

After defining the settings for the virtual machine, you have two options: place the virtual machine on a host or store it in the library for future deployment. If the virtual machine is stored in the library, then the virtual machine will need to be placed on a host before it can be started. For this walk-through, select the option Place The Virtual Machine On A Host, and click Next.

FIGURE 11.12
Hardware configuration options in SCVMM

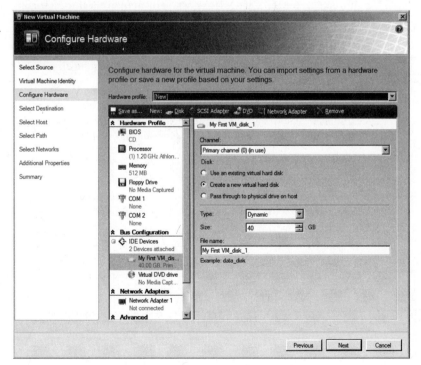

The Select Host window helps you choose the optimal host for this newly created virtual machine. SCVMM monitors the utilization of the host and provides a star rating for all the hosts in your environment. The star rating can be influenced by clicking the Customize Ratings button and adjusting the Resource Importance sliders.

NOTE Generally, accepting the recommended placement is a best practice.

The Select Path screen is used to enter where the virtual machine will be created on the target host. By default, it uses the value that was defined when the host was added to SCVMM.

NOTE If the host is part of a failover cluster with Clustered Shared Volume (CSV) enabled, the Virtual Machine Path should be the CSV volume such as `c:\clusterstorage\volume1`.

After you confirm that the virtual networks are set up correctly and specify the operating system that will run in the guest, the virtual machine will be created on the host.

Installing the SCVMM 2008 Self-Service Portal

The self-service portal is an excellent tool for creating self-service test and development environments. It allows you to target development environments for individual developers or entire development groups. The self-service portal lets you set policies and granular access that provides self-service flexibility while giving you control over virtualization capacity. If that doesn't excite you, consider that it also uses AD to authenticate and authorize users on the portal. The requirements for the self-service portal are an Internet Information Services (IIS) server and an existing SCVMM installation.

You can scale out a self-service environment by using a hardware load balancer such as F5 or Cisco SS. Those load balancers allow you to create a virtual IP (used to direct requests to the real web servers) that fronts various real web servers all pointing to the same instance of a SCVMM server.

WARNING A self-service portal installation must point to a SCVMM instance. This can cause trouble in SCVMM environments with multiple SCVMM instances. You have to know what SCVMM instance a user is storing VMs on and make sure users are routed to that instance.

After you've configured and installed the self-service portal on a web server, you're ready to move to the next configuration steps.

USING THE SCVMM ADMINISTRATOR CONSOLE TO CREATE A SELF-SERVICE USER POLICY

For users to leverage the self-service portal to control and create virtual machines, a self-service user policy must be created. The self-service user policy is used to shape the actions that an end user can perform when using the self-service portal. Consider the self-service policy as the blueprint that shapes the self-service environment for an end user. Let's walk through the steps to creating a self-service policy:

1. Open the SCVMM administrator console, and select the Administration tab.

2. Select the User role, right-click Profile Type, and select the New User role.

3. Assign a name for the user role, and select User Role Profile: Self Service User.

4. Add user-role users or groups from AD.

5. Select the scope of hosts that this self-service user profile can use. The scope of hosts maps back to the host-group layout that you as an administrator create. Each host group contains specific managed hosts. You can use host groups to segment managed hosts by location or purpose (for example, development or testing) or for purposes of migration, like a cluster.

6. Assign the granular actions that users can perform when logged into the console. Figure 11.13 shows the self-service policy rights you can assign to users.

FIGURE 11.13
Granular rights assignment for self-service

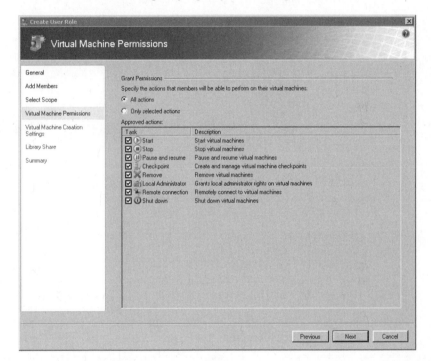

7. Decide whether you'll allow users to create VMs from the portal, and assign a template to the user or group for provisioning VMs.

8. Decide whether users can store VMs in a SCVMM library server, and assign the self-service policy to a specific set of one library server.

9. Create a self-service policy.

10. Log on to the portal by going to `http://nameofwebserver:assigned port`, as configured in Figure 11.14.

FIGURE 11.14

Self-service portal configuration

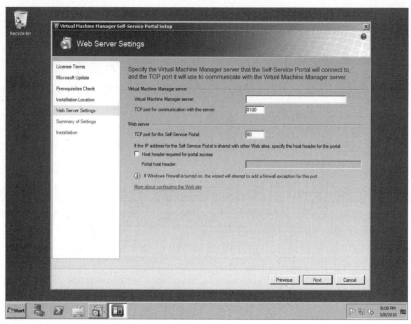

USING POWERSHELL TO CREATE A SELF-SERVICE POLICY

You can use a PowerShell script to create a self-service policy that gives a user on the domain access to the self-service portal. For example, the following scenario adds `stewartnet\test1` access:

```
$VMPermission = 511
$AddScope = Host group
$AddMember = @("STEWARTNET\test1")
Set-VMMUserRole -VMPermission $VMPermission -QuotaPoint 0 -AddScope $AddScope
-VMMServer 192.168.2.101 -JobGroup
2c0c9c4e-ce57-49f2-b98d-727ff8516823 -AddMember $AddMember
New-VMMUserRole -Name "New_User" -Description "" -UserRoleProfile SelfServiceUser
-JobGroup 2c0c9c4e-ce57-49f2-b98d-727ff8516823
```

Integrating SCOM 2007 and SCVMM 2008

One of the most compelling features of SCVMM 2008 is the connector established between SCOM 2007 and SCVMM. This PRO functionality highlights the ability to perform actions that map to specific applications. The ability to handle performance and application issues directly from the virtualization console is a compelling scenario that requires you to use several management consoles to find out information about the applications running in the virtual machine. You can not only perform normal virtualization actions but also implement rich application actions.

If you turn your attention from the VM to the applications running in the VM, you'll see we're bridging the two worlds into a cohesive management approach. PRO provides the infrastructure for alerts triggered by applications or the OS running on the VM. You need certain components: a SCOM agent in the VM and management and PRO packs for the applications and operating system running in the VM. The PRO infrastructure is built such that software vendors and line-of-business application developers can create PRO packs, thus expanding the infrastructure to support any application.

NOTE   You can find information about authoring PRO packs for applications at www.microsoft.com/downloads. Search for *VMM2008 R2 – Building PRO-Enabled Management Packs*.

The out-of-the-box PRO components include the ability to trigger VM workload balancing based on the resource-consumption triggers. The initial management packs include the following elements:

SCVMM PRO VMware Host Performance   The VMware Host Performance pack provides monitors and rules for monitoring the performance of VMware ESX hosts managed by SCVMM 2008 to support PRO in SCVMM.

SCVMM PRO Virtual Machine Right-Sizing   The Virtual Machine Right-Sizing management pack provides monitors and rules for monitoring the performance of VMs managed by SCVMM 2008 to support PRO in SCVMM.

SCVMM PRO Library   The Library management pack provides the base class and group definitions that are used by PRO in SCVMM 2008.

SCVMM PRO Host Performance   The Host Performance management pack provides monitors and rules for monitoring the performance of Microsoft Hyper-V and virtual server hosts managed by SCVMM 2008 to support PRO in SCVMM.

The PRO functionality requires an existing SCOM 2007 environment (see Chapter 13 for planning guidance). PRO ties the SCVMM environment to a SCOM 2007 environment to form a two-way information flow in the form of PRO *Tips*. These consist of information and actions detected by SCOM 2007 and triggered by a condition on a managed virtualization host or VMs with a SCOM 2007 agent. This information is forwarded into the SCVMM console with the condition and action that you can use to clear the condition. See Figure 11.7, earlier in this chapter, for a PRO Tip view.

Enabling PRO Functionality

Let's dive into the steps required to set up the PRO functionality. We'll assume you have an existing SCOM 2007 SP1 and SQL Server infrastructure.

1. Install a SCVMM server, and install the SCVMM administrator console on the server.

2. Install the SCOM console on the existing SCVMM server.

3. Import the following management packs into SCOM:

    ◆ Microsoft SQL Server 2000/2005 management pack:

        ◆ Microsoft SQL Server Library

        ◆ Microsoft SQL Server 2005 Monitoring (recommended)

        ◆ Microsoft SQL Server 2005 Discovery (recommended)

◆ Microsoft Windows Server 2000/2003 IIS management pack:

   ◆ Microsoft Windows Internet Information Services Common Library

   ◆ Microsoft Windows Internet Information Services 2003

4. Run the Configure Operation Manager option from the SCVMM setup screen on the SCOM root management server.

5. Add the default action account to the SCVMM server as an administrator user role.

6. Enable remote running of PowerShell scripts on all servers running the VM administrator console. Start the PowerShell console, and select A for Always Trust Remote Signed Scripts.

7. On the SCVMM Server, configure the Operations Manager server name on the Administration tab, as shown in Figure 11.15.

FIGURE 11.15
Configuring the Operations Manager server in SCVMM

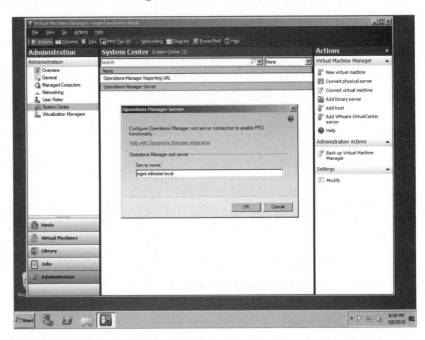

8. Test the integration by clicking the diagram view in the SCVMM administrator console, as shown in Figure 11.16.

You can also verify that PRO has been configured in SCOM by ensuring that the SCVMM and SCOM connectors are configured. To do this, open the SCOM console, click the Administration option, and then click Product Connectors (see Figure 11.17). You should see several SCVMM connectors in the format SCVMMConnectorSCVMM *ServerName - Connector number*. You have several connectors to divide the workload of forwarding alerts in the form of PRO Tips to SCVMM servers. Figure 11.18 shows the Product Connector Properties screen.

FIGURE 11.16
Successful SCOM integration

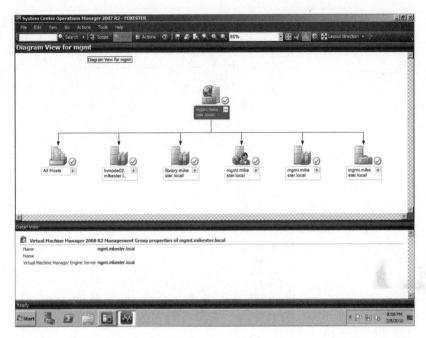

FIGURE 11.17
SCVMM PRO connectors in SCOM

FIGURE 11.18

SCVMM PRO connector properties

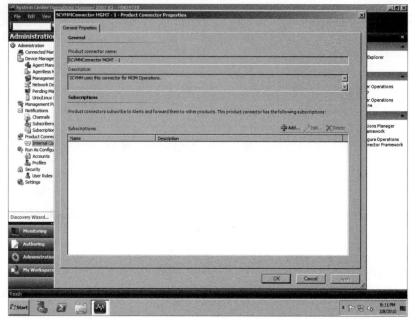

Customizing the Base PRO Monitors

Now that you have the out-of-box PRO functionality configured, you'll want to customize the base PRO monitors. Customizing the PRO alerts comes down to configuring overrides on management pack monitors in SCOM. Remember that the PRO infrastructure uses the SCOM infrastructure and adds management packs to SCOM. Those management packs contain the knowledge, triggers, and alerts that drive PRO. Let's dive into customizing some of the PRO management packs.

One of the scenarios you may want to customize is the host CPU utilization threshold. Most virtualization hosts achieve high rates of CPU usage. The default threshold is set to provide a critical alert at 75 percent CPU usage. You might want to customize it to 80 percent for your Hyper-V environment so as to maximize your host utilization.

NOTE   Remember that SCVMM manages Hyper-V, Virtual Server, and ESX environments and provides PRO packs for each environment. This gives you granular PRO capability so you can set thresholds for each environment selectively.

Follow these steps to customize the CPU utilization alert threshold:

1. Open the SCOM console with a user account that has author rights.

2. Select the Authoring tab, click Management Pack Objects, and then click Monitors (see Figure 11.19).

3. Scroll down to find each PRO-related monitor, and click through each one to find the monitor labeled PRO CPU Utilization (under Performance). Or, use the search box labeled Look For to find the CPU monitors.

FIGURE 11.19
PRO CPU monitors
by host type

4. Under PRO Hyper-V Host Target, select PRO CPU Utilization, right-click, select Overrides, select Override The Monitor, and then select For All Objects Of Type: PRO Hyper-V Host Target (see Figure 11.20).

FIGURE 11.20
Selecting an override for the Hyper-V CPU host target

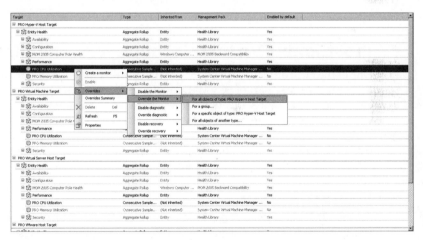

5. In the CPU Override Properties screen, select Threshold, and enter the new CPU threshold in the Override Setting column (see Figure 11.21). You may also want to change Alert Severity, which is set to Critical, by selecting Alert Severity.

You can use the same process to configure memory thresholds as well; of course, the target will be PRO memory counters. It's also important to note that if you want a threshold to apply to all virtualization-managed host types, you must perform an override for each type.

FIGURE 11.21
Changing the PRO
CPU threshold for
Hyper-V hosts

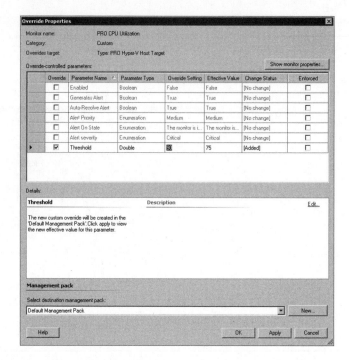

Provisioning Virtual Machines from the Library

One of the most attractive functions of virtualization is the ability to rapidly provision new VMs. This is a core part of SCVMM functionality. Provisioning a new VM will be one of the tasks that you as a virtualization administrator most frequently perform. It's important that you understand how to use SCVMM to do this.

As a virtualization administrator, you'll be called on to decide which VMs are placed on which virtualization host. You can use performance counters, the number of VMs on each host, or your gut feeling to make the decision.

VM Host Placement

Because VM host placement is critical to the health of the virtual environment, SCVMM provides functionality to aid you. The Intelligent Placement functionality helps you by looking across all the virtualization hosts or specific host groups and using capacity-planning algorithms to place the VM on the most appropriate host.

Intelligent Placement uses the following elements to decide on VM placement on a host:

◆ CPU utilization

◆ Free memory

◆ Disk I/O

◆ Network utilization

You can tweak this Intelligent Placement algorithm by choosing which virtualization host resources are prioritized during placement. To configure Intelligent Placement properties, follow these steps:

1. In the SCVMM administrator console, select the Administration tab, select the General option, and then highlight Placement Settings (see Figure 11.22).

FIGURE 11.22
Configuring
Intelligent Place-
ment options

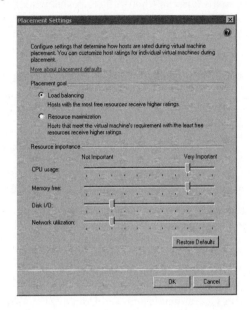

2. Change the sliding bar of each resource you want to change; the range isn't important.

Changing the placement settings prioritizes the selected resources during the VM placement process.

TIP Remember that Intelligent Placement happens not only during new VM provisioning but also during migration of VMs from host to host using Quick Migration, Live Migration, or over-the-network movement. This ensures the best host is always selected for a specific VM's resource requirement.

Using SCVMM Templates

It's important to understand how to use SCVMM templates to provision VMs. You can use templates to create new VMs repeatedly with standardized hardware and software settings. A VM template is a SCVMM library resource consisting of the following parts:

Hardware profile To define a standard set of hardware settings, you can create a hardware profile and associate it with a template. When you create a new template or create a VM from a template, you can specify the virtual hardware settings or reuse an existing hardware profile from the library.

Virtual hard disk   You can use a generalized VHD from the library or create a VHD from an existing VM. If the source VM for your template has multiple VHDs, select the disk that contains the operating system.

Guest operating system profile   To use the same product key, administrator password, time zone, and so on, in a set of templates, you can create a guest operating system profile and store it in the library. When you create a new template or create a VM from a template, you can specify the settings manually or use an operating system profile associated with your answer files.

CREATING A NEW TEMPLATE FROM AN EXISTING HARD DISK

To create a new template from an existing hard disk, you can use the default blank hard disks created by the SCVMM installation in the default library or another VHD stored in any SCVMM library server. Follow these steps:

1. In the SCVMM administrator console, select the Library tab.

2. In the library, choose a VHD object that you want to use to create a template. Right-click the object, and select the New Template option.

3. From Active Directory, add an Active Directory Identity, User, or Group owner to the template, and add a description of the template.

4. Configure a new hardware profile, or select an existing hardware profile for the VM.

5. Configure a new operating system profile, or select No Customization Needed. The options you can fill in are Machine Netbios Name, Admin Password, Product Key, Time Zone, Operating System, and Domain/Workgroup.

You can now use the new template stored in the SCVMM library server to create VMs.

NOTE   Always use the No Customization Needed option for templates that provision Linux VMs, because the operating system profile options apply to Windows systems only.

Let's move on to the provisioning process. We'll explore the different types of provisioning capabilities in SCVMM.

PROVISIONING VMS WITH BLANK OR EXISTING VHDS

One method of provisioning allows you to provision a virtual machine with a blank or existing hard drive. In the blank hard drive approach, you can provision and install an operating system at a later time. In the case of leveraging an existing virtual machine hard drive file, you can use this virtual hard drive to create new virtual machines. Let's explore the steps:

1. Open the SCVMM administrator console.

2. Select New Virtual Machine to start the New Virtual Machine Wizard.

3. Select Source For New Virtual Machine. Create the new machine with a blank hard drive.

4. Select the name and the owner of the VM (AD user or group), and enter a description of the VM.

5. You can now set up the VM's hardware profile (see Figure 11.23), including the VHD, processor count, network adapters, and either IDE or SCSI adapters.

FIGURE 11.23
Hardware properties for a new VM

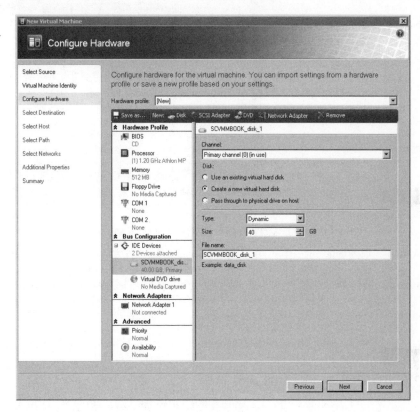

6. Select a destination. You can either deploy directly to an existing host or store the VM on a SCVMM library server.

7. Intelligent Placement determines the best host for the workload using the star rating system (see Figure 11.24). The host with the most stars represents the best host for placement of this VM (driven by the Intelligent Placement settings shown in Figure 11.22, earlier in this chapter).

8. Click Create The Virtual Machine, and verify that the VM is created on the selected host.

FIGURE 11.24
Intelligent Place-
ment in action

PROVISIONING FROM TEMPLATES, VHDS, AND VMS IN THE LIBRARY

Provisioning virtual machines from templates is one of the most popular methods. The template provides a blueprint for creating virtual machines. Important virtual machine properties, such as the number of virtual processors assigned to a virtual machine and the size and type of virtual hard drive (dynamic or fixed), are specified in the template.

1. Open the SCVMM administrator console.

2. Select New Virtual Machine to start the New Virtual Machine Wizard.

3. Select the source for the new VM. Choose Use Existing Virtual Machine, Template Or Virtual Hard Disk.

4. You have the option to select a template, an existing VHD, or a VM stored in the SCVMM library (see Figure 11.25).

5. Select the name and the owner of the VM (Active Directory user or group), and enter a description of the VM.

6. Depending on your selection, you can configure various hardware properties. If you use a template, those options are predefined. If you select a VHD, you can configure all options except the VHD for the VM.

7. Select the destination. You can either deploy directly to an existing host or store the VM on a SCVMM library server.

8. Intelligent Placement determines the best host for the workload using the star rating system. The host with the most stars represents the best host for placement of this VM (driven by the Intelligent Placement settings shown in Figure 11.22, earlier in this chapter).

9. Click Create and verify that the VM is created on the selected host.

FIGURE 11.25
Selecting objects from the SCVMM library

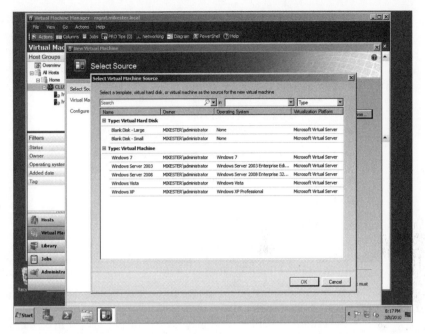

Provisioning Systems via P2V Functionality

One of the great capabilities of the virtualization environment is the ability to take a physical system running on physical hardware and capture that configuration to make the physical system a VM. This action is called *physical to virtual* (P2V). As the name implies, the process converts a physical system to a VM. This process is very popular for several reasons:

Server consolidation   Server consolidation is by far the most popular use of P2V technology. In this case, underutilized physical systems are converted to VMs. This saves power, cooling, and data center footprint.

Disaster recovery   The P2V process captures an exact copy of the physical system as a VM that can be started and run at any time. Think of a disaster scenario in which the physical system or the data center where the server is located goes down. If you have a P2V of the physical system, all you need to do is start that VM. The services will be up and running in a short time.

SCVMM P2V functionality provides two options for doing a P2V: online or offline. Offline P2V uses the Windows Pre-installation Environment (Windows PE) to capture an exact copy of the physical system. This process deploys a SCVMM agent to the source machine and restarts the source machine into Windows PE to capture the image. The following operating systems without the VSS infrastructure have to use offline P2V:

◆   Windows 2000 Server SP4

◆   Windows 2000 Advanced Server SP4

NOTE   If you need to perform a P2V of a Linux physical system, you have to use a third-party solution like Novell Platespin.

The online functionality uses the VSS infrastructure to take a disk snapshot of the source machine. The VSS infrastructure allows the P2V process to perform the disk capture without any system downtime. Online P2V is ideal because it doesn't cause user or service interruption. It works only for Windows operating systems that have the VSS infrastructure:

◆ Windows Server 2008 (32-bit)

◆ Windows Server 2008 (64-bit)

◆ Windows Server 2003 (32-bit) SP1 or later

◆ Windows Server 2003 (64-bit) SP1 or later

◆ Windows XP Professional (32-bit) SP2 or later

◆ Windows XP Professional (64-bit) SP2 or later

◆ Windows Vista Service Pack 1 (32-bit)

◆ Windows Vista SP1 or later (64-bit)

◆ Windows 7 (both 32-bit and 64-bit)

After you've identified the server for which you want to perform a P2V, you need to understand what type of P2V you'll be performing—offline or online—because offline P2V affects system availability and may have to be performed in off-hours. Now you're ready to start the P2V process.

PERFORMING AN ONLINE P2V

An online P2V leverages the VSS infrastructure in Windows machines to capture the physical system data for inclusion in the new virtual machine. The VSS infrastructure provides you the ability to take a backup of the actual virtual machine as well as the applications running in the system, provided each application has a VSS writer.

1. From the SCVMM administrator console, select the Convert Physical Server option.

2. Provide the IP address or machine name of the source machine, and provide administrator credentials for the source machine.

3. SCVMM scans the system. During this process, a SCVMM agent is deployed to the machine to gather system information.

4. On the Volume Configuration page, review the lists of volumes and determine whether you want to make any changes.

5. Select volumes to copy. Initially, all volumes appear in the results pane and are selected for duplication to the new VM. The new VM must contain the system volume and the boot volume from the source machine, but any other volumes are optional.

6. Adjust volume settings. You can change the following:

◆ VHD Size (MB) field to adjust the size of any volume (NTFS volumes are automatically expanded to the size indicated)

- VHD Type field to adjust the type (Dynamic or Fixed) of any volume
- Channel field to adjust the channel (for both IDE devices and SCSI adapters) of any selected volume

7. Select the number of processors and amount of memory for the new VM.

8. Intelligent Placement provides the best host to host the machine. Select the host.

9. Choose the path for the VM to be stored on the virtualization.

10. Attach to a network on the virtual host, or select Not Connected (you can connect the VM to a network later).

11. Review any issues reported by the wizard; the P2V won't process with any reported issues. Click Create to start the P2V process.

PERFORMING AN OFFLINE P2V

Follow the same process as in the previous section for online P2V, but select the conversion options, and select Offline P2V. You need to provide configuration information for the Windows PE environment. To do so, on the Offline Conversion Options page, select one of the following methods to provide an IP address to the boot environment on the host:

- Obtain an IP address automatically via DHCP.
- Use the following IPv6 address to specify a IPv6 address, subnet prefix length, and default gateway of the host.
- Use the following IPv4 address to specify the IPv6 address, subnet mask, and default gateway of the host.

If you attempt to perform an online P2V of an AD Domain Controller, you are warned to perform an offline P2V (see Figure 11.26). To avoid AD update sequence number issues, always perform an offline conversion.

Creating Highly Available Virtual Machines

One of the most important provisioning options is the ability to make a VM highly available. Doing so provides availability in the event that the virtualization host experiences planned or unplanned downtime. Planned downtime can occur when you perform maintenance on a host; unplanned downtime can occur when a virtualization host goes down completely for any reason.

In the event of planned downtime, the VM is migrated to another virtualization host in a Hyper-V cluster. If a virtualization host crashes and it is part of a cluster, the VM and associated resources are restarted on another Hyper-V host in the cluster.

To provision highly available VMs, you first must have set up a Live Migration cluster (see Chapter 8, "Achieving High Availability"). Then, you're almost ready to use SCVMM to create highly available VMs. You have to make SCVMM aware of the host cluster the same way you add any host to SCVMM for management. Let's walk through the steps for making a VM highly available:

1. Open the SCVMM administrator console, and add the cluster to SCVMM via the SCVMM administrator console using the Add Host option. SCVMM detects that you're adding a

node to the Quick Migration cluster and adds SCVMM agents to each host in the cluster. A cluster object is created and available in the SCVMM console. See Figure 11.27 for a view of the new cluster object.

FIGURE 11.26
Online P2V domain controller warning

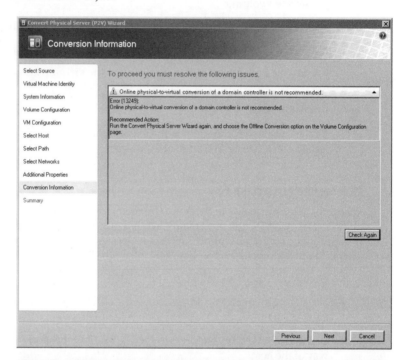

FIGURE 11.27
SCVMM cluster object

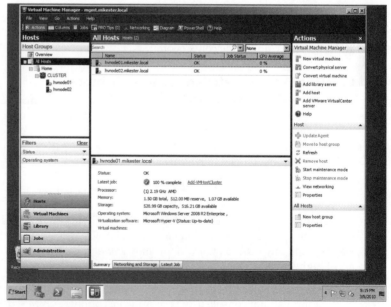

2. Select New Virtual Machine to start the New Virtual Machine Wizard.

3. Select the source for the new VM. Create the new machine with a blank hard drive.

4. Select the name and the owner of the VM (AD user or group), and enter a description of the VM.

5. Set up the hardware profile of the VM, including the VHD, the processor count, the network adapters, and either IDE or SCSI adapters.

6. The most important step is to scroll down to the Availability option and select the check box to make this VM highly available (see Figure 11.28).

FIGURE 11.28
Making the VM
highly available

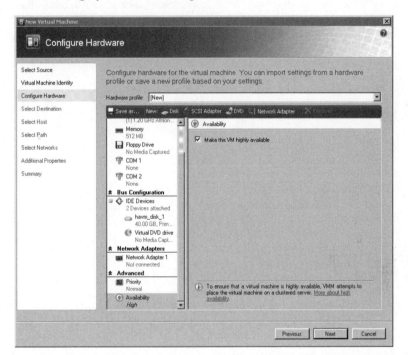

7. Select the destination. You can either deploy directly to an existing host or store the VM on a SCVMM library server.

8. Intelligent Placement determines the best host for the workload using the star rating system. The host with the most stars represents the best host for placement of this VM (driven by the Intelligent Placement settings shown in Figure 11.22, earlier in this chapter).

9. Select a VM path that is in the cluster and a SAN volume.

10. Click Create The Virtual Machine, and verify that the VM is created on the selected cluster node.

11. Verify the high-availability configuration for the VM by right-clicking the VM and performing a migration of the VM to another node in the cluster.

Summary

In this chapter, we provided the knowledge you need to begin using SCVMM 2008 with Hyper-V deployments. Any Hyper-V deployment without SCVMM 2008 doesn't truly exercise the flexibility that the virtualization environment provides.

Virtualization management will continue to evolve and add new capabilities; the first glimpse of the future is the PRO functionality included in SCVMM 2008. Look for the virtualization management mind-set to change from provisioning individual VMs to provisioning entire applications and services as a unit/model.

In addition, as the underlying virtualization platform evolves with new capabilities, Virtual Machine Manager will continue to evolve functionality to take advantage of new Hyper-V and managed hypervisor capabilities. Remember the formula for successful virtualization deployments: virtualization platform capabilities + functionality-rich management software = a flexible, dynamic virtualization deployment.

Chapter 12

Protecting Virtualized Environments with System Center Data Protection Manager

There's a motto that says, "If you're going to put all of your eggs in one basket, you better have a good basket." Certainly this applies to virtualization: if you're going to put multiple servers on a single piece of hardware, then you need a reliable way to protect that host.

In Chapter 7, "Backing Up and Recovering VMs," we reviewed common issues and manual methods to back up Hyper-V–based virtual machines. Although those options and techniques work well with Hyper-V, they are not optimal, because they require manual intervention and don't easily address complex scenarios or multiple servers. This chapter will explore how you can use System Center Data Protection Manager to protect virtualization hosts, guests, and the configuration between them.

In this chapter, we'll cover the following topics:

◆ Overview of Data Protection Manager

◆ Protecting your Hyper-V environment

◆ Configuring protection of Hyper-V hosts

◆ Considerations when protecting virtualized environments

◆ Restoring your virtual environment with DPM

Overview of Data Protection Manager

Data Protection Manager (DPM) 2010 is intended to be *the* enterprise backup and recovery solution of choice for all core Microsoft production workloads, including Hyper-V. DPM was designed around three core premises:

◆ Provide an optimized backup and recovery solution for Microsoft-based technology that ensures supportability, reliability, and customer satisfaction with the core operating system or application. In part, DPM is intended to ensure that customers are confident in their Hyper-V (or other Microsoft server platform) deployment because they're assured of reliable protection and recovery.

◆ Use only approved backup and recovery mechanisms within the production workloads, such that each application is backed up as intended by the application designers. This means DPM uses only those constructs provided by Hyper-V in order to protect Hyper-V.

◆ Demonstrate additional value by choosing a comprehensive Microsoft portfolio, instead of using one Microsoft operating system or application server and then choosing non-Microsoft add-on components. In this case, DPM, like the other System Center components, is intended to offer "best for Windows" capabilities: it was designed by Microsoft with Microsoft applications as its top priority, and it incorporates lessons learned and feedback from the platform teams. Specifically for Hyper-V, DPM is intended to be "the best protection for Windows virtualization."

History of DPM

DPM was first introduced in 2005. At that time, it provided backup and recovery for common Microsoft application services. DPM 2007 was enhanced to support more applications and scenarios, including Hyper-V. The release of DPM 2010 builds on the capabilities in previous versions. DPM 2010 not only protects Hyper-V virtual machines on stand-alone Hyper-V hosts and VMs hosted on failover cluster nodes but also protects VMs residing on Cluster Shared Volumes. DPM 2010 also introduces Item Level Recovery (ILR), which allows you to restore files hosted *inside* Hyper-V virtual machines to a share or disk on a Hyper-V host. It also includes increased PowerShell support and robust replication for cloud-based backup.

All versions of DPM are native disk-to-disk-to-tape (D2D2T) solutions. In other words, to create a backup, DPM replicates data from the source server disk to the DPM server disk (referred to as the *replica*) and then to DPM tape. This gives you fast recovery (via the DPM disk) as well as long-term retention (via tape). Because DPM can replicate from one DPM server to another DPM server, you can technically have D2D2D2T—or what Microsoft refers to as DPM 2 DPM 4 DR (disaster recovery). Figure 12.1 presents the complete DPM solution for Microsoft backup and recovery for Microsoft workloads, with integrated disk, tape, and disaster-recovery replication.

FIGURE 12.1
Solution diagram for DPM

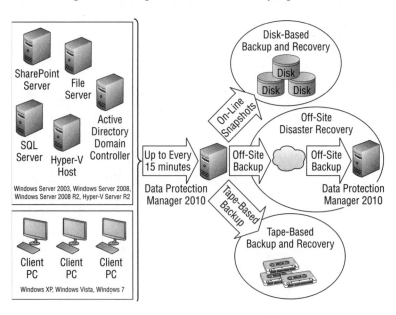

In the case of Hyper-V, this means the virtual hard disks (VHDs) from the production host are duplicated on the DPM disk replica and can be replicated to an off-site DPM server. VM backups can also be moved to tape, for long-term retention. To do this, DPM installs a single DPM agent on each production "platform" to be protected.

NOTE By *platform* I mean physical Hyper-V hosts as well as SQL Server, Exchange Server, SharePoint products and technologies, Windows file servers, and Windows desktops.

The agent, using a filter driver, monitors the physical storage blocks that are being updated on the production disk volumes. As production workloads—in this case, the Windows hypervisor—write to disk blocks within the VHDs, the DPM agent tracks which blocks have been updated. On a predefined schedule, DPM captures just those blocks that are reported as changed by the filter and propagates those blocks to the DPM replica.

Backup Alternatives

The best method for protecting virtualized guests from a Microsoft virtualization host is to use the Hyper-V Volume Shadow Copy Service (VSS) writer. By using the APIs provided by VSS and delivered through a VSS writer from the Hyper-V development team, you can do backups and recoveries of your virtual infrastructure in an application-consistent and supported way. The details of the VSS writer are covered in Chapter 7.

However, not all backup solutions use VSS writers, which can lead to potential supportability issues, possible data corruption in the guest operating systems and the physical VHDs, and backups that may not be restorable. With those worrisome considerations in mind, you may ask, "Why would any backup solution not use VSS?"

Often, third-party tape technologies use a generic architecture in their agent/server model that allows them to back up anything and everything from a laptop to a mainframe computer. This flexibility gives them a broad reach in their marketplace. However, it also often precludes them from using API sets or other original application-provided methods for data backup and recovery (such as VSS). In fairness, an application's VSS writer may not address every backup and restore scenario. Sometimes, third-party tape backup vendors ignore VSS in order to create additional capabilities not provided by the native writer. Although this may satisfy some customer desires, it results in the same concerns about supportability and potential data corruption.

DPM, as a Microsoft product, is committed to using only approved backup and recovery methods (such as VSS) from Microsoft application teams (like the Hyper-V development team). This ensures the most reliable and supportable backup and recovery solution.

TIP There's a great book out, *Data Protection for Virtual Data Centers* by Jason Buffington, that goes into much more detail regarding DPM and virtualization backup and recovery than we will cover here. Jason is the "data protection guy," and if you are serious about virtualization backup and recovery, check out his blog at http://blog.jasonbuffington.com.

Understanding DPM Storage

The DPM server or appliance is usually installed with one defined NTFS volume for the bootable operating system, as well as the DPM application and its supporting SQL Server database. In addition, the DPM server or appliance should have a significant amount of unallocated storage and possibly a tape drive or library. The additional disk storage can be local direct-attached storage

(DAS) or a storage area network (SAN)–attached via Fibre Channel or Internet SCSI (iSCSI); but it must appear as *locally mounted* via the Windows Disk Administrator. Removable disk media such as USB hard drives aren't directly supported because DPM presumes that any disk medium is always connected. In addition, DPM uses VSS, which isn't available for removable media types.

For each production data source being protected by DPM, the DPM server allocates two NTFS volumes out of its raw storage, one for the replica and the other for recovery points:

◆ The *DPM replica volume* is a real NTFS volume, usually defined to be equal in size to or slightly larger than the production NTFS volume that holds the virtualization VHDs. Within the replica, you can find the VHDs for a given virtual machine (VM).

◆ The *DPM recovery point volume* holds the block-level changes between a given synchronization point and the previous one. Specifically, whenever DPM synchronizes the production volume against the DPM replica, the changed blocks that are overwritten within the replica are moved into the recovery-point volume.

Consider the following scenario:

1. **Day one**: The original VHD (or any other data object protected by DPM) contains eight blocks on disk (ABCDEFGH).

2. Upon initially protecting the VHD with DPM, two volumes are allocated for the replica and recovery points. Immediately after that, DPM creates its initial baseline, which populates the replica volume with an exact copy of the production VHD (ABCDEFGH).

3. **Day two**: During the day, two blocks (*IJ*) are updated, resulting in AB*IJ*EFGH.

4. At the next scheduled synchronization, referred to by DPM as an *express full backup*, the two changed blocks (*IJ*) are identified and replicated from the production VHD to the DPM replica—resulting in the replica also having AB*IJ*EFGH. The two displaced blocks (CD) are then moved from the replica into the recovery-point volume (in case they are needed in the future).

5. **Day three**: After another day, three more blocks (B, J, G) are overwritten (*KLM*) and synchronized, resulting in A*KILEFMH*. Again, DPM replicates just the three changed blocks within the VHD to the DPM replica, and the displaced blocks are moved to the recovery-point volume.

This process can occur up to 512 times—based on a limit of 512 snapshots via VSS. This may represent 512 daily synchronization points (almost 1.5 years worth)—or, at 4 per day, 128 days (four months) of changes.

DPM Data Storage

It's important to recognize that the *full* (complete copy) of the VHD happens only once and is always maintained. Previous points in time are held strictly as the changed blocks from one iteration to the next, which results in a very efficient form of storing past data without consuming inordinate amounts of space.

Another nuance of this behavior is that it's *exactly the opposite* of a traditional tape backup. In a traditional tape backup, you do a full backup that copies the entire data set. From that point on, the full ages, meaning that after a day, the full backup is one day old. Because of this, most environments do an incremental or a differential backup of simple changes since the full backup was completed. After another day, subsequent incremental or differential backups are also done. The result is that if you need to recover data after four days, you start by recovering the full and then layer over the top each of the subsequent daily backups to reconstitute the most current state of the production data set.

DPM changes this paradigm completely:

♦ In the case of DPM, the full is the replica and is always current within one synchronization window. Each synchronization refreshes the full and creates a differential between the current point in time and the backup before it. This means that after a catastrophic failure, you don't have to go back to an aged full and then layer one or more differentials over the top of it. Instead, to restore the complete server to the most recent backup, you need only restore the full (replica).

♦ To recover to a previous point in time, DPM still doesn't require any kind of layering between the full and the differentials. Instead, because DPM uses a native disk on which all the data is held as individual disk blocks, DPM simply selects the specific blocks from whichever point in time is requested by the DPM administrator.

In the earlier example, if you want to recover to day two (step 3 in the scenario), DPM requests the eight blocks ABIJEFGH. Although some of those blocks still exist in the disk replica, other blocks are held in the recovery-point volume. Because both volumes are disks in the DPM storage pool, no additional disk I/O or layering is required. DPM simply selects the appropriate eight blocks. Thus, the recovery-point volume is not only extremely efficient for storing previous points in time but also enables a very rapid restore based on how the previous points in time are retained.

DPM STORAGE AND HYPER-V PROTECTION

To put all of this together, the DPM disk is your first line of defense (or recovery) for recovering VMs that are lost due to, for example, a hardware failure on a Hyper-V host. DPM gives you a calendar- and time-based view to select a point in time to which to recover the VHD(s). DPM then selects the blocks from both the replica and recovery-point volumes that constitute those VHD(s) to that particular point in time.

Beyond the disk-based protection of a DPM server, DPM can replicate the replica to another DPM server for off-site disaster recovery. Microsoft commonly refers to this as *DPM 2 DPM 4 DR*. (Yes, many of us have an acronym issue!) Pragmatically speaking, the secondary DPM server treats the primary DPM server as a protectable workload. On a less frequent schedule, it replicates those changed blocks in the primary DPM replica as if it were the production VHD volume. On a separate schedule, the secondary/off-site DPM server retains an additional replica and points in time. For example, the primary DPM server might protect the production VHD 4 times per day for 2 weeks, while the secondary DPM server protects the primary nightly for 60 days.

In addition to disk-based protection, DPM offers native, tape-based backup. To do this, you configure a traditional tape-backup retention system on the DPM server, which backs up the DPM replica to tape. This means Microsoft customers don't require third-party tape-backup software in order to protect their Windows hypervisors (or any other workload protectable by DPM). As a general rule of thumb, any tape drive, library, media changer, or virtual tape library (VTL) that is visible from the Windows Device Manager can be used with DPM.

NOTE You can find a list of tested tape devices at www.microsoft.com/DPM. This list isn't exhaustive; it just includes devices whose original manufacturers have chosen to run the DPM-provided test utility on their tape device(s) and report the results to Microsoft. Many other devices whose manufacturers haven't chosen to run the test utility may also work.

Because of the transparency that DPM provides by using most devices that are visible from the Windows Device Manager, you may find that even deduplication appliances that present themselves as VTLs are usable for long-term retention.

DPM and Cluster Shared Volumes

DPM 2010 is among the first software-only solutions that automates host backup of virtual machines housed on a Cluster Shared Volume (CSV). We mentioned CSV backup in Chapter 7 and introduced how to use CSVs in Chapter 8, "High Availability," but we didn't provide much in the way of details on how to back up and recover VMs homed on them.

CSVs add a layer of complexity to the backup and recovery of VMs. The issues are described well in the DPM Insider blog (http://blogs.technet.com/asim_mitra) in the post dated December 11, 2009, and titled "Snapshot Provider Considerations While Backing Up a CSV Cluster." Simply put, host-based Hyper-V backups rely on VSS, and using VSS with a CSV is a complex task because multiple hosts are accessing a single disk. The bottom line recommendation is this: *if you want to create host-based backups with CSVs, use DPM.* You should also use a hardware VSS provider to create hardware-assisted snapshots, if at all possible. Relying on the software VSS provider may lead to extremely long backup times and may have other implications on your implementation related to volume pinning and redirected I/O (detailed in the blog post mentioned earlier).

Protecting Your Hyper-V Environment

Deploying DPM 2010 to protect a virtualized environment involves three primary phases:

1. Setting up your first DPM server, including software installation as well adding disk and/or tape media

2. Deploying DPM agents to the production servers, meaning the Hyper-V hosts and/or inside the virtual machines

3. Configuring one or more protection groups, which define what is to be protected and how

Setting Up Your First DPM Server

The DPM 2010 server should be installed on a dedicated system running x64 Windows Server 2008 or Windows Server 2008 R2. As an alternative, you can acquire a *data protection appliance*, which is usually a Windows Storage Server (OEM version of Windows Server) that is preinstalled on server hardware and includes a preinstallation of DPM.

RELEASE NOTE

At the time of writing, DPM 2010 has not yet been released. We're referring to and using the release candidate (RC) of DPM 2010, which was made available in February 2010. The RC is very stable and close to the final product, but some of the information presented here may not reflect the final release.

HARDWARE REQUIREMENTS FOR **DPM 2010**

As we mentioned earlier, your DPM platform should have one production disk with the operating system and capacity/performance for the DPM application and related SQL Server. After you insert the DPM installation DVD, DPM performs a minimum requirements check, or *preflight inspection*.

NOTE Check out the "How to protect Hyper-V with DPM 2010" white paper available at `www.microsoft.com/downloads`.

Not all the guidance for DPM 2010 is available at this time, and the hardware guidelines have not been finalized, but the hardware requirements are generally similar to those for DPM 2007. You can check the adequacy of your backup hardware by comparing it to the requirements for DPM 2007. Table 12.1 shows an abridged version of the DPM 2007 requirements (for the full version, see "DPM 2007 System Requirements" at `http://technet.microsoft.com/library/bb808832.aspx`).

TABLE 12.1:   DPM 2007/2010 Server Hardware Requirements and Recommendations

COMPONENT	MINIMUM REQUIREMENTS	RECOMMENDATION
Processor	1 GHz or faster	2.33 GHz quad-core CPUs
Memory	512 MB RAM	4 GB RAM
Disk space for DPM installation	Program hard drive: 410 MB; database files drive: 900 MB; system drive 2650 MB	2–3 GB of free space on the program files volume
Disk space for storage pool	1.5 times the size of the protected data	2–3 times the size of the protected data

INSTALLING **DPM 2010**

Starting the installation presents you with a menu of installation choices (Figure 12.2). Clicking Install Data Protection Manager should move you along to the obligatory licensing screens and then to the Welcome page (Figure 12.3).

DPM does an extensive prerequisites check to ensure that the correct versions of all required software components are installed (see Figure 12.4). The following Windows Server optional components are required for DPM 2010 (and are pre-installed with Windows Server 2008 R2):

- ◆ .NET 3.5 Service Pack 1
- ◆ Windows Installer 4.5
- ◆ Windows Single Instance Store (SIS)
- ◆ PowerShell 2.0

FIGURE 12.2
DPM initial menu

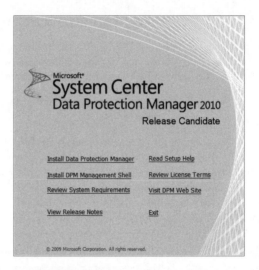

FIGURE 12.3
DPM Setup
Wizard's
Welcome page

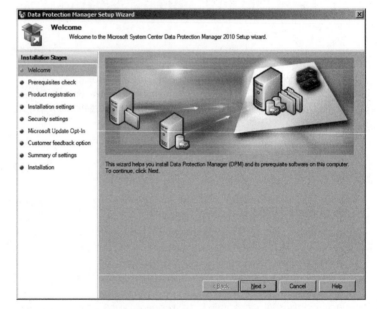

DPM 2010 is heavily dependent on PowerShell version 2. If you are installing the server on Windows Server 2008 with PowerShell 1 already installed, you will need to remove (uninstall) it and install version 2. DPM's prerequisites check will let you know whether the wrong version of PowerShell is installed, as well as where you can find PowerShell 2.

After you make it through the prerequisite validation, you can enter your name and company, select where the DPM application will go, and choose whether to use the included SQL Server or an existing SQL Server (see Figure 12.5).

FIGURE 12.4
DPM Setup
Wizard's
Prerequisites
Check page

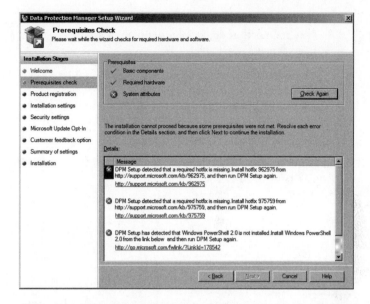

FIGURE 12.5
DPM server
installation—
choosing which
SQL Server to use

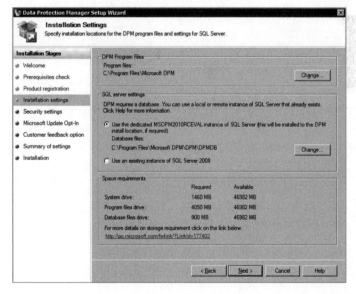

◆ DPM 2010 includes SQL Server on the DPM DVD or as downloadable installation software that can be automatically installed on the DPM server. This is the default choice and doesn't require a separate SQL Server license; nor is there a SQL client-access license (CAL) requirement, because the end user license agreement (EULA) and software allow DPM to use only this included instance of SQL Server.

◆ Alternatively, you can use an external SQL Server database, with the proper permissions.

NOTE For most scenarios, the included SQL Server instance is adequate; however, for high I/O environments or deployments with multiple DPM servers, an external and centralized SQL Server may be desirable.

The next screen requests authentication information for SQL Server and/or its reporting services.

The remaining installation screens walk you through all the components to be installed from this point forward, and then the wizard displays a summary once you've completed the installations (Figure 12.6).

FIGURE 12.6
DPM Setup Wizard
Installation page

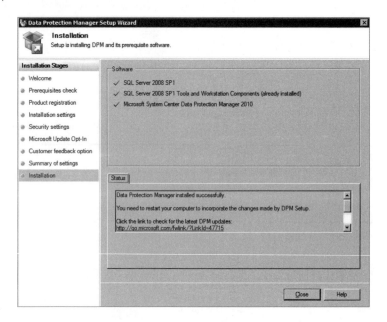

After the prerequisite check and moving through the wizard, you'll watch a status bar for about a half hour—with the only interruptions being a possible request early on for your Windows Server installation media for some initial components. After installation completes and you reboot, you have a DPM 2010 server.

The remaining setup steps are performed in the DPM Administrator Console (after the initial software installation), which are discussed in the next section. The high-level steps are as follows:

1. Allocate one or more disks for the DPM storage pool.

As mentioned earlier, this can consist of any internal/external, locally attached disks (DAS), Fibre Channel, or iSCSI storage solutions. It can't include removable disk media (such as USB hard drives), remote file shares from network-attached storage (NAS), or other filer-type appliances.

2. Attach tape-based storage to the DPM server (optional).

After you confirm that the tape device is visible from the Windows Device Manager, the DPM server should be able to "find" it and use it.

That's it! You now have a data protection server with disk and perhaps tape—and you're ready to protect your production environment, including physical servers, virtualization hosts, and guests.

Introducing the DPM Administrator Console

When you first fire up the DPM Administrator Console, you should intuitively understand the core functionality based on previous Microsoft Management Console (MMC) snap-ins and similar System Center interfaces.

Across the top of the DPM console is the *Ribbon*, which divides the five views of DPM administration:

◆ *Monitoring* presents the active and previous jobs as well as status/completion/failure information that may be necessary during troubleshooting.

◆ *Protection* (shown in Figure 12.7) allows you to view and configure what is protected and how.

FIGURE 12.7
The DPM Administrator Console—Protection tab

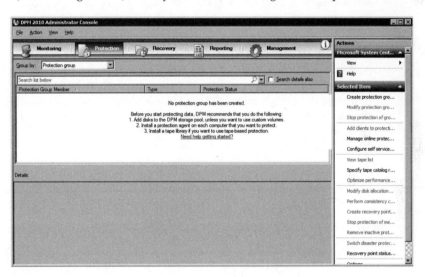

◆ *Recovery* is used for data restoration and is discussed in "Restoring Your Virtual Environment with DPM" later in this chapter.

◆ *Reporting* utilizes SQL Server reporting services to provide information about tape and disk usage, job status, protection compliance, and so on.

◆ *Management* is used for managing the DPM server, including three subtabs for agents (discussed in the next section), disk storage, and tape devices/media.

Deploying Agents and Application Workload Prerequisites

At this point, you still have some work to do before you actually protect your virtual environment. You'll start by deploying agents on the production servers (the Hyper-V hosts and/or the guests) and then move on to configuring the storage attached to the DPM server.

DPM Agent Licenses

Every production server, physical and/or virtual, that is to be individually protected requires its own DPM agent. DPM uses a single agent to protect all workloads so that you can use the same agents and installations for protecting Hyper-V that you use for protecting Exchange Server, SQL Server, or components of a SharePoint farm.

You can purchase several different agents for the production servers' DPM licenses (DPMLs):

Client DPML   For protecting files on Windows XP, Windows Vista, or Windows 7

Standard DPML   For protecting files on Windows Server 2003, Windows Server 2003 R2, Windows Server 2008, and Windows Server 2008 R2

Enterprise DPML   For protecting files as well as application workloads, including SQL Server databases, Exchange storage groups, SharePoint farms, and virtualization hosts and guests

DPM agents can be pushed from the DPM Administrator Console or from any automated software-deployment mechanism, including System Center Configuration Manager, Group Policy in Active Directory (AD), or preinstallation in a Windows operating system base image.

Deploying DPM Agents Through the DPM Administrator Console

Although there are different DPML agent price tiers and capabilities, you install only one agent package, which has variants for x86 and x64 systems. For this first installation, we will show how to push agents from the DPM console—although you can also deploy them en masse from your favorite software distribution solution. In either case, the agent communicates with the DPM server as well as with whatever VSS writers are on each production server (Hyper-V host or virtual guests, in this case). Follow these steps:

1. In the DPM Administrator Console, click the Management button on the ribbon, and then select the Agents tab (Figure 12.8). Click Install in the Actions pane on the right to start a wizard that will push the agent to multiple production servers at the same time.

FIGURE 12.8
The Agents tab in the Management view

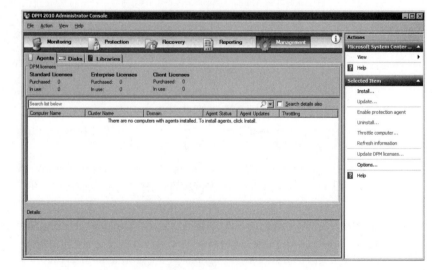

2. The first page of the Protection Agent Installation Wizard (Figure 12.9) allows you to select the agent deployment method. You have two choices:

♦ Install Agents pushes DPM agents to systems in trusted domains that are not isolated behind a firewall.

♦ Attach Agents connects your server to an already deployed agent that may be on a system in an untrusted domain or behind a firewall.

Select the Install Agents option and move along.

FIGURE 12.9
Selecting an
agent deployment
method in the
Protection Agent
Installation
Wizard

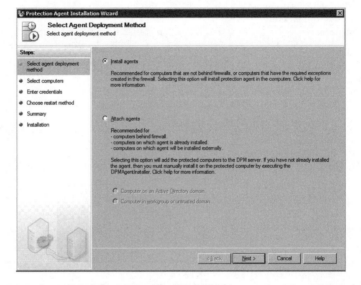

3. Select which production servers to protect. For a smaller environment, the list of production servers in the same AD domain as the DPM server will appear in the Selected Computers box (Figure 12.10). For a domain with many servers, it is more efficient to enter the fully qualified domain name of servers to be protected (this is how we populated the Selected Computers box on the right of Figure 12.10).

4. On the Enter Credentials page, you're asked for an administrator-level username and password. The user must have appropriate rights to install the DPM agent on the production machines (Figure 12.11).

5. On the Choose Restart Method page (Figure 12.12), you are able to choose whether the production machines will be automatically rebooted after agent installation. This is an important consideration. Because the DPM agent uses a filter technology, the agent is initialized after a reboot; however, this reboot can be done later during off-hours. This screen offers no default choice for post-installation reboot behavior, so you can't accidentally (for example) click Next, Next, and Finish and reboot your production server farm. Here are the options:

♦ Yes. Restart The Selected Computers After Installing The Protection Agents (If Required).

This option enables each production server to independently reboot when its agent installation is complete. This is often done during off-hours or in large deployments where you don't have direct access to the production servers.

◆ No. I Will Restart The Selected Computers Later.

This option deploys the agent to all the production servers, but you must intentionally and individually reboot each server.

FIGURE 12.10
Selecting which production servers to protect

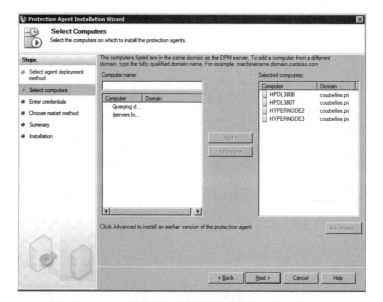

FIGURE 12.11
Entering administrator credentials

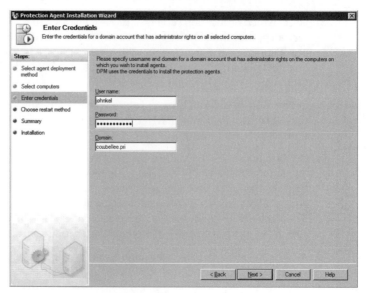

FIGURE 12.12

Choosing the restart method

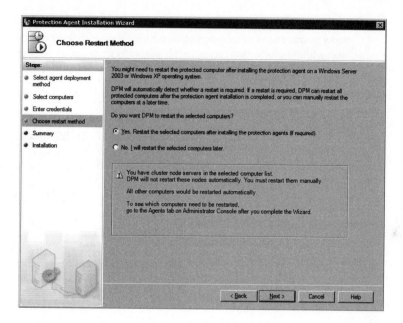

The dialog box is sensitive to failover clusters and detects agent installation on cluster nodes (as shown in the middle of Figure 12.12).

The wizard finishes by showing you the status of installation on the servers you selected (Figure 12.13).

FIGURE 12.13

Installation status

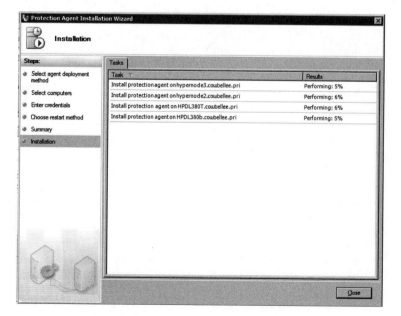

NOTE You can close the installation status window with a good level of confidence if all the agents show greater than 6 percent complete, which indicates that the DPM server has been able to connect with the production server, isn't hindered by most firewalls, and appears to be authorized to install software on the server. Of course, you can also wait until 100 percent to be sure.

The Agents tab of the Administrator Console's Management view shows what did or didn't complete (Figure 12.14).

FIGURE 12.14
Agent status as shown in the Administrator Console

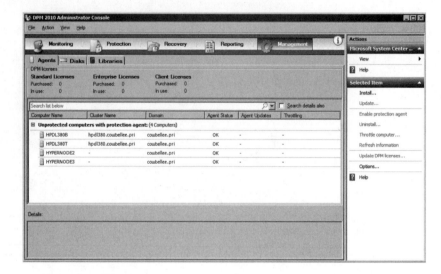

APPLICATION VSS UPDATES OR HOTFIXES

With the DPM agent(s) installed and the appropriate updates or hotfixes from the application (for example, Hyper-V) applied, your production environment, including your Hyper-V hosts, is ready to be protected.

NOTE Individual hotfixes may be required for each application being protected by DPM. In this case, Hyper-V (for Windows Server 2008–based versions; not necessary for R2) VSS hotfix KB959962 (or an update that supersedes it) is required in order to allow online backups using the Hyper-V VSS writer.

Adding Storage to DPM

Before you can back up your Hyper-V hosts, you need to allocate storage to hold your information. Locally attached storage (including SAN and iSCSI) can be assigned to the DPM server to store protected data. Remember that removable disks (USB or IEEE 1394) can't be used. Any volumes used must be dedicated to the DPM server. Disks are assigned to DPM in groups referred to as *storage pools*. To add disks to a storage pool, click Management in the navigation bar, and select the Disks tab (Figure 12.15).

Clicking Add in the Actions pane opens the Add Disks To Storage Pool dialog box, which will display available storage and allow you to allocate disks (Figure 12.16).

FIGURE 12.15

Empty Disks tab

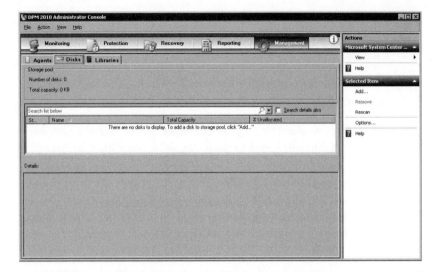

FIGURE 12.16

Adding disks to
the storage pool

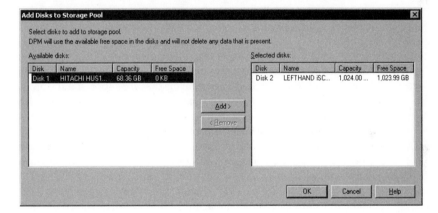

Your organization's corporate retention policies (often dictated by industry regulation such as Sarbanes Oxley (SOX), HIPAA, or CO-OP/DOD 5015.2) may require retention of data beyond what is feasible within your disk-based DPM storage pools. If so, you can configure tape devices for the long-term, remote retention of backup data by selecting the Libraries tab in the Management view of the Administrator Console.

Configuring Protection of Hyper-V Hosts

The DPM server is installed, agents are deployed, storage is assigned—now you need to protect your virtual machines! DPM was designed to allow you to gather similar resources requiring protection into groups. A *protection group* is a policy defining what you want to protect and how you want to protect it. This section focuses on protecting VMs. Virtual machine protection groups should be created to collect and protect VMs that have similar retention and recovery requirements.

You can define a protection group by selecting Protection from the Ribbon and clicking Create Protection Group in the Actions pane. Like other tasks within DPM, the process is wizard-driven.

What Do You Want to Protect?

On the first page of the Create New Protection Group Wizard, the left pane lists the production servers that are currently running the DPM agent. By expanding any server, you see common data object types and data sources that are specific to the workloads running on that machine. On all production servers protected by DPM, you can select the following elements:

Volumes   A traditional view of a production server, whereby you can select individual directories for protection in a Windows Explorer–like view.

Shares   Typically for file servers but available on all protected machines. This view lists all the file shares on a production server. Selecting an individual share for file server protection makes DPM identify where the directory is in the production server and protect from that directory down within the volume filesystem.

NOTE   As an interesting side note, if you select multiple shares that reside on the same physical volume, DPM is intelligent enough to protect that volume only once and also discern only those directories as appropriate from the shares that are selected.

System state   Protects the registry, metadata, and other operating system–specific information necessary to re-create the configuration of the production server. Again, because DPM is intended to use only those mechanisms that are supported for protecting its various workloads, DPM protection as system state uses the built-in backup utility provided by the operating system. This built-in backup utility (NTBackup or WSBackup) provides a native capability to back up the system state on the local machine. DPM automates this process by presenting system state as a logical workload or data source within the production server to be protected. Behind the scenes, when protecting system state, DPM invokes the native utility, which first protects system state to a local file on the production server. Then, DPM replicates the captured or *dumped* system state to the DPM server so that its information can be secured along with the other data objects from that machine. This also gives you confidence that you can restore the system state locally using the native utility for minor recovery scenarios or that you can restore the system state along with the other server data after larger calamities.

In addition to these three common protectable object types, the DPM agent exposes any additional application workloads that are protectable by DPM, including the virtualization workloads that are hosted on Hyper-V.

When expanding a virtualization host, the DPM UI presents host-specific information as well as a single item for each VM currently defined on that host. These have different names as exposed from the Hyper-V VSS writer, but their function is similar.

When protecting VMs from the host, note that you can't select any granularity other than each entire VM. In addition, the DPM UI selects the VMs for protection with a few qualifiers, as shown in Figure 12.17. For Hyper-V, the VMs in the left pane are noted as being backed up using either saved state or a child partition snapshot.

Notice that the entire process for selecting what you want to protect occurs on one screen. You can choose one or more VMs, along with any other directories or shares on the virtualization host, the host configuration, and data from any other protectable workload visible by DPM—all on one screen.

FIGURE 12.17
Configuring protection: data source selection

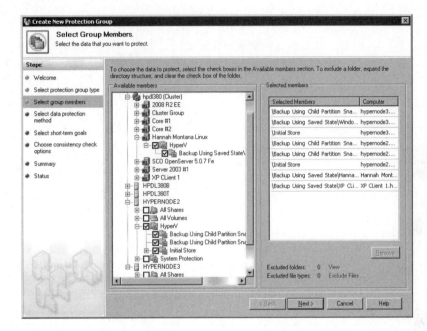

How Do You Want to Protect It?

You use the Create New Protection Group Wizard to choose how to protect the data you selected, by configuring the following:

♦ Disk-based protection

♦ Tape-based protection

♦ Initial synchronization

Configuring Disk-Based Protection

Disk-to-disk protection in DPM can be as simple as answering two business-driven questions:

♦ How long would you like to keep the data on disk (for fast recovery)?

♦ How often would you like to synchronize the data to disk?

You specify the retention window on the Specify Short-Term Goals page of the wizard (Figure 12.18). Typical values are between 5 and 14 days but may often be 30, 45, or even 60. This is the number of days worth of data you can restore from the DPM disk. For example, if you select 30, you'll be able to restore to any previously synchronized point in time for a complete month, with no need for tape-based restore.

FIGURE 12.18
Configuring protection: disk-based retention

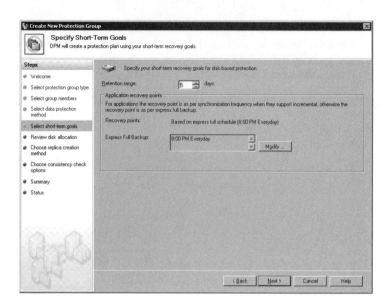

If you've selected additional workloads for protection besides virtualization hosts, you may see a second question on this screen about synchronization frequency, presented as a dropdown list with selectable options from 15 minutes to 24 hours. However, this drop-down list is generic to DPM and the protection group—it isn't entirely applicable to virtualized environments. If your protection group includes only virtualization hosts, then this selection might be predefined as Immediately Before An Express Full or might not appear. If your protection group includes not only virtualization hosts but also transactional applications such as SQL Server, 15 minutes is the default and most common answer (although it won't apply to the protection of the virtualization hosts themselves).

POWERSHELL SCRIPTS HELP AUTOMATICALLY CONFIGURE BACKUPS FOR YOUR HYPER-V HOSTS!

PowerShell scripts are available for automating common tasks within DPM. If using the DPM GUI becomes tedious for repetitive tasks like configuring protection of VMs, check the Microsoft Download Center for "DPM 2010 PowerShell Script – Hyper-V Auto-Protection," available at this link:

```
www.microsoft.com/downloads/details.aspx?displaylang=en&FamilyID=46d51b5a-5827-
43f6-84f5-ce33f4a8e6c3
```

UNDERSTANDING DPM DISK-BASED PROTECTION

DPM uses two different processes to protect Windows data sources:

◆ For all workloads protected by DPM, you can do an *express full*. This is a block-level resynchronization at predetermined points in time, usually between one and six times per day. For details, see "Understanding DPM Storage" earlier in this chapter.

♦ For transactional applications that are protectable by DPM, such as SQL Server and Exchange Server, DPM can synchronize the backup of transactional logs between express fulls—up to every 15 minutes. The second question on the disk-to-disk protection screen addresses the configuration for these transactional applications.

Unfortunately, VHDs don't have transactional logs and therefore can't be protected every 15 minutes. Instead, to configure the schedule for VHD protection, you should configure one or more express fulls per day. The frequency for VHD protection is determined in part by whether the VMs can be protected while online or offline:

If all the VMs selected for protection can be protected while online (without downtime), then it may be reasonable to select one to six express fulls per day, which would allow you to recover a VM to multiple previous points in time without interrupting production users during the backups.

If one or more VMs selected for protection can't be protected online, perhaps because they are running Linux or an older Windows operating system, then these VMs will be taken offline during the backup (saved state and later resumed). In this case, you would normally configure a single express full to be run during nonproduction hours.

For your first protection group, schedule one express full for after-production hours. Later, by right-clicking the protection group and selecting Modify Protection Group, you can change this or any other setting for protection.

ALLOCATING DISK-BASED STORAGE

On the second disk-based protection screen (Figure 12.19), you review the disk allocation for protecting your data sources (the VMs). As discussed earlier, for each data source protected by DPM, two NTFS volumes are allocated out of the DPM storage pool. On this screen, you define how large each of those volumes (per data source) will be—specifically, the replica volumes and the recovery-point volumes:

Replica volumes should be at least as large as the production data file set (not the production volume), but with some room for expansion. For example, if one VM currently has 3 GB of VHDs on a 10 GB volume, it isn't necessary to define 10 GB for the DPM replica. If the VHDs are fixed size, the replica need be only slightly larger than 3 GB to allow for the natural expansion as blocks are overwritten. However, if the VHDs are dynamic, the replica should be larger—big enough to accommodate the anticipated growth of the VHDs.

Recovery-point volumes should be sized based on the number of days you want to retain previous point-in-time backups. This may take more experimentation to better define, because daily growth depends directly on the data change rate. DPM retains all the previous points in time if either of the following two conditions is met:

♦ When DPM reaches the maximum number of days as defined in the protection group policy (for example, 30 days), then on the next day (day 31), the oldest block-level changes (those more than 30 days old) are discarded from the recovery-point volume.

♦ When the recovery-point volume is full, the block-level changes consisting of the oldest day are retained or discarded as a whole. This means that if the recovery-point volume is undersized, DPM may be able to hold only 24 or 16 days of data regardless of the policy (because of lack of capacity).

FIGURE 12.19
Configuring protection: disk allocation

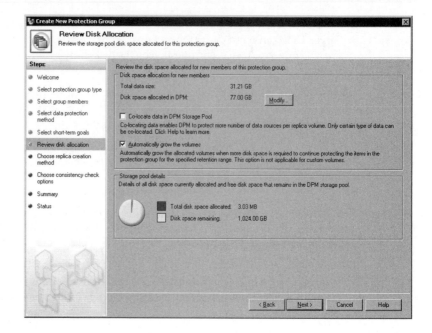

NOTE Typically, DPM volumes can be expanded later—but they usually can't be reduced, so over-allocation of disk space isn't recommended.

You can modify disk allocations individually for each data source or for an entire protection group, as shown in Figure 12.20.

FIGURE 12.20
Modifying disk allocation

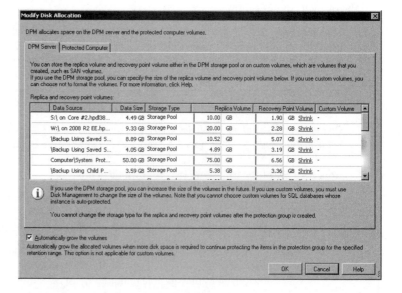

Configuring Tape-Based Protection

The Create New Protection Group Wizard defines the DPM disk-to-disk protection by asking the following questions:

- ◆ How long should the data reside on disk?
- ◆ How frequently (and on what schedule) should the data be synchronized?
- ◆ How should the medium be configured for retention?

In the section of the wizard dealing with tape-based protection with DPM, you must answer the same three questions plus one more:

How long should the data reside on tape?   The default is three months, but you can easily alter this setting by choosing a different number of weeks, months, or years. Often, this question is best answered by referring to the corporate retention policy that is defined by senior management or perhaps in an industry regulation such as Sarbanes Oxley (SOX), HIPAA, or CO-OP/DOD 5015.2.

How frequently should tape backup occur?   The default value and often the best choice is Weekly. Other choices include Daily, Biweekly, Monthly, and Annually. However, because most of your recoveries will now come from disk, tape backups (and recoveries) will be far less frequent and can be done less often. A best practice here is to schedule at least two tape backups during your disk retention window. This ensures that you have at least two different tapes (in case of tape media failure) to restore data from, above and beyond your disk storage pool.

On what schedule should tape backups occur?   After you select the maximum retention time as well as the frequency of tape backups, DPM automatically configures a traditional *grandfather, father, son* tape-rotation system that typically comprises weekly, monthly, and annual tapes. You can configure exactly when the tape backups occur for each of the three tiers or define a custom schedule based on business practices that may be less typical.

Which tape device(s) should be used?   Similar to allocating storage in the disk protection screens, you need to define which tape device(s) will be used for this backup. If your tape library has multiple drives, you may choose how many of those tape drives should be allocated for this particular protection group. This allows you to create some load balancing; for example, in a four-drive library, this protection group may be allowed to use two of the drives, while a different protection group protecting SQL Server or Exchange Server servers uses the other two drives.

Additionally, you may want to create copies of some tapes so that one tape resides in the tape library (on-site) and a copy is available for off-site courier services or vaulting. Additional options include the ability to encrypt or compress the tapes.

Setting Up the Initial Baseline

Because DPM is natively a disk-to-disk solution, all of its protection capabilities are based on the requirement that the DPM replica has a complete copy of the production data set.

The Choose Replica Creation Method page in the Create New Protection Group Wizard (Figure 12.21) determines how the initial synchronization, or *baseline*, occurs:

◆ *Now* is the most common choice, particularly in cases where the VMs can be protected while they remain online. Within the data center and without significant production load, it may be reasonable to immediately start popping the data from the production virtualization host(s) to the DPM server.

◆ *Later* allows you to schedule the data synchronization to occur during off-hours. You can configure the data protection group during your typical day, without affecting the production user base, and you can schedule the baseline to occur during off-hours and finish before the next business day. Selecting this choice displays simple calendar and time-based controls.

◆ *Manually* provides for branch-office scenarios and other circumstances where pulling the production data may not be appealing. For example, if you are in a remote office with a significant amount of data, you can do an offline backup of the branch office server (using tape, USB hard drive, or other portable media) and ship the media from the branch to the DPM server location. Then, you can complete the baseline by restoring the offline backup into the DPM replica partition.

If you select the manual option, you notify the DPM server that the data already resides in or has been manually copied to the DPM replica. In turn, DPM performs an immediate consistency check, which does a block-level comparison of what is on the remote production server and what is in the DPM replica. This allows the DPM server to replicate those block-level changes that have occurred over the past few days since the initial backup was taken—making it ideal for the initial setup of branch-office or remote servers with large amounts of data.

FIGURE 12.21
Choosing the replica creation method

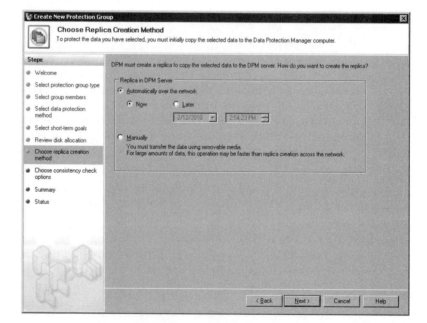

After selecting the desired consistency check options, you will see a confirmation screen that summarizes the choices you've made (Figure 12.22). This screen shows that DPM intends to allocate the appropriate storage for the replica and recovery-point volumes, defines the protection group, configures the protection schedule(s), and initiates the baseline copy or consistency check.

FIGURE 12.22
Summary page

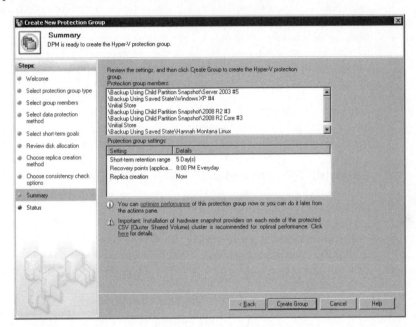

Clicking Create Group on the Summary page will kick off all these processes. During a consistency check, each data source initially appears as a green OK and then later turns to a yellow warning while the block-level comparison happens. For the baseline copy, the object appears with a white informational note for notifications until the baseline is complete. After either case, the data source changes back to a green OK, and begins synchronizing on the schedule you've defined.

Congratulations! You've now protected your virtualization environment.

Considerations When Protecting Virtualized Environments

Just because you can protect your virtual infrastructure from the host perspective doesn't necessarily mean that you'll always want to do so. There are reasons to protect VMs from the outside (using a host-based agent). Similarly, there are reasons to protect your VMs using the same methodology you use to protect physical machines from the inside (using a guest-based agent). We'll revisit some of the topics discussed in Chapter 7 from the perspective of a DPM-protected environment.

Virtual Machines, Hosts, and Guests

Virtualization gives you new backup and recovery options through encapsulation, but that doesn't mean you have to abandon other backup and recovery approaches. You can continue to protect VMs as if they were physical systems by running a DPM agent inside each virtualized production server. Fundamentally, there is no difference between protecting a virtualized Windows Server running an application such as SQL Server and protecting a physical server with the same operating system and application. There are reasons you may choose to do this—most notably, if you want the most granular data selection options during backups and recovery.

Assume for a moment that you have five virtualization hosts, and each happens to be running approximately 10 virtualized Windows Server and SQL Server application platforms. If they're all generic database platforms, then protecting their entire machine set may have you protecting 50 copies of essentially the same Windows Server operating system and 50 copies of the SQL Server application, when all you really want is the 50 database sets. In this scenario, in the case of a crisis, you may consider restoring only a select subset of those databases onto a few consolidated SQL servers for recovery purposes. But if complex applications are installed on each of those 50 database servers, then perhaps the best resolution method is to protect the machine sets and bring all 50 virtualized application platforms back online.

Choosing What to Protect and How to Recover

The previous scenario illustrates the primary question for which you need a clear answer when you're deciding whether to protect your virtual infrastructure from a guest perspective or from a host perspective: what will you want to restore?

If your primary requirement is protecting the data—that is, specific SQL Server databases, Exchange Server storage groups, SharePoint farms, or Windows file server home directories—then the appropriate choice may be to run DPM agents in each guest and protect strictly those data objects.

But it isn't quite that simple. You must also ask, what is your recovery goal?

If you're primarily protecting application data sets with the anticipation of being able to roll back to previous points in time in anticipation of user error, hardware calamity, or ad hoc point-in-time requests, then you'll be predominantly restoring individual data objects and therefore should protect those individual data objects (from within the guest).

If you're primarily protecting application servers in anticipation of whole-server failure or as part of your disaster recovery or business continuity preparedness plan (or you have other requirements for being able to restore an entire server's application set in a very short time frame), then you should protect the entire virtualized server (from the host).

The two choices aren't mutually exclusive, and we'll discuss a hybrid approach later in the chapter.

If you do choose to protect each virtualized server as if it were physical, then you should plan not only for how the virtual data will be protected but also for the aggregate impact to the host and overall I/O. For example, although protecting transactional applications like Exchange Server or SQL Server may be fairly transparent and nonimpacting during the production day, it's not zero impact. Plan for some amount, albeit minor, of network/disk/performance impact during the backup windows themselves. Also, recognize that if you have 10 virtualized SQL Servers on the same host and you've configured them to be in the same DPM protection group, then your host will see a significant increase in network traffic every 15 minutes (or as often as you're set up to synchronize)—the aggregate of the backup traffic that might normally be seen on 10 separate physical servers. Consider dedicated network segments (physical and virtual in those cases), or stagger the replication with multiple protection groups on different schedules).

Protecting Virtual Machines from the Host

When the VMs' operating system is Windows Server 2003, Windows Server 2008, or Windows Server 2008 R2 and they're running Microsoft application server platforms, then you may have the choice of protecting from the host or guest.

The opposite corollary is also true. If the VMs aren't running a Windows operating system, DPM isn't a choice for protecting them within the guest(s) and therefore makes a compelling argument for protecting from the host. At that point, DPM provides a crash-consistent backup of the VM, regardless of the operating system. As a twist on this idea, for secure environments as well as outsourcing situations, this enables you to back up entire VMs from the host without any visibility of the contents or data inside.

Aside from the VMs' applications and operating systems, there are other considerations when choosing whether to protect from the host or the guest.

GUEST OPERATING SYSTEMS AND APPLICATIONS

Similarly (but not exactly), if the VMs are running a Windows operating system but the applications aren't currently protectable by DPM, there is merit in protecting each VM from the host-based perspective. To make the decision slightly more blurry, some Windows applications, which may not be explicitly defined as protectable by DPM, may have known recipes allowing them to be protected by DPM using its pre-/post-backup scripting method. In this case, it still comes back to "What do you want to protect?" and "How do you need to restore?"

STORAGE CONFIGURATION OF GUESTS

If the guest operating system isn't using VHDs for its data volumes but instead is using the Hyper-V capability for pass-through disks, then the Hyper-V VSS writer doesn't have access to those data volumes and can't protect those volumes using a host-based backup.

Similarly, if the guest operating system is using an iSCSI initiator or storage not visible from the hypervisor host, then a *host-based backup of those volumes isn't viable.*

Interestingly, some administrators consider this an ideal scenario—the operating system and application volume are in a VHD that can be protected from the host, but the data sets are conveniently missing. Instead, many administrators choose to protect the data volumes by protecting the actual data objects using a guest-based DPM agent. This provides the best of both worlds, where you can protect and recover the whole machine (operating system and applications) as a single VHD while still providing granular data restoration from within the data volumes.

Choosing Guest or Host or Both

Let's summarize the decision points we've presented so far:

◆ VMs running VSS-capable Windows operating systems and applications can be protected from the host or the guest (in general).

◆ VMs *not* running a VSS-capable operating system or application should generally be protected from the host. This scenario is most commonly seen in DPM environments where a significant majority of production physical and virtual servers are protectable by DPM; however, the business requirements mandate a minority of non-Microsoft platforms to be backed up as well. By virtualizing those platforms, you enjoy the benefits of DPM for the majority of your servers while getting at least a crash-consistent external backup of your few non-Windows machines in order to maintain a single backup and recovery solution for their entire environment.

◆ Storage architectures that preclude the Hyper-V VSS writer from having direct access to the VHD enclosed data may not be protectable from the host.

Often, the ability to restore a complete (virtual) machine, similar to the desire to do a bare-metal recovery of physical servers, is the primary reason to protect and recover from the host.

The other primary reason for protecting from the host is cost. DPM is often one of the most cost-effective backup and recovery solutions for Windows environments or for providing enterprise-type backup capabilities (such as D2D2T and DR) without enterprise prices.

Restoring Your Virtual Environment with DPM

And now for the fun part. After all, no one intentionally purchases *backup* software—you purchase *recovery* software, where backup is simply a preparation task. That twist on words isn't entirely meant as a joke, but it's intended to demonstrate that DPM is designed as recovery software and not backup software. Often, backup software is just that: software intended to conduct backups and typically used only for whole-server recoveries or as a proof point to confirm that backups are occurring for compliance or retention purposes. DPM really is *recovery* software.

Overview of the DPM Restore UI

Similar to the wizards for protecting data, DPM uses restoration wizards to provide recovery with the same ease-of-use goals.

1. In the DPM Administrator Console, select Recovery from the Ribbon (see Figure 12.23). The left pane provides a tree-based view of all the production servers that have been protected by this DPM server.

FIGURE 12.23
Restoring data: the DPM Administrator Console's Recovery view

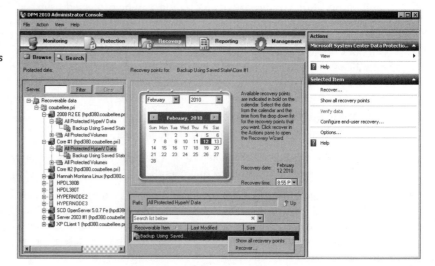

When you expand each of the servers, you see the same kinds of data objects that you can select for a protection group, such as volumes, system state, and application workloads.

2. Expand the Hyper-V host, and you can see the virtualization workload being protected, including the host configuration as well as each of the VMs.

3. Click a protected data object to refresh the calendar and detail panes in the center.

The calendar presents a typical monthly view. The dates in bold have recovery points available for restoration.

4. Select any bold date on the calendar, and a pull-down menu to the right presents any points in time from that day that are available for restore.

5. Click a desired time, and the details pane in the lower-right corner displays the VM for restoration.

6. Right-click the VM, and select Restore.

You can select any data object for recovery to any point in time in as few as four mouse clicks:

1. Select the data objects from the left pane.

2. Select the date you want to recover to.

3. Pull down the time you want to recover to.

4. Right-click the data object in the right pane, and choose Recover.

TIP Remember that restoring a virtual machine requires not only the VHDs used by the VM but also the configuration information. DPM allows you to recover just the VHD files or the entire virtual machine. Be certain that you are choosing the appropriate type of recovery for your needs when you restore.

Restoring a Virtual Machine from the DPM UI

Following the steps described in the previous section, you can select the VM to restore from the DPM UI. Doing so invokes a Recovery Wizard (see Figure 12.24) that walks you through the remaining steps. After the introduction screen, you'll move through several different recovery choices, some of which are specific to the workload being restored (in this case, a VM); others are generic to all DPM recovery scenarios.

DPM allows you to easily restore a virtual machine to the original host, to another Hyper-V system, or to a network share. You can also recover to tape (Figure 12.25).

The last two recovery options are generic for all DPM data sources:

Copy To A Network Folder   The Copy To A Network Folder option restores the files that make up your data source to any file share or directory that is accessible from the DPM server. The intent is to provide the files in such a way that an application owner can then manually act on them. In the case of SQL Server or Exchange Server, you may choose to manually mount the database for some particular recovery scenario.

In the case of a VM, you can create a directory that will receive the VHDs. You can then choose to manually create a new VM or perhaps use SCVMM to automate that VM creation.

Copy To Tape With the Copy To Tape option, the files of the selected data source are *restored* from the DPM repository onto their own tape. This approach is normally used for IT environments that must periodically ship data off-site to an auditor, a vault, or an e-discovery judicial proceeding. A typical (and nonoptimal) method has been to copy an existing backup tape from the nightly library, which includes not only the requested data but also other, unnecessary information.

This DPM capability improves on the typical method by letting you select only the data object you desire at the specific point in time that it's required. Copy To Tape *restores* the data to its own individual tape. This tape can then be sent off to the auditor, vault, or attorney.

FIGURE 12.24
Review Recovery
Selection page
of the Recovery
Wizard

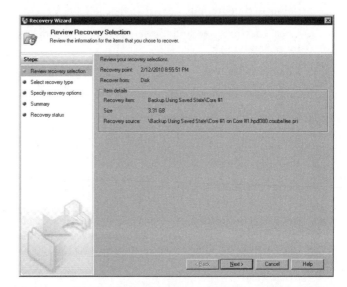

FIGURE 12.25
Selecting the
recovery type

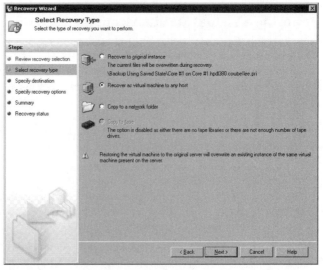

The other restore option(s) are specific to the type of data being recovered. For applications such as SQL Server, Exchange, and SharePoint, you may see multiple choices for restoring the data back to the original location or alternate locations, and additional options based on the granularity of the data being restored. In the case of Hyper-V (as shown in Figure 12.25), the choice is to restore the VM on an alternate host.

If you select Recover To Original Instance, you restore the VM to the original Hyper-V host server, overwriting the configuration and associated VHDs. To restore to an alternate Hyper-V host, you choose Recover As Virtual Machine To Any Host. From there, you'll select an appropriate Hyper-V host and a destination directory. Note that when restoring to an alternate host, the recovery process appends the recovery date and time to the name of the folder where the virtual machine will be recovered (Figure 12.26).

FIGURE 12.26

Specifying the destination of a recovery

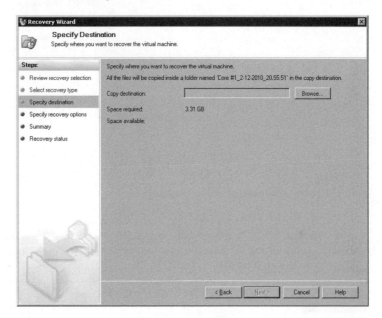

You are able to browse hosts that have the DPM agent installed and select (via volume or share) an appropriate destination for the recovery. Once the destination is chosen, you can move on to configure additional DPM restoration options (show in Figure 12.27).

Some of the options are as follows:

◆ *Network Bandwidth Usage Throttling* ensures that the restoration activity doesn't overwhelm limited-bandwidth segments between the DPM server and the restoration target. If you select this option, DPM provides Kbps and Mbps settings, including variations for time of day, so you may use partial wide area network (WAN) bandwidth during the production day and all available bandwidth during nonproduction hours.

◆ *SAN Recovery* uses a SAN that is shared between the DPM server and the Hyper-V host. This option invokes a SAN-specific script that instructs the SAN to make a mirror of the DPM replica volume within the shared disk array and then to remount the mirror on the host. This can be a powerful feature if the production server(s) and the DPM server are on the same SAN, because terabytes of data can be restored in a matter of seconds.

◆ *Notification* uses a Simple Mail Transfer Protocol (SMTP) mail server and notifies the appropriate systems administrators when the restoration process is complete.

FIGURE 12.27
Specifying
recovery options

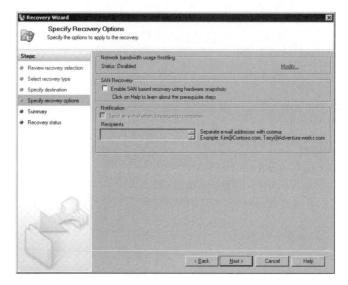

On the Summary page of the Recovery Wizard, you see an overview of what will be restored (see Figure 12.28). Note that in this example, the VM consists of three components, each of which must be properly recovered. Here you see each of the VM components, including its one VHD and the VM definition information (noted by the GUID).

FIGURE 12.28
Summary page
of the Recovery
Wizard

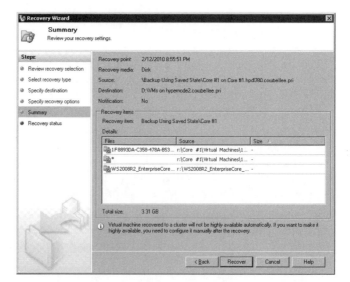

Summary

Microsoft System Center DPM 2010 is designed, in part, to complement Hyper-V in the larger scope of the Microsoft virtualization portfolio. As mentioned at the beginning of this chapter, if you're going to put all of your eggs in one basket, it had better be a good basket. DPM helps ensure that Hyper-V is a "good basket" for your virtual infrastructure:

◆ In contrast to the backup capabilities provided by other virtualization vendors, DPM doesn't require a SAN or third-party tape backup software to protect its VMs.

◆ In contrast to third-party tape-backup software for Hyper-V, DPM provides an all-Microsoft backup and recovery solution that is wholly supportable and uses only protection and restoration methods that are directly supported by the Hyper-V development team and customer service organization.

◆ In contrast to a third-party replication technology for Hyper-V, DPM provides on-site and off-site protection of VMs and the host configuration, and does so at a fraction of the cost of most replication software and in a more supportable way.

◆ In contrast to the solutions and examples presented in Chapter 7, backup and recovery tasks are easy to accomplish across multiple servers in an enterprise environment.

Chapter 13

Using System Center Operations Manager 2007

In this chapter, we'll cover System Center Operations Manager (SCOM) 2007 and the role it plays in the Microsoft virtualization infrastructure for managing both physical and virtual systems. This chapter isn't designed to be an install or design guide for SCOM 2007—several very good guides are available for installing core SCOM 2007 functionality. Instead, we will describe how you can use SCOM 2007 to manage a Microsoft virtualization infrastructure. This is only a small part of what you can do with SCOM 2007—SCOM is designed to handle all aspects of IT operations. SCOM is a feature-rich platform for IT management, with functionality that maps to specific operational areas defined in the Information Technology Infrastructure Library (ITIL), the Managed Operations Framework (MOF), and the Microsoft Operations Framework. It's important for you to spend time getting up to speed on all aspects of SCOM 2007 that aren't covered in this chapter. We recommend that you read the book *Mastering Microsoft System Center Operations Manager 2007* by Price, Mueller, and Fenstermacher (Sybex, 2007). In addition, the SCOM 2007 white papers located at `http://technet.microsoft.com/en-us/opsmgr/bb498235.aspx` should be considered required reading. Specifically, the Operations Manager 2007 R2 Design Guide and the Operations Manager 2007 Deployment Guide are useful documents to help in the initial deployment and configuration of SCOM.

This chapter covers the following topics:

- Introduction to System Center Operations Manager 2007
- SCOM technical overview
- Using SCOM for your virtualization environment
- Monitoring and reporting

Introduction to System Center Operations Manager 2007

SCOM provides health/service models, real-time alerting, monitoring infrastructure, and the reporting environment, all of which let you manage physical and virtual environments as well as Microsoft and non-Microsoft platforms. SCOM provides the following functionality:

- End-to-end monitoring
- Comprehensive views of health states

◆ Rapid response to events for managed systems

◆ Application-specific management packs

◆ Automated tasks per application

◆ A comprehensive automated reporting infrastructure

An SCOM management pack provides application-level knowledge and custom tasks tailored to the specifics of an application. The end-state goal is to bridge application alerting and monitoring into the virtualization management framework. System Center Virtual Machine Manager (SCVMM) and SCOM provide a system connector to share information about managed virtual machines (VMs) and applications. The functionality providing deep integration between SCOM and SCVMM is called Performance Resource Optimization (PRO) and is described in detail in Chapter 11, "Using System Center Virtual Machine Manager." This enables SCOM management packs and PRO packs installed to exchange information with SCVMM 2008.

NOTE The current version of Operations Manager is 2007 R2. All the content in this chapter applies to both 2007 and 2007 R2.

SCOM Technical Overview

In this section, we'll introduce the key concepts that all virtualization administrators should be familiar with before deploying SCOM. SCOM 2007 forms the backbone of monitoring, reporting, and alerting services in the Microsoft virtualization infrastructure. SCOM 2007 integration with SCVMM provides 360-degree monitoring, real-time triggers, and alerting of not only the physical systems but also VMs and the applications running in VMs.

All hardware, software, services, and other logical components that you want SCOM to be aware of are described in a model. A *model* is a consumable representation of software or hardware components that captures the nature of the components and the relationships between them. For example, monitoring Microsoft virtualization services involves keeping track of a variety of components such as Hyper-V hosts, clusters, operating system components, disk subsystems, and SCVMM components. The diagram view shown in SCVMM and SCOM is an example of how all the Microsoft virtualization components in a model are monitored and displayed in a single view. Some would call this *service-level monitoring*, and that's accurate; but all service management begins from a model. To fully monitor Microsoft virtualization services, you must discover and monitor the interaction and interdependencies between these systems, such as whether PRO tips and alerts are flowing through the system. In SCOM 2007, a health model for the service can alert you when one component of the service is unhealthy and can change the state of the overall service until all components are functioning correctly.

SCOM uses management packs to model and monitor software and hardware components. In SCOM, management packs contain the models required for the software to interpret the structure of an application and determine the health of the application. This knowledge is expressed as an XML document and uses a predefined XML scheme understood by SCOM.

The model-based design uses this standard specification language to tell SCOM about important elements of your application or component. Objects in your model can represent hardware components, such as whether a physical switch that connects into a virtual switch is running;

or they can represent software, such as whether a particular application in a VM or service is running. By combining different objects and relationships, you can create a distributed application model that spans different components, applications, and hardware. Understanding models helps you make the best use of SCOM 2007.

Core Components of SCOM

The following SCOM components make up the core SCOM functionality that provides alerting, reporting, monitoring, and service-modeling capabilities.

SCOM Database

The SCOM database is the first component to be installed in all management groups. It must be installed on a Microsoft SQL Server (either SQL Server 2005 with SP2 or SQL Server 2008). This database holds all the configuration data for the management group, and it stores all the monitoring data that the agents collect and process.

To optimize the performance of SCOM, you must optimize the performance of the SCOM database. You do so by controlling the size of the database. Testing has shown that 50 GB is a good upper limit. To control the database size, SCOM 2007 automatically weeds out older, unnecessary data according to parameters you set.

Because there can be only one SCOM database in a management group, it must be functional in order for the management group to work. To prevent the single instance of the SCOM database from being a single point of failure, you can place it in a failover cluster.

Root Management Server

The root management server (RMS) is a specialized type of management server in a management group, and it's the first management server installed in a management group. There can be only one active RMS per management group.

In brief, management servers are the focal point for administering the management group configuration, administering and communicating with agents, and communicating with the SCOM database and other databases in the management group.

The RMS performs all these functions plus some additional ones. It serves as the target for the operations console and the preferred target for the web console.

In addition, the RMS hosts the SCOM software development kit (SDK)/System Center Data Access services and the SCOM Config/System Center Management Configuration services. These services run only on the RMS. The SDK service provides a communication layer between the SCOM database and the rest of the management group. The Config service calculates the configuration of all agents, which management packs they should receive, and the overall configuration of the management group.

Like the SCOM database, you can install the RMS role into an failover cluster to make it highly available. In addition, you can manually promote other management servers in the management group (if you have them) to the role of RMS.

Operations Console

The operations console provides a single, unified user interface (UI) for interacting with SCOM 2007. The operations console gives you access to monitoring data, management-pack authoring tools, SCOM reports, all the controls and tools necessary for administering SCOM, and a customizable workspace.

To allow a user to access the operations console, you must assign the user's Active Directory (AD) user account to an SCOM 2007 role. A *role* is the combination of a scope of devices to which access is granted and a profile that defines what the role can do within its defined scope. For example, you can use a role to define a virtualization administrator for a specific set of Hyper-V hosts. Role-based security is enforced in the operations console so you can define what any given user can see in the console and what actions the user can take on those items.

Agent

An SCOM 2007 *agent* is a service that you deploy on a computer that you want to monitor. Once a machine is managed by SCOM, the SCOM health service is listed in the Operations Manager console. Every agent is owned by a management server in the management group, and this server is referred to as the agent's *primary* management server. Agents watch data sources on the monitored device and collect information according to the configuration sent from its management server. This data is used to calculate the health state of the monitored object. When the health state of a monitored object changes or other criteria are met, an alert can be generated, which lets you know that something has gone awry and requires attention.

Agents can also take many types of actions to help you diagnose or correct issues. It's most important to note that agents feed a constant stream of data back to the management server about the monitored device so that an up-to-date picture of the health of the device and all the applications that it supports is always available.

NOTE It's also possible to monitor devices in an agentless fashion. In this case, an agent on a management server performs the monitoring remotely.

Management Packs

Management packs contain the definition of an application's health as defined by the application developers. When you import management packs into SCOM, the agent can then monitor the health of an application, generate alerts when something of significance goes wrong in the application, and take actions in the application and its supporting infrastructure to further diagnose the application or restore it to a healthy state. Without an application, operating system, or device-specific management pack, SCOM 2007 is unaware of those entities and is unable to monitor them.

Optional Server Roles and Components

These additional server roles extend the functionality of a management group. Most of these components are installed separately from the required core components, but you can install some at the same time as the core components.

Management Server

A management server isn't the first one installed into a management group; it's automatically configured as a regular management server and doesn't perform any of the special functions of the RMS. You can promote this type of management server to the RMS role if the RMS fails, as long as the server was present in the management group prior to the RMS failure.

You can install multiple management servers in a management group to provide extra capacity for agent management. In addition to providing scalability, introducing additional management servers into a management group allows agents to fail over and start reporting their data to another management server if they lose communication with their primary management server.

Management servers that aren't in the RMS role are used primarily for agent administration. One additional role for a management server is to host the Audit Collection Service (ACS) Collector role, which collects audit records from systems that are managed by Operations Manager. These records can then be analyzed by Microsoft SQL Server, allowing administrators to look for unauthorized attempts to access data, failed logins, and other security risks. The ACS Collector can be installed only on a management server.

Gateway Server

An SCOM 2007 gateway server can drastically reduce the administrative overhead required to maintain communication between agents and management servers that are separated by a trust boundary.

SCOM 2007 requires that agents and management servers authenticate each other and establish an encrypted communication channel before they exchange information. Kerberos is the authentication protocol used for the agent-to-server and server-to-agent authentication. When the agent and the management server are in the same Active Directory (AD) domain or in domains that share a two-way trust relationship, mutual authentication occurs automatically. This is because Kerberos is the default authentication protocol in AD.

Web Console Server

The web console server provides an administrative interface to the management group that is accessible via a web browser. It doesn't have the full functionality of the operations console, however. The web console provides access to all the monitoring data and tasks that are actions that can be run against monitored computers from the operations console. It also exposes the operator's personalized My Workspace. Access to data in the web console has the same restrictions as access to content in the operations console.

Reporting Data Warehouse

The Reporting Data Warehouse stores monitoring and alerting data for historical purposes. The management servers write their data to the Reporting Data Warehouse at the same time they write it to the SCOM database, so the reports generated always contain the most up-to-date information. The Reporting Data Warehouse automatically aggregates performance data on an hourly and daily basis. This lets you run long-term trending reports much more quickly than would be possible otherwise, and far less data needs to be retained to support long-term trend reporting.

The Reporting Data Warehouse can receive data from multiple management groups, thereby allowing for an aggregated view of data in your reports.

Reporting Server

The reporting server is an important part of the managed virtualization infrastructure because it provides reports for virtualization functionality, like Virtualization Candidate reports. SCVMM 2008 uses the reporting server functionality to report on critical SCVMM services.

The SCOM reporting server is installed into an instance of Microsoft SQL Reporting Services. It builds and presents the reports using data queried from the Reporting Data Warehouse. All reports can be accessed from the SCOM operations console; and when SCVMM is integrated with SCOM 2007, you can view the reports directly from the SCVMM administration console. This is great because you don't need to move out of the same console you use to manage VMs.

AUDIT COLLECTION SERVICES (ACS)

ACS is a high-performance, secure solution that collects and stores events from the security event logs on monitored computers. Events are stored in a separate ACS in Microsoft SQL Server. ACS collects all events written to the security event log on computers for which you've enabled the ACS Forwarder. Events are forwarded from monitored computers to the ACS Collector, which runs on a management server. ACS Collector processes the events and writes them to the ACS database. Forwarders transmit events in an encrypted, near-real-time fashion to the collector. A separate component, ACS Reporting, is then used to generate reports from the stored ACS data.

PROXY AGENT

SCOM 2007 can monitor network devices via Simple Network Management Protocol (SNMP) v2, computers that aren't running a Windows operating system, and computers without agents. In these cases, another computer that has an agent installed is performing the monitoring remotely. The computer that performs the remote monitoring is called a *proxy agent*. The agent that acts as a proxy for monitoring other devices is a standard SCOM agent: you merely configure it differently by using the Agent Properties dialog box and selecting the option Allow This Agent To Act As A Proxy And Discover Managed Objects And Other Computers. Then you configure the agentless managed device to designate the proxy agent it should to use.

SCOM 2007 Command Shell

The SCOM 2007 PowerShell command shell interface includes an interactive prompt and a scripting environment that you can use independently or in combination. The command shell is a grouping of more than 200 individual cmdlets that have been specifically developed for automating SCOM administrative tasks. You can install the command shell on any computer that will have the Operations Console installed, which ensures that the prerequisites for the command shell are loaded on the system. You can query the cmdlets on any system in the command shell installed by typing **get-OperationsManagerCommand**; this gives you a list of the cmdlets. Each cmdlet comes with detailed help information.

We've gone through a lot of concepts, but each SCOM component fulfills specific roles with needed functionality. It's important to understand the roles each component plays in providing rich management functionality. Now that you have the SCOM 2007 core concepts under your belt, it's time to concentrate on enabling SCOM to manage the Microsoft virtualization infrastructure.

Using SCOM for Your Virtualization Environment

Either you're deploying a Microsoft virtualization environment or you're far along in the planning of the environment, and it's time to consider how the virtualization environment will work with

SCOM. Consider the two most common deployment scenarios for SCOM 2007 for managing virtual environments, each with various levels of effort associated to integrate SCOM 2007:

Scenario 1 You're deploying a new SCOM 2007 environment to manage existing servers/ applications and new or existing virtualization components. This scenario requires you to deploy an SCOM 2007 infrastructure for physical and virtual systems, and you must go through the SCOM 2007 architecture design, scalability, and topology processes. By following these processes, you'll design an infrastructure that not only meets the existing systems' management needs but can also scale to new requirements for managed systems.

Scenario 2 An SCOM 2007 environment is already deployed in the enterprise for monitoring existing systems. In this case, you're going to add any management packs for applications that you'll run in VMs. The next step is to configure SCVMM PRO functionality that uses SCOM 2007, which will add more management packs and reports for the virtualization environment.

TIP   In most large enterprises, the virtualization engineering function and the system management team are separated. So, any discussion about deploying a new management platform is a joint exercise between groups. This can become a long process, full of engineering rigor and integration of the new management platform into existing IT processes. Don't assume it will be quick.

NOTE   The assumption is that you are deploying not only Hyper-V or Virtual Server 2005 R2 SP1 but SCVMM as well. Deploying SCVMM is a critical component in managing a Microsoft virtual environment. SCVMM is generally the first management software deployed unless you have an existing SCOM environment.

Before we walk through the processes associated with these scenarios, let's identify the critical virtualization components that SCOM 2007 will manage and the components needed to manage them effectively. SCOM needs a management pack that has knowledge, rules, tasks, and reports associated with the managed component.

It's important that as a virtualization administrator, you separate the management packs needed to manage the Microsoft virtualization environment from other application and operating system management packs. You can download the base operating system management packs as well as management packs for Microsoft Server applications at `http://pinpoint.microsoft` `.com/en-US/systemcenter/managementpackcatalog`.

The management packs needed for the Microsoft virtual environment are shipped with SCVMM. The process of configuring the PRO functionality to work with SCOM 2007, covered in Chapter 12, adds those management packs to the SCOM 2007 infrastructure automatically. See Table 13.1 for all managed components and associated SCOM management packs that must be added to SCOM to manage the components.

TABLE 13.1:   Managed Microsoft Virtualization Components

MANAGED COMPONENTS	SCOM MANAGEMENT PACK	ADDITIONAL COMPONENT DETAILS
Hyper-V hosts	Hardware-specific management packs from server vendors (Dell, HP)	Management pack for monitoring physical hardware attributes.

TABLE 13.1: Managed Microsoft Virtualization Components *(CONTINUED)*

MANAGED COMPONENTS	SCOM MANAGEMENT PACK	ADDITIONAL COMPONENT DETAILS
	Windows Server Hyper-V management pack	Management pack for monitoring coverage of Hyper-V host servers, including critical services and disks, and Hyper-V virtual machines, including virtual components and virtual hardware.
Windows Server 2008	2008 operating system management pack	Management pack for the core operating system and base performance rules and thresholds.
SCVMM 2008	SCVMM 2008 management pack and Reports pack (installed as part of PRO setup)	Management pack includes all SCVMM components: database server, self-service portal, SCVMM server, library servers, and rules and thresholds for all managed virtual platforms. This also includes the virtualization reports that are available in the SCVMM administration console.
Quick or Live Migration clusters	2008 cluster management pack	Specific to failover clusters, not Quick Migration or Live Migration directly.
VM application workloads	Various application management packs, Exchange, SQL, SharePoint	Deployed management packs depend on applications running in the VMs. These include any PRO packs made for specific applications.

NOTE Tools are available to help you determine what existing systems you have in your environment and which systems are good virtualization candidates. Those same tools can help you with VM density planning as well. An excellent tool to use is the free Microsoft Assessment and Planning (MAP) tool. The MAP tool inventories existing systems via an agentless discovery mechanism and makes recommendations about the number of physical Hyper-V hosts and VM density. You can also use MAP to determine the number of virtual hosts and VMs you'll need to account for in SCOM deployments. You can find MAP at http://technet.microsoft.com/en-us/library/bb977556.aspx.

Scenario 1: Deploying a New SCOM Environment

When you deploy a new Microsoft virtualization infrastructure and a new SCOM 2007 infrastructure to manage that environment, you must consider the planning and design aspects. Certain tools are available to facilitate the planning process, which can help you determine the physical server's needs for a new SCOM 2007 environment. Determining the number of servers to manage is critical to determining needed SCOM 2007 capacity, because each managed machine, physical or virtual, needs an SCOM agent.

NOTE   Microsoft has released a tool to help in planning your SCOM 2007 R2 deployment. The OpsMgr 2007 R2 Sizing Helper helps identify the ideal hardware configuration and infrastructure necessary to support your new SCOM 2007 R2 deployment. Refer to "Operations Manager 2007 R2 – Sizing Helper" at `http://blogs.technet.com/momteam/archive/2009/08/12/operations-manager-2007-r2-sizing-helper.aspx` for more information.

If you're deploying a new SCOM 2007 environment to manage existing servers/applications and new or existing virtualization components, you need to determine the number of hosts for which you need management capacity, including virtual and physical systems. Strictly from an SCOM perspective, it doesn't matter if the managed host is physical or virtual. If the needed management packs are imported into the SCOM infrastructure and an SCOM agent is deployed to the endpoint, all systems are considered under management.

Determining the number of Hyper-V hosts and VMs to be managed by SCOM 2007 is an important step because this number may drive the deployment of additional SCOM servers. Although this step is important for SCOM, planning it is usually tackled during normal virtualization deployment planning.

After identifying the different features that you're going to utilize with SCOM, it's time to get started. For this walk-through, we're going to install everything on a single server, which will work for smaller deployments. Larger deployments will be more complex given the multimachine dependencies.

1. Install and configure SCOM 2007 servers and roles. We won't cover the detailed SCOM installation process in this chapter, but you can find detailed instructions in the TechNet article "How to Deploy an Operations Manager 2007 Management Group on a Single Computer Using the Setup Wizard" at `http://technet.microsoft.com/en-us/library/bb381350.aspx`.

2. Import management packs into the new SCOM 2007 infrastructure. This is a critical step: you want to make sure you have the latest reports and health models for applications you plan to run and manage in your environment. Use Table 13.1, earlier in this chapter, as a guide, but remember that the SCVMM management packs are loaded automatically when you configure the integration between SCVMM and SCOM.

3. Determine the SCOM agent deployment process for new physical and virtual machines. Because you're doing a new deployment and there is no existing process for installing SCOM agents, you should consider the SCOM agent as base software that is installed on each server (physical or virtual) in your environment. Agents can use the current process you have for installing antivirus and backup software. Those software agents are typically integrated directly into the build process and ecosystem.

Even if you install the SCOM agent manually, you still need to run the discovery process before you add the managed endpoint to the management group. For automated agent installation from the SCOM console, we recommend that you use the automated discovery process provided by SCOM.

4. The Computer And Device Management Wizard lets you choose between two options: Automatic Computer Discovery, which scans an entire domain for all systems, or Advanced Discovery, which lets you specify types of systems to look for (servers or clients; see Figure 13.1).

FIGURE 13.1

Computer And Device Management Wizard scan options

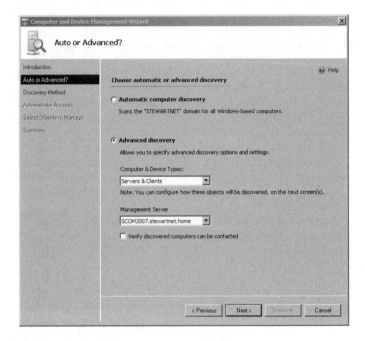

5. The last part of the process is specifying an account to use to install the SCOM agent: either the default actions account or another domain account with administrative privileges on the system or device to be managed.

For VMs, because we're talking about an existing SCOM 2007 deployment, an agent deployment process is already in place. Either you're using the standard domain-discovery process, or you're installing the SCOM agent as part of a standardized build process.

The VM build process offers some additional flexibilities. Typical VMs are built from a Sysprepped VHD file that's already created. (We covered the creation of a Sysprepped VHD in Chapter 4, "Utilizing Virtualization Best Practices.") In this instance, you can stage the SCOM agent on the VHD file and silently install it after the mini-Sysprep wizard runs. After the agent is installed on the system, manual and automated SCOM discovery can discover the system and add it to the relevant computer group.

You can configure SCVMM PRO functionality to work with the existing SCOM 2007 deployment. Determine whether PRO packs are available for applications you'll run in VMs, and deploy the PRO packs into the SCVMM and SCOM 2007 environment. (See Chapter 11 for detailed instructions for setting up SCOM and SCVMM PRO functionality.)

Scenario 2: SCOM Already Deployed

Now, let's dive into the deployment process for SCOM 2007 for a Microsoft virtual environment. If you already have an SCOM environment deployed into your infrastructure, you'll be interested in the components you can deploy into your environment for additional or new capabilities. SCOM can be used as the single console solution for doing enterprise management or as the driven, task-oriented component that can forward rich alerts into an existing enterprise management solution.

To deploy SCOM, you must work with your systems management counterparts to deploy the necessary components. If you're deploying a new SCOM 2007 environment, then you may require more detailed collaboration between groups. If you work in a small to medium enterprise, you may be in charge of not only the virtualization deployment but the operational management tools as well.

We'll drill into this scenario to make sure we cover all bases. You've decided to deploy virtualization in your environment because of all the great things it provides: better server-asset utilization, workload migration, and deployment flexibility. You're going to deploy Hyper-V and SCVMM to manage the Hyper-V environment, and you want to use your existing SCOM 2007 environment. Let's walk through the process of connecting SCOM and your virtualization deployment.

You must determine the number of Hyper-V hosts and VMs that will be managed by SCOM 2007. This is an important step because this number may drive the deployment of additional SCOM servers. Although this step is important for SCOM, planning it is usually tackled during normal virtualization deployment planning.

In this scenario, you already have SCOM 2007 deployed, so you can use the Virtualization Candidates report to find under-utilized servers that are being managed by SCOM 2007. To use the Virtualization Candidates report, follow these steps:

1. If you don't already have Reporting Services installed in SCOM, you'll have to install it before you can use the Virtualization Candidates report. You can find detailed Reporting Services installation instructions in the TechNet article "How to Deploy Operations Manager 2007 Reporting Using the Setup Wizard," available at http://technet.microsoft.com/en-us/library/bb381267.aspx.

2. Download and install the SCVMM 2008 Reports management pack. If you're using SCVMM 2008 R2, this management pack is installed automatically when you integrate SCVMM + SCOM.

3. Import the SCVMM 2008 Reports management pack into SCOM (see Figure 13.2).

4. You're ready to run the report either from the SCOM console under the Reports section or from the SCVMM administration console. Running reports from the SCVMM administration console requires that you've configured the Reporting option in SCVMM (see Figure 13.3).

5. Select the Virtualization Candidates report, and fill in the parameters (CPU, Memory, Disk, and Network) for what you consider an underutilized physical machine (see Figure 13.4).

You can use the Virtualization Candidates report to determine the number of physical systems you'll virtualize. In addition, to give you an idea of the number of potential VMs, you can use this report to generate P2V lists.

6. Create a list of additional management packs that need to be deployed into an existing SCOM environment to support the virtualization components. This process comes down to understanding the types of server applications you run or will run in the virtualized environment.

FIGURE 13.2

Importing the Reports management pack

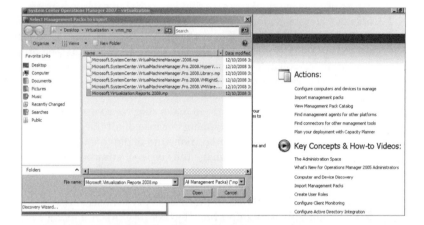

FIGURE 13.3

Virtualization reports

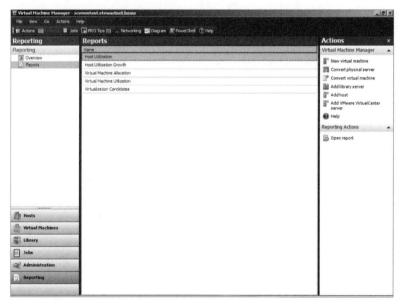

In this scenario, because you have an SCOM 2007 environment running, you already have management packs imported in the environment and managing server applications. The only additional management packs you need are any for new server applications and SCVMM management packs for managing the virtual environment. VM management packs are added automatically when you configure the PRO functionality. (See Chapter 11 for the steps involved in configuring PRO.)

7. Coordinate with the SCOM 2007 administrators to review the additional number of systems identified that need SCOM 2007 agents. Either the needed capacity fits into the existing SCOM environment or you add existing management servers to meet the additional demand.

FIGURE 13.4

Virtualization Candidates report

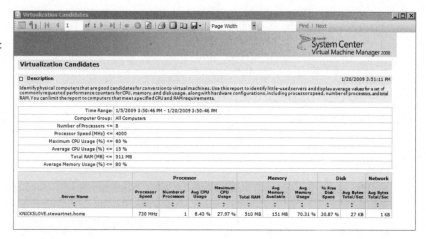

Consider the agent deployment process for VMs. Because we're talking about an existing SCOM 2007 deployment, an agent deployment is already in place. Either you're using the standard domain-discovery process or you're installing the SCOM agent as part of a standardized build process.

The VM build process offers some additional flexibilities. Typical VMs are built from a Sysprepped VHD file that's already created. In this instance, you can stage the SCOM agent on the VHD file and silently install it after the mini-Sysprep wizard runs. After the agent is installed on the system, manual and automated SCOM discovery can discover the system and add it to the relevant computer group.

You can configure SCVMM PRO functionality to work with the existing SCOM 2007 deployment. Determine whether PRO packs are available for applications you'll run in VMs, and deploy the PRO packs into the SCVMM and SCOM 2007 environment. (See Chapter 11 for detailed instructions for setting up SCOM and SCVMM PRO functionality.)

Monitoring and Reporting

Now that you've deployed agents to all the physical and virtual machines, all machines with an agent are being managed by SCOM. What does it mean to be *managed*? All the talk about models and management packs starts to come to life now. The knowledge from the management packs is deployed to the managed systems.

Take, for instance, a managed SQL Server. The rules and health model from the imported SQL management pack are deployed to the system, and all SQL events and services are monitored for health. If one of the SQL components isn't functioning correctly, the SQL service shows up as unhealthy until the condition is corrected.

Let's explore managed systems and the systems' health. Now that you have managed systems, you can look at the initial state of the managed machines by going to the Administration tab on the SCOM console and selecting Agent Managed (see Figure 13.5).

You can also get a quick overview of the systems' state by selecting the Monitoring tab (see Figure 13.6). This view shows you alerts, the state of the managed systems, and specific types of managed services and applications.

We've been discussing the idea of a health model; but how do you drill into the health model of a managed endpoint? You can do so by using the Health Explorer in SCOM (see Figure 13.7), which you access from the Action menu. It lets you drill into the monitors for the managed systems and determine health. You can see the exact monitors that run and determine which monitor specifically is failing if the service or system is listed as unhealthy.

SCOM also allows you to run tasks on all managed systems. If you're alerted to a problem on a system, you can perform some tasks directly from the SCOM console to discern and pinpoint issues. You can even use the remote-desktop functionality directly from the SCOM console Task menu to troubleshoot an alert generated in SCOM. You access the tasks from the Action menu (see Figure 13.8 and Figure 13.9).

FIGURE 13.5
Managed
system state

FIGURE 13.6
Monitoring view

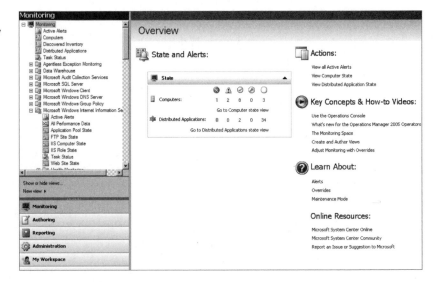

FIGURE 13.7
Health Explorer

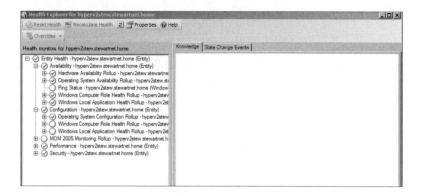

FIGURE 13.8
Tasks for managed
systems

The SCOM reporting infrastructure provides rich reports for managed endpoints. It's important to understand that these structured reports come from the management packs for specific applications and services. Most, if not all, management packs provide reports with the health models and service-application knowledge. When the reporting infrastructure is in place, each time you import a management pack with reports, those reports are available to be run from within the SCOM console on the Reporting tab.

For this section, we'll concentrate on reports for the managed virtualization environment. System Center Virtual Manager provides the Reports management pack that is imported into the SCOM environment. For SCVMM 2008, this management pack isn't imported automatically during the configuration of SCOM SCVMM integration like the PRO management packs; virtualization reports must be downloaded and imported separately. This functionality is included by default with SCVMM 2008 R2.

After you import the reports into the SCOM infrastructure, they're available to run. You can run them from within SCOM console; or, with the integration between SCOM and SCVMM, you can run them directly from the SCVMM administration console. Before you can run the reports from the SCVMM console, you must configure the SCOM server, enable reporting, and add the reporting server URL (see Figure 13.10).

FIGURE 13.9
Completed
SCOM task

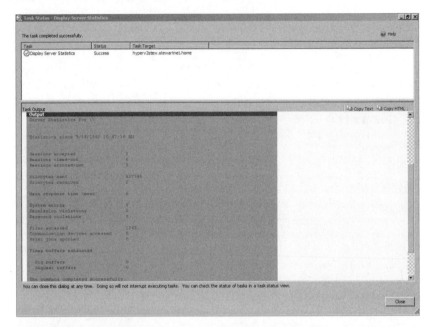

FIGURE 13.10
Configuring
reporting in
SCVMM

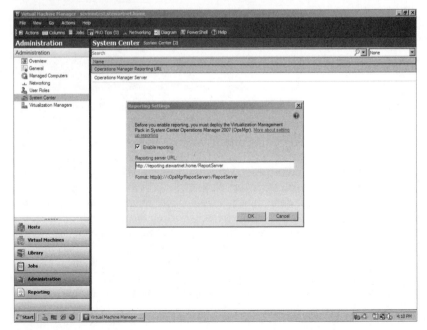

After you add the reports, they're listed on the Reporting tab in the SCVMM administration console (see Figure 13.11).

FIGURE 13.11
Reports in SCVMM

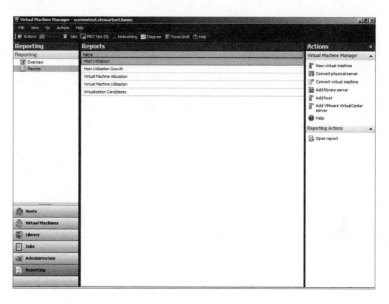

The following virtualization reports are available:

◆ Host Utilization (see Figure 13.12)

FIGURE 13.12
Host Utilization report

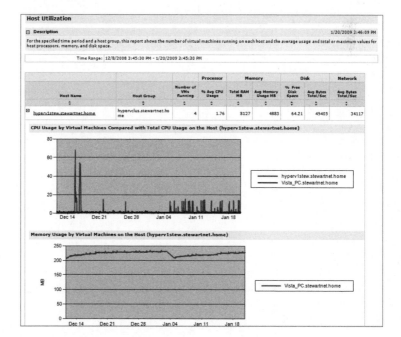

◆ Host Utilization Growth (see Figure 13.13)

◆ Virtual Machine Allocation (see Figure 13.14)

◆ Virtual Machine Utilization (see Figure 13.15)

◆ Virtualization Candidates

FIGURE 13.13
Host Utilization
Growth report

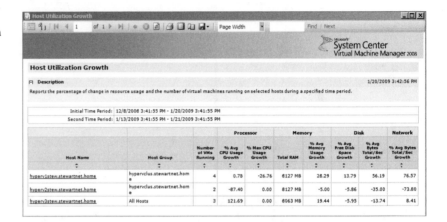

FIGURE 13.14
Virtual Machine
Allocation report

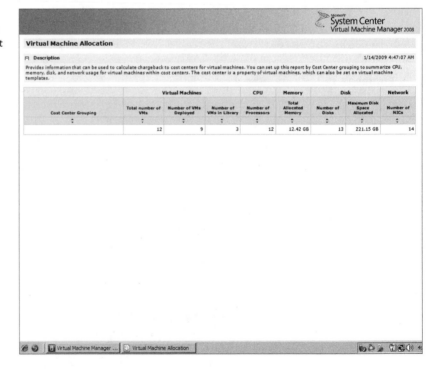

FIGURE 13.15
Virtual Machine
Utilization report

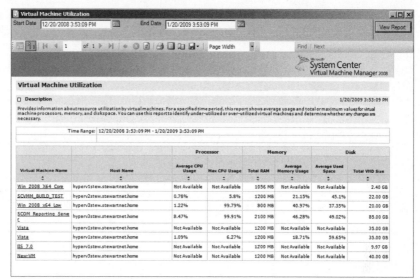

You can use all of these reports to make proactive decisions about the capacity needed or used in your Microsoft virtualization environment. Additionally, you can use the Dynamic Datacenter Toolkit for Enterprises (DDTK-E) to help implement chargeback, where individual groups can be charged for virtualization infrastructure that a central group provides. You can find out more information on the DDTK-E at the Dynamic Data Center Alliance Blog at `http://blogs.technet.com/ddcalliance/default.aspx`. On the Host Utilization report, you can drill into the performance charts and VMs running on a host.

Summary

SCOM 2007 brings critical functionality to managing the Microsoft virtualization environment, such as real-time alerting, reporting, and application knowledge. As you can see from this chapter, planning the SCOM 2007 environment with your virtualization deployment in mind will help ensure that you have the needed management capacity. SCOM 2007 in combination with SCVMM and the PRO functionality provides a rich 360-degree view of your VMs and other critical virtualization components.

Index

Note to Reader: **Bolded** page numbers refer to definitions and main discussions of a topic. *Italicized* page numbers refer to illustrations.